Real Law Stories

Real Law Stories

Inside the American Judicial Process

RICHARD A. BRISBIN, JR.
West Virginia University

JOHN C. KILWEIN
West Virginia University

New York   Oxford
OXFORD UNIVERSITY PRESS
2010

Oxford University Press, Inc., publishes works that further Oxford University's
objective of excellence in research, scholarship, and education.

Oxford   New York
Auckland   Cape Town   Dar es Salaam   Hong Kong   Karachi
Kuala Lumpur   Madrid   Melbourne   Mexico City   Nairobi
New Delhi   Shanghai   Taipei   Toronto

With offices in
Argentina   Austria   Brazil   Chile   Czech Republic   France   Greece
Guatemala   Hungary   Italy   Japan   Poland   Portugal   Singapore
South Korea   Switzerland   Thailand   Turkey   Ukraine   Vietnam

Published by Oxford University Press, Inc.
198 Madison Avenue, New York, New York 10016
http://www.oup.com

Library of Congress Cataloging-in-Publication Data
Brisbin, Richard A.
    Real law stories : inside the American judicial process / Richard A. Brisbin, Jr., John C. Kilwein.
        p. cm.
    Includes bibliographical references.
    ISBN 978-0-19-973359-0 (pbk. : alk. paper)
1. Judicial process—United States.   2. Justice, Administration of—United States.
3. Civil procedure—United States.   4. Criminal procedure—United States.
5. Lawyers—United States—Interviews.   6. Judges—United States—Interviews.
I. Kilwein, John C.   II. Title.
    KF8700.B76 2009
    347.73—dc22   2009025234

Printed in the United States of America
on acid-free paper

CONTENTS

PREFACE

The law is omnipresent in the United States. Every year more than one hundred million Americans and American businesses find themselves engaged in some form of legal action. Untold millions more consider legal action but settle their conflicts out of court or seek advice from an attorney as they seek to prevent becoming involved in a lawsuit. Through law and legal actions Americans regulate family life, business and financial relationships, employment, land and the environment, criminal conduct, the use and misuse of motor vehicles, and even sexual behavior. Law affords potential relief for all sorts of injuries, whether physical, economic, psychological, or social. Law provides a means to protect political rights, economic interests, and even the wishes of the deceased.

Additionally, stories about law and courts saturate the American media and expose the public to the significance of law. Newspaper headlines scream out with stories of about horrific murders, child abuse, and criminal trials. Television devotes dozens of hours each week to fictional dramas about crime and lawyers, to reality trial shows such as *Judge Judy*, to news reports of crime and politically important legal actions such as the bankruptcy of General Motors, and to programs devoted to discussion of specific crimes, such as *Nancy Grace*. Law appears to be an inescapable element of the American social fabric.

Why the attention to law, lawyers, and courts? Because of various cultural and historical circumstances, in the United States much of the public has decided that following the rule of law—as enacted by elected representatives and interpreted by the judiciary—should define moral responsibilities and the scope of personal rights. People respect law and the legal process as ethically sufficient and politically efficacious means for managing conflicts among people and institutions. People have a shared faith that the legal process can protect their rights and interests and produce what they regard as justice and moral order. The law, therefore, has come to shape everyday life. It has come to define how we see ourselves and others and how we envision a just future. As anthropologist Clifford Geertz asserted, the law is a "part of a distinctive manner of imaging the real."

Academic studies suggest that Americans, despite living in a legalized society, have only a crude knowledge of how the legal system works. Because of the tendency of the mass media to ignore the legal problems of the ordinary person, the knowledge that the public possesses is also often skewed or inaccurate. Instead of covering the divorce and auto accident cases that bring people into the legal process, the media cover Supreme Court decisions and the prosecutions of homicides—the rarest of crimes. Further affecting Americans' knowledge of the law is the fact that attention is given only to rules and trials, in many school curricula and the tendency of undergraduate university courses to focus primarily on the decisions of the Supreme Court of the United States. There often is little concern about what Patricia Ewick and Susan Silbey (1998, 15–32) have called "the common place of the law."

In *Real Law Stories* we offer a series of interviews designed to furnish a partial corrective to the lack of education about how law works. The objective of the book is to provide real-world interviews as a supplement to the more academic discussions about courts contained in judicial process textbooks and to correct the mistaken stereotypes of lawyers and police often conveyed by the mass media. The interviews especially describe how the legal process works from the perspective of lawyers, judges, and police. Told to us in the interviewees' own words, the interviews provide students of judicial politics with insights into the "real world" of the law. The interviews also emphasize the routine and typical functions of American legal professionals rather than describing exceptional or famous cases.

Through the interviews and brief descriptions and explanations of legal processes, the book endeavors to assist university students in learning about the law and the legal process in the United States. The first section of the book supplies the student with a brief introduction to the importance of American law and legal processes, the politics of the law, and the values of reading interviews. Subsequent sections contain explanatory introductions and interviews with lawyers in civil or noncriminal practice; with police, prosecutors, public defenders, and lawyers engaged in the criminal legal process; and with judges involved in the adjudication of different categories of cases. Also, the book offers a section to guide students in conducting their own interviews to gain knowledge about the frequency of use and operations of the judicial process, the roles of judges, lawyers, police, and other legal professionals, and the outcomes of litigation. Through the stories told in interviews, we believe that students can acquire a richer understanding of the importance of the world of law in the governance of social, economic, and political life in America, can grasp how law affects the everyday lives of ordinary people, and can learn how law might affect their own futures.

As an effort to teach about the legal process from the bottom up, this book germinated from our experience in requiring students in an undergraduate judicial process class to conduct interviews with legal professionals. Richard Brisbin derived this requirement from a similar project assigned by Marvin Downey in a state and local politics class at West Virginia Wesleyan College. Brisbin adopted the assignment when he began to teach about law and politics in 1974, and John

Kilwein adopted it in 1990. Together we have found that students regard it as a critical learning experience in the introductory judicial politics class.

We especially thank the persons whose interviews appear in this book. We also thank Claude Teweles for his initial support of this project and the staff of Oxford University Press for their guidance and support in the completion of the book. Jeff Worsham of West Virginia University gave us the idea for the joint interview that appears in the book. Melissa Butler of Wabash College, Chuck Epp of the University of Kansas, Ed Heck of San Diego State University, Susan Hunter of West Virginia University, Greg Noone of Fairmont State University, Jami Myers of West Virginia State University, and Pat Pierce of Saint Mary's College helped us arrange the interviews. The Eberly Family Foundation and Office of the Dean, Eberly College of Arts and Sciences of West Virginia University, and the Eberly Family Charitable Trust provided assistance with travel costs. The Institutional Review Board for the Protection of Human Subjects at West Virginia University has approved the collection of interviews presented in this book. In addition, we wish to thank the following reviewers for their comments: Paul Wahlbeck, George Washington University; Timothy M. Hagle, The University of Iowa; Jennifer Segal Diascro, American University; Kathryn A. DePalo, Florida International University; Herbert M. Kritzer, University of Minnesota Law School; Jim L. Riley, Regis University.

I

The Real World of Law
and Courts

In America lawsuits seem to be popping up everywhere. The crimes of celebrities such as Paris Hilton, Michael Vick, Britney Spears, Michael Jackson, Lindsay Lohan, Kobe Bryant, and Martha Stewart are recounted in excruciating detail by the media. Each day television programs such as *Judge Judy*, *Judge Joe Brown*, and *Divorce Court* present courtroom *litigation*, or lawsuits and trials, about a host of often bizarre conflicts. Newspaper stories tell of teenage girls who, when jilted by their prom dates, sued them for the costs of their dresses and accessories. Because they claim that the firm's supersized French fries brought on their health problems, obese persons sue McDonald's restaurants. When television personality Rosie O'Donnell filed a civil suit to control the revenues from the *Rosie* magazine, she held impromptu press conferences and spewed invective at her opponents. Representations of law and courts pervade other aspects of popular culture also (Mather 2005). However, are such infamous cases telling the real story of the workings of American law and courts?

In the real world of law and courts, half of marriages end in divorce suits, nearly one million persons seek bankruptcy each year, federal and state courts convict more than one million Americans of a serious crime or *felony* each year, and almost every death brings *probate of an estate,* or the distribution of the property of the deceased by lawyers and court personnel. *Real Law Stories* presents interviews that describe the jobs of, and offer comments on the law by, a range of legal professionals—judges, lawyers, police, and other court personnel. In their own words, the interviewees offer insights on the "real world" of the law. The objective of this collection of interviews is to supplement the more abstract academic discussions about courts contained in standard judicial process textbooks and to correct the mistaken or skewed stereotypes of lawyers, police, and litigants conveyed by the mass media. The interviews emphasize the more routine functions of law, rather than exceptional or famous cases. They attend largely to how law operates, not the definition of the law or issues of justice and prescriptions of what the law ought to be. From this approach it is possible for readers to better grasp how law affects the ordinary lives of people and how law might affect their own futures.

This book opens with interviews of attorneys involved in *civil,* or noncriminal, conflicts. This choice of civil cases is deliberate. Civil cases make up approximately 70 percent of the business of American courts. These cases include disputes between spouses and among family members. They involve such problems as vehicular accidents; unpaid debts to financial institutions and retailers; the terms of loans, mortgages, and wills; the ownership, sale, or use of real estate; taxes; and government regulations of business and the environment—problems much like those handled by the attorneys whose interviews appear later in this book, including those of Anne Becker, Jeffrey Byer, Paul Cranston, Dan Cooper, Robert Eye, Scott Friedman, Scott Himsel, Earl LeVere, Deborah Pascente Lifka, Salene Mazur, and Linda Rice. The next section of the book contains interviews conducted with Traci Cook, David Godwin, J. Luis Guerrero, Cynthia Short, Rita Peerenboom, and Michelle Reichenbach. These interviews address criminal justice issues from the perspective of police, prosecutors, and defense counsel. A final set of interviews with Dan Hogan, Steven King, Rick Savignano, Larry Starcher, and Richard Stearns afford the reader a view of the legal process from the vantage point of federal and state judges of trial and appellate courts. To aid the reader, this introduction illustrates how a critical reading of the collected interviews can help avoid misconceptions and comprehend the routine business of law and courts in the United States. Although the subjects of the interviews stress the infrequency of trials in a world full of potential lawsuits, the interviews contained in this book detail a process that is an accepted means of attempting to resolve problems. Americans use law and courts when they need protection of their interests, security, or rights from others; compensation for injuries; stability in their business transactions; or expansion of their personal freedoms. Often they recognize that law and courts are a valuable public resource available for settling disputes. Finally, they know that law trumps other ways of ordering social and economic life. Therefore, despite the infrequency of trials, law is an integral part of American life.

LAW STORIES

Because this book presents a series of stories told by ordinary people and legal professionals, it cannot present a comprehensive overview of the complicated workings of American law and courts. Telling stories is a natural form of human behavior, and the study of stories can provide insights into lives and events. By presenting collected stories, this book effectively becomes a *scrapbook* composed of a collection of personal tales about the workings of law and courts. Through our arrangement of this collection of personal stories from diverse locales and institutional settings, this scrapbook offers selected insights about the everyday, real-world behavior and images of order and value of people who participate in the legal realm (see Katriel and Farrell 1991). The tales or stories in this scrapbook are what scholars define as narratives, or selective accounts, of experiences related by legal professionals that offer a glimpse into how they see themselves and explain how they act (Ewick and Silbey 1995, 200). The stories reveal their desires, aspirations, social interactions, knowledge and use of the law, application of legal rules and procedures, and other calculations as they cope with conflicts and try to manage or govern problems. Through these actions at the street level, office level, or courthouse level, legal professionals help construct the distribution of political, social, and economic power in ways often more important for the lives of individuals than the actions of the President of the United States or the U.S. Congress.

Why Read Law Stories?

American social science has developed two approaches to the study of courts and law. Perhaps the most common approach involves the collection of data about people's attitudes and behavior at a point in time. Through the collection of quantitative data through devices such as survey questionnaires, scholars can propose and test hypotheses about specific attitudes and behavior. For example, surveys conducted as part of the Civil Litigation Research Project at the University of Wisconsin (Trubek et al.1983) asked persons questions about their problems and legal experiences. Among other things, the researchers asked litigants about their socioeconomic status and what they wanted in a case, and they asked lawyers how complex they rated a case and their specialty as part of an effort to assess hypotheses about the impact of fee arrangement on case outcomes. Contemporary social science also uses historical data to spot patterns or changes in legal behavior. For example, a study by Lawrence Friedman and Robert Percival (1976) studied the numbers of kinds of suits in Alameda and San Benito Counties, California, to assess hypotheses about how time changes people's use of the courts for different problems. Although valuable, the data collected from surveys and documents tend to reduce complex life experiences of complex individuals to simple quantitative bits of information about categories of behavior or status, known as variables. It simplifies human behavior to provide a valuable snapshot of what law and courts care about within the world of disputes.

Stories, however, offer another kind of perspective on law and courts. They provide a "thick" description of human behavior and afford the opportunity for analysis of an individual's actions. Because it focuses on one person, a legal story is not reducible to a series of hypotheses that explain the behavior of persons in similar situations. Stories can reveal only how specific persons *experience* the world of law and courts and the nature of their *associations* with other persons. In ways similar to other case studies of political events, collected stories offer insights into the complexity and interactions that mark legal activity. Lumped together, several stories can also furnish insight into concepts that mark litigation, such as plea bargaining or discovery procedures; can provide information that might be used to develop theories and hypotheses about the behavior of legal professionals; and can supply data for future studies (see George and Bennett 2005).

For our interviews we developed a series of questions so that the persons we interviewed would provide a comprehensive story about their experiences or their legal life stories. However, the reader must recognize that each courthouse is its own separate universe (Eisenstein, Flemming, and Nardulli 1988). Each court develops its own norms of behavior and informal rules of legal practice. These varying norms and practices often require unique questions to generate a more complete picture of the activity of the legal professionals who work in it. Even a scrapbook composed of stories gathered from interviews cannot fully account for this diversity of legal activity in the United States. Nonetheless, we believe that it does offer a window for the interested reader into the meaning of law and legal procedures in their home communities. To assist other researchers and students in the collection of stories and the composition of a scrapbook about the law, we have included a description of how to conduct an interview and question litigants and legal professionals in the section "How to Conduct Interviews and Gather Legal Narratives" that follows the interviews. The questions endeavor to gain information on the life stories of the interviewees; their social interactions in legal proceedings; the role of law and norms and conventions of legal behavior and activity in their careers; their perceptions of key people, institutions, and events in their legal lives; and their interests and concerns for the future. These are the *when*, *what*, *how*, and *why* that any social scientist or journalist asks of the persons that they interview.

WHAT IS IMPORTANT IN A LEGAL STORY?

Before reading legal stories, it is important to gain a richer understanding of what composes a story. A legal story contains a two-part recounting of how law constitutes reality and reality constitutes law. First, a story conveys an *instrumental* or *practical* message. In many of the interviews in this book, the message is often recounted as a series of events involving how legal professionals go about their daily tasks in an attempt to resolve conflicts among people. The explanation of their routine business and interactions with other persons conveys information about how they employ law and discretion as instruments that shape the world in which we live. Law can, however, be an instrument to achieve a "new reality" such as the protection of rights or the enhancement of a litigant's sociopolitical importance or economic interests (see Epp 2008). For example, when confronted by institutionalized and legalized racism, the National Association for the Advancement of Colored People (NAACP) undertook a series of lawsuits to change the status of African Americans. Even after achieving a legal victory that required an end to racial segregation in the public schools, the organization had to press forward thousands of additional lawsuits, seek a Civil Rights Act from Congress, and demand enforcement of the law and decisions in lawsuits from the federal Justice Department. They practiced a "politics of rights" (Scheingold 2004) as a tool to achieve political empowerment and equal rights. As with the girls who sued when their prom dates jilted them, people use law and courts to resolve their conflicts. Just as with the girls, who did not use gossip to defame or have their brothers beat up the cads who did not show up in white limos wearing powder-blue tuxedos and carrying wrist corsages, litigation appears as the legitimate means to handle disputes.

Second, people's perceptions of the world shape their understanding of why law is important. As revealed in several of the interviews in this book, people end up resolving problems by using law in an effort to empower themselves in conflicts about liberty and responsibility (Ewick and Silbey 1995, 211–17). In the United States, ordinary persons also commonly refer to law and legal rights and assume that right and wrong, order and disorder, and property and common space are matters of law and for courts to address. Acquired early in their lives, their perspective of reality assumes the value of legality, "the rule of law," or "the ethical attitude that holds moral conduct to be a matter of rule following, and moral relationships to consist of rights and duties determined by rules" (Shklar 1964, 1). The mental construction of the importance of law provides a "distinctive manner of imagining the real" (Geertz 1983, 184) and makes legal ideas, rules, norms, and behavior seem "if not invisible, perfectly natural and benign" (Sarat and Simon 2003, 14). Americans' reliance on law indicates that they envision law as a central element in their lives and as a tool for improving the world about them (see Sarat and Kearns 1993; Brigham 1996). The popular acceptance of legality causes people to seek out legal remedies for personal and social problems.

Americans also learn that disobedience of the law, even for just religious, moral, or philosophical principles, can result in a penalty. Americans thus rarely lapse into what are called "subversive" stories that resist the law or the judicial settlement of disputes (Ewick and Silbey 1995, 217–22). Relatively few studies have found groups of Americans turning away from law and treating their grievances as matters to be settled by prayer or violence, and most of these individuals have reasons to distrust the ways powerful people have used the law against their interests (Brisbin 2002, 2009; Greenhouse 1986; Wagner-Pacifici 1994). If the law does not comport with their personal morality or sense of justice, they may ignore the law, such as laws that restrict teenage drinking or marijuana use; they may adopt practices that circumvent the law, such as the establishment of foreign headquarters by U.S. corporations seeking to avoid U.S. tax laws; or they may complain to politicians and seek changes in the law, such as with religious traditionalists who seek to repeal the inclusion of abortion within the right to privacy. Thus interviews can generate a thick description from which the reader learns not just the nature of legal activity but the dimensions and depth of the legitimacy of the law and the commitment to legal remedies for problems held by American litigants and legal professionals (see Ewick and Silbey 1995, 202–3).

The Collection of Stories

Through a variety of contacts, we located the people interviewed for this book. Although we have known some of the interview subjects for many years or had interviewed them for other research projects, mostly we relied on colleagues, former students, and friends to recommend potential interviewees. Most of the interviews in this book extended more than an hour. To fit them into allocated space and for pedagogical purposes, we have edited the transcripts of the interviews. Unlike some books that use legal stories, however, we have not cut them into pieces to illustrate theories of behavior nor subjected them to evaluation of their grammar, use of vocabulary, or social and political assumptions. Also, we have largely reported the exact verbal statements of the subjects of the interviews. Although the head note to each interview contains information on the context of the interview, in the interest of brevity we have included only limited comments on the location of the interview, the appearance of the subject, and nonverbal gestures and behavior by the subject. Despite these limitations, these are stories for the reader to evaluate both on their own terms and with the assistance of questions found in Part V of this book, "How to Conduct Interviews and Gather Legal Narratives."

THE POLITICS OF LAW AND COURTS

When appraising the following interviews of legal professionals, readers should attend to issues of political power. Politics matters in judicial proceedings, but the ways in which it matters are not always obvious. If politics is the story of the possession and use of power or of having a reputation of holding power to affect the interests of other persons in a community or nation, then law and courts are political. The politics of law and courts, however, is often a struggle over power that lacks the overt simplicity of the partisan battles that mark elections. In this section we briefly recount how politics affects law and courts (undergraduate students will find much more detail on these topics in texts such as Baum 2008; Carp, Stidham, and Manning 2007; Neubauer and Meinhold 2010; and Melone and Karnes 2008).

The Legal Context
The actions of the legal professionals interviewed in this book occur in a context defined by a host of laws and rules that they largely consider to be legitimate and that they follow in their everyday activity. However, political decisions that have resulted in a federal system of government and the adoption of a variety of federal, state, and local laws and legal procedures have created a bewildering institutional context for the operation of the law. The laws and procedures that legal professionals follow consequently vary from community to community. There is diversity of *procedural law,* or the required stages and processes that govern the operation of the dual system of federal and state courts that exist in the United States. The *substantive law,* or the rules of behavior stated as law, such as the definition of a contract (sales or employment agreement), will, or crime, includes federal and state constitutions and their interpretations by judges; *statutes* or acts of the Congress and state legislatures; state-to-state interpretations of the *common* or judge-made law; and differences between federal and state administrative rules and regulations. Because of the American constitutional commitment to federal government, names of courts and offices vary from state to state and from state to federal government (see the National Center for State Courts website, listed in the reference section of this book, for information on the names and arrangements of American courts). Also, the state and federal systems vary in terms of their arrangement of duties, or *subject matter jurisdiction,* among minor courts, trial courts that consider the facts of an alleged civil wrong or crime, and various appellate courts that review the application of the law at trial. Although the federal courts apply the U.S.

Constitution, acts of Congress, and federal regulations, and state courts apply state constitutions and state legislation, rules, and regulations, federal supremacy and legal overlap can confuse even lawyers.

Procedural Law

The complex rules of procedure used in American courts are not designed to confuse. They have a political source and a political function. Some of the rules come from the federal and state constitutions and legislation enacted by the people or their representatives, such as the rules on warrants for searches and seizures in the Fourth Amendment of the U.S. Constitution. Politically selected judges establish other procedural rules through their interpretations of constitutional rights and constitutional concepts, such as due process of the law, and by their power to establish rules of procedure in the federal and many state judicial systems. Ideally, these rules function to ensure that a person is not deprived of liberty or property without a fair opportunity to present his or her case before a judge and jury. The rules thus promote democratic political values and function to prevent the arbitrary arrests and the secret proceedings so common in authoritarian political regimes.

Because procedural rules are complicated, some persons regard them as a maze of indecipherable technicalities. To address this concern, the U.S. Supreme Court required that indigent defendants be afforded lawyers. Although some civil and criminal litigants will attempt to argue their cases *pro se,* or without a lawyer, most individuals recognize that, in the words of Justice George Sutherland, "Even the intelligent and educated layman has small and sometimes no skill in the science of law. He lacks both the skill and knowledge adequately to prepare his defense, even though he had a perfect one. He requires the guiding hand of counsel at every step in the proceedings against him" (*Powell v. Alabama* 1932, 69). Indeed, scattered evidence also suggests that "haves" who can pay or pay more for a lawyer's time and skill receive more favorable outcomes.

The complexity of procedural rules, especially those about the admissibility of evidence, also creates the opportunity for judicial interpretation. Procedural rules thus empower judges. As there is substantial evidence that political values and roles affect judicial decisions, judges can shape the procedures that govern the adjudicatory "playing field" in terms of the assumptions of what is politically appropriate for the protection of rights. Usually this influence of politics passes unrecognized even by judges. However, as conflicts about search and seizure and self-incrimination rights before the U.S. Supreme Court illustrate, political ideology sometimes overtly affects the definition of procedures.

Substantive Law

In the United States political actions define the substance of the law—the definition of rights, a will, a crime, an injury, and the availability of a remedy, such as money damages or a protection of rights of free speech. However, depending on whether the law is constitutional, statutory, common, or administrative, the influence of politicians and the political function of substantive law vary in several ways.

Conventions of public representatives wrote and approved the United States Constitution, the "supreme law of the land." Federal and state legislative bodies have amended it. The Constitution's function is political. It defines political rights, especially those related to free political expression and freedom from arbitrary arrest and punishment. It establishes procedures for the operation of political institutions. It both encourages certain kinds of political actions, such as legislating for the general welfare, and prevents other actions, such as the taxation of exports. State constitutions, adopted and amended either by conventions or legislative actions or by public referendum, also serve the political functions of protecting rights and defining the authority of state and local governments. The interpretation of constitutional law is frequently an activity of appellate courts. The justices selected through some sort of political process, therefore, define the meaning of constitutions.

The laws enacted by Congress and state legislatures make up the *statutory law.* They are supplemented by *ordinances* enacted by local councils. Statutes emerge from the political processes of lobbying, logrolling, hearings, committee actions, and legislative efforts to appease constituents that characterize American legislative decision making. Therefore, the bulk of American law is a political product. As Judge Richard Stearns indicates in his interview, an ever-expanding statutory law serves innumerable political functions. The law of contracts, which all states base on a compilation of the law of sales and financial exchanges called the Uniform Commercial Code, serves to support orderly markets and a capitalist economy. Statutes permit states to license corporations, protect investors, and regulate the enormous financial and political power that corporations hold over their employees, consumers, and the general stability of the economy. As discussed in the interviews with Jeffrey Byer, Scott Himsel, and Salene Mazur, commercial law and bankruptcy law protect the interests of creditors and debtors in a market economy. Statutes specify the taxes paid by individuals and corporations. Statutes define crimes and regulate the intimate details of family life and the welfare of children, provide for marriage and divorce, and protect the interests of deceased persons to prevent the social disorder caused by family feuding, as described in the interview with domestic relations lawyer Scott Friedman. The interpretation of statutes is frequently an activity of judges. Thus judges selected through some sort of political process help define the meaning of statutes and support and bring order to the American market economy and the American family. Finally, the criminal law is found in statutes. Thus the definition of crime is a legislative task and is shaped by legislative politics and judicial interpretation of the words of legislative acts.

Once the core of American law, legislatures have replaced much common or judge-made law with statutes. Nonetheless, judge-made law continues to supplement statutory law. With personal injuries, or *torts,* the common law furnishes rules for decisions about responsibility for accidents and careless behavior. Tort law decisions by publicly employed judges serve important political functions. Because governmental regulations cannot prevent all injuries, the threat of tort suits can force people and businesses to exercise care to prevent injuries from an enormous range of activities, from owning a dog and driving an auto to producing pharmaceuticals and selling chicken. Also, tort suits provide compensation for injuries. They alleviate the need for charities or government to pay for injuries. To protect themselves against the risk of injury lawsuits, people purchase insurance. The insurance industry invests their premiums and creates a pool of investment capital for construction, business and job creation, and loans. Consequently, tort law has fostered an industry and provides resources for economic development for the economy. The joint interview with Paul Cranston, a plaintiffs' attorney, and Dan Cooper, a civil defense lawyer, exposes the reader to both sides of tort law.

Administrative law comprises the rules and regulations established by federal and state executive bureaus. Congress and state legislatures have delegated this lawmaking power to bureaus. Administrative law thus is a product of political decisions by legislators and the executive branch of government. Today this is a body of law that is far more detailed and extensive than the statutory law. As illustrated in the interviews with Anne Becker and Linda Rice, disputes about the rules and regulations normally are negotiated or adjudicated before administrative law judges or hearing panels rather than trial judges and juries. Administrative law also has innumerable political functions. Administrative law includes regulations of the environment, occupational safety, and food processing and selling; the practices of the professions; the administration of government assistance programs such as Social Security, Medicare and Medicaid, and unemployment compensation; the responsibilities of public college and university faculty and students; and the operation of pension plans.

Finally, a mix of statutory, common, and administrative law affects some aspects of the lives of Americans. Legislatures and courts protect interests in homes and other real estate through common law and statutory law about title to property and the transfer of real estate. They also govern how real estate can be used for investment purposes or leased to others. Through administrative rules and regulations, municipalities can zone real estate and allow its use for only certain purposes. Each of these kinds of rules is a product of political decisions, and each serves to promote certain political values, such as a right to own a residence or the protection of a person's home from nuisances caused by the other property owners.

THE BUSINESS OF COURTS

Having a case in court is a rare experience for many Americans. Despite the media's attention to crime, a very small number Americans become defendants in a criminal case. Nonetheless, this book includes interviews with criminal justice professionals. Studies of criminal processes suggest that trials are quite rare. The United States Department of Justice (2008b, Table 3.33; cf. Table 4.20) has found that only about half of violent crimes and as few as 5 percent of petty thefts are reported to police. Because they cannot find a perpetrator or lack evidence, police cannot make arrests in a substantial proportion of reported crimes. Prosecutors or district attorneys find that evidentiary problems cause them to dismiss about 20 percent of the arrests forwarded to them by police. Because prosecutors will then negotiate a guilty plea and a penalty in most cases, they go to trial in only about 10 percent of the cases they decide to prosecute. Trials occur for about two or three of every one hundred crimes or five to seven of every one hundred arrests.

In noncriminal civil disputes, also, Americans are not litigation happy or out to change American society, economy, or politics through lawsuits. There are several reasons why this is true. Some persons lack a consciousness of the law. They regard the problems they have with others as the workings of fate or God's will. They believe that use of lawsuits is a stigma. They regard the use of law to be socially divisive, a cause of unneeded conflict with other persons with whom they might have to deal in the future, and as evidence of unreasonableness. They do not want outsiders to intrude into family problems. They believe that direct action—such as a physical confrontation with a victimizer, as when a child fights a bully or an abused wife burns the bed in which her husband sleeps—can solve their problems. They do not understand how to use law or contact a lawyer. They cannot name the source of their injury. They see courts as inaccessible because of a lack of money or time (see Engel and Munger 2003; Ewick and Silbey 1998, 57–107; Felstiner, Abel, and Sarat 1980–1981; Merry 1990, 37–63).

Even when conscious of the power and utility of law to protect their interests, most Americans cope with their potential legal problems out of court with and without the assistance of a lawyer. A national study of American civil litigation found that about 40 percent of American households each year experience a *grievance,* or sense that a blameworthy person or organization has injured their welfare. Of those experiencing grievances, about three in ten "lumped it," or took no action; but seven in ten made some demand—a *claim*—on those they thought had harmed their welfare. When a claim was rejected, a *dispute* arose. This occurred in just under five of every ten grievances, or just over six of every ten claims. However, only about 22 percent of disputants hired lawyers, and only 10 percent of the disputants filed suits (Miller and Sarat 1980–1981).

Often the persons who did not litigate employed a means of alternative dispute resolution, such as personal negotiation with their opponents' insurance companies, mediators such as state governments' consumer protection agencies, or private better business bureaus. Others sought the intercession and mediation afforded by legislators' staffs, debt reorganization services, clergy, or family counselors. Still others used preestablished arbitration schemes, such as the provisions for salary arbitration provided in the contract between the major league player's union and major league baseball (see Nader 1980). Consequently, only 5 percent of grievances resulted in suits. Other evidence indicates that few suits end in a trial. As many of the interview subjects reveal, the chance of a civil suit ending in trial is about one in ten. It is much lower for divorces and vehicular accidents without physical injuries. In these cases, either lawyers or insurance companies or both will negotiate a settlement. The bottom line is that in a world full of perceived grievances, fewer than one in two hundred ends with a trial (Miller and Sarat 1980–1981). Americans, therefore, appear to be adept at avoiding courts and litigation. They are not litigation crazed. Instead, they selectively use the law to empower themselves when other avenues of redress for their problems or their security are less useful.

Personnel

Politics, patronage, and partisanship affect the selection of the personnel of American courts. Governments use political processes, tax money, and fees to employ or regulate American legal professionals. Judges are elected or appointed by elected executives and legislators. Lawyers who work for governments and address a wide range of noncriminal matters can be political appointees or merit-selected civil servants overseen by political appointees. Although federal prosecutors (called United States Attorneys) and some state prosecutors are appointed by elected executives with attention to their political party affiliation, prosecutors are usually elected by people of a county on a partisan ballot that discloses their party affiliation. Public defenders who represent poor criminal defendants, clerks, police, sheriffs, and support staff for judicial proceedings are public employees selected through executive or judicial appointment, civil service merit selection, or partisan election. The interviews with Anne Becker, Traci Cook, Robert Eye, David Godwin, J. Luis Guerrero, Dan Hogan, Steven King, Rita Peerenboom, Rick Savignano, Richard Stearns, Cynthia Short, and Larry V. Starcher illustrate the many and varied linkages of partisan and bureaucratic politics with American legal processes.

Also, lawyers generally have a political status. After earning a bachelor's degree and graduation from law school, in most states they must pass a bar examination, be admitted to practice, and follow the regulations established by a state bar association. By assigning these powers to the state bar association, in the majority of the states the state legislature or its judiciary has created a professional monopoly over the governance of lawyers. The state bar association is thus *integrated* into government, and all lawyers are quasi-public officers of the court.

Finally, governments maintain the courts. They design and fund the facilities, police, and support personnel who assist the judges' and lawyers' efforts at conflict resolution. Even many alternative dispute resolution processes, such as the mediation services offered by state and federal consumer protection agencies, are managed or funded by governments. Insurance companies, so critical in personal injury cases, must be licensed by government and are heavily regulated by the states. In brief, some dimension of politics permeates the selection or regulation of the professional participants in American courts.

LOYALTY TO LAW AS POLITICS

Another way to understand the linkage of law and politics is to ask litigants and legal professionals about the changes they would favor in law and the judicial process. As is illustrated in many of the interviews in this book, usually they prefer small-scale or incremental changes in the selection of personnel, the management of court operations and court procedures, the financing of courts, or the substantive law. Such recommendations for change not only indicate a loyalty to the idea of the rule of law, but they are also proposals that assume that the improvement of legality is often a matter of legislative action. Indeed, studies of legal reforms find that change is most likely when the bar or associations of judges lobby the legislature for changes or, in a few instances, sponsor state constitutional amendments. Even the Chief Justice of the United States sends a yearly formal message to Congress on the need for change in the operations and funding of the federal courts. Often, also, a sense of crisis must galvanize the legislature into action (Cook 1969–70; Feeley 1983, 191–207). When the legislature does change the judicial process, the change is often not implemented. For example, efforts to ban plea bargaining have only caused prosecutors, public defenders, and judges to find other ways to ensure guilty pleas and avoid trials.

However, it is striking that Americans hardly ever abandon law and legal procedures or "exit" legality. In the early twentieth century legislators endeavored to take cases concerning worker's injuries out of courts and assign them to expert boards for compensation, but within a few decades the worker's compensation boards had become adversarial legal entities in which all key personnel were lawyers (Nonet 1969). Today, calls to remove some issues from the realm of law and courts usually fall on deaf ears. Despite calls by everyone from Grateful Dead fans to Libertarian Party candidates to the late conservative Republican author William F. Buckley, Jr., to cancer sufferers seeking medicinal relief, polls indicate that a majority of Americans support the courts and desire to keep marijuana use a crime (PollingReport.com 2009; Gonzales v. Raich 2005). Indeed, drug users of all stripes are commonly penalized under the law rather than given therapy or treatment with neurochemicals.

CONCLUSION

Politics helps constitute the power and defines the importance of law and courts, and law and courts cannot escape being political instruments in the hands of the public and its government. As the reader peruses our scrapbook of interviews or collects his or her own set of life stories, he or she should always ask, How is this person's professional or personal life shaped by assumptions about the value of law, and how is he or she using law to shape his or her world? How does the law affect people's lives and their identities, as workers, mothers, victims, criminals, or lovers, in the eyes of others? How does law encourage people to seek out solutions to their grievances, to challenge their economic, social, or political status, to influence how judges and juries resolve disputes, and to provide leverage against corporate and political power? Finally, students need to ask the ultimate political question. Do their interviews show that the law serves to protect those who have power, money, and status or that it provides an avenue for victims, the less powerful, and the dispossessed to acquire what they regard as justice? Who is empowered and disempowered by the legal management of resolution of conflicts? (For possible answers to these questions, see Engel and Munger 2003; Galanter 1974; Mather 1995.)

II

Civil Litigation

The interviews presented in this section offer discussions of the conduct of civil legal conflicts. These are the conflicts that most Americans are likely to experience. We begin with a joint interview with two lawyers, Paul Cranston and Dan Cooper. Their business centers on different sides of personal liability, or *tort,* cases, cases that are mostly about vehicular accidents. As with more than 90 percent of cases filed in the United States, their cases are about a matter of state law and therefore are heard in a state rather than a federal court. However, usually lawyers' efforts keep disputes about accidents from ending up in court. Much as in Akira Kurosawa's classic 1951 Japanese movie *Rashomon*, in which a rape and murder are filmed in sections that depict the independent recounting of events by four participants, these two attorneys have a different story to tell about the same events (for commentary on the legal aspects of this movie, see Kamir 2000). Because these lawyers either settle most disputes out of court or take no action, the informal rules and practices of settlement they describe are vital to understanding how law shapes the welfare of many Americans. Their stories also recount the reasons that the parties could not achieve a negotiated settlement. That is the reason we asked questions about the events that make up the *pleadings,* or procedures and documents that initiate a case. These events include the filing of a court *complaint,* which is a legal document alleging the defendant's liability for an injury and a "prayer" for the judge to afford a remedy for the injury. It is also the reason we posed questions to help the reader understand the response of the defense to a complaint—whether they defaulted, filed a formal legal document called an *answer* to the allegations in the complaint, or sought to have a judge dismiss the complaint because of a lack of an asserted injury or the lack of authority or *jurisdiction* of the court over the subject of the complaint.

The stories told by these two lawyers also contain discussions of how each party experienced the pretrial and trial process and their assessment of outcomes. Through these interviews the reader can see the progress of the case from *discovery*, a process that permits each side to evaluate the evidence in the case collected by the opposition, through *pretrial conference* with the judges to jury selection, the trial, the judge's charge to the jury, and the verdict. The assessment of outcomes focuses not just on who wins and loses or on who is *liable* or *not liable* in legal parlance but on how each side perceives the fairness of the trial process. For most participants in litigation, the assessment of the fairness of the outcome has two dimensions: what scholars call *distributive justice,* or the fairness of the outcome achieved by negotiation or ordered by the judge, and *procedural justice,* or the fairness of the process by which the outcome is achieved (Tyler 1988, 1990).

The Cranston and Cooper interview also illustrates the importance of interpersonal relations. The legal process is not normally a process captured and directed by rigid rules. It is a fluid and dynamic process in which participants' power, roles, norms, and practices adjust to changing circumstances. In this process, lawyers try to influence their clients, and clients try to influence their lawyers. Lawyers negotiate and try to settle the conflict without the time and costs of a trial for their clients and the taxpayers. The judge must often act as a broker between adversarial interests. Jurors must reach a consensus. Even the outcome of the case does not strip one side of all of its interests. Sometimes scholars and courtroom participants refer to the judicial process as a game. This is true; as in a game, the parties interact in a restricted combat in which they defend or advance their interests.

CIVIL LITIGATION: THE VARIOUS PARTICIPANTS

Although the stories from the joint interview with Cranston and Cooper shed light on the reality of the law, as noted earlier no single set of stories can convey what goes on in American courts. We offer additional interviews to cast further light on civil litigation. In these other areas of legal conflict, various forms of law and informal norms shape a community of practice. Therefore, at each courthouse the judges, private lawyers, court clerks, administrators, and other staff often regularly interact, learn about one another, and develop routines for the management and resolution of specific categories of conflicts (see Mather et al. 2001, 41–63). Several of the interview subjects discuss some of the norms of cooperation and mutual respect among lawyers and the people they interact with to settle conflicts, and this section generally describes the people and interactions that can shape who gets what from legal processes.

Litigants

If a person or business is locked in a conflict with other persons, businesses, or government, has suffered a physical or psychological injury, or perceives a deprivation of rights, the first decision they face is whether to "mobilize the law." A complicated mix of community associations, social status, rights consciousness, knowledge of legal procedures, access to lawyers, procedural rules of a court, and severity of physical and economic injury affects the decision to file a complaint and initiate a lawsuit (Bumiller 1988; Engel and Munger 2003; Ewick and Silbey 1998: McCann 2008; Merry 1990; Yngvesson 1993). In these situations, interactions or expectations about the behavior of other persons or governmental institutions especially affect the decision to dispute and pursue a legal remedy for a grievance.

Although the media and politicians often complain about "frivolous" litigation, there is no empirical evidence that the public generally bears the costs of individuals' filing of civil complaints for irrational, casual, or inane reasons. Calling a suit frivolous is a value judgment usually made by someone who lacks empathy with the suffering of a person or who fears the economic, political, or social costs of such suits. For example, calling a suit by a teenager against the prom date who jilted her "frivolous" ignores the mental anguish suffered by a girl who cannot attend the most important social event of her young life and gives legitimacy to males' disrespect of females. Moreover, most American judges have the power to penalize litigants and their counsel if they file lawsuits that lack a substantial claim that the court has the power to redress.

Often persons who mobilize the law employ an attorney. Middle- and working-class Americans, as illustrated in the interviews with Paul Cranston and Dan Cooper, Deborah Pascente Lifka, and Scott Friedman, sometimes contact an attorney when injured, especially in an auto accident or on the job, when purchasing real estate, or when seeking a divorce. As indicated in the interview with Linda Rice, some clients might not contact an attorney until long after an injury occurred or a dispute arose. There is sparse published information on client-attorney interactions. There often are few face-to-face meetings of lawyers and clients; much business is transacted by telephone or letter. Nonetheless, lawyers attempt to manage client expectations and behavior. Studies of divorce actions depict the efforts of lawyers to gain control of a client's emotions and expectations, inform them what is legally possible, and guide them to a negotiated settlement (Mather et al. 2001; Sarat and Felstiner 1995). Other studies have found that some lawyers who deal with "one-shot" clients in a high-volume practice leave their clients feeling rushed and their problems unheard (Van Hoy 1997, 72–75). Through this process, as described in the interviews with Scott Friedman, Deborah Pascente Lifka, and Linda Rice, the lawyer gains partial control of the client's preferences, permission to seek a settlement that conforms to local norms of reasonableness, and an ability to transform, at least in part, the emotional trauma of a personal crisis or injury into the impersonal language of the law (see also Kritzer 2004, 188–226).

Lawyers

The interviews with lawyers largely present the stories of the daily activities of lawyers involved in different kinds of civil legal practice and their interactions with clients and other legal professionals. As the interviews indicate, people from a diverse set of backgrounds become attorneys. Some came to the law only after other employment experiences or public service. Some have longed to be lawyers since childhood, whereas others seem to have drifted into the profession and into their current practice because of events in their lives. Some also faced new personal issues when becoming lawyers. This is especially true for female attorneys, as mentioned by Anne Becker, Deborah Pascente Lifka, and Salene Mazur.

Private Practice

All attorneys pay some attention to a core set of tasks and interactions with clients, other lawyers, witnesses, government employees, and judges. In these relationships they often act as brokers between the interests of clients and opposing parties or government (Kritzer 1990). Consequently, attorneys in private practice first must have clients. Law firms, some composed of several hundred lawyers, will require lawyers to generate business, or engage in "rainmaking." As Scott Himsel describes the large law firm in his interview, senior lawyers, or *partners,* in these firms have long-standing clients they keep because of the previous services they performed. Many of these clients are large firms or nonprofit organizations who can afford their services. Junior lawyers, or *associates,* in these firms work with the clients of the partners, but over time they acquire their own clients. Smaller firms, such as the one in which Jeffrey Byer is a partner, have used personal contacts and word of mouth within the community of lawyers to develop a long-standing business clientele. As he and Scott Himsel note, smaller firms also can serve as local representatives for the law firms of national or regional businesses. Robert Eye attracts business through word of mouth and through media coverage of his high-profile cases. Smaller partnerships and solo practitioners, such as Paul Cranston, Scott Friedman, Deborah Pascente Lifka, and Linda Rice, will use personal contacts with individuals, small businesses such as real estate firms, and psychologists and other mental health professionals, participation in social and community activities, word of mouth, and advertising to acquire clients who need legal services for only a single, specific need (Kritzer 2004, 47–67). Although advertising was once severely restricted by state bar associations, judicial decisions have permitted lawyers to advertise (*Bates v. State Bar of Arizona* 1977). Although advertising by personal injury lawyers has become much more common, many lawyers appear to be reluctant to advertise through the mass media and rely instead on their professional reputations (Bowen 1995).

Most lawyers will screen clients or review their claims before taking them as clients (Kritzer 2004, 67–89; Mather et al. 2001, 92–96). Deborah Pascente Lifka describes how this occurs with possible sexual harassment clients, as does Scott Friedman with potential clients seeking representation in family law cases. Also, as Lifka notes, it is not unknown for lawyers to "fire" a client who is uncooperative or who misleads them (Mather et al. 2001, 104–7). Regardless of the organization of their practice, most lawyers try to maintain a "portfolio" of cases—from a few to hundreds—to ensure a steady flow of income. The lawyer in a larger firm in civil practice, such as Scott Himsel, has fifteen to twenty active matters that require some attention; real estate lawyer Deborah Pascente Lifka has fifty active cases; and workers' compensation attorney Linda Rice has more than five hundred active case files. Cause lawyer Cynthia Short, whose work is provided for free, usually takes less than a half dozen cases at a time.

Often the clients of law firms are corporations who will pay them a fee called a *retainer* so that the corporation can consult with the law firm as its legal needs arise. Additional work is paid for at an hourly rate, as Jeffrey Byer and Earl Levere note. Small partnerships composed of a few lawyers and solo practitioners tend to provide legal services for middle- and working-class Americans. For some of their services, as described by Deborah Pascente Lifka, such as writing a will, closing a home purchase, or negotiating a divorce, lawyers will charge a *flat fee* for the one-time client. However, in personal injury cases, or torts, as Paul Cranston notes, lawyers will charge the client a portion, often about a third, of what they win for the client through negotiation or trial. Because this fee depends on winning, it is called a *contingency fee*. Linda Rice also reports charging a 20 percent contingency fee in workers' compensation cases. Regardless of the method of payment, as are other small businessmen, lawyers are very concerned with securing payment for services (Kritzer 1990, 55–67).

Lawyers service their client's needs by *advising and counseling* them about the meaning of the law, ways to prevent becoming involved in litigation, and the consequences of legal strategies and tactics. Although they do it differently, Jeffrey Byer, Earl LeVere, and Linda Rice note that this is an activity in which they engage. Those in private practice also must be concerned with both finding clients and keeping them protected by the provision of advice that keeps them out of lawsuits. As discussed in the interview with Scott Himsel, advising the nonprofit organizations that are his clients on the disposition of gifts and churches on employment and effective management, helping them operate in ways that avoid disputes and lawsuits, and educating them about federal policy are an important part of his work. Earl LeVere discusses how he helps corporate leaders to understand the legal implications of buying other companies or the ownership of new inventions. Likewise, Deborah Pascente Lifka explains how she must educate individuals and employers about sexual harassment law. She also finds that she must sooth their emotions and "bring tranquility and peace" into their lives. Finally, lawyers must manage client expectations and be able to convince clients to see rewards in any settlements that they negotiate.

Related to this effort, most lawyers spend much of their time *reviewing* and *drafting documents*. Contracts, deeds, wills, motions, briefs, agreements about the settlement of a case, and other documents require skillful drafting lest the attorney put his clients' interests in jeopardy. Deborah Pascente Lifka details the wide range of document review and drafting required for even the purchase of a home that requires meticulous care. Linda Rice's practice, she states, is very dependent on the routine preparation, processing, and management of assorted documents that must be submitted to the Worker's Compensation Commission or its administrative law judges. However, as Scott Himsel indicates, in larger firms much of this work is delegated to associates.

As attorneys Himsel and Lifka note, lawyers will spend extensive time on the telephone discussing issues with clients and the attorneys of other persons or firms. Often, as described by Jeffrey Byer, they will summarize their understanding of the conversation in a memo or letter to the opposing party. Also, lawyers can draft letters to threaten parties who might offend their clients' interests so that those persons will cease injurious activity. For example, the attorney for a restaurant called "Deceased Poultry" could threaten a hip-hop band that calls itself "Deceased Poultry" with a suit for violation of the restaurant's legally registered trademark. In preparation of these documents, the lawyer might employ investigators to substantiate their client's claims through the collection of evidence from witnesses. They also, as Jeffrey Byer, Earl LeVere, Robert Eye, Scott Friedman, and Linda Rice indicate, will hire experts to assess technical aspects of the claim, such as financial records and scientific, medical, psychological, and technological evidence. Private investigators also can be employed. Lawyers recognize that proper preparation of documents and the conduct of research is often a key determinant of the outcome of the case.

Usually lawyers *negotiate settlements* to disputes. Paul Cranston and Dan Cooper offer detailed perspectives on negotiation with the lawyers of the opposing party or, sometimes, with an unrepresented opponent (called a *pro se* litigant). Lawyers recognize that through negotiations they can protect a client's interests without the costs of trial preparation and courtroom time and, as Robert Eye notes, the uncertainties associated with trial. Much negotiation, however, is not a complicated strategic process of give and take. The negotiation, instead, assumes the liability of one of the parties and focuses on the amount of a settlement. It is a cut-and-dried process in which there are informal rules and a few exchanges of offers and demands very close to a "going rate" for money damages for similar kinds of cases (Kritzer 1991; Ross 1980). Negotiations especially tend to follow a going rate for two reasons. First, most lawyers specialize, and, because of the local organization of American courts, they thus bargain with opponents on a frequent basis. They learn what offers and compromises normally can be expected when dealing with other lawyers, insurance companies, or lawyers for government agencies. Because they will work with some of these people in the future, as Jeffrey Byer and Deborah Pascente Lifka indicate, they want to protect their reputations as "reasonable" and as cooperative, efficient, and honest negotiators (see also Mather et al. 2001, 48–56). Lifka and Scott Friedman also note that less experienced lawyers who do not know the informal rules of exchange can make the negotiation process more difficult.

Second, most lawyers think that adversary contests should have limits. Although they will defend their client's interests in the case, they recognize that settlement often serves the client's emotional or economic interests in a way that is more beneficial than any marginal gains in divorce litigation or from victory at trial in a debt or accident case. As indicated in the interviews with Jeffrey Byer and Scott Himsel, lawyers will also use alternative dispute resolution, such as mediation or arbitration, to settle disputes. The mediation can be court ordered or agreed to by the parties, but lawyers such as Byer and Himsel find that it often is beneficial. Additionally, Robert Eye lists some of the benefits of mediation: satisfactory outcomes for both parties, saving of time and money, and greater control of the parties over the outcome.

Because many executive branch agencies of the federal and state governments regulate businesses, professions, and property owners and provide service and payments such as social security to citizens, disputes can arise about these regulations, services, and payments. Both the government and private parties will employ lawyers to *represent* their interests before the agency. For example, a private lawyer can represent a client who is seeking social security or, as illustrated in the interview with Linda Rice, workers' compensation benefits from government agencies for injuries suffered at work. In her case the representation largely consists of the submission of documents to government administrators or a private company hired to administer a public policy. Also, a private lawyer can represent a property owner who wants a permit to build a garage before a local government's zoning board. A private lawyer can represent a businessman who is seeking a license to operate a tavern from a state alcoholic beverage regulatory agency. As discussed in the Scott Himsel interview, lawyers also can attempt legislative solutions through efforts to get state or federal legislators to change the meaning of the law. In this situation the lawyer becomes a lobbyist.

Finally, lawyers can *litigate,* or prepare for trial and argue cases at trial. As discussed in the interviews with Jeffrey Byer, Robert Eye, Earl LeVere, and Scott Himsel, *discovery*, or the process of reviewing evidence before trial, requires that a lawyer permit the opposition to examine the witnesses and evidence possessed by the opposition. As part of this effort, the lawyer seeking to examine the opposition's case must carefully devise *interrogatories,* or written questions about the case to be answered by his or her opponent; take *depositions,* or sworn oral testimony from the witnesses to be presented by his or her opponent; and file requests for the production of physical and documentary evidence and the medical or physical examination of allegedly injured parties. Often, preparation for litigation involves the preparation for judicial consideration of *motions* to exclude or include evidence and testimony produced through discovery. A failure of the opposition to supply evidence can cause a lawyer to go the judge and seek an *order to produce* or a *subpoena* to compel access to the evidence or witnesses. The lawyer might also participate in a *pretrial conference* or conferences with the judge to discuss motions, the nature of contested issues in the case, possible out-of-court settlement of the case, and issues related to the conduct of the forthcoming trial. In the section of this book on judges, Judge Rick Savignano further describes this conference. By eliminating surprise evidence and creating conditions for lawyers to estimate the strength of their cases, these discovery procedures attempt to turn litigation from an adversarial contest into a search for a way to dispose of the case.

As a result of norms of negotiation and pretrial discovery, most lawyers have experiences similar to those of Jeffrey Byer, Scott Himsel, Deborah Pascente Lifka, Salene Mazur, and Linda Rice. They hardly ever see the inside of a courtroom. Less than 5 percent of civil cases filed with most courts go to trial. The interview with Earl LeVere shows that he is in the minority of lawyers who spend a significant portion of their careers preparing for litigation and trying cases. As with his cases trials tend to occur when settlements are not possible because of the seriousness of the matter, the potential larger size of a monetary remedy, or untested legal arguments or imprecisely worded new laws. As Jeffrey Byer and Earl LeVere describe it, the key to a lawyer's success at trial is preparation. At trial the aim of the lawyer is to pose questions that clearly articulate the legality of the injury or harms suffered by his or her client and to impeach the credibility of the opposition's assertions and witnesses. To this end, as Byer notes, the attorney tries to find and appeal to jurors who will like him or her and treat the case without bias.

Government Lawyers

American federal, state, and local governments employ more than one hundred thousand attorneys. Those lawyers who work for government must satisfy their superiors' requests for sound legal information, success in adjudication, or justification of governmental policy choices. Most of these attorneys are civil servants who are selected for their jobs on the basis of the merit of their credentials. However, the attorneys who manage public agencies and who supervise the work of lawyer civil servants often are political appointees of the president, a governor, or a mayor. Until recently Anne Becker was such an attorney. Her interview illustrates the political selection process for some government attorneys, the political pressures on them from the executive and legislative branches of government, and the politics of dealing with governmentally regulated enterprises. In the interview Becker also stresses how her expertise as an attorney in the field of public utility economics permitted her some degree of independence from political pressures that might affect her duty to the public interest. Her interview also describes how attorney-public managers must acquire both technical knowledge beyond the law and skills in personnel management and the delegation of authority to subordinate technical staff and attorneys. Finally, the interview illustrates how important administrative or regulatory law and legal institutions are in the governance of the firms that affect the daily lives of Americans (for an additional perspective on administrative legal practice, see Schmidt 2005).

Cause Lawyers

Sometimes lawyers will do more than try to defend their clients' interests. As with Robert Eye and Cynthia Short (whose interview is found in the criminal litigation section of this book), some lawyers possess a political or moral passion that will induce them to seek out cases that permit them to challenge public policy. These *cause lawyers* usually have a specific political agenda and a strong commitment to either a liberal or a conservative ideology (Sarat 1998). By searching out clients with problems affected by governmental abuses of rights or victims of the malfeasance of corporations, they attempt to question the constitutional or legal correctness of legislative and executive actions, corporate behavior, trial court decisions, or past judicial judgments. Cause lawyers can undertake to correct such abuses through *class action* lawsuits that present a claim on behalf of a group of people who allegedly suffered the same injury but who otherwise have no connection to one another. For example, civil rights cause lawyers have organized suits by African Americans who claimed that school district policies denied their children equal protection of the law by segregating them in a few schools. Also, cause lawyers have organized class actions that proved that negligence by pharmaceutical manufacturers led to the distribution of drugs and medical appliances that injured groups of people. Cause lawyers also can represent clients in criminal cases that have broader or long-term political significance, such as Clarence Darrow's famous defense of John Scopes for the crime of teaching evolution to students in Tennessee in 1925.

There are different styles of cause lawyer practice (Kilwein 1998). Robert Eye is an example of an "individual client" cause lawyer. He has on occasion taken on environmental cases for ad hoc organizations and civil rights cases for individuals allegedly subjected to police misconduct to secure what he believed was a just outcome of policy controversy in which the client was enmeshed. His experience with the Wolf Creek nuclear plant and other environmental cases and police misconduct cases illustrate how complex and politically charged the litigation of a cause can be. As he points out about the wetlands case, such matters can persist over many years. He also takes criminal cases pro bono, or without charging the client (many states' bar rules require lawyers to provide pro bono services to some poor clients each year). As Eye indicates, this kind of practice is difficult, but it pays benefits when the lawyer realizes he has helped people and made a difference in their lives.

Although she is not engaged in civil litigation, Cynthia Short is another kind of cause lawyer, an "impact" lawyer. She practices the narrow specialty of death-penalty-mitigation litigation in an effort both to remedy a specific client's fate and also to establish legal standards to affect similarly situated clients in the future. Usually working pro bono, she often works as part of a team or network of lawyers who try to prevent the imposition of the death penalty on their poor clients.

Other cause lawyers can try to do more than argue cases. They can try to "mobilize" a group of persons and use legal arguments to advance their interests through litigation, legislative lobbying, or challenges to regulatory actions of administrative agencies. In an interview located in the section of this book on the judiciary, Justice Larry Starcher describes how, when he was a Legal Services attorney, he organized a poor people's organization and mobilized the poor to file divorce cases.

***

Although American lawyers work in different contexts and offer different services for different kinds of clients, they are the key participants in the American legal universe. Their special knowledge of the formal law and legal procedures and of local norms and their skills ensure a powerful place in the adjustment or resolution of their client's cases.

THE TRIAL PROCESS

In the United States there are a wide variety of courts that hold hearings and trials. In some courts judges hear cases about minor crimes and civil suits, often called *small claims,* with low amounts of money at stake. The names of these courts vary among the states in what are sometimes called magistrate, justice of the peace, or district courts. In many states the judges of these courts are not attorneys. Many states also have specialized courts for family or juvenile cases staffed by lawyer judges. Traditionally, their procedures in these courts are less formal, and lawyers might not appear for the parties. These courts rarely or never have jury trials. Instead, they serve as forums for the ratification of divorce settlements arranged by lawyers, disputes about child support and child custody that occur after a divorce, and the assessment of the delinquency of a juvenile. Often the procedure of these courts is less adversarial, as the judge seeks to ameliorate a conflict in an ongoing family relationship or to assess the character of a juvenile. More serious civil and criminal cases are bound over to the jurisdiction of the trial judge who is a lawyer.

Preliminaries

Prior to trial the judge and attorneys interact on several matters. Attorneys can offer motions about the *pleadings,* such as requests for the court to reject the plaintiff's (the party initiating a lawsuit) complaint, and discovery issues, such as motions about the collection of evidence or motions filed by parties to collect and admit or exclude witness testimony and other evidence in their hands or the hands of their opponents. In response to motions by an attorney, the judge can issue *subpoenas* and *orders to produce* so the parties have full knowledge of each other's cases so that there are no surprises at trial and the parties can focus on key points of conflict. The judge will also consider motions for a jury trial. At the same time the attorneys will prepare their arguments and evidence for their clients' cases, and sometimes they will continue to negotiate settlements in the case.

The Jury

In the rare cases that escape the pretrial process without settlement, the first question is whether a party is engaged in a civil dispute "at law" that permits her or him to request either a jury trial or a *bench trial* before a judge but without a jury. Except in small-dollar-amount claims, in many jurisdictions about two-thirds of litigants opt for a jury trial. Often states preclude the use of juries when a party seeks an *equitable remedy,* or specific relief from a court for an alleged injustice, such as an injunction prohibiting interference with a party's life or business or an order of protection against contact with the party by a former lover or spouse, and in civil claims over small amounts of money. If the case qualifies for the exercise of the right, the trial or *petit* jury serves as the public's direct representative in the judicial process. Although the jury traditionally must have twelve members and must decide a case by unanimous vote, the U.S. Supreme Court has permitted smaller juries and non-unanimous verdicts in state courts. Several states have adopted such requirements for civil cases. The Supreme Court of the United States has, however, adopted various standards that require courts to disregard race and gender in the selection of potential jurors.

Using various methods, court clerks, jury commissioners, or other court employees summon potential jurors from the geographic jurisdiction of a court. From this pool of jurors the court randomly calls potential jurors, called a *venire*, to the courthouse. When a trial is to occur, a random selection of the venire is taken to the courtroom, where they are interviewed in a process called *voir dire*. Usually after questions posed to potential jurors by the judge, the lawyers can ask questions. Lawyers can ask the judge to dismiss potential jurors *for cause,* or evidence of obvious bias elicited during the interview, such as knowing a party or witness in a case. Also, the two lawyers possess a limited number of *peremptory challenges* that permit them to move for dismissal of a juror without giving a reason. Nonetheless, even with the use of professional jury consultants, as Robert Eye explains, lawyers' decisions during jury selection are usually more a matter of intuition than applied social science. However, when the stakes are great, as in Cynthia Short's death penalty cases, jury selection becomes a long and intensive process of questioning prospective jurors.

The Trial

After jury selection American trials have five distinctive stages. First, the attorneys for the plaintiff and defendant offer *opening statements* that outline the conflict, explain their clients' versions of events, and identify the witnesses and evidence that will prove their clients' claims. Second, the plaintiff's attorney offers his or her client's *case in chief.* Witnesses provide statements about the conflict based on their direct observation or hearing, and they testify as to the veracity of any physical evidence that supports the plaintiff's claim. For example, a witness could testify that he saw Al's auto smash into Betty's truck and that the fender to be introduced as evidence came off one of the autos. Expert witnesses also can be called to testify about the circumstances of an event they did not witness if they have special knowledge recognized by both parties. For example, a police officer could testify about the length of skid marks observed on the road at the accident site. To test the truthfulness of their testimony, the plaintiff's witnesses are then subjected to cross-examination by the defense counsel. Third, the defense offers its case in chief by calling witnesses to rebut the plaintiff's witnesses and, sometimes, to offer an alternative explanation of events (an *affirmative defense*). The plaintiff's counsel can cross-examine these witnesses. Fourth, the attorneys sum up the evidence supporting their client's claims in a *closing argument*. Finally, the judge charges the jury. He issues *instructions to the jury,* or explains the law applicable in the case, and fixes the *burden of proof.* In most civil litigation the judge will inform the jury that the plaintiff must prove his or her claim by a *preponderance of the evidence.*

As Robert Eye indicates, judges vary in how they address and process cases. Lawyers, therefore, often try to predict how a judge will react toward issues such as the admissibility of evidence. Often lawyers share such specialized knowledge or use it to inform clients about the probable outcome of their case if it goes to trial (Mather et al. 2001, 99–100).

The trial usually concludes with the verdict of the jury. Simulations and other studies of jury decision making suggest that usually a few jurors dominate discussions in the jury room. They reach most decisions with limited debate and little acrimony, focus on legal factors, and make a decision that is often what the judge would have given. Few juries cannot reach a decision, or are *hung*. There also is little evidence that lawyer tricks or emotional appeals will have a significant effect on the liability and remedy decisions of the majority of jurors (see Hastie 1993; Vidmar and Hans 2007). As Judge Steven King comments in his interview in the judiciary section of this book, most jurors take their task seriously and do a "terrific" job.

The decision of the jury can hold the defendant *not liable* and uphold the claims of the defendant. If the defendant is held *liable* for the plaintiff's asserted injuries, the jury can assign a *remedy*. Most frequently the remedy is the award of money damages. In a sample of state court cases from 2005, the plaintiff won approximately 56 percent of civil trials, but a higher percentage of plaintiffs won in contract (66 percent) than in tort cases (personal injury; 52 percent). In the sample of tort trials, plaintiffs were most likely to win in cases involving an animal attack (75 percent), followed by motor vehicle accidents (64 percent). Plaintiffs won far less often in medical malpractice trials (23 percent) and product liability trials that involved manufactured goods other than asbestos (20 percent). Mortgage foreclosure cases in which the plaintiff was either a mortgage company or other financial lending institution had the highest percentage of plaintiff winners (89 percent) of all varieties of tort and contract cases. The median amount won by plaintiffs in tort and contract cases was only $28,000 ($24,000 in tort cases and $35,000 in contract cases), from which the plaintiff usually had to pay lawyer's fees. Only 5 percent of civil cases resulted in awards of punitive damages as penalty for an injury or "pain and suffering." The median amount of punitive damages was $64,000. Plaintiffs won more than $1 million in only 4.4 percent of cases that went to trial (U.S. Department of Justice 2008a).

Although the jury renders its decision, the decision is not final until it is accepted by the judge. In very rare circumstances the judge can set aside the finding on the issue of liability, especially if he or she discovers errors in the conduct of the trial or the actions of the jury. In such circumstances the judge can order a new trial or direct a verdict. Also, the judge can modify the remedy by reducing or increasing the money damages awarded by the jury.

Finally, once a trial has concluded or the parties have negotiated a settlement, it is not always over. Whatever remedies a settlement provides or a judge or jury awards can cause additional conflicts. A divorced parent might violate a child support order, or a debtor might fail to pay the winner in a creditor-debtor case. In these situations the parties can petition the judge for *equitable relief,* or the enforcement or modification of the remedy. Judges make such judgments and grant various forms of equitable relief on the basis of "sound judicial discretion" and without jury trial. However, litigation is rarely so decisive that it terminates a conflict. As Robert Eye notes, collecting money won in civil cases can be difficult and can involve additional legal actions and expenses. As Scott Friedman mentions, in ordinary divorces and other family law matters, the parties can return to court again and again to adjust child custody, child support, or alimony settlements. The history of the litigation of many constitutional rights is frequently less a history of a decision settling the scope of a right than a story of how a decision opens up a whole new arena of disputes. For example, in *Roe v. Wade* (1973), the Supreme Court of the United States determined that the Fourteenth Amendment to the Constitution protects a woman's right to an abortion. But the decision only resulted in new legislation, new lawsuits, and many more adjudications of the right (Epstein and Kobylka 1992, 203–98). The lesson, thus, is that litigation and the more general reference of Americans to law and courts is but a part of a dynamic, ongoing effort to keep social, political, and economic order. Each time a court opens its doors or a lawyer welcomes a client, people repeat the never-ending story of efforts to use law to bring order and some sense of justice to a fractious society.

The Role of Court Staff

Various court personnel support the civil litigation process. Courts have clerk's offices that accept filings and keep the records of cases. Sheriffs or private process servers deliver *summonses* that inform the defendant of the filing of a complaint. Bailiffs and tipstaffs furnish security and order in the courtroom. Court reporters type or record transcripts of testimony and motions made during trials. In some larger jurisdictions professional court administrators oversee the assignment of cases to judges and manage jury pools, court finances, security, and the employment of court personnel. Judges can employ young lawyers to serve as personal law clerks who assist them with research and document drafting. Some courts hire staff attorneys to administer cases and provide drafts of documents and opinions for judges. In addition to these staff employees, volunteers assist the courts. In the criminal process, separate offices supervise probationers, and sometimes there are victim-witness assistance programs, victim compensation programs, and drug or alcohol counseling programs. The CASA volunteers (court-appointed special advocates) mentioned in the interview with Judge Steven King are citizens trained to assist and to speak for the interests of abused, neglected, or foster children who are affected by the decisions of courts.

CONCLUSION

The interviews and the brief description of the civil process in this section cannot capture the variety of people, conflicts, activities, procedures, and rules that affect litigation. As a scrapbook of stories and a generic description of the civil process, it is only a guide to understanding law and courts. The items listed as references at the end of this book are intended to encourage the reader to delve more into the complex and dynamic world of civil litigation.

Paul Cranston and Dan Cooper

Perspectives on Personal Injury Lawyers

MIDDLE-CLASS AND WORKING-CLASS Americans usually employ lawyers for a single dispute—they are "one-shotters." This interview and the
following interviews with Deborah Pascente Lifka and Scott Friedman
present the perspectives of lawyers who address the most common legal
needs of ordinary Americans: compensation for injuries from accidents,
the purchase of a home and real estate transfers, and divorce and associated family issues. The following joint interview with Paul Cranston,
who represents injured persons, and Dan Cooper, who at the time of the
interview represented the insurance companies of the persons who allegedly caused the injury, discusses how these disputes are managed. Both
men have long experience in personal injury law. Usually they address
these disputes after the injured party has refused a settlement offer from
a nonlawyer employee of the insurance company, known as an adjuster.
The interview was conducted in the offices of Cranston and Edwards,
a two-attorney partnership located in a suburban Morgantown, West
Virginia, office building.

Dan, could you describe your practice?
> DAN: I guess I tell people that I do commercial litigation because usually my
> clients tend to be insurance companies being sued. Lately I've been defend-
> ing insurance companies when they get sued. The general description is
> just litigation. We do all kinds of litigation. I tell people that I'm charging
> for fussing and fighting. And that's what we do, any type of litigation that
> comes down the pike.

And you work for what firm?
> DAN: I'm at Steptoe and Johnson.

What's the size of that firm?
> DAN: We have about one hundred fifty lawyers now.

Throughout the state?

    DAN: Right. Probably a third of those people are doing litigation; another third are doing business and transactions.

When you came into the firm, did you go right into litigation?

    DAN: Well, I was going to go into the business department. I just decided that I couldn't stand doing that kind of work. I thought it might be kind of boring, so I went into litigation.

    PAUL: Dan and I started at the same time. I graduated from law school a year before Dan; we clerked together. I had the same idea as Dan. I graduated with an accounting degree. I was thinking about becoming a tax lawyer or getting into business law. When I started at the firm, I kind of observed what the lawyers did. I thought the litigation practice looked a lot more exciting and more enjoyable. Basically, I was doing the same thing as Dan is doing now.

    DAN: I've doubted myself a few times over the years because litigation can be pretty stressful from time to time. It seems to me sometimes that some of the business partners don't lead quite as stressful a life. They might say otherwise, I guess; I don't know what causes them stress. They have a lot of deadlines and that sort of thing. But I think overall that was the right thing to do. I think litigation has not been boring. I always thought that whatever I did in life is something that you have to do every day. You have to go in to work. You have to do it every day. I always thought that wouldn't it be horrible if what you did is boring. I don't know how anybody could stand to do a boring job day after day. I guess a lot of people can stand it. It really never has been too terribly boring. From time to time you end up with a few tedious periods of time, but overall I think that was a good decision, going into litigation.

    PAUL: I agree. Like Dan, sometimes, particularly in recent years with the kids growing up when you've got all these activities going on, I think litigation practice is much more stressful, unpredictable, where a business practice, the lawyers that I see doing a business practice have more of a regular schedule, at least that's my perception. Our schedule is pretty erratic. We may have a case where we have an expert out in California, Florida, or somewhere where in a week's notice we've got to fly out there and that makes it difficult, but the plus of litigation is, I think, it's not boring. Every case and every person you meet is new, and there are always a lot of turns and twists. I do a lot of personal injury and car accident cases on behalf of individuals who are hurt. They all seem—generally you think they're all pretty much the same, but there are always little twists and turns, things are different, and everybody you meet is different. That keeps you wanting to come to work.

Dan, your clients, you mentioned, are insurance companies. Does your firm have those clients for long periods of time? Are they on retainer to your firm?

    DAN: It's really very competitive nowadays with insurance companies. There are lots of people doing what we do, and some of the work can be price sensitive. They'll more or less go with the lowest bidder. It isn't like it used to be, where the firm can count on having these institutionalized clients; it's not like that anymore. They go with the cheaper provider. There are several reasons for this. One of them is that the turnover in these companies is higher than it used to be. People coming and going, moving around from place to place; it used to be that personal relationships could always be counted on to keep the work flow going. Sometimes it's not quite that way anymore. In what I'm doing, though, in defending the insurance companies, you tend to get hired by the people in the corporate office. So you are able to maintain those relationships a little easier than when you're defending their insurers. A lot of places refer to that as commodity work, defending the insured party versus defending the company. You tend to keep those relationships going if you do the work for them, if you do a good job. They're looking for the result. They're looking much more carefully at the result when their name is under the v. instead of their insured's name.

PAUL: I think it's difficult for a defense lawyer, what Dan does. I think what he's saying is that in some cases you're just going to represent the insurance company if the insurance company is being sued. But then you've got other cases, such as a car wreck case, where the insurance company hires a lawyer to defend the insured. That's really an interesting relationship there because the insurance company is paying your bill. As a defense firm, now that it has gotten so competitive, you want to maintain a good relationship with the carrier. At times there is a little bit of a conflict situation they can put you in—if the insurance carrier wants you to do something, and you want to do something else because it's in the best interest of the insured, then that puts the lawyer in a tough situation.

[To Dan] Don't you think?

DAN: I hear that all the time, but I have to say I've never really experienced that. In my experience, the people you're working with, the claims adjusters have the same interest that their insured does. They want to get the best result that they can for the insured. I guess I've just been lucky and not experienced that situation. What he's describing, if you're defending the insured for an insurance company, your client is not the insurance company, but you have a business relationship with the insurance company that you need to maintain so that you can get work. And I have not really experienced a big problem with that. I have heard people talk about it a lot, though.

DAUL: When I was at the firm, maybe a year or so out of law school, I had one situation—it wasn't really a problem with the client, but I remember a client, the insured, asking me a lot of questions when they weren't real happy with what the insurance company wanted to do. In that particular case, the insured had a personal attorney. I don't know if I told him to do that or if he already had a personal attorney, but it seemed to get resolved when the insured talked to his personal attorney and then everything seemed to be fine. That was the first time I can ever remember thinking about that, but that was something since that time that I have always been conscious of, and I think it's difficult for a defense attorney in that situation. Dan and I've had some cases. I know that when you ask for information you try to get in a case, some of it is really in control of the insurance company. How do you get that information? Does the insurance company have to provide it, or does the individual have to provide it? There are some confusing situations there.

Dan, you've talked about this being a more competitive environment and that you have to keep these insurance companies happy if they're going to come back for business. Is that on your shoulders individually, or does the firm take care of keeping those relationships healthy with the insurance companies?

DAN: No, it's on the lawyers' shoulders.

So the clients come back because they've dealt with you and they like you as opposed to their coming back because they have this ongoing relationship with the firm?

DAN: There's a little bit of both of that. I've been working for one company since the day I walked in the door. And actually a couple of them are like that, I've done their work for sixteen years, and that's because they know me. They come back to me. When you first start out, you're working underneath a senior lawyer, by and large, and they're sending you the case, and you're doing the nuts-and-bolts work on the case and talking things over with them. Most cases that I handle now, I'm really not primarily responsible for the day-to-day handling of the case. The file might come in to me, and I'll look at it and see what's going on and sort of do triage on it, and then send it to one of the five or six different associates who I work with, and they'll take over primary responsibility for handling that file. There are some days where I spend the whole day just going from office to office talking about what's going on in the various files. I can't bill a thing on those days! [*laughs*]

Paul, can you describe your practice?

PAUL: As I said, I started out with Dan's firm. Since I left that firm, my practice comes down to basically representing individuals rather than companies. And ninety-nine percent of what I do is probably personal injury work, which includes car accidents, some medical malpractice cases; and I've sued insurance companies for claims in addition to personal injuries. But it's basically a personal injury practice—any kinds of injuries, wrongful death. I've handled some labor and employment cases. And I do those occasionally, but not as much. I did a few, probably more [than] five years ago. But, unlike how Dan gets paid, I get paid on a contingency basis, which there has been a lot of discussion about in the news. One of the reasons why I think that a contingency fee is good is because most of my clients do not have the ability to pay an attorney if they're hurt. It doesn't matter that they have a legitimate claim that they want to pursue, because they wouldn't have one hundred or two hundred dollars an hour to pay a lawyer to handle their claim. So the way I get paid is that I take a percentage of what I recover for the client. I get a percentage of that fee in the end. And I think it's very good because it allows people who have legitimate claims to pursue them when they couldn't otherwise afford a lawyer. Dan has mentioned how he keeps his clients and the competitiveness in the insurance defense business. My business is very competitive as well. The biggest problem that I face is the legal advertising that we have today. There are things on TV that raise ethical concerns for me. I don't think that a lot of this advertising does us any good, not me or any lawyer. I tell law students who I teach to be very careful about this. I think that it needs to be very tasteful. There is a potential out there that you have a lawyer, just a new lawyer who doesn't know what they're doing, and if their dad or somebody has some money, they can put on a big advertising campaign. That, unfortunately, is how these people get most of their cases. And they are not necessarily the best cases. When you go on this big advertising campaign, you may get the case where somebody had a fly in their sandwich at Hardee's [a fast food outlet] and they want to sue somebody. I don't handle cases like that. Some of these folks on TV, they might be able to do that. I guess what I'm saying is that they've got freedom of speech, which everybody is entitled to, but I'm proud to be a lawyer and I'm proud of my profession and I think it should be an honorable profession. I think that some of these advertisements out there don't cast a good light on our profession. There are people out there getting work not because they're better attorneys, but because of their advertising.

Dan, do you agree with that?
DAN: Yes, I do.

How do you get your clients, and who are they?
PAUL: I would say ninety-nine percent of the good cases that I have are people who know me or who have been referred to me by former clients or attorneys. If Dan would get a call, for example, on a case that I would handle, a personal injury case that he couldn't handle, some lawyers that I've had some cases against will think I do a pretty good job [and] refer me some cases, but most of them are people I know. If I handle a case and do something well for a client, then that's word of mouth. Very rarely do I get a significant case just out of the phone book or just out of the blue. We get some car accidents, some smaller car accident cases, and my partner Bryan Edwards does some criminal defense work. And he gets some of his criminal clients who call on the phone, but the good cases come by a recommendation. Most people check out the lawyers and want to find somebody they have good information about.

Can you describe your clientele?
PAUL: Through the years I've represented all types of people. I've represented doctors in personal injury cases. I've represented people who aren't working,

who never had a job. Most of my clients are probably moderate- to middle-income people, ordinary people who had a car accident or have something happen to them. It's anybody. And I've found that one of the things that helps me relate to some of these folks is that I grew up a middle-class person. My mom was a teacher, and I worked my way through school.

Did you grow up here?
PAUL: I grew up in Marietta, Ohio.

When your clients first come in, what do you do?
PAUL: Well, to me, and Dan will probably appreciate this, the most important thing to me is to get a description of the case before you set up the appointment with the client. And you would hope that a client, if they're intelligent, they're going to be interviewing the lawyer to make sure that the lawyer is competent and understands their needs. But the most important thing to me is that I have a credible, likable person when they come in with a personal injury case. When I was younger and just starting out on this side of the fence, you get a good case, say the damages were good, you knew that you could obtain a pretty significant recovery, but you might get some bad feelings about the client. It might be someone you don't necessarily want to be around a lot, or it's just, there are little indications that this person is going to be hard to handle; they're not going to listen to you. That's important. If I'm going to represent someone, I need them to listen to me; otherwise they don't need me as a lawyer. I really want to evaluate the client, to make sure he or she is someone that's credible and trustworthy. It's a continuing process; that first interview you have to decide whether you're willing to enter into a fee arrangement or agreement with the client. Then we will proceed to investigate the case and see if there is something there. As time goes by, you're still picking up on information from the client and kind of figuring out if this [is] somebody I really want to represent. Generally, though, once somebody retains me as their lawyer, I stick with it. I can't remember a case that I have withdrawn from because I've later on had any problem with the client. So the initial interview process, my interview with the client is critical. You really need to get to know them, assess them, at that point in time.

Have your clients already been made an offer by the insurance company for settlement by the time they reach your office?
PAUL: That's changed a little bit in recent years. In years past, I would say most of them did. It depends on timing and the case. Some folks, if they suffer something pretty significant, a real significant injury where they're hospitalized for a long time, they are going to have somebody contact a lawyer because they know it's going to be an important, lifelong decision they are making early on. And generally at that point there hasn't been an offer, other than possibly their own insurance company paying some of their

medical bills. But most of the time they've usually had some communications with the insurance company, and some type of offer has been made to them. When the folks come to me at that point, it's because they're not happy with the offer that's been made.

And that offer has been made by the insurance adjuster?

PAUL: Yes. For example, say Dan and I are in a car accident and it's my fault. My insurance company would get a copy of the accident report and get in touch with Dan at some point. We understand that you were injured in this car accident. Please send us your medical bills and let us know what happened to you. And then they would proceed to evaluate the claim and try to make an offer to Dan as to what they think is fair and reasonable compensation. That's what's supposed to happen, and sometimes it does and sometimes it doesn't.

How do you proceed with the case?

PAUL: For what I do on a personal injury case, first thing I do is I have a pretty standard form where I get information from the client, a lot of background information. I also want to know anything bad that's happened to them in the past, including injuries, whether they have a criminal record—things like that, which are intrusive, but you have a private relationship with the client. I need to know these things because, before I send a letter to Dan's client, I want to know my client, and I don't want to tell them that I have someone who is just a wonderful type of person when they've got a long criminal record, so I need to evaluate them. So what I do is get the client in, get their information. Another early step in a personal injury case is to obtain all relevant medical records. For the person who's been off from work, I try to develop a rapport with the employer, at least obtaining information from the employer about their wages, what they did, what their loss is going to be. So the first step is really about getting the medical records and getting the medical bills. Then I try to get those to the insurance company as soon as possible, to avoid a lawsuit. As I was telling Dan, over the past couple of years most of my cases that I have are resolved through the process of getting the information, evaluating that information, putting it together, engaging in settlement negotiations with the insurance company, and obtaining a settlement without having to file a lawsuit.

DAN [to Paul]: If people call your office and want to hire you as a lawyer, you have to do a triage with them at that point, where you're making a judgment whether you even want to schedule an appointment with them? Or do you just sort of take all comers?

PAUL: No. The way we work it here is the receptionist will answer the phone, and she'll pass the call on to my assistant. She talks to them and gets some information.

DAN [to Paul]: So she makes the first judgment call about whether it's somebody you might want to talk to?

PAUL: Anybody who calls, I want to know about it. They let me know. For example, if a call comes in, and if I am available, what my assistant would do is call me and describe the case to me. I try to talk to everybody, but being so busy, and it's really busy, I'm not as good as I used to be about that. So, based on the information that I get from my assistant, sometimes I'll tell them to please let the person know that I can't handle this case but that they may want to call so-and-so. I always tell people that I'm not the end for them and that if they feel they have something or want something to contact another lawyer. In a good portion of the potential cases, I don't end up talking to the people because you get a lot of calls.

PAUL: You asked me about employment calls?

Yes.

PAUL: There are very few employment calls that I get where I think there is a good case there because of our laws on employment. We have an employment-at-will doctrine in West Virginia. Basically, an employer can fire an employee for any reason as long as it doesn't violate some established type of policy. Employers may not be nice to an employee, and they fire them just to be mean, but that doesn't always give you a lawsuit. There's got to be something else. We get a lot of those calls.

DAN *[to Paul]*: Did you ever hear of any of them that you've turned down that later somebody else picked up and made something good out of it?

PAUL: I've heard of cases that I have turned down where clients have gone to another lawyer, but to be honest with you, I've never heard of a case where a client did this and anything real good came out of it. I've had some smaller cases that I haven't had the time to handle, that I've referred to other lawyers, and I think they've done okay with, but it hasn't been because it was a case that I've rejected because I didn't think it was a good case.

DAN *[to Paul]*: I would think that one of the clues would be, you get a call and they tell you, yeah, I've talked to so-and-so and so-and-so, and they told me they were too busy to take the case. Every now and then we'll get a *pro se* plaintiff on a case. They are the most difficult to deal with from the defense perspective, because they've been turned down by three or four lawyers, but all the lawyers tell them, "Well, yeah, you've got a great case, but you know I'm just a little to busy to help you. Why don't you go see that guy?" [*laughs*]

PAUL: And that's something when I start interviewing clients I always try to find out, whether they have contacted another lawyer or not. I have actually rejected cases because I didn't think the person gave me an honest answer, where you can look at them and sense that they have contacted another lawyer, where they say, "I'm not sure." How can you not be sure about that? I'm going to scrutinize a client a little bit more if they tell me, well, they've talked to four different lawyers. And here's what you typically get is, "I talked to this lawyer and he told me I had a really great case, but he doesn't have time to handle it, so he said to call you" [*laughs*]. What I generally tend to tell people is, "If Joe Lawyer thought you had a great case, he would find time to handle it."

DAN: [*Laughing*] Because, you know, they don't trust me, I'm the defense attorney. I tell them that they don't have a good case against my client, and they tell me that same story—a lawyer said that they had a good case, but he was too busy to handle it. If it's a good case, the lawyer will keep it!

PAUL: In malpractice cases, here's something that commonly happens. I have people who come in and say one Dr. Jones screwed up and that they went to another doctor and this doctor told them that Dr. Jones screwed up. That happens a lot, and I tell them that they need to get that second doctor to call me or send me a letter and tell me that's the case. I have one case right now where the client told me that, and the second doctor actually did say to me, "Yeah, I did tell him that, this doctor did screw up." That's the only case that I can remember having where a doctor would actually come forward and confirm that was the case. I think sometimes doctors do give people the impression that they do feel that maybe another doctor screwed up in some way. But they're colleagues of one another and they're reluctant to publicly criticize another doctor.

When these cases come in and you gather this information, you said you have these records collected. I assume you write letters, or does the client do that?

PAUL: That's a major process. People don't understand what we do, and sometimes that's hard for clients until they come in and see their file and see all the letters. It's a very complicated system of obtaining medical records. Basically, we have a statute that allows clients, or a lawyer working on their behalf, to request copies of medical records and to get bills. So we have to send letters to the health care providers. Many of these health care providers now use what they call outsourcing services, where they may have a company in Georgia that will actually provide the medical records. Some providers will immediately send you the medical records with a bill and allow you to pay them at that point. Some of them, they outsource, and you'll get a letter from their outsourcing company saying this is how much it's going to cost you, and you have to pay us before we send the records, unless you've established a prior relationship with them. It's complicated, and I've had some cases over that. I was involved in a class action lawsuit a few years ago against about all the hospitals in the state and some of these copying companies for charging people too much for copies of their own medical records. We entered into a settlement with all the providers in those cases and the outsourcing companies where they agreed to reduce their charges to people in the future. It was a good benefit to the people in West Virginia, but it's complicated. That's something that has changed a great deal since we've been practicing. It used to be simple.

DAN: When we first started sixteen or seventeen years ago, you could get an injury case, and Paul might call me on the phone. We would be talking about the case, and we might say, let's just get the doctor on the phone. We would call him up on the phone and ask about the case, and the doctor would just tell us about the injury and the treatment and that sort of thing. Not anymore.

PAUL: Some doctors just refuse to treat personal injury patients because they do not want to get involved at all in the legal process. Some doctors who do treat those patients make it very difficult on themselves because they won't call you back, they won't talk to you. They'll say, "You've got to talk to my lawyer." For example, what Dan just said, there are some doctors who I can call up on the phone, as long as I've gotten a release from the client, they'll tell me what I need to know, but that's very rare anymore. And when you're dealing with the West Virginia University hospitals for example, it's such a corporate form that you can't even talk to the doctors. To talk to the doctors, they send you a letter that says this is how much it costs to talk to our doctor. If you want to talk to Dr. Smith, you have to send me a check for five hundred dollars, and Dr. Smith will talk to you. If you want Dr. Smith to write you a report telling you what he's going to tell you over the phone, it will be another one thousand dollars. It frustrates me because sometimes I just need to know whether she's going to get this surgery or not. It's just a real quick question. The client is telling me that she needs surgery, and I don't see it [in] the medical records, so I want to find out if that's true or not because the insurance company wants to know and we'd like to settle the case. I don't really want to spend five hundred dollars. Dan's represented some insurance companies that I have cases with now. One insurance company in particular I think I have a real good rapport with, although we're obviously adversaries in our cases. What we have had to do in many of these cases where we can't get good communication from many of these doctors, we developed a letter that the insurance company is willing to pay to have the doctor complete. It's a form where the doctor checks off little boxes, but what's happened recently is now the doctors aren't allowed to use that form. They have to dictate what's on the form and their answers. Half of the time they don't answer half the questions, so the insurance company or me is paying a lot of money and not even getting our questions answered.

Do you employ investigators or anything like that?

PAUL: Sometimes, we both do.

DAN: We have a couple employed in the firm.

Back to the settlement. When you do settle cases, basically, it's you and the insurance company, and Dan doesn't really come into that equation.

DAN: Presuit. If I would file a lawsuit, most of the time there is no lawyer involved for the insurance company. It's me dealing with the adjuster, and these adjusters are educated people, and they know what they're doing,

I mean they're supposed to know what they're doing. What generally happens is the insurance company will have made an offer, or I've made a demand, and at some point we agree to settle the case. I can only agree to settle the case after speaking with my client and obtaining their consent. I tell people, I've got a hundred cases. This is your only case, so you've got to think long and hard about that. So after I've talked to the client and the client agrees, I would call the insurance adjuster, and then I would confirm it in a letter that we've agreed to settle for x amount. And what happens, the insurance company would then send a release that my client would need to sign saying that we're settling this, this is over, we can never sue you again on this, and send a check.

And the client pays his or her contingency fee from that to you?
PAUL: Yes.
DAN: All this stuff adds expenses, and that means they have to get more money from us to want to settle.
PAUL: That's right. I advance expenses, too. This is another thing with our system now in medical malpractice cases. I was telling Dan how hard the laws have made it for lawyers and people to have these cases because for me to try a medical malpractice case, it could cost me a lot of money. I'm looking at between thirty thousand to fifty thousand dollars in expenses in an average case that I need to spend to prepare the case and maybe take it to court. I would need to advance that out of my pocket. The way I work it, I advance those expenses, and if I represent you, you don't have to pay me those expenses back, reimburse me those expenses unless I win. Now some lawyers will take cases where they obligate the client to reimburse them for the expenses regardless of what happens. I don't do that.
DAN: As a practical matter, you're not going to get that money, even if you do say you're going to charge them for it.
PAUL: No. If you've got a client, say someone who does have some money where they have agreed they would pay all the expenses, but it would be a different type of fee arrangement. But Dan's right. That's one thing that is nice about my practice, doing things on a contingency fee. I don't have to send bills out to clients. When I get the check from the insurance company, the check's made payable to my client and me as the client's attorney. We have trust accounts [for the client's share] that I cannot put my own funds into. It's client funds, it's going to be separate. So I would have the client come into the office to sign the check, I would sign the check, and then deposit it in the client trust account, and then I would disburse checks from there. I would give the client his share of the settlement, I would write a check to myself for my fee and my expenses. I also try to find out if there are any medical bills that the client owes, and I pay those. I found through the years that I'm better off if I get this in my fees agreement, that the client is giving me authority to pay off bills when the

settlement is over, because people sometimes they say they'll take care of the bills and then it's a major headache for me, but more so for the individual. I think they're better off in the long run if they allow me to pay those bills. It also helps me try to maintain a good relationship with the health care providers.

As to the settlement amount, could you discuss who contacts whom and whether or not there is some kind of understanding of the range of settlement that might occur?

PAUL: Who knows? [*laughs*] Cases are different, but the way the procedure is supposed to work in West Virginia is that the insurance company is required to make a good-faith, a fair and reasonable settlement offer to the victim, or the injured person, based on the information that they have. And they have to investigate that to try to find out what injuries and damages the person has suffered. The easier damages, for example, a rear-end car crash where there's no question about somebody's injuries, the medical bills. If the person has five thousand dollars in medical bills, that is something that would go into that evaluation that shouldn't be contested. If the person had to miss three days of work because they were in the hospital right after the accident, the wage loss that the person had during that time should not be contested. Let's say you have seven or eight thousand dollars there. The ambiguous aspect of it is the general damages for pain and suffering, annoyance and inconvenience, those types of things. That's something that differs in every case. You may have somebody who suffered the same injury, but because of their status in life, because of whatever reason, they didn't suffer as much as somebody else. I've represented some poor people not too long ago, and the guy got in a car accident, and he had to go to work, but he couldn't go to work, so he ended [up] losing his job, getting all these collection notices. They were going to turn off his electric, his power at his house. He was trying to do the best that he could, but he had a real tough time. He and his wife started having problems as a result of it. It was real difficult on him. They almost had to declare bankruptcy. That put him in a position where he might compromise what his claim was really worth just to get some money to be able to go on with his life. Whereas a doctor, or somebody in a higher economic status, they may be able to afford to wait because that wouldn't be as disruptive on his life because they have other financial resources. Just because their car has been totaled they can afford to go out and get a rental car and not worry whether the insurance company is going to pay for it. They've got enough in their savings, and they probably have enough in their income policy while they're recovering from their injuries that will help them support their family. Those are some of the things that people don't realize work into the strategy over settlement.

Some of the texts talk about a going rate for settlement for different kinds of injuries. Do you think that's a fair assessment?

PAUL: Dan would probably be better than me at that.

DAN: Everything goes into an evaluation of what the claim is worth. One of the factors that goes into it is what do they think their claim's worth. That's why I have to talk to the insured. I ask them what they think their claim is worth.

PAUL: When Dan and I settle a case, we don't know for certain what the value of that claim is. The only way you find out is to try it in front of a jury.

DAN: And that would only tell you what those people thought it was worth.

PAUL: I do a thorough analysis of all aspects, like Dan said, everything. I've got to factor everything: the medical bills, the wage loss, and the specific losses that this client has suffered. Are they getting collection notices, has their credit been damaged? Whatever problems that would be compensable, those are all factored in. What I try to do is come up with my best evaluation of what would be a fair amount to compensate somebody for that. For example, annoyance and inconvenience for loss of your car, how do you value that? One way I've used through the years to value that is: What would it cost this person to get a rental car of the same type of car? And that's, maybe that's thirty dollars a day. That might be some value, and I think some insurance companies agree with that. It's not just poking out in the air and picking a number. What the claim settles for is based on what the insurance company is willing to pay and what the individual is willing to accept. That's the settlement value. Sometimes for one claim that might be fifty thousand dollars for the same injury and it may be ten thousand dollars for the same injury in another case because you're dealing with different people, different insurance companies. Somebody may be willing to accept ten thousand dollars and move on with their life and somebody else can't afford to do that. I've got to get what I really think this is worth.

So most cases settle, then?

PAUL: Yeah, most of my cases do, and I think that's the same for other lawyers. I'm going to say over ninety percent of the cases I handle.

It sounds like for both of you it's important to know who's on the other line when you're calling up for negotiations. Also, it seems that when you two know each other, when you know the lawyer's a quality plaintiffs' attorney, negotiations are going to go much better than when you don't know them?

DAN: I think that makes all the difference in the world.

PAUL: I agree.

[To Paul]: And the same with the claims adjusters?

PAUL: Claims adjusters and defense lawyers.

DAN: We don't have a lot of confrontation among the lawyers. I don't get into fights with the other lawyers, there's no point in it. There are people out there who just seem to want to fight, don't you think, and they'll fight about anything; it doesn't help.

PAUL: I agree.

But what makes a dispute one in which you will file a complaint?

PAUL: When I reach a point with the insurance company, those types of cases that we've determined that we can't agree. And sometimes I have insurance companies that are just very difficult. You find that you have some incompetent adjusters. You find you have some nasty adjusters. A lot of them are suspicious of plaintiffs' attorneys. I would say I have a very good success ratio as far as settling cases with insurance companies and adjusters that know me, that have dealt with me in the past, that feel that they can trust me and that I'm not withholding anything from them. That I've given them all the information and that they know I know what I'm doing. You've got some companies that may not do a lot of business in this area, and I find those adjusters and those companies are the hardest to ones to deal with. More of those cases I end up filing suit with than the ones with, say, State Farm Insurance that I deal with a lot. A State Farm agent in Fairmont [West Virginia] who I deal with all the time, he can tell me, "Paul, I think you're crazy. I don't think this is the value of this case. Have you seen this medical record here where this person had this same injury five years ago?" I'll look at the medical record, and if he's right, I'll agree and go back to talk to the client. He and I usually have that dialogue. The adjusters I don't know, we don't have that dialogue, and that makes it much more difficult to settle.

Once the complaint is filed, then you're going to find out who is going to be opposing you. Let's assume it's Dan. What happens at that point?

PAUL: It's a strategic thing. Some lawyers, and this is a credit to Dan, if I have a case that I think is a legitimate case and the ones I file, I do. The first thing I usually get from Dan is a call to ask what's going on here. I think every case we've ever had, there has been an attempt early on to get it resolved before it costs your client a bunch of money. I think Dan does a good job at that. Dan is busy. The best lawyers I want on the other side are the best lawyers, the busy lawyers. Because Dan doesn't have the time to fool around with a bunch of stuff, he's not going to just grind out a case because he needs the work. But the defense lawyers who need the work, those are harder, because that case is going to drag on a long time. But if I'm dealing with someone like Dan, if the case is assigned to Dan, Dan is going to call me, and we're going to be pretty straight with each other.

Can you talk about that, Dan?

DAN: To give a little bit of perspective about what we've been talking about, there are all kinds of different people working for insurance companies, different backgrounds, levels of intelligence, levels of experience, and all of those things factor into it, but the same thing goes for the lawyers. You're in here talking to Paul Cranston, and Paul doesn't know this, but I do. The other side thinks Paul is a very good lawyer. He does work up all these cases, and he does gather up all the information. Well, not all lawyers do that.

Some of the plaintiffs' lawyers out there are operating a whole different way. They're getting cases in the door, they'll do nothing with the case for months and months, then all of a sudden they're like, oh my goodness, the statute's running [out] (state statutes often require a lawsuit be filed within a specified time period after an injury), and they'll file a lawsuit. And they've sent no information to the adjuster, and all they've done is write nastygrams to the adjuster saying, "You've got a duty to settle this case. How come you haven't paid me?" And the adjusters will say, "Because you need to give me information." And they'll give them a list of stuff that they don't know about the case. And the lawyer won't give them that information, but they'll write back a few months later still looking for payment. It's a much different thing when you have a lawyer that takes the case and does what Paul does, which is collect all the information and get the package to the adjuster; it's going to be a whole other thing. That's why you see a whole lot of cases going into litigation. The adjuster is doing the same thing I'm doing; he's trying to settle it. My first thought when a case comes in the door is how I am going to get rid of this.

I guess that's counter to what we were talking about, when he's saying since I'm paid by the hour, I'll be thinking how am I going to do a bunch of work. I just don't do that, never have, never will. When it comes in the door, I'm thinking what's the cheapest way to get rid of this case? When you get that file and start looking at it, you have to figure out why. Is the reason because the lawyer didn't do his work and had to file? I need to know this. Or is it just a case where there is a disagreement over the value of the case? Parties couldn't agree? What broke down? Because by the time I've gotten to the case, something's broke down. A lot of times someone's looked at it and decided they won't pay what they're asking. What's the reason for that? So we look at the case and try and decide what we need to know to be able to get rid of this case, and to get rid of it usually means settlement. Some cases are so bad that you just look at it and say, we might as well just plan on pushing this one through because there's no point in paying them money. In almost every case, by the time it comes to us, the company will pay something to get rid of it. Because they've got to pay me to get it to trial, they might as well pay a few thousand dollars to the plaintiff to get rid of him.

So strategically, simply filing a complaint shows more seriousness, and that might cause the company to increase its offer to get rid of it?

DAN: That does happen, I think. Why that happens, I don't know, but I think a lot of times they'll take a harder line, and then a lawsuit is filed, and then what usually happens is that the company gives the case to another adjuster, and they look at it with different eyes. Don't you find that?

PAUL: I haven't filed many cases, I told you, in the past year or so because I've been settling.

DAN: So you don't meatball, if you're doing your job and they're doing their job.

PAUL: I think so. There are a number of things in getting cases settled, and lawyers have different opinions of this. I try to talk to my client and educate my client on the benefit of getting a matter resolved without going through a lawsuit. Because it is one of, if not the most, stressful things that any person will ever go through. We went to school to do this, and this is our job. For a person to go through a lawsuit, it is a heck of an ordeal. So if there is an offer that's made to my client prior to suit, and it may not be what they want, but I feel obligated to tell them what I think we can potentially get at a trial. It could be this much more or that much more. What you need to do is go home and discuss with your family and really decide would it be worth it for you to go through this experience for a year or two. You've got to make a decision on that.

DAN: You've got the same thing on the other end. They'll come in the door and we'll say, well, we might get a defense verdict if we try this case, and we might not. If we lose, it might cost you X. What can you settle it for? Well, that's a factor that goes into the value of the settlement.

PAUL: Our laws on third-party bad faith in West Virginia changed. Dan's probably happy that they abolished it, but I don't think it was a good thing. It was important in a few cases where I thought the insurance company was screwing the plaintiff around and not willing to do things fairly, do what they were supposed to do. But what third-party bad faith used to allow me to do is, if you were trying to rip my client off and you weren't dealing with my client fairly, then I could basically sue the insurance company and punish them. I could recover the additional harm that you put my client through by not paying him what you should have in the beginning. Unfortunately, Dan will tell you, he saw some of these lawsuits where plaintiffs' lawyers filed these where they didn't have a basis for doing that. I think it was something, like anything else, if it was used properly, which I thought I did, and most of the lawsuits that I knew of on third-party bad faith were appropriate, but there were some apparently that weren't.

DAN: There sure were!

PAUL: But I'm like Dan. I try to figure out how to resolve the case. I don't want to file a lawsuit. I don't want to have to sue an insurance company for bad faith because I'm hoping I'm going to get more cases in the door to keep me busy. But that law helped people get fair settlements for their claims.

Dan, when you were talking about settling cases and assessing what you were going to do, you implied that some cases were nuisance cases and that you try to settle them and clear the books of them.

DAN: I don't know about that. There are a lot of cases that when you look at them you realize that there's not much merit to it. They don't have a very good claim, nothing's happening to them, but you have to bring in the case anyway.

I would call that a nuisance case. You're walking a tightrope there, and it depends on the particular philosophy at the time. If you get into a situation where, from an insurance company's standpoint, you will pay something for anything, well, the plaintiffs' lawyers out there who are scrounging around for work and talking to clients who walk in their door with these kind of silly cases figure that out and they say, well, I guess I'll take the case because I know I can get a couple of thousand dollars just by knocking on the door. Insurance companies really have to walk a fine line there about what they do. Do they pay something for anything that someone comes looking for, or do they make people prove their case? Then it gets cyclical. One company will be making people prove their case this year, and next year they'll be paying people something for anything. What we're doing, we're just doing an assessment of the case, and we're just providing advice to the people who are paying us. We'll go back to them and say the case doesn't have much merit. They all want you to do an early evaluation of the case. Everybody wants that now. It didn't used to be that way. It used to be they'd send you the file and you could do whatever you want to do. You could do discovery and take some depositions and then maybe get around to telling them what the case is worth. Everybody these days, all the insurance companies, wants you to do early evaluations on the file. So you take whatever information you have and you make an assessment of what you think that claim or that case is going to be worth. Does it have merit? If it doesn't have merit, how much are the damages? Then what's it going to cost you to prove that it doesn't have merit? Like I said, what do we need to do to get rid of this case as cheaply as we can?

So you might pay off a case because just simply investigating it further would cost you more money?

DAN: Sure. That happens. You can look at it and say we can offer them some small sum right now because we're going to spend that sum over the next couple of months investigating. Sometimes that's all they want, and they'll go away.

Are there some cases in which there's more pressure to settle than other cases? Or are all cases pretty much the same?

DAN: I can't think of any examples where there's more pressure to settle the case.

What about a case that is complicated, with a large amount of loss, or something like that?

DAN: Sometimes you think the bigger the cases, the easier they are to get resolved.

How much discovery do you do?

PAUL: In my cases I generally do a lot. I probably do more than most lawyers. I probably drive defense attorneys crazy because it's usually on the other end. And I can tell you, when I was defending cases and I saw a plaintiff's lawyer not doing discovery, that showed me he wasn't serious about the case. I still did my work and got my stuff together to be ready, but that tells me something about the lawyer, it tells me something about the case. What I like to do is to file my complaint and file an initial set of written discovery with my complaint, so it sends a message to Dan and his client that I think this is a pretty serious matter. I want to get things moving, I want to schedule depositions as soon as possible. That's written discovery: you get answers, you get documents, you take depositions of important people. Usually they want to talk the same people that I do. The discovery process helps us to evaluate our ability to get the case resolved. In West Virginia we also have court-ordered mediation. Basically, we have to sit down at some point with another lawyer who we both agree upon and the judge appoints to see if we can get the case resolved. I've had a lot of success getting cases settled with those mediations, too. A lot of times that depends on who the mediator is. What I like to do is have Dan pick the mediator because, hopefully, I have control of my clients. I don't say that in a mean way, but basically clients are listening to me, and I would rather the mediator have more influence over the insurance company, so the insurance company respects this person, their judgment. So I would rather have a mediator who is a defense lawyer, who the insurance company trusts. If I'm going to hire a plaintiffs' attorney to be the mediator, I'm afraid that the insurance company's going to say, "Wait a minute, that guy is a plaintiffs' lawyer. He's just going to try and get Paul and his client some money."

PAUL [to Dan]: What percentage of the cases that get filed are settled?

DAN: Almost all of them, it's a high percentage of them.

PAUL: I don't know a lot of lawyers who are trying a lot of cases right now.

With your discovery you're asking for documents. What sort of documents are important for both of you?

PAUL: I guess what Dan's going to want from me is all of my clients' medical records, all their wage-loss information. In one case that we had Dan kept asking me and asking me for my client's tax returns because my client worked for a company. The company was filling out reports and indicating that my client was making a heck of a lot of money. I was talking to them, and they told me that. Dan kept asking me for tax returns, and I got him the tax returns. Dan was able to use those basically to show that things didn't seem to add up. So that's one of the reasons why you want those things: because an employer may give you something, but we don't know the employer, so you have to make sure they are reliable. What I want is pictures. In a car wreck case, I want any pictures the insurance companies have. What I like to request in a car accident case is the other driver's medical records. I want to confirm that they weren't tested or in the hospital or anything within forty-eight hours of the time of the accident. I've had cases where I've had defendant drivers who had cocaine and had alcohol in their system that the police did not note in the accident report. Their driving record, sometimes that's relevant.

DAN: Basically when you look over it in the beginning you're going to form a list of questions that you have about the case and from that you can decide what records you have to have. The thing I don't understand is why we run into folks who don't want to give us that. If you're an injury case, and anybody can look at it and say, there's a question about whether you've had this condition before the accident, obviously they're going to want to see your preaccident medical records, and yet you end up getting into a fight about your preaccident medical records. Well, that's not relevant. We're not going to give you that. Well, then, we're going to fight about it, because I've got to see it. Sometimes you see them and they're right, there weren't any preaccident conditions, and a lot of times, you see them and there was a whole bunch of preaccident.

PAUL: I agree. I'm one of the plaintiffs' lawyers, and I have absolutely no problem with Dan Cooper, if I file suit, getting access to my client's prior medical records. That's something that I try to get in any case where I think there can be something, like back injuries. If you get a back injury case, I really want to look through the client's history, because the first thing an insurance company says is they hurt their back many years ago. So I at least want to look for myself and confirm for myself that they didn't have a prior injury; or, if they did, I want the doctors to be able to explain how this is different, is this related or anything like that. I don't have any problem with that. What I get on the other side, too, my side is, for example, I've got a medical malpractice case right now, and one of the causes for malpractice that I see anymore is that the doctors have too much going on. Their negligence is because they're seeing too many patients, they're everywhere. I ask the doctor for their calendar for a month or a few weeks. Well, actually, I wanted a month because I wanted to see what his regular routine is. I want to see what his patient load was. And I'm fighting with a lawyer because they won't give me that. So that tells me, I know why they wouldn't want to give it to me, because it's not going to look good, but that's something I should get. I had another case where I ended up getting the calendar of the doctor, and I think the doctor ended up seeing eighty patients one day. It was an unbelievable amount. It was an infection case where the doctor missed an infection in a lady's knee and she ended up dying from the infection. I think the guy's a good doctor, but I think he was just too busy.

DAN [to Paul]: *Are they objecting on privacy grounds? Or are you telling them to redact the identifying information?*

PAUL: I told him to redact any personal names or anything. The objection I got in the case was from a lawyer who isn't as specific as he needs to be in his objections, basically throwing up all these objections, nonspecific objections. I called him up and told him I'm entitled to this. He told me he was going to reconsider it. That was three months ago, and I hadn't heard back because we've got some delays in the case, but I have a feeling that I'm going to have to file a motion to compel, which is something I don't like to do.

You don't file many motions in discovery?

PAUL: It depends on the lawyers. The cases I've had, it's been hotly contested. In litigation cases, we've filed them, and Dan and I have had some cases he's objected to giving me stuff, and I think he believed he had valid ground to do that. I disagreed with him, and sometimes you file motions on that and sometimes you win, sometimes you lose. I don't have a problem with a lawyer who's got a legal basis, who really thinks that he has. The problem that I see is, some defense lawyers, and probably some plaintiffs' attorneys, will give you an answer to your discovery. It's a form response where they object to virtually every single question you ask, and then they say without waiving the objection, here's what I'll give you. Well, they don't give you anything. That makes it difficult, and I take the approach that I'm going to try and answer every single one of Dan's questions, because I'd rather give him everything from my client so he can't say that my client hid anything from him. It goes back to credibility, because if he finds something that I didn't give him, he's going to use that against my client at trial, and they're going to look like a liar, or dishonest. And that's the worst thing that can happen in my opinion for a plaintiff's case.

DAN: The worst thing that can happen for us is for them to be totally honest.

PAUL: When you're defending a case, a soft-tissue injury case, for example, where it's subjective, where it's not shown on an X-ray, you can't see a picture. What I think he wants to do is find anything where my client didn't necessarily tell the truth where the jury might not think they're credible. With me, I want the opposite. I tell them, "If your arm didn't hurt that day, that's okay. Tell the jury it didn't hurt. Be totally honest with them because if they find anything...." I had a case one time I tried with another lawyer, and I believe this lady was telling the truth, one hundred percent. But her records indicated that she didn't have any restriction in her range of motion. It was a soft-tissue injury case, and the lawyer I was trying the case with, cocounsel, asked the client the question, "Did this injury restrict your range of motion?" I'm like, "Why would you ask that question, because it doesn't look like it did." The client said, "Yes, it did. I can raise this arm this high and this arm only like this." She cringed a little bit on the stand, and I think it really did hurt her. The next thing we know, the defense lawyer got another one of her treating physicians to come in and proceeded to say that he examined [her] for an entire year and there was never any restriction of range of motion. That didn't help me much! [*laughs*] At that point in the case I was sitting there thinking, that's not good.

DAN: I've found that almost everybody will exaggerate their claim. And the other thing that works in conflict to the whole process is that everybody honestly thinks that their claim is worth more than it is.

Do you take many depositions, and, if so, from whom?

DAN: You almost always have to depose the plaintiff in a case to find out, if nothing else, just what kind of witness they're going to make. That can make a difference to a jury. I just had a deposition the other day. It was just a little car accident case. We've offered them what we thought was fair value. They're saying, "We need a little bit more money. Why don't you take my client's deposition, and I think then you'll see that you need to pay a little more money." So I sat down and took his deposition, and after the deposition, the plaintiff's attorney said he would take our original offer, because his client didn't make a very good witness. He just didn't come off very well. And neither one of us knew that was going to happen.

PAUL: My client's appearance, my client's demeanor, the way they act at their deposition, whether they go crazy, get angry at you, just how they respond has a big impact on the settlement of the case. Dan and I had a case once. His client was an elderly man, wonderful guy, just wasn't paying attention and rear-ended my client. I didn't get as much of a recovery in that case as I think my client deserved. And one of the reasons I think was because he had a very likable client. The jury looked at him—and we have negligence, we're entitled to recover—but for jurors to really award someone a full recovery I think they have to look at the defendant and the plaintiff, they have to like the plaintiff, think it's a good person, and look at the defendant and say, this wasn't just a simple negligence, this is somebody who is the type of person that would be speeding around town, running stop signs, not paying attention. Not an old man who just made an innocent mistake. I think they discount their damages because of that.

DAN: I guess that works for any witness that you're deposing. One reason why we depose them in person and not on the phone is because we want to make those judgments. Are they going to be likable, are they going to do well in front of the jury?

PAUL: Doctors, expert witnesses. If you don't see them, you don't know what kind of witness they're going to be. They can sound good over the phone, and then I meet them and I wonder why I retained this person. That's important. The problem is how busy we are doing all these things. This is the way you should do it, but unfortunately you can't always do all these things timewise. You've got other lawyers at your firm who can assist you and then do those things for you. But for me, I've got myself and two other lawyers here, and it keeps us hopping to do all those things.

DAN: There are always things that don't get done that you wish you'd got done in the file. Sometimes it makes a difference and other times you never know what type of difference it's going to make.

What do you think of the way courts handle those cases?

PAUL: I think our court system is great. I'm not saying it's perfect, but I think our system of justice is the best in the world. I think there's a myth out there that basically says our system's out of control and people say that we need all this reform. The judges we have in this county, the judges in Harrison County, Marion County, these are good judges, they're intelligent judges, they're fair judges. They want to do the right thing. Most of the judges that I've been in front of in the state of West Virginia have been very competent individuals who I think are trying to do the right thing. They make preliminary rulings that decide what evidence Dan and I are allowed to introduce into the trial, and these rulings help to determine the general outlines of the case. So there's some regulation right there. Then we've got the ability to have six members of the community sit there and listen to all our evidence that we present—I'm talking about civil cases—and to make a decision based on the instructions that they get from the court. Some people tell you that they don't think the jurors listen to the instructions. I think they do, and when I've interviewed jurors afterwards, they told me the instructions were important. Let's say that they give the plaintiff way too much money, something that the law wouldn't allow. You have a judge right there who can look at that and say, "Wait a minute, we have to correct that." Dan's going to file a motion, or the judge is going to do that on his own. Ninety percent of the time or more, the judge is going to make that decision and correct that verdict. And if he doesn't, then we have the ability to go to our Supreme Court and appeal that. I think the system is already in place to prevent abuse. You've heard a lot of discussion in the press about frivolous lawsuits and that's been a big thing. We have procedures in force to curtail frivolous lawsuits. If I file a lawsuit against Dan's client that there is not merit whatsoever, I have no basis whatsoever for filing, just a harassment-type lawsuit, I could get sanctioned by the court. You don't see that remedy under Rule 11 used very often, but I think that's probably because there is some basis for the lawsuits that are being filed. [*Paul to Dan*] : I'm sure you've probably seen some you think are frivolous, but....

DAN: I really can't think of any that I can name you that didn't have merit at all, what is truly frivolous, as having no basis. There have been plenty where they filed it, and I'm sure they thought they had an argument. It turns out that they didn't, they were wrong, or they're going to lose on their argument; there was another side to their story. But that shouldn't stop people from thinking that they can file a lawsuit just because there could be another side to the story.

Dan, what about this notion that the juries walk in biased against your client; do you buy that argument?

DAN: When I walk into a courtroom, I've got two strikes against me. I'm usually defending an insurance company. There's a bias against my client. But I'm not sure that it's not justified. They're a large company and oftentimes they have billions and billions of dollars and people can't relate to that at all. And that is something that is difficult to overcome.

PAUL: See, everybody at some point in their life has had some bad experience with an insurance company. Paying too much money on their premiums. Or they file a claim, like I had, I had a flood in my house, and they paid it, and they ended up raising my rates. I think there is some general dislike for insurance companies. I think it's justified. [*laughs*]

DAN: Well, what the people don't realize is that insurance companies don't have any of their own money; they have your money and my money and his money. You can't fix a system that you're upset with by hammering an insurance company and taking some of their money and giving it to Paul and his clients. That doesn't fix a system that you don't like. I'll tell you, the court system is not perfect. Neither is the system we have of insurance and claims; it's not perfect. There's constant conflict there; people always think their claim is worth more than what it is. Adjusters are always working pretty hard; they have a lot of work to do. They're regular people, too, and they've got things going on in their lives, and they're not perfect, and some are better than others. Paul thinks it was a bad idea to eliminate that cause of action. I made my living off of that cause of action for years, and let me tell you, West Virginia could not afford that cause of action, and it needed to be eliminated. It's a bad thing to have that cause of action. You don't need it.

If you're not getting a fair offer from an insurance company, you've already got a perfectly good dispute resolution system. File a lawsuit and take it to court and prove that they're not offering you enough. What's wrong with that? There's nothing wrong with that, and it's a good thing, like we just heard. Jurors, by and large, do the right thing. They want to do the right thing, and even if you disagree a time or two about a particular verdict, the overall system is good. In West Virginia, our system is perceived by the business community as not being fair to them. I personally think that you can change one thing in our system and make a huge difference in the way that it's perceived. And that would be to give people a right of appeal. In West Virginia there is not a right to appeal. Every appeal is done by cert [a request to the Supreme Court of Appeals to use its discretion to hear the appeal]; you ask the court to take your appeal. And I think what happens a lot of times, and I've seen this myself, if a company got the short end of the stick, in the company's view, they file the appeal with the West Virginia Supreme Court of Appeals, and the justices just don't take it. They say they're just going to leave that alone. Now if you had a right to appeal, where a group of judges had to put in writing why you lose, then people would perceive that as fair.

PAUL: I don't disagree with what Dan's saying, but I was thinking the next thing is now we've got to have more judges, because our judges won't be able to handle it. But what he's saying is frustrating. I've filed petitions for appeals and they've been denied, and what happens is basically so many people voted yea and so many voted no, but they don't tell you why. That is hard and it's costly. And you can re-petition, and that costs more money.

DAN: We need a midlevel appeals court, where you have the right to appeal and where someone passes on it, in writing, whether you should win or lose. In writing. I think that's one problem we have in our system in West

Virginia and the way it's viewed from outsiders. By and large, there is nothing wrong with our jury system; it works very well.

Even given what you just said earlier, that they walk in with a bias, you think they are going to give you a fair shake once the trial has started and the instructions have been given?

DAN: Well, it depends what you mean by a fair shake. I think that bias is part of what's fair. People come in there with whatever experiences they've had in life. I don't think that's a bad thing, and I don't think that it makes the overall system a bad thing. I think its okay if people come in and have a bias against a company if they listen to the whole case, even if they make their decision with that bias built into it. In the overall scope of the justice system, that's still okay. It doesn't put these companies out of business; there are other safeguards in place. There is court precedent that prevents that. You're not going to put an insurance company out of business by giving away a million dollars of their money. It doesn't make it a right thing to give away a million dollars of their money. But does that mean we scrap the system? No, that doesn't mean we scrap the system, just because that might occasionally happen. And the other thing that can happen, too, you can get jurors sitting there that can drive the other ones back. You're very seldom going to end up with all of your jurors with the same bias. One person might be sitting at the table saying, "We've got to give them twenty million dollars!" and somebody else is over there saying, "Forget that." They work it out.

PAUL: Right now there's a different bias. There are a lot of people with a bias against filing lawsuits. And that's something I have to deal with. That's why we have voir dire. What Dan's trying to do, and what I'm trying to do, is pick out the jurors who are most favorable to our client, who relate to our client the most. And we have to exclude people who we think are biased against our client. It's a real difficult procedure, and there's a lot of strategy involved. Do I ask the question of the panel if there is anybody among them who thinks there are too many frivolous lawsuits? And then what if I have a guy raise his hand and say, "Absolutely. I know of twenty in this county." He's possibly poisoned my whole jury pool, and I have to follow up with that and make sure that the other people think he's full of it. With malpractice, suing doctors, people don't want to believe that doctors do these things. And the way the jurors look at it is that a doctor is there to help a person; they would never intentionally injure a person, but in an emergency situation when they're trying to save a person's life, mistakes can happen. The jury's first of all thinking, well, this guy's trying to save your client's life, now you're blaming him for something that went wrong. So it's got to be something pretty egregious, because I don't think that people want to find against doctors in general.

DAN: I think these days you're liable to run into a juror who's biased against someone who's trying to collect for a back injury from a car accident, because they've heard these things in the press, and they see their own premiums and think, "My goodness. I'm already paying more than I want to pay, and here's this guy and he doesn't have any more back pain than I do." So they have some bias against the plaintiff. But, I think people these days, because of whatever's been in the news or whatever they've seen happening, they're going to think of corporate America and look at it with a little suspicion on that side, too. That's why the lawyers are there. You know, we've got to even that out. We show them that our clients aren't lying, our clients aren't bad folks, our clients were doing their job, and the jury's going to make the decision they think is right.

PAUL: One thing in the jury trials that you can't control is the married juror who goes home every night. The judge is going to tell you that you're not allowed to discuss the case. You and your wife may have the same opinion of lawsuits and various things, but you've gone in and listened to this trial, and I may have changed your opinion, or Dan can change your opinion, even if you're predisposed in a certain way. Then the juror goes home and has to explain sometime to his spouse why he ruled this way. We may be able to do our work in the courtroom and really convince somebody, explain that this is the way it is, and they may really believe that. Then when they go home, they get convinced to go back to their predisposition because of their spouses. In a perfect world, you would sequester the jurors, every time.

DAN: Well, when you interview jury you find that oftentimes when they sit down to hear the opening statement they're thinking that that's the person who's wrong here, but by the time they hear all the evidence, they've switched, and they decide that this other side's right.

PAUL: They tell you in law school [about] primacy and recency. Your opening statement helps people to form their opinions and then your closing's got to be good. Maybe they make up their mind on some things early on, but I think most people are willing to listen.

DAN: I think they're willing to listing. I tried a case defending a police officer who shot somebody in the line of duty, and so we're going to trial now. I think this happens, too: I think a lot of folks think that the court wouldn't let it get to a jury unless it had some merit. And I think that's a bias that works against defendants, because that's not really true, either. The way it works, you can get just about anything in front of a jury if there is a factual question. And I think that's what worked against me in that case at the beginning. When we walked into that courtroom, the court security and all the officers who are in a federal court, they were very cold to us. I thought we had done something wrong at the very beginning, but by the time they heard two weeks of trial, they were all rooting for us. When the jury announced the defense verdict, the court officer picked up his mike and was shouting that it was a defense verdict, and you could hear cheering throughout the courthouse. Because they knew by the time we walked in there that this guy must have done something wrong or they wouldn't be here. By the time they heard the evidence they knew that wasn't true.

Deborah Pascente Lifka

Lawyer for the Middle Class

THE LAW FIRM OF LIFKA and Lifka occupies part of a commercial building between the commuter rail line to the Chicago Loop and the large homes with beautifully manicured lawns in upscale suburban Downers Grove, Illinois. The firm, consisting of Debbie Lifka and her husband Dan, occupies adjoining offices separated by a glass partition. Their practice is dedicated to the legal needs of the American middle class and small local businesses, especially protection against litigation and the management of their legal needs when they buy a home or a family member dies.

Why did you decide to become an attorney?

I am a graduate of Saint Mary's College, Notre Dame, Indiana. Some time during that four years' experience I made a jump from teaching to lawyering. I am not sure how or why, but something happened. I am pretty sure my parents had something to do with that decision. My dad had owned his own business for many years. Lawyers were not his favorite people. So he figured if I was one of those folks, he could rely on me. So I went to law school at DePaul University and graduated in 1988. There was no gap between college and law school. I went from frying pan one to frying pan two. I took the bar and passed it on my first try. I started working at Garritson and Santora in Chicago. It was essentially defense insurance work. That's where I got my taste of litigation. I did that for two years until I gave birth to child number one. After a one-year, nine-month sabbatical, I went in-house general counsel with Garrard and Company, which is a mid-size steel company in Des Plaines, Illinois. It was there that I got my taste of what lawyering was about. Then I started my own private practice.

What is the nature of your current practice?

I have been in this practice for about eighteen years. My husband joined me seven years ago. I started the practice. He came on board when he felt it was safe to do so—financially safe. He went to law school after we were married. He went to night school and didn't tell his employers he was even in law school until his fourth year of night school. He quit his very good paying job [in corporate finance], and he moved my desk over and put one next to mine. That was the start of Lifka and Lifka on a permanent basis.

We have a civil practice with some litigation, not a lot of litigation. He does our estate planning, wills, trusts, probate. I do real estate, corporate work in conjunction with him, and also our employment law. We don't do divorce. We don't do bankruptcy. We refer that work out. We are a suburban, local, family firm.

How do you find your clients?

We have advertised in the yellow pages. We advertise in our church bulletin. We get a lot of mom-and-pop corporations that initially want us to incorporate them. They want service and some hand-holding on things from A to Z. They want to be our best friends. That is typically the type of corporate client we will see. Sometimes they have some employment issues. I will assist them with those. Dan takes care of some of their tax-based problems that are filed with the secretary of state, board minutes, resolutions, all that kind of stuff. Anything of a complex litigation nature we refer out.

The real estate practice involves transactions on behalf of buyers and sellers, from soup to nuts. Depending on the time of the year, it depends on how much of the time of my practice is devoted to that specialty. Pretty much in the spring heavy market, ninety percent of my time will be spent on real estate transactions. We will probably close between thirty and forty files a month, which for a single office is a lot. I am bright enough to have a realtor base that spans from as far east as Lake [Michigan] and Chicago to St. Charles and Aurora [to the west]. That's a good forty miles. I found that having contacts in all that area helps me in real estate. Depending on the season or the year, you can have a good market one place and not in another. So I can balance what I do because of the span that I have. The other real estate work I do comes from my husband's files. Many of his clients are dead [*smiles*]. We take care of the executors. They may have some property to sell on behalf of the deceased. The rest of them are referrals. If I have handled your file, I'll handle your brother's file, your mother's file, your neighbor's file, your cousin's file, your coworker's file. If you are a repeat customer—I have just had one come my way. It will be their fourth house in two years. I'm not sure what those folks are doing, but they like me, so I'm stuck with them.

What does real estate work involve?

People think of real estate as being a Mickey Mouse function. I have learned so much since I first got into it. You are not taught how to do it in law school. You are taught how to think. The mechanics of what you do comes with on-the-job practice. From a seller's perspective, I order title. I order a survey. I procure all the papers. Title [deeds and other documents that evidence the just possession of property] is an interesting being. I had no idea what it meant. I am an agent for a number of title companies. I do work for them. I review title. I have to clear all title issues—any mortgages and liens [claims against the property owner, usually because of nonpayment of debt] by way of association, by way of county, by way of sanitary district, by way of possible judgment against folks. It's fairly challenging when you get something that is complex—a lot of survey issues, a lot of encroachment issues, a lot of variance issues [requests for an exception to local land use law or zoning requirements]. I don't do zoning.

Some cases are pretty matter of fact. You start it. You finish it for a flat fee. Certain contracts give attorneys an opportunity to modify or disapprove a real estate contract, so that brings you into some interesting areas of case law and litigation. It is not as cut-and-dried as people think.

Do you deal with realtors and the attorneys for the other party in the real estate transaction?

My contacts with both groups are voluminous. I talk to those people all the time. Some lawyers have very closed-door policies with regard to speaking with realtors. I have a team philosophy. I kind of view it as a triangular team: the client, the realtor, and myself. I have a very open relationship with realtors. They enjoy my company. Real estate can be so boring. We try to make it fun, we try to spice it up. We take a vested interest in the people, we make it a personable thing. I am seated as a seller's attorney on one side, and seated on the other side is the buyer. But I tell their folks we're at a round table. We are working toward the same goal. I try to keep things very upbeat, very light. If I have issues with the attorneys or with the realtors, my goal is to resolve them before I get to the table. The table is for signing. That is my philosophy. The reality of it is that it doesn't always work that way, but that is our goal. Chicago is a large metropolitan area, but we all know each other. It's amazing. Ninety percent of the folks I deal with are normal, genuine, and honest. Everybody is a little quirky, but quirky makes life a little spicier and interesting, and that's okay! Sometimes we will get heated, but there is also a mutual respect that underlies the dispute, and it always can be resolved.

My title company serves cookies now. The philosophy is that they are trying to create a homier environment. When those cookies are getting done and clients are getting cranky, I go in, I put the cookies in the oven, I pop them out of the Easy-Bake oven, and I serve them. I go next door to the people I have nothing to do with. They think I work for the title company. We have fun.

What other types of legal matters do you handle?

I do employment law. Sexual harassment and age discrimination law are the biggest things that come my way on a fairly regular basis. Terminations happen on a Friday, so by Monday morning everybody has read the yellow pages and has decided they need a female lawyer. They call me on Monday for free advice. Because I'm a female, I get a lot of calls, but I don't necessarily bring them in. I can tell in about five minutes if somebody has something worth my time. I don't bring a lot of folks in, but I do hear a lot of complaints.

People are confused as to what sexual harassment really is. Or people drop the word *sex* off and consider the word *harassment* something interesting. You know that some people have personalities that are just harassing, but that is not illegal. There is no cause of action for just someone being a pain the neck or being rude or disrespectful. Illinois is a state where we have employment at will. It means that one can be fired for any reason so long as it's not a discriminatory reason. Lots of times people get terminated because its, "He didn't like me." It is very difficult to tell people that it is legal and maybe you're not likable. That is not protected under any statute or any type of federal regulation.

What you get more is age discrimination, so we can educate employers to build a paper trail. So the real reason may be one of age but on paper, it doesn't look like age. It looks like performance. Lawyers are responsible for training how to make something look like what it's not. Those are extremely difficult to prove.

How many cases do you have on your desk at any point in time?
I would probably say fifty. My workload is very different from my husband. He's the one who works for dead people, so he works at a different rate of speed. His work is more methodical.

Do you counsel clients?
Counseling clients I do a lot of. Sometimes I am not sure if I am counseling clients from a legal perspective or a psychological one. I wear both hats. I wasn't prepared for that, but that's what I do. We do a lot of hand-holding. Sometimes I speak to someone as an attorney. Sometimes I speak to someone just as a friend. Sometimes I speak as a business person to give counsel and advice. Everyone who calls me wants my counsel and advice on some different level. People who come to me for advice are usually in a predicament. An unemployment predicament, or they are folks who have never bought a home or haven't done it for a long time. It is overwhelming when people are thrown into a financial world, or document world, [with] which they are unfamiliar; they are very nervous. I am the calming force that settles them through periods of time. Even when I am not confident that what I am doing will make them happy, I have to portray the confidence to keep them sane. I think I do bring some sense of tranquility and peace to some people's lives.

You spend a great deal of time on the phone?
I will be buried with my phone. I buried my dad with his phone, and I will be buried with my phone. My husband buys a new package for my cell phone on a regular basis, and he constantly says, "Who the hell are you talking to?" I utilize my time well. I am always on my phone. I connect more in writing

now as an older attorney because covering your backside is what it is about. My license is much too important to me not to [record my actions].

Do you deal with experts?

I don't deal with experts. I don't deal with any great litigation. I deal with clients on a regular basis. A lot of hand-holding on all levels of matters. I swear I have people who come in because they have no one else to talk to but me. A lot of client counseling, early and late. Someone called me the other day at midnight. They say, "You're there?" I said, "And you're calling me. You're just as nuts as I am."

Do you draft many documents and letters?

Yes, especially in real estate. It takes up a lot of time—meticulous time. Errors are frequent. Not only my drafting, but my review of someone else's drafting takes the bulk of my time, especially in the spring.

I was told in college that the thing I needed to improve was my writing. I now am the master of letters. I write the best, concise letters. I have this rule of thumb. If you can't get it on a page, it can't happen. It's called less is more. You have to be very succinct. It is about what you don't say as much as what you do say. It is an art.

Do you use letters to clarify points or to threaten legal action?

All of the above. I don't like to use the word *threaten*. I like to plant a seed. I am a seed planter.

Do you settle disputes through negotiations?

I am the queen of negotiations. If it can be negotiated, it's going to happen. I tell my clients, especially the employment clients, when you walk into a courtroom, even in the best-of-case scenario with a great case, your chances are fifty-fifty. It is a crap shoot. If you have me on your team as a negotiator, I can assure you that you've got better odds of getting something out of it that's tangible that you wouldn't have had otherwise and sooner rather than later. Negotiation is an art.

What goes into that art?

Confidence. There are folks that try to negotiate who don't know the rules. They are not as successful. BS-ing only gets you so far. You really have to know what you are talking about. Mutual respect at the beginning of a negotiation [is important]. Reputation—it can matter. It can matter as a positive or negative. Everything these days is about the small firm, and it is about service. It is about how you personally service a client. Large firms take a big rap for not being able to do that. Folks come to smaller firms for service. So that's what we give them, because that's their expectation. People may not know Debbie Lifka as a great employment attorney, but once we are through a negotiation, what they will probably remember is she's a nice lady. Being respectful will get you a lot farther than the reverse. In my way of negotiating, it has been extremely successful for me.

Are most attorneys cooperative during negotiations?

I would say the rare situation is the lawyer who is not cooperative. I remind people that we are not solving world peace, we are just involved in a real estate transaction. That brings them to the level they should be at. Interestingly enough, you are going to find that folks in Chicago take a little more adversarial position in their transactions. That isn't naturally so. They have to posture in front of their clients, and so by rocking the boat a little it can make them look important. That's not true of most of my colleagues here in the suburbs—we usually try to knock those folks down a peg. We just remind them they are not as important as they think. It's fun. What attorneys forget is that a long time ago the job of lawyering was very big on mentoring, so older and more experienced attorneys had an obligation to mentor the younger persons. It is not rare that I will jump to the other side of the table for a new, newly licensed lawyer who let somebody's parent or father or somebody's sister get sucked into a real estate closing when they had no business being part of it. The proper way of doing it is not one of disrespect but one of mentoring. Our profession has lost touch with some of that. You see it coming back a little bit. It's a good thing. The only way you learn is hands-on, it is experience. So if you have it, you must share it. It's an obligation.

Do you engage in court-ordered mediation?
[That] is with regard to divorce, but that's an area I don't practice in.

Do you litigate many cases?
I have litigated one case in my seventeen years of practice. It was a sexual harassment case. I took that to federal court. We settled after my opening statement. It was a damn good opening statement.

Are the sexual discrimination cases therefore settled out of court?
The charges of discrimination start with the EEOC [the federal Equal Employment Opportunity Commission]. Any Tom, Dick, and Harry can file a charge. EEOC has to take your charge whether they believe it is meritorious or not. The EEOC is overworked, underpaid, and understaffed. They have an internal system of ranking. They don't disclose that to you. I can come in with a case, let's say my client was an employee of Ford. If they [the EEOC] think this is hot and give us some good press, your ranking is higher than the ranking of somebody else. Knowing how this ranking system works, knowing that there are only seven days in a week and twenty-four hours in a day, I am selective about what I take—extremely selective. I tell my clients if I can win in litigation, and, if I can negotiate for you, I will reserve the right to review the case from a litigation standpoint. What I find out with a lot of folks—I don't know if it's intentional–leave out a lot of information. They may come to you and give you their spiel. Their spiel is one in which they have worn blinders for a period of years, and so they are going to give it to you and miss all the stuff on the side. Once the employer comes in, you pick up the fuller picture. Then, of course, you are in a better position to make a decision with regards to [the case's] litigation value. So very few cases will I even consider. I tell folks that up front. I was threatened once because the expectation from a client was that, because I filed the charge, I was obligated to litigate. My engagement letter was not specific enough.

What would you tell students are the most demanding aspects of your practice?

Time—how much time they have in their day to dedicate to the profession, because it requires a lot and people expect a lot. They are big on calling me on Saturday. Their expectations are that you are a doctor who is on call seven days a week, twenty-four hours a day. It is a huge undertaking. If you like to have a family, twenty-four hours in a day just does not cut it. Ten more hours a day would probably get me to be where I want to be. You have to learn how to give some stuff up. If you are willing to make this sacrifice to practice law, then welcome.

It's a crazy world we live in. Everybody's got a pager. Everybody's got a BlackBerry. Everybody can fax you immediately. Everything moves at a quicker rate than it did five or ten years ago.

What advice do you have for women who want to go into the law?

The law thing for women? What happened to all the women I graduated with? I don't know where in the heck they are. The majority of people I practice with are male, but my graduating class was close to fifty-fifty. They may be doing different things because law practice is draining, and folks that do litigation have it even worse.

They have to be really willing to work for this. When I was in seventh grade, I knew I wanted to do litigation. I do some of Dan's contested probate work, so that does keep me in the courtroom on a limited basis, but if you want families fighting over money, dysfunctional families—I always wanted to do it. I love the fact that I have the degree and it has given me respect. I hope that everyone who comes has a passion for the law, has respect for the degree, and has a desire to help those who are first starting in the profession.

Does being a lawyer pose problems for raising a family?

It is the same challenge that any working parent has in raising a family. It all depends on what kind of example you want to give to your children. You produce money to create a lifestyle that makes everybody comfortable, but you've got to demonstrate the small stuff with what I do and try to raise three children while concentrating on the bigger picture. The good news for my kids is that I am the most organized person I know. If I wasn't as organized as I was, I would miss more than I miss. I do miss, but I don't miss as much as I could miss. I am there for the big stuff. It's amazing how God always finds a way to help me out. Usually when I think I can't do it, something gives. I always think that He has the upper hand in giving me a little pat on the back so I can be at a game or I can be at a meet or I can be at park day. I am amazed at how blessed I am.

Working with your husband makes this is an unusual legal practice. How does that affect your life?

It wasn't my plan. If someone had asked me years ago in my wildest dreams would I be practicing with my husband, I would have laughed. First, I had no clue he had a passion for the law. And I don't think I appreciated his decision for corporate life. He now is the best attorney. He is the best thing that happened to my practice. He brings with him a wealth of business experience that I just don't have. In terms of our interpersonal relations, it works because we try. What we try to do is go home and not talk about work. It's a huge effort.

What do you consider to be the minuses of your kind of legal practice?

Dealing with very mean and crabby people makes my life as difficult as it can be. It is hard to be professional when you're faced with someone that's obnoxious and that has no degree of respect for you. I was sitting in a closing one day. It was an attorney I had dealt with before, and he was pushing my buttons and pushing my buttons and screaming at me over two hundred fifty dollars. It was so ridiculous. Apparently I was having a bad day and I used a bad word. I told him where to go, "F___ you," which was fine if it had been just him and me. What I forgot was the realtor sitting next to me was called the "church lady." As it was coming out of my mouth, I could see her slithering under the table. I thought, she isn't going to work with me again. He threatened me. I thought "grow up." That's hard to deal with.

Have you ever fired a client?

Yes, it was a lawyer. When I was a younger attorney, I was poorer than I am now; we took more clients because we thought we had to. We don't have to. My husband would be the first to say, "If it looks goofy, don't get yourself involved." So I am free to tell them to go jump and find somebody else. We have a rule. If somebody has been working on a file, it comes to me, and they fired their first lawyer, I won't go there.

What are the positive aspects of your practice?

I have seen a lot of horror stories. I have seen a lot of lives be devastated by losses of jobs and families without insurance. When people come to see me they are desperate, they are just desperate. I have a great deal of faith which I don't wear on my wrist, but I try to focus on it; there is good that comes out of every situation that maybe on its face doesn't look so good. My confidence is bringing that to them very often will give them some more hours of sleep at night. I think if we all did as part of our job that we could make the world a little bit better place.

That is the rewarding aspect of it. The people I meet—they laugh at me because I am the kissing attorney. I kiss everybody. When I shake someone's hand on the way out the door, I always tell them, "I wish you all God's blessings." I started doing that the last couple of years. It felt good, and it's kind of what I do and what I am known for, and I mean it. I think I am blessed by getting to meet people and hoping their meeting me has brought them some degree of blessing as well.

Scott Friedman

The Family Law Attorney

SCOTT FRIEDMAN IS AN ATTORNEY in the firm of Friedman & Mirman Co., LPA, in Columbus, Ohio. Mr. Friedman's firm is housed in a suburban neighborhood located just minutes from Columbus's dynamic city center and courthouses. The seven attorneys of the firm exclusively practice family relations law. In the United States family legal problems are perhaps the most common reason that people contact an attorney. Often these cases involve intense emotions as couples seek to end their marriages.

Could you please describe the nature of your practice?
What we consider family law consists of everything surrounding a marriage termination: divorce, dissolution, and the issues that arise as a result of those, which include child custody, child support, spousal support, division of property. And then everything we call postdivorce. There are many times when people will have problems after the divorce is over, so we address those issues as well. We also do prenuptial agreements for people. We do not do wills, trust, and estates. We do not do adoption work; we leave that to other people. We do some juvenile work, and the distinction in Ohio is people who have a child together who are not married, if they have disputes over the child, that falls under the jurisdiction of the juvenile court. I won't do things such as juvenile justice for a youngster who commits a crime. I'm not a criminal lawyer. Our focus is primarily divorce.

What is the gender of your clientele?
I think overall my personal practice is a little bit more female, probably sixty percent/forty percent. I think that's probably the case in our general practice as well because one of my partners is a female. And I think we have a reputation of being prepared, knowledgeable, and tough, and I think sometimes women feel they need that, so they will go to a stronger reputation law firm.

Now we do represent many men, but it just seems like there's a sixty percent/ forty percent split.

How do your clients find you?

We've found that most of our clients get to us by word of mouth. That can be word of mouth from other clients or from other attorneys in town who do not practice in our area and from some who do but have a conflict. We get a lot of business from mental health professionals who have counseled couples and the marriage is not going to last and they need legal advice. We also get referrals from financial people, planners, CPAs [certified public accountants] who are involved in advising families about the nature of their financial planning, and then one of the parties asks the financial planner for a referral to an attorney.

Do you foster and develop those relationships with mental health professionals and financial planners?

We do. I either develop them by picking up the phone and taking them to lunch if I've never met them before. I get to know that person and trust them, and they refer me business, and vice versa.

You don't rely on advertising?

We do very little advertising. We do no paid advertising other than a very small listing in the Yellow Pages. That's changed over time, where we used to have much bigger ads in the Yellow Pages and other things like that. We have stopped that because we've found that our best marketing strategy is fostering the relationships I talked about. We do spend dollars on the Internet. We have a website that's pretty nice. We're listed in *Martindale Hubbell* and a couple of other directories that focus exclusively on family law.

How is a client treated when he or she walks into your firm?

When a client is referred here, the first thing that happens when they call is that we set up an appointment. We charge a small flat fee for an initial appointment. We do that because we feel if we have a free initial consultation, people won't take it seriously. This meeting is an opportunity for them to interview us and us to interview them and for us to make sure we're comfortable with the client and vice versa. We have them fill out some paperwork, similar to what you do when you first visit a doctor. We ask them about their marriage, their income, kids, and things like that. That initial meeting usually lasts about an hour. I get an idea of what their situation is, talk through their concerns and questions, and give them general advice about the process if they are going to terminate their marriage. If that's not why they're here—for example, [for] a second opinion—I'll go through and figure out where they are in their marriage and what they need to know. They leave here with a big packet of information from us that they will need to complete if they want to retain us and information about fees and a fee assessment.

In that initial meeting, is the client usually sure that he or she wants a divorce?

I think that seventy-five to eighty percent of people come in here ready to end their marriage in that circumstance. I think the other twenty or twenty-five percent are here for advice, like the "what if" scenario. I always ask that question. It's a great question. This morning I met with a lady who was ready to start divorce proceedings, but after all was said and done I got the sense she was still a bit confused about whether she wanted to do this or not. And she was, because life is different when your marriage ends. She would probably have to go to work, and she hadn't worked in a number of years, and there are all sorts of considerations that she had to weigh. What would be better for her, for her family, and for her children? But, I'd say that seventy-five percent of them are ready to go forward.

Once they return with their paperwork and they become your client, what happens to their case?

It depends on which direction their case is going to take. If the case is going to be what is called a contested divorce, someone has filed or is going to file a case in the court system, then we'll take that road, which is more contested in terms of its adversarial nature. There will be court hearings. Depositions will be taken. Witnesses will be subpoenaed. This is not unlike what you see on television with a trial.

What about what in some other states is called an uncontested or no-fault divorce?

Ohio has something called a dissolution, which is an agreed divorce, an agreed termination of your marriage. Some would call it an uncontested divorce, although that's a little bit of a misnomer, because if someone files a divorce case in Ohio and later that divorce case gets agreed to, that's also called an uncontested divorce. We distinguish it, because in a dissolution you never go to court until everything is agreed. Whereas in an uncontested divorce, as we call it in Ohio, it's settled after a divorce case has been filed. I would tell you that probably eighty to eighty-five percent of what the firm handles are settled eventually. They don't see a trial.

But of the cases that walk in the door, how many are dissolution cases, the simpler cases?

Probably fifty percent. But a lot [of] people come in not even knowing what a dissolution is. A lot of people come in not knowing if a dissolution is right for their situation. For example, a dissolution, in my opinion, is really based on good faith. You have to trust your spouse to come in and disclose everything, no one is hiding anything, or taking any money, everybody's on the up-and-up. When someone comes in and that's not the case, or there's a suspicion that that's not the case, I'd be less inclined to recommend a dissolution, and I'm afraid that this person has no understanding of his or her financial situation. I don't want to stereotype, but maybe it's a stay-at-home mom who hasn't handled any of the money issues and just spent what she needed to spend. She went to the grocery and there was always money there.

So is that what you do in those initial visits, a legal triage, or assessment of what the client needs and his or her understanding of this?

Absolutely. My job in the initial interview is to read the person, read the case, and take that and give that person advice. So yes, that's a great term, triage, as there are different steps for different cases. To be a domestic relations lawyer, you have to know how to read people. I'm lucky because I practice with my father and I learned it from him, how to sense people. Sense what's driving them. Sense that there's somebody else in their life, there's an affair, whatever. You sort of learn that pattern. You learn to tell when people are telling you a load of crap.

So after you listen to them and size them up, do you present them with these three divorce options, or do you present them with the one you think best fits their needs?

I always want to know what they think. I always tell clients that they are my boss. I work for them. They pay me. I take their direction, and I will do what is necessary for your case, as long as it's ethical. And if you ask me to do something unethical, I won't do it, and if you insist, I'll quit your case. But I always want to hear from the clients. Then I tell them I'm entitled to give them my advice. There are people who go against my advice. When that happens, I write them a letter, and then we go forward, and I advocate strongly either way because that's my job. Still, I want to hear from them and have them tell me how they think things are going, because people are generally pretty honest with me. If I ask a client if he or she thinks they could sit down with their spouse and work out a parenting plan for their kids and whether they can be fair with each other, there are people who will say yes, and I think they're being truthful. Then there are people who say absolutely not because we can't communicate; we can't agree today's Friday. In that case, I tell them that we shouldn't be wasting your money by trying to get a dissolution; we need to go to a court and have that court give us direction. Because the beauty of going to court, and the way most of those cases settle, is that the judge, for the most part, will give you his or her opinion after they've heard all the facts. They don't wait for a trial. For example, a judge will ask me to tell him what my case is all about. I tell him, judge, we have a woman who stayed at home for thirty years and raised six kids. Her husband is a doctor who makes five hundred thousand dollars a year. She's fifty-nine and he's sixty-one. Well, I'm painting a picture of a long-term marriage, long-term support case, et cetera. The judge will give you some direction of the outcome. If you have smaller issues where both sides can't agree, hopefully the judge can give you some direction of how he or she will come down on the case. Of course, the judges all say that these predictions are based on the evidence coming in as the lawyers presented it.

How do you handle the divorce using each of the three tracks, starting with dissolution?

Typically we will seek a disclosure of financial information. That may mean I write a letter to that person's spouse, or, if he's being represented, I'll get in contact with the other attorney and give him or her my list of information I need, tax returns, bank statements, et cetera. We eventually exchange that information. I end up sitting down with my client and try to determine what's fair, then I go back and forth with the other side to try to settle. In some cases, we will use four-way settlement meetings, and those seem to be becoming more popular. We'll have the parties and both counsels meet at one of the offices, and we might spend a half a day and go back and forth on all the issues and come up with a resolution.

In that four-way meeting, is there a lot of two-way discussion between the two lawyers?

Yes.

Is the four-way fairly contentious?

Let me go back and say something. It depends on the complexity of the case. If they have both have a 401(k) [retirement annuity] and they own a house and they make equal money, there isn't a lot of complexity. [If] I'm dividing lots of assets, liabilities, et cetera, it's going to be a more complex thing. The other thing, no matter what kind of divorce I'm doing, if there are assets that need to be valued, one side or both sides have to take the time to do that. So, if I have a medical practice, that has to be valued. I would get an appraiser to do that. Real estate gets valued. Retirement plans get valued. All of these assets get valued by experts who can come to court if necessary and testify as to what they are worth. All of this has happened before any kind of divorce case goes forward and, in a dissolution, before we have the meeting with the other side.

Does the law make this division of assets a fairly mechanical process?

Ohio is an equitable-division state, meaning the division should be equal unless there's a legitimate reason why it shouldn't. Yes, so in the perfect case, if two people come in with matching retirement plans, pretty equal incomes, it's a simple deal. What isn't so simple is when you can't agree on values or on someone's income. You know, we have a lot of individuals who come in and their income is one thing on their tax return and another in terms of actual income. For example, they get the use of a car from their business; shouldn't we count that as income? All those issues come up. So it's not as simple as it may seem.

When you do this kind of law, you get very involved in tax issues. I'm constantly needing to look at someone's estate. My client's going to take x, y, z assets, I need to figure out what the tax implications are. Because it's not the same for someone to take one hundred thousand dollars in a money market account versus that same amount in a retirement plan they can't access for twenty years. So there are different values of money, different tax effects, different penalties associated with the assets and/or liabilities that one takes. All those things need to be addressed. That's why people hire lawyers, or one of the reasons why. So to answer your question, yes, the law is helpful, and we have case law that directs us on certain issues, like how to we treat retirement plans or social security benefits, but it is never clear-cut. The unfortunate thing is that a lot of people come in with high-valued assets, but they don't have the cash to pay out the difference. For example, you own a car dealership valued at a couple million bucks, but you don't have a million dollars to pay your spouse to get her out of her interest in the business. So then you, as a lawyer, have to figure out creative ways to get that done. Whether it's going to the bank and borrowing money to buy her out or trading off other assets to come up with the deal. I tell people I'm just trading horses. My concern is whether I'm trading the right horses.

When the four-way has been completed, is the finished agreement then presented to the court?

Yes, the process in Ohio is that the parties first sign a separation agreement. Then, if there are children and they're going to be what are called shared parents, which in Ohio is the concept of joint custody, then they sign a shared-parenting plan. Those documents, along with other documents that we prepare, are filed at the courthouse, and then thirty days thereafter—no later than ninety days after the separation agreement has been signed—they will go in front of a judge, and the marriage will be dissolved by dissolution.

Do children in a marriage make it less likely that a case will be handled by dissolution?

Not necessarily; it certainly complicates things. I'd much rather, to settle a case, have it without the children, because children issues can complicate it. But we certainly do many dissolutions with children. I always say to people, I don't know your kids, and quite honestly, if I were going through a divorce, I wouldn't want a complete stranger like a judge to be making decisions like when my kids see mom, when my kids see dad. You know, who's going to have them for Christmas or New Year's. I'd rather the parents sit down and figure that out. Now, there are many people who are incapable of doing that, and so then they need lawyers. There's a professional in our court system called a *guardian ad litem*. That's a lawyer who is appointed by the court but paid by the parents to look after the interests of the children. I actually do some guardian work to get a different perspective on cases and to see what kids have to say in these situations. I go out and talk to children about mom and dad. I go talk to schoolteachers, counselors, or therapists to be able to understand the children.

Can we talk about those cases that start out as contested cases that eventually become uncontested?

I have a different level of legal power. I can subpoena records. I can use discovery. For example, I will send out subpoenas to the employer to get what I want in terms of the compensation summary for an executive and/or in terms of stock options for that person or retirement contributions. Those are the kinds of things that in a contested divorce I can get directly from the source, rather than in a dissolution. For example, I have to say to the husband to give me his executive summary and he won't give it to me, or he'll give me half of it or whatever. That's a big part of what's different in a contested divorce. The other thing is that I can take depositions. A deposition is a process where I take a witness and question him under oath in an office with the other lawyer and a court reporter. Presumably, if I'm speaking the truth to your questions, when I'm asked those questions again if we have a trial I better give those same answers again. It's a fact-finding mission for attorneys to find out the truth about certain things. I can't do that in a dissolution. There it's all good faith. I've got to trust you. You've got to trust me that we're laying it all out on the table and we're doing a fair deal.

When does the court become involved in a contested divorce?

Court connection is almost instantaneous after filing. The first thing that happens most of the time in a contested divorce is the court will issue temporary orders; those are orders that are put in place while the case is pending. These include temporary custody of children, a child support order, a spousal support order, if applicable, and what we call temporary allocation of debt and expenses. For example, determining who's going to pay the mortgage while this case is going. Who is going to pay the car payment? The court addresses attorney's fees and expert fees and whether these are necessary. Is one side going to help the other side with that? For example, you've got the housewife at home who hasn't worked and has zero income and you've got the doctor making nine hundred thousand dollars. He's probably going to be paying a good portion of his wife's attorney's fees.

Are these preliminary court decisions used to leverage the other side into settlement?

There's constant leveraging in getting a leg up in negotiations. You know one thing I see more and more, which is unfortunate, we've become more of a violent society. Domestic violence is the buzzword around, and I get into a lot of those issues if it's applicable with a client. What I mean is that this is an emotional, emotional deal. I can't think of anything more emotional than your marriage. I mean people kill over it. And people do some crazy, crazy things in a divorce. I've had clients go home, get upset, and do something they shouldn't have done; it's uncharacteristic for them. It's like when you have that one drink too many and drive and you get pulled over. So those kinds of things bring leverage. You know, you get a good temporary order award that the other side doesn't like, that brings leverage. You just sit tight for a while. You get a good psychological report in a custody case; you're going to sit on that for a while potentially, until the other side wants to come to bat. Ultimately, and this is what laypeople don't understand, your case is only as good as the evidence you can present. I always tell clients evidence is in court testimony and documents. Just because you say something, that doesn't make it true. I very rarely have a divorce case where she says one thing and he doesn't say the complete opposite, so I need other, credible witnesses to come in. That's why expert witnesses in what I do are so important. Claims are much more credible coming from a psychologist rather than from one of the parties or a neighbor because there's a different level of education, experience, and objectivity. I say to people you can say he's a horrible dad and you're the greatest mom, but until a psychologist really agrees with that opinion, it's useless. So the evidence is important. People come in, and they say all these things about their spouse, and I say great, how are we going to prove it? Because your case will never be worth anything if I can't prove it. I can't prove it without witnesses or documents or something credible to show the court that is truthful and that's important to your case.

As you're working with the opposing counsel, do you both have a pretty good sense of how the case is going to end up?

It depends on my opposing counsel. There's another firm here that is probably our biggest competitor. I was over at that lawyer's office Wednesday, and we sat down for an hour and had the whole case resolved. He knew that if I had to try the case, I knew how to try the case, and I knew the same about him, so that help us cut through all the BS. I have other lawyers who I have cases with where we don't have the ability to do that. It's unfortunate. I'm not blaming it on them. I'm not blaming it on anybody; it's just the reality of the situation. What I find often, and once again I've learned this from my mentor, is that when I first started and there was someone across the seat and he or she was crying, I felt bad. My reaction was we're going to go get the other side, even if that wasn't the right thing that would make my client feel better. What I've learned is sometimes I have to let them cry and say I'm really sorry that you're going to lose custody of your kids, and I'm really sorry that the psychologist thinks you have a lot of mental health problems that you need to attend to, or I'm really sorry that your drug test came back positive for the third time in a row—I'm really sorry, but that's the reality. I feel that in my job, I constantly have to tell people things that are unpleasant, because I don't think very many people win divorce cases.

Let me put it this way, I think that nobody ends up winning all that often because it's a court of equity. A couple of years ago I tried a big, big money case. I won every point on the property division, so everything I wanted I got, but I got slammed on the support decision. So I won one thing, lost on the other, so it all worked out even in the end, and I think that's what the judge wanted to do because we the lawyers and the parties couldn't agree on how to settle the case. So anyway, getting back to telling clients unpleasant truths, there are a lot of lawyers who won't do that. I don't know if it's a fee issue or they just can't tell people bad news. And some people fire me. I've had clients walk out the door and tell me they think I believe their spouses more than them. I'll tell them I'm sorry that's what you think, but I'm just being honest with you because you're paying me a lot of money and [I'm] not going to fight for something that is unattainable. Or if I do fight it, I want you to understand that it's really like a zero chance, so let's make this deal and it's a little bit better. Going back to your original question, there are a lot of lawyers who don't have that kind of relationship with their clients, so it makes it hard to work with them to settle the case.

Columbus is a big city. Do you know all of the opposing counsel well?

There is a handful, let's say a dozen, ten to twelve, law firms in town who specialize in what we specialize in, in a boutique setting. So I know all those attorneys well. But the unfortunate thing for the public is that there are a lot of lawyers who think they can do this work as long as you can divide by two, and that's where I can take advantage of the other side. I settled a case three or four weeks ago, and the other side had no idea of the tax ramifications for his client on a deal we were doing, and that saved my guy about seventy-five thousand dollars and to the detriment of his client. It happened because I do this every day; he doesn't. I think he was helping out a friend. There are lots of lawyers out there doing it because there's so much business. I mean about fifty percent, fifty-five percent of all first marriages are ending in divorce, and it doesn't stop. It's not like we're on some decline; the religious right is not having an effect, and divorce is thriving as it ever was.

If someone comes to me, or there's a conflict in a case, I'll refer them out to one of the other lawyers who I trust, and vice versa. Like some people come in, say my spouse and I want to do this, and they want the name of a good lawyer, who would you like to work with? It doesn't happen that often, but it happens a few times a year, and I love it because they're being reasonable. Because most people would say whatever lawyer my spouse's lawyer recommends, I'm going to go the opposite because there must be some bad faith message there. I'll say go see so-and-so, and I can tell you we can get your case done much sooner, much cheaper.

What's the role of the judge in moving a contested divorce to a settlement?

It depends on the judge. Most of our judges encourage settlement because they don't have time to hear every case. They will be mediators, in a way. A lot of judges will say we're going to have a settlement conference. They'll have both parties and the lawyers down at the court on a particular day with all of what we call trial notebooks, the file you'll need for trial. You'll lay out your case that way. You'll sit in the conference room with the judge and the parties and you'll say, judge, this is our balance sheet, this a financial statement and what we've stipulated to it, and we can agree to everything but the value of the real estate. I have so-and-so as my expert to come in and talk about the real estate, and they have so-and-so. Then the judge will ask how far off we are, or what's the difference in the value. A couple of years ago my dad and I tried a case where the value of the husband's business was about eight million bucks. We couldn't just meet in the middle. This was one of those cases that had to be tried. That's quite different than a case where the real estate experts differ over the value of property by ten thousand dollars. In that case, the judge can say, come on, five thousand dollars? You're spending more than five thousand dollars on your lawyers. Let's split down the middle and get it done. So some judges will do that. Judges will also give you an idea on spousal support, which is also a pretty contested issue. In Ohio we have factors that the judge looks at, but there are no guidelines. In child support you basically spit the number into a formula, and it spits out a number. It's not like that with spousal support [also called *alimony*]. The judge may say, under these circumstances and with all this information, I'm likely to go five thousand dollars a month for three years and then you know.

Does the judge ever play "bad cop" to an obstinate party who doesn't want to settle?
I was in a conference the other day in a different county where the judge looked at the other side and said, there is no way I am going to go with your proposal, it's way too high. Now the parties weren't there for that, but that's also an example of a lawyer I don't know very well. I went out and told my client truthfully everything that was said. I don't know whether or not this other lawyer did, but I could settle the case based on what the judge told us in there. My client would go for it. Her client is not, and they're digging in their heels. I just heard from my client that his wife is going to fire her attorney and get a more aggressive one. I don't think that's going to change the judge's mind.

Can you talk about the tougher cases that have to go to trial?
Being in trial for me is like the ultimate high. I love being in trial. I don't go to trial just to go to trial, but if you're prepared it's just a great feeling. It's fun to seek the truth. It's fun to test your legal skills as an attorney. The process is that you have witnesses. They get examined both on direct examination and cross-examination. You put documents into evidence. You argue your case. You don't have a jury in what we do. One thing that is important to understand, throughout the process in divorce and postdivorce litigation you may have a lot of mini-hearings. You may have an issue on temporary child support, or should the husband be thrown out of the house for being violent or being detrimental to the children, and you may have a trial on that. It may be like a half a day, and you may bring in a neighbor and your client. So you're getting trial work that way, but the big long-term divorce cases that go on to trial probably are only in my practice about seven to eight a year, at most. My partner is up in another county right now trying a divorce. She's been gone two weeks, and it will probably go another two weeks. Those are rare.

What are the characteristics of those rare cases? Why do they defy settlement?
Usually a lot of money. Without giving names, my partner's case probably involves a hundred million bucks, lots of corporations, lots of sham stuff going on, and lots of potential hidden assets.

So going to trial is not a function of the level of hatred between the spouses?

It can be. I tried a case earlier this summer, seventeen days, and it was all on the issue of relocation of a child. Mom wanted to relocate from Columbus with the child to a different state. Dad didn't want it to happen. You know, a postdivorce issue. So some people fight over their child, which is legitimate. My client, who wanted the child to remain here, felt that if the child were permitted to go, his relationship with the child would be affected forever. So different reasons make people dig in their heels.

I find that for the most part, though, that the reason trials take a long time is because of the complexity of the finances. You know when you've corporations and money flowing in and out from all different deals and whatnot, then it just needs to be explained in detail, and you need to put everything up into evidence. The other thing to understand about trials is that in order for the court to technically consider it, it has to be put into evidence, so although we may be dealing with what sounds like the most basic thing, we still have to put it into evidence. Otherwise, if there is an appeal and it's not in the record, the appellate court can't consider it. So it might be as basic as here's your 2005 tax return and we have to put each line on the record, for example, line 31 says, line 32 says, et cetera; I'm going to put it on the record. Now sometimes it's not that deliberate, and that's a bad example because people are familiar with tax forms. With detailed documents that are not so familiar, you might have to go through that so the judge can understand.

Since you have these pretrial conferences, how often is the outcome of the trial a surprise?

That's a great question. I would say that, overall, I end up within the ballpark of what I expected. But as a litigator, there's always that sense of doubt, that for some reason you missed something, or you had a bad witness, or they had a better witness on the other side. I was the kind of student who walked out of every test thinking I flunked, and—maybe it was psychological—then it felt great when I did ace it. So there's the same sort of feeling when you're in trial. You're often not aware of how you're doing. I tried a case last week, just a little mini-custody case in a different county. You know, I walked out of there thinking I'm going to win, but I don't know, maybe I'm not, and I'm waiting for a decision. I thought I had all the good evidence on my side. The magistrate in that case didn't give us any clue; she said, I really need to hear all of the evidence about it, and that's what we did.

Studies show that many times clients want to explain to their lawyer why they are not responsible for the failure of the marriage, but the lawyers are focused on the legal issues that will resolve the case. At other times, lawyers may use the clients' stories to keep them focused on completing the divorce rather than reconciling with a spouse who has caused them so much trouble. Is this a fair representation of your practice?

I'm probably a different type of lawyer. I don't think you can be in this business and not be a part-time armchair mental health professional. I actually listen to my clients and don't just jump to the legal parts of the case. I want to listen to them. I want to figure out if there's a different way. One of the first times I ever sat in on an interview with a client with my dad, I was a young lawyer, you know, a wife came in and her husband was having an affair. You know, at that age, I think I had just been married, I thought if your spouse is having an affair your marriage was done. Instead, my dad said to the client, here's the name of a psychologist. I want you to go see him and take your husband. You have a young child, and you have a strong future if you can get this issue resolved. Go try to do it. Don't come back until you at least try. Now if you try and your husband won't, then we'll go forward. Well, you know what? They're still married. They have two more children. They're very happy; I see them in the community. Now that takes a different kind of lawyer. I learned from that, so that I'm listening. I'm making sure that that's what they want to do. Then when I do jump to the legal part, we're going to get to the legal part. It's true that, anymore, the issues of adultery or fault are not considered much in Ohio.

But do you find that clients want to come and make it clear to you that they're not at fault?

Absolutely, and I listen. I remember the first Friday afternoon, I'm sitting in my office, and some woman started to tell me stories—intimate details about her sex life and blah, blah, blah; and I just sort of looked up at the window, it was 4 P.M., and I thought to myself, I'm listening to this woman's personal sex life stories, it's a Friday afternoon, I'm getting paid, I'm like, this isn't a bad deal. It wasn't like I was being perverted or something. My first job was at a big law firm, and I was one of those guys who had to bill hours, and you researched, and it wasn't for me. I never saw a client. I remember on that job counting the hours until I could leave, because it was just painful, and it was just the opposite on this first interview. It was like I was watching an episode of *Desperate Housewives* or something.

   Also, I really want to say this about this practice. I've seen a lot of people who get into it and burn out. I didn't know what to expect for myself. You need to take it seriously, but you also need to live a life. I mean, you can get too wrapped up in other people's problems, in trying to help them, and then you screw up yourself. I did that for the first couple of years. I didn't sleep. I didn't eat well. Every problem was my problem, and I had to solve it. And I realized that I'm taking other people's problems and making them more important than they are making them. That isn't right. That's something you need to know about this practice. It's an emotionally draining practice. You're always on, and I get calls at home all weekend with different people going through different crises. You need to be able to love to be in court, to have good trial skills, to be really good and be able to tell people good and bad news. I think a lot of people go into this work thinking either that they're going to make a lot of money or for whatever reason; some people have that quintessential need to help people. You do help people out of a process, and certainly that's important. You help people fight for their children, and that's important, but you also have a lot of grief, and you have to have a strong will.

Can you tell me what is the best part of your job?

The best part of my job is that I get to meet a ton of people and that there's no day that's the same. Every one of my days is different. I never know who's going to call with what issue or concern, including existing clients. For me that's a joy, because I cannot be routine and bored in what I do. And the other thing is owning a small business. If it's a beautiful day and I don't have anything on my calendar and I want to golf, I can go, and nobody cares. When I was at a big law firm, I always felt like someone was watching me. I felt like if I left before certain partners, even though it might not have been true, that that wasn't appreciated. And I have a family, I have three young kids, and I want to go to their games, their things, et cetera.

What's the worst part of your job?

The worst part of the job is having to tell people really bad news. It's just not an easy thing. You know, if you get a decision—and fortunately for me I haven't [had] a lot of these horrible situations—but it's tough. It's tough to watch people break down in your office or on the phone. And combined with that is feeling attached. There are many people who hire me who are just in a horrible situation, equivalent to the death of a loved one, and they don't treat you well, they don't show you respect, they argue over how much they pay you, the time you take on their case, et cetera, et cetera, and it's hard for me to deal with that because I'm really trying to help them. It's hard for me to understand why this person is screaming and yelling at me or arguing over a hundred fifty dollars I charged them, if I'm ultimately helping them. I always say to people, it's sort of like I'm your doctor, and if a doctor helps me, I wouldn't scream and yell at my doctor. Anyway, that would be the worst thing. But I think, as I've gotten older, I've learned to deal with that better, and it doesn't affect me as much and I really like what I do, I really do.

Scott Himsel

The Lawyer in the Large Firm

THE OFFICE OF BAKER AND DANIELS is on the top floors of the tallest building in Indianapolis, Indiana. Floor-to-ceiling glass windows in the reception area provide the visitor with a more than 180- degree view to the horizon. The firm's law library occupies an adjoining space in two open floors of the skyscraper. As with many large firms, its clients are corporations who often seek ways of preventing legal problems from arising. The firm provides this service on a continuing basis. Its clients are not one-shotters. The mild-mannered Scott Himsel is a partner in the firm. He also teaches part time at Wabash College.

Could you please describe your career as an attorney?
I grew up on a farm in southern Indiana. I decided to go to law school because I had always thought I wanted to be a lawyer—probably starting in the fourth grade. I did my undergraduate work at Wabash College and then went to law school at Northwestern University. Right after a clerkship, I came to Baker and Daniels. So there was one position in between. I graduated law school in 1988, and I was a law clerk for the United States District Court from 1988 to 1989. I came to Baker and Daniels in 1990 and have been here ever since.

Is this a large firm?
We have well over three hundred lawyers. We have offices in Indianapolis, Elkhart, South Bend, Fort Wayne, Washington, D.C., and we have a couple of offices in China. We have had offices in China for a number of years. We were one of the first firms to get a license from the [Chinese] government to open an office.

What kinds of clients do you have, and what problems do they bring to you?
I involve myself in general litigation, civil litigation. My clientele is primarily made up of nonprofit organizations. Of the nonprofit organizations I work with, the largest single group would be religious organizations of all types

and denominations. But I have also worked for college, universities, and charities. I have also done a significant amount of work over the years for estates, for trusts, and then also I have done work for large corporate clients of various types in commercial transactions and when they get involved in litigation matters. Insofar as how people find me, when you start off at a firm of this size, typically you are just working for more experienced lawyers. The clients come to you through more senior lawyers. Over time, as you do more work, clients frequently find you through your other clients. Particularly in the nonprofit and religious worlds, clients will talk to one another. Frequently, that is how they will find you—because of prior work you have done.

What sorts of legal problems do nonprofit organizations have?
All the types of problems everyone else has. They have problems with employees. They have problems with business dealing, and they have internal issues. Issues of internal discipline that can sometimes spill out into outside dispute-resolution mechanisms. So, for example, someone may be disciplined [by a religious body] and may seek to take that up in the courts later.

Do the problems involve disputes between congregations and church leaders?
Yes, or a member of the church who is employed in some capacity by the church. If they are disciplined, they might even lose their position, and then they seek to litigate.

Do such cases present issues of First Amendment religious free exercise?
Sometimes. For example, I was just mentioning that sometimes the church will employ a person to teach. We have had circumstances where employees of the church were terminated because of differences of opinion on matters of theology with the church. Then they [teachers] seek to litigate that matter in the courts. The courts, however, have no jurisdiction to resolve theological and religious disputes. This can occur in the situation I have just described. It can also occur in situations where there are splits within congregations over various matters of doctrine and polity, or church government. The U.S. Supreme Court has made clear for many years that it is not in a position to resolve those disputes, because to do so would be in effect to "establish" the church or its government, which the courts can't do (see Presbyterian Church in the U.S. v. Mary Elizabeth Blue Hull Memorial Presbyterian Church 1969; Serbian Eastern Orthodox Diocese for the U.S. and Canada v. Milivojevich 1976).

What kinds of legal problems do charities face?
Charities can have issues in interpreting the meaning of a gift and the restrictions upon it and how those might apply when circumstances are very different in the future than they were at the time the gift was made. Sometimes those changes can occur decades after the gift was given. Then there are circumstances where family members become intensely interested in an estate

or trust and will seek to challenge the use of those gifts or stop them from being made effective to the charity. So then we get involved defending the charity in a will contest or a trust dispute to make sure the charity gets the bequest the deceased intended.

Do you deal with other clients or problems?

All kinds of problems. We have clients who come to us with regulatory issues, such as how they are supposed to comply with some of the extremely detailed and specific requirements that relate to matters of lending, for example, and disclosure in the area of lending. I had a lawsuit that went on for a number of years in that area that we were able to resolve successfully. I have had clients who have had their billing practices questioned. In many ways those types of what I would call non-brass-tacks, run-of-the-mill legal disputes are very helpful in exercising the mind and understanding how you get from point A to point Z in terms of dealing with the practical problems of how business is conducted.

What sort of advice and counsel do your clients seek?

What they are asking for are good mechanisms for resolving disputes internally. For example, Indianapolis is blessed with being the headquarters for many nonprofit organizations. The Lilly Endowment is here. We have represented them; in fact, we incorporated them many years ago. There also are a number of fraternities and sororities that have their national headquarters here. I do a lot of work for sororities. What they are interested in having me do is helping them come up with better bylaws, articles, rules and regulations for handling procedures, so that they can achieve their mission. Frequently the same is true of our religious clients and denominations. They are looking for guidance about how to resolve disputes more effectively and how to make their rules clearer.

Most of that is litigation-based, but I like to think of myself more as a dispute resolver rather than a litigator. The truth of the matter is that there just aren't that many cases that get tried these days. They get resolved, but they get resolved in other, more efficient ways, so I like to think of what I do as all being related to that principle. A sorority, for example, might call with an immediate issue with one of their chapters somewhere in the United States. Of course, you have to immediately resolve the issue, whatever it is. But often that leads to further thought and further discussion about how we might improve what we do within the organization to avoid any further occurrence of the problem. Sometimes it doesn't have anything to do with how the procedures are written, sometimes it does.

Does politics enter into the kinds of problems or cases that you address?

Particularly when you have done some First Amendment work as I have, politics matters. What you are often doing is reminding the court that it matters. To give an example, I remember arguing a case in a county in Indiana, a religious case, and reminding the court that although the way the case came to the court was as a breach of contract and tort case, that was nothing more than a thinly veiled effort to get the court to reverse the church on a religious issue. We were successful in getting the court oriented toward that way of looking at the dispute, which was the correct way of looking at it. I think helping the court in the midst of its busy work when you are dealing with a situation like that is very helpful. Another way in which I think there is an impact comes to mind because the legislature has just been in town. One of the things you have to learn to do when you are counseling clients is to broaden your perspective when it comes to possible solutions. We litigators have been getting used to that through alternative dispute resolution. For our clients it is also important that there can be legislative solutions to problems. Let us say that we have a statute that is not perfectly clear or is now being applied to a problem that the legislature hadn't foreseen. You have to include on the table the option that might be effective to also draw into the discussion one of our lawyers who works in the area of legislation. Then when that person is brought into the discussion, they can explain time frames and likelihoods of success and who the interested people are going to be in such a legislative proposal during the next session.

For our nonprofit clients, especially our schools and universities, we have lawyers in Washington who are very effective in figuring out how they interface with the federal government. It is particularly for our nonprofit private-sector colleges and universities. We represent a group of Christian schools, and they are especially interested in learning what the federal government is doing. In all of those ways I think the political realm is immediately relevant.

On a typical day, how do you spend your time?
When you litigate you have to be able to respond to that immediate need whenever it comes. Because I also teach part time, it would depend. On my teaching days, I am involved in that enterprise until eleven or noon, two days a week; then I will probably be at work until seven that evening. On the days when I am not teaching, I'm starting at work at about eight in the morning with a similar ending time. I typically don't work weekends. As to what happens during the course of that day, it just depends. I spend a fair amount of time on the phone with clients addressing questions. I spend a fair amount of time with our associates, delegating assignments to them: research, writing, asking them to follow up with clients on various points. We like to involve our associates as much as we can in all aspects so they continue their development toward partnership.

I don't do as much research as I used to, which I regret, because I enjoy it. I also don't spend as much of my time writing as I used to. I have more client contact now. But I still spend a fair amount of time writing or revising the writing that is done by others, because most of our practice is based on paper—by fax. So a lot of work is done preparing for a way to resolve the cases as quickly and inexpensively as we can.

How many issues do you have on your desk at any time?

It's hard to say. Some lawyers who are public defenders or prosecutors can tell you they have a hundred active cases, and they are not lying. I would never have that many. I typically at any time probably have between fifteen and twenty active matters pending. Some of them are not only on the back burner, but they are off the stove and in the freezer. Others are on the front burner and require immediate attention. The practice of law is largely about managing the stove and making sure everything gets prepared properly and in the right order. That juggling process is one of the greatest challenges in practicing law.

Do you have frequent contact with attorneys for the other parties in disputes?

Quite a bit. Telephone combat is one of the most common forms of litigation warfare today. That's simply because it is more efficient and often more effective because you don't have to come to court at the same time and you can do the contracts in person. We spend a lot of time with opposing counsel on the telephone.

Do you keep records of the information conveyed in the calls?

I always have notes of some sort. I might dictate a memo to the file. If I don't do that, I always take notes of every conversation I have.

Do you find that other attorneys are cooperative and fair?

I find that other lawyers are generally above board and operate fairly. In those rare circumstances where you come across a person with whom you have had a bad experience, it is often made more effective to communicate in writing.

Do you often see opposing attorneys' clients?

No, but we do when necessary. For example, one of the purposes of mediation is to require the parties to see one another much earlier in the process than would have been the case otherwise. That can often be effective. It's not a convivial thing, often because we as litigators often see people only when they are unhappy, but typically people conduct themselves responsibly. In this room just a few months ago opposing clients were here, and I think it's helpful in the mediation process to have the clients in the room. It helps you understand it's a real, human problem with various perceptions. You get all kinds of important and useful information just by having them in the room talking about the likelihood of settling something.

Does the preparation and discovery involve preparing interrogatories and conducting depositions?

Sure, so we are preparing discovery, and we are also responding to the other side's discovery. At each point we are tying to figure out what the most efficient way is to resolve the dispute. Sometimes is it through those traditional means. Sometimes it isn't. Sometimes it can be through a prompt presuit mediation, or just a discussion between counsel, or simply our preparing a letter explaining why there is no claim here and seeking to resolve it that way.

Is the mediation of cases common?

Very common. It is court-ordered, but we have also done it on our volition when we thought it would be an effective way to reach a resolution. We have had a lot of success with mediation, and I favor it in many cases. I am not interested in engagement when we have got a case that is clearly frivolous or where I think the parties are at such loggerheads that it is just too easy for it to be useful.

So trials are uncommon?

I think that the last statistics I saw for the (federal) Seventh Circuit—Indiana, Illinois, and Wisconsin—I think we have a trial rate of less than two percent.

Are your cases federal or state matters?

Our practice is a mix, but it's mostly state court. That's because the types of thing I do are between individuals who are in the same state at the outset. So we end up in state court for a fair amount of what I do. I also, however, in addition to the litigation work, am increasingly involved in doing the other side of the law—advice and counsel work for our nonprofit clients. So that whole area of work doesn't involve the courts at all. It is directed toward preventing us from going to court.

Do you practice before governmental regulatory bodies?

No, I don't.

Do you use experts?

Yes, we use experts. My area of practice doesn't involve as many experts as other areas of practice. For example, product liability lawyers use experts a lot more than in our area.

Do you interview or depose witnesses?

Oh, sure, and we interview witnesses and try to figure out what the most effective way is to preserve testimony or to have it in line if we need it.

In your practice, are contacts with judges infrequent?

This has been an unusual week for me because I had a hearing on Monday and a hearing on Tuesday. I was with judges on both occasions. On Monday we were in the courtroom, and it was fairly formal process that we went through, although a friendly one—a short hearing. Yesterday I was all prepared to agree to a hearing in a case, and at the last minute I thought of a way to resolve it without having to have a hearing. I printed that order up, took it with me to another county, and was able to talk to everyone in the hallway before we went in, and we reached a quick agreement. It was signed and we were done in fifteen minutes. I had not met that judge before, but I had local counsel, which was helpful.

Does your firm employ local counsel to assist you outside the local area?

Indeed, I think it's a good idea. We do a lot of cases here in Indianapolis, where it is necessary, but this was two or three counties away. Local counsel is extremely helpful in understanding our audience and understanding the court and what practices it prefers.

What do you regard as the pluses of practicing law?

I think there is satisfaction that comes with helping clients achieve their goals. I especially think that is true when you are working with the nonprofit sector. These are organizations that have really good missions. Sororities, for example, can help young women learn the benefits and burdens of making tough decisions. If you can help them design systems by which they can do that more effectively, then you are helping them achieve some real-life education experiences in the undergraduate years, which I think are extremely valuable. They worked for me in my fraternity, and I feel the same way about our sorority clients. The religious clients, perhaps even more so. We have a number of religious clients that are interested in mission work. Anything that we can do to avoid disputes or problems so that they can focus all of their attention on that, that makes you feel very good about what you are doing. I think in general the intellectual challenge of whether it's in lending practices or collection practices or any of those matters, to be able to throw yourself into a field that you know nothing about is a true liberal arts sort of challenge. You have to first learn it as a student, and then you have to eventually be able to teach it as an advocate. Those, in a nutshell, are some of the pluses.

What do you regard as the hardest aspects of practicing law?

Often in an area where there is very little law to guide you and you are a bit on your own. And, also, I think, where people's emotional reactions to problems can mask what should be the best course of action for them. This is [why it is] often said [that] a man who represents himself has a fool for a client. There is something to be gained by taking the problem to someone else who is your advocate but who can often view it outside that emotional charge that the clients themselves have when they have been accused of something.

I don't have a whole lot of problems. I think that the system works pretty well. I think that sometimes clients need to adjust their expectations as to the length of time it takes for disputes to be resolved. Our courts, despite using alternative dispute resolution, are still very busy. It simply takes time to resolve disputes. I think clients find that very frustrating, and I can't blame them. But it's a difficult problem to resolve unless we double the size of our system. I think that's a challenge.

Since you teach undergraduates, what is your advice to those who aspire to be attorneys?

I think it is really important for undergraduates to work hard and to seize the opportunities they have as undergraduates to learn how to learn. It's not so much being able to recall the substance of individual courses, although there is a lot of merit in that. It's the process of reading comprehension, organization of materials, and clear communication that an undergraduate curriculum provides a wonderful opportunity to develop. If it is developed, it can be put to very good use in the practice of law. [Law] is very much a profession for good liberal arts students. I think that if they can develop those skills, they can continue to enjoy the challenge of using them as lawyers. I think law is a very interesting and challenging field.

I think what is important for undergraduates to do is to continue to ask questions. They will be given many opportunities, sometimes more than they want, to meet alumni, and if, like me, they come from families that don't have any lawyers, they need to ask questions, corner lawyers, and not just hear the war stories but to ask them day-in-the-life questions. They still won't know until they immerse themselves in the practice of law. Nonetheless, I think it is very valuable for them to ask as many lawyers as they can find in their alumni organizations, fraternities and sororities, clubs, and what have you. Ask, "What is it you do ?" and "Do you like it?" Those questions can lead to much valuable information.

How important is the ability to write effectively?

I can take this week as an example. I am writing a summary judgment brief in a case in the medical field. It's not a medical malpractice case. It's a case about how medical organizations are put together these days. In the managed care field. Then, after that, I'll be writing an amicus brief in the United States Court of Appeals for a nonprofit client that is essentially an organization in a particular trade or industry. The writing style you need to develop is an advocacy style. What that means, it is hard, is to write with short, crisp, declarative sentences in the active voice. This is a real challenge for all of us. It is a particular challenge for undergraduates, I have found. But what it means is, without overstatement or exaggeration, which is never effective, to be able to get to the essence of the matter quickly and to communicate with confidence. My favorite example—I wish I could claim it were mine—is in a brief that was written to our district court here in Indianapolis by another lawyer in this office, in a case where there had been one discovery dispute after another. He began his brief—most people begin their briefs by saying, "This brief is submitted in support of our motion to compel." That's not very effective. It's not very exciting. It's not very interesting. Instead, this lawyer began his brief about his opponent's misconduct with the following sentence: "They're at it again." You have got to be able to get the attention of the court quickly. The extent to which you will be effective depends almost entirely on the extent to which you can express the idea succinctly. If you can't, that's very telling for the court.

I really hope we can find more ways to help our undergraduates and our law students learn that skill, because the opportunities to appear in court are diminishing every year. If you are going to get their attention, you better be able to do it on paper.

What challenges should budding lawyers prepare to face?

A problem is areas of law where we have little guidance from the courts about what the proper resolution ought to be. I was in court on Monday in what is a case of first impression on a particular point. So, going to the other states, getting their law, seeing how it fits into the existing fabric of Indiana law is a challenge.

The other challenge, which is more of a long-term challenge, is figuring out how you are going to put a brief together. Judge Learned Hand once said something about writing is the most difficult thing he did, and of course he was a great writer. You also have to figure out how to put the puzzle together when you are going through the boxes of documents for the first time. When you are trying to digest what a client is telling you for the first time—that is a real challenge, because it requires being adept at processing information and figuring it out. You go through many drafts or many hours of trying to sort that out. Once you have a handle on it, it becomes a lot more enjoyable.

Jeffrey M. Byer

The Commercial Practice Attorney

THE LAW FIRM OF SANDLER, Lasry, Laube, Byer, and Valdez, LLP, occupies much of the seventeenth floor of an office tower in downtown San Diego, California. Entering the office, the interviewer notes the abundant use of wood paneling, both on a wall bearing the name of the firm and around the receptionist's desk. Jeff, in his late thirties, ushers the interviewer into a conference room. Around a large conference table with a stunning view of the harbor and Mission Bay, this attorney discusses a broad-based civil practice in what some might call a "boutique" law firm.

Could you please describe your background and education?
I was raised in Los Angeles. I went to school at San Diego State—undergrad— and then I went to law school at Boalt Hall—the University of California at Berkeley. I was fortunate to come to San Diego with my family. I really liked it. One of my brothers went to San Diego State, and I had an opportunity to see the area a little closer. But I was not mature enough to get too far away from home, so it seemed like a good fit at the time.

Why did you decide to go to law school?
I had been encouraged about being a lawyer by my father, who is not a lawyer. He thought it would be something I would be interested in. Also, an English teacher sort of encouraged me. I was focused on it without really knowing too much about it. I had the [legal] career in mind. I chose Boalt Hall because it was a terrific school, and I could get in.

Where did you begin your practice?
Here in San Diego. When I was in my second year of law school, I worked for a local firm here in San Diego. I knew that I wanted to come back to San Diego after graduation from law school. I wanted to work as a summer clerk with a

San Diego firm with the idea that I could get a job the day after I graduated from law school. That's what I did. During my second and third years I worked for a large firm [about forty lawyers] here in San Diego for the summer, and then I received an offer and started working for the firm after I graduated.

How long did you practice at the larger firm?

Ten years. My four partners and I were at the old firm. We started this firm in 2000. We brought clients with us. I am at the younger end of the scale of us. The three more senior lawyers had been practicing for fifteen to twenty years when we moved to this firm. I had worked with them at my old firm. In terms of the clients we have, they mostly came from those relationships with the more senior of the partners. Also, we had a pretty loyal group of clients that wanted to follow us as a group when we moved over here.

How large is your current firm?

There are just the five of us. No associates. We really wanted to avoid doing that if we could. We wanted to limit the number of employees that we had and not have the responsibility for associates. The way we planned it was that, if the practice grew to the point where we couldn't handle the work by ourselves or with contract lawyers who we use occasionally, then we would consider hiring an associate. But our business plan, if you can call it that, did not involve growth. It involved keeping our nice group the way it is without injecting the risks with different personalities and employees.

How is work managed in the firm?

We each have our own caseloads. To an extent, we are all doing the same thing on cases. There are certain cases that we collaborate with each other on. I have a few cases that I am working on with some of my partners. I am helping them— that's the best way to put it. With certain matters I can come in and help with tasks, but, for the most part, everyone is doing the same thing on other cases.

What kinds of clients do you represent?

They are a very, very broad group of clients. I represent a bank, and I represent a woman who was run over by an SUV. The very two ends of the spectrum. We represent probably—the bank is probably our largest client—but we also represent some pretty large corporations all the way down to individuals with specific legal problems. The bank is local. The national clients we represent typically result from our being brought into a matter as local counsel. For example, we represented a fairly large company that manufactured latex gloves. There was national litigation against this manufacturer and others. Some of the cases, obviously, were in California and in San Diego. So the national firm in Chicago needed to find local counsel. So we do serve in a local-counsel role, which is particularly suitable to a firm our size. Also, we represent several public entities in San Diego—an agency of the county and quasi-public entities in real estate and commercial disputes.

How do clients locate your firm?

The bulk of our individual clients are referrals from either past clients or lawyers that we worked with or that we have relationships with. We don't do advertising.

With such a range of clients, do you see yourself as a specialist?

No, I don't, which maybe makes me a little unique from some of my partners. I am a specialist in the sense that I am a civil litigator, but that's really not a disciplinary specialty. If I had to say what my specialty would be, I would probably say that it is commercial and real estate litigation. That tends to be the bulk of my practice, but there are many different types of disputes that would fall into those categories. Some of my partners have very specific types of cases that they handle, but not exclusively. We sort of hold ourselves out as a general civil litigation practice.

We're typically paid on an hourly basis. As most firms, with new clients, depending on the client, we ask for a deposit. There are a small number of cases we handle on a contingency basis.

You practice largely before state courts?

I do. One of my partners is in federal court because he handles cases involving the Americans with Disabilities Act, which is a litigious federal law. But in most case I find myself in state court.

Could you please describe a routine workday?

I wouldn't say there is a routine. It is driven by what cases I happen to be working on and what tasks I have to do on a particular case. I will say that one routine thing I do every day is write letters. That is something we have to do, communicate with clients and other counsel.

Do you also write letters after discussing topics on the phone?

It depends on the phone call. Sometimes, yes, if you want to memorialize what has taken place, if there is any reason to doubt that the person you are communicating with would interpret what you discussed differently, or just generally to confirm things. For example, if I were to request an extension from another lawyer to provide a response to something, I would routinely confirm that in writing, even if it was a lawyer I had worked with and had no doubt that they would not go back on their word. That's just the routine confirmation letter.

What are the topics of letters to clients?

Status of the case, recommendations. If the client needs to participate in certain tasks—responding to discovery in a civil case—the client needs to participate in that, they need to review the responses. They need to verify the responses are accurate. That would be a certain kind of communication I would have with the client. If something happens of interest in a case that would potentially affect the case. That would be something I would write the client about.

What other documents do you draft?

Settlement agreements, complaints, answers, motions, all types of pleadings that need to be filed in a court case.

These activities occupy a considerable portion of your time?

Yes, I would say so.

How important are discovery activities for you?

Discovery is a means to an end. If in a particular case you know all the facts and you have full control of the facts, then there is no need to get information from the other side. In the typical case, though, you do want to get information from the other side. At a minimum, you want to ask the other side what their contentions are and what facts support their contentions.

Is taking depositions a part of this process?

Yes. In most cases I take depositions unless there are economic considerations that come into it. Depositions can be very expensive, so in a dispute where there is a relatively modest amount of money involved relative to what you would spend taking depositions, then my recommendation to the client would be "don't take the deposition." Or, here is the pros and cons of it.

Who else do you contact during discovery or case preparation?

Expert witnesses. We use expert witnesses in cases where there are issues that require expertise. For example, in a personal injury case where you have injuries to your client, then you might need a physician to be able to explain the injuries. In a real estate case where the value of property is an issue, then you need to obtain an appraiser who can give an expert opinion on what the value of the property is. Most cases have experts.

If it is an area where I have used experts, I like to use experts that I have used in the past. If it's not somebody that I have used before, then I'll ask my colleagues, my partners, for recommendations, or sometimes I'll go outside the firm and ask other lawyers for recommendations or other experts for recommendations to track somebody down.

Anyone else?

Private investigators. We hire private investigators in certain cases to do witness interviews, to investigate if there are certain facts that require some work that a private investigator would be good at doing.

Do you have to file motions to secure access to evidence held by the other side?

I would say it is rare. In my practice it has been rare over the past few years. But certainly I have had to do it. Judges hate those motions, so you like to get [the access problem] resolved if you can. Certainly it does happen.

What sorts of contacts do you have with opposing lawyers?

It depends on the stage of the case. Certainly when you get closer to trial you are in touch with them constantly—daily sometimes in the short period of time leading up to trial. But before that, at the initial filing of the lawsuit through discovery, it just depends on what happens. There are certain cases in which nothing can happen. Then you won't have any communication with the other lawyer. So it is really task-dependent.

I would say that I have been pretty fortunate in my practice to have had, for the most part, dealings with reasonable lawyers on the other side. *Reasonable* is a word I would use to describe most of the lawyers I work with. There are some exceptions to that. Having a license to practice law is a license to create a lot of misery, and some people take advantage of that. I have dealt with a fair number of difficult lawyers over the years, but overall I have been pretty fortunate. The community in San Diego, the legal community in San Diego is still a small legal community—if not in numbers—so reputations develop easier than they would in a city like Los Angeles, which is much larger and there is not as much personal accountability.

What sorts of contacts do you have with opposing clients?
The contact with the other side of the case is generally through the lawyers. I can't communicate directly with the other lawyer's client. So the interaction usually comes if I am taking that person's deposition or see them at mediation or see them at trial. Generally, I would say, in cases where the other side is a large entity, the client on the other side knows how litigation works. It isn't personal with them. As a result, they don't like me or dislike me. They just reject the position I take or what have you. But it is not a personal thing. Whereas when you are dealing with people on the other side who are individuals, where the dispute is very personal to them, then there is an immediate dislike to me.

Do you settle most cases through negotiation?
Yes, I'd say so.

When and how do you negotiate?
It depends on the case. Litigation is a notoriously bad way to resolve disputes. It is very expensive. It is very emotional. In almost all cases, settlement is the best way to resolve the dispute. If there is an opportunity to get a case resolved sooner rather than later that would benefit the client, then I would seize upon that opportunity. In some cases the parties are too far apart, the dispute is too emotional, or whatever the reason might be—in those cases you have to track a different course. Increasingly, most disputes are resolved by mediation—unless the parties are so close [to settlement] that it doesn't justify the expense of hiring a mediator.

The mediator is a private third party who tries to settle the case?
Right, either an attorney or a retired judge. In San Diego the court has a list of mediators that will agree to reduce their hourly rate. They are capped at a certain rate for the first four hours, and then after the four hours charge their hourly rate. That's a way to—sometimes it makes sense to go through the

court list. A lot of the good mediators don't need to reduce their hourly rate for the first four hours.

Is mediation becoming more common?
I think so.

Do you engage in arbitration?
We do go to arbitration sometimes. I will have an arbitration hearing, which is the equivalent of a trial. Arbitration is an alternative to the litigation system. Once you get into arbitration, you pretty much have left the court system. It [arbitration] is typically by agreement among the parties. Typically, there will be a contract between the parties that has a clause in it that says, if there is any dispute between the parties, they will agree to submit the dispute to arbitration. That is—unless there is no contract—the parties can agree voluntarily to go to arbitration instead of by way of a contract they happened to sign.

There are different arbitral bodies, different organizations, that do arbitration. Sometimes the contract will say which of those organizations you have to go to. The biggest is the American Arbitration Association. They have their own set of rules on discovery and their own set of procedural rules like you have in the courts. So you are in that system, and you have to follow their rules. Typically, discovery rights are pretty limited in arbitration when compared to what they are in litigation. Once you complete your discovery, you have your "trial," which is not a trial. It's a hearing before the arbitrator or a panel of arbitrators. Sometimes there is a panel of three arbitrators. Typically, it occurs in someone's office or a conference room, or some of these organizations have their own offices. They make their decision. They generally have no obligation to explain how they reached their decision—you can't compel them to. Then the other party has the right to take the arbitrator's decision and go to court and then have it confirmed as a judgment. The distinction of arbitration and trial is that the grounds for appeal are extremely limited from the arbitrator's ruling as opposed to the judge's ruling or a jury finding.

Do you represent clients before administrative bodies?
I have represented several cases before the labor commissioner here in California which involved salary disputes. Somebody was terminated, and they were trying, they were claiming they weren't paid the salary they were owed.

Do you frequently appear before judges?
At trial, infrequently. Courts here regularly have status conferences to go over with the judge what is happening in a case. Then the judge will set deadlines and trial dates and so on. And, if you ever find yourself in front of a judge for a motion, which isn't that unusual; it's a regular part of the practice.

What do you do to prepare for trial?
I'm really a bad person to ask because my experience is a little unusual. I haven't had a jury trial in about three or four years—which is unusual.

Whereas in the year preceding that I had three or four trials. The two real important tasks in getting prepared for trial are determining what evidence you are going to present through witnesses and documents and presenting the legal arguments, which in a jury trial shape the jury instructions. There is a fact side and a legal side. By the time I get to trial I generally have pretty much my opening statement and my closing statement—some of my closing statement—done. I have thought through what the other side is going to argue and developed responses to those arguments and considered what evidence I am going to put on.

Are the trials before juries?

Most of the trials I have had are jury trials. I have had a few bench trials, but the majority are jury trials. I would say there are two things I try to do during jury selection. One is, I try to pick a jury with people that I think will respond to me personally. People that will like me—because I think that part of my job is to project that I believe in my client and that [I am] sincere in the presentation of the case. I need to connect with the jurors. I look for jurors that I think will like me, which is hard to determine sometimes. I also like to try to eliminate the jurors who I think will be biased against my client's position for whatever reason.

How would you assess the quality of the judiciary?

I think that the judiciary—there are certain judges that I think are better than others. There are certain judges that I have direct contact with that I don't think are particularly well suited, for one reason or another, to be on the bench, but I think generally justice is served by the judiciary here. The results aren't always as what you want them to be or you think they should be, but that's a product of the system.

Have you handled appeals?

Yes. I smile because I am two and zero. There are lawyers who just specialize in appellate law. We have a lawyer in our office, we have a person in our office who is "of counsel." That means he is not a partner in the firm, but we have a professional relationship with him. He is an appellate lawyer. So, if it is a very complex issue or a large appeal, I wouldn't get involved; I would let this appellate lawyer do it. But there have been certain cases I have had that have discrete enough issues that I felt comfortable handling the appeal. In both cases I had prevailed earlier, so I was not appealing. I was responding to the argument that was being made on appeal. I then had a hearing before the appellate court—an oral argument. I was less interrupted than the other side in both cases, but interaction with the judges is part of it.

What changes would you like to see in the legal process?

I think that generally the legal process is efficient. One of the problems I have found is where there is a dispute among lawyers. The courts [judges] are beleaguered by these, and there is a tendency of some of the judges to assume that both sides are being unreasonable, so they say, "Why don't you work that out?" I think maybe a little more intervention earlier on by the court if you have a problem. You could access somebody at the court to be a problem solver rather than having to go to the judge. That would be a valuable reform.

I also think that—and I don't know if there is a solution to this—I think that the quality of the legal decisions that are made by the court—this is more in state court than in federal court because it has more resources and more clerks to do the work—needs to be improved. Sometimes in state court you find that you are dealing with a judge who has twenty other matters. So your case cannot get the attention it probably deserves. That is not the fault of the judge. They just don't have the time to do it. It would be nice to have more resources, more judges. That comes down to a question of money that isn't always there.

What do you regard to be the pluses and minuses of being an attorney?
The pluses are the ability to problem solve for people who need problem solving. Having a satisfied client is really the best, is the greatest reward of the job. The other aspect—certainly another plus—would be that there are certain things that I find intellectually challenging and interesting. So, while I may gripe about having to file a motion, by the time I am done with it I generally like the fact that I did it and the thought process that I did to do it. Those are probably the biggest pros.

The cons are, it is a hard job. Not in the sense of—compared to laying bricks, obviously. Also, dealing with difficult people is very unrewarding and not satisfying at all. It is a part of the job I don't particularly like. But it is a well-compensated job for most lawyers.

Does it consume considerable time?
That varies depending on my caseload. Generally, the most time I spend is getting ready for trial. That is a highly intense period of time. I tend to be very obsessive about trials because there is so much you can control by just being prepared. So preparation is the key. The hours can be long and time-consuming.

But you enjoy being a lawyer?
Yes, overall I do. The reason I enjoy it is because of the partnership I am in and the people I work with and because of the ability to help those in need. If I were in another setting, I might not enjoy it nearly as much. For me it is very important to be somewhere I feel comfortable, and the big firm is not that.

Earl LeVere

The Litigation of Intellectual Property

THE FOLLOWING INTERVIEWS WITH EARL LEVERE, Salene Mazur, Linda Rice, Robert Eye, and Anne Becker describe various forms of specialized legal practice. Located in Columbus, Ohio, Earl LeVere, of the firm of Brickler and Eckler (at the time of the interview), has an intellectual property law practice. It involves litigation, or arguments before courts, and transactional work, or arranging business agreements. However, his focus is more on litigation. This interview took place at the firm's downtown headquarters, a stately former federal courthouse located very near the historic Ohio Statehouse.

Can you define what intellectual property means?
It's a general area of law that includes traditional and nontraditional areas of property law. The traditional "big three" are patent, copyright, and trademark. The less traditional ones are trade secrets, rights to publicity, rights to privacy, and confidentiality arrangements. Intellectual property as a genre refers to those things that the law recognizes having property rights associated with them, but things that you can't really touch.

Can you give some examples?
Sure. If I invent the perfect mousetrap, I apply for a patent. That prevents others from making, using, offering for sale a mousetrap that falls within the confines of my patent. The patent is a written document; it's granted by the federal government, and it allows me to exclude others from making, using, selling, offering things that are described and disclosed in the patent. Intellectual property patents and copyrights trace their origins back to the U.S. Constitution. There is a clause in the Constitution [Article I, Section 8, Clause 8] that says that the government can issue to individuals limited monopolies for their writings and discoveries.

Most people generally understand the notions of patents and copyrights. But isn't there a new, cutting-edge aspect to intellectual property law? In other words, is this area of the law evolving?

The law is evolving. I'm more of a traditionalist when it comes to intellectual property law. But it is true that the law is always chasing, trying to keep in step with the way technology is developing. Traditional notions are being applied to new technologies. For example, a few years ago you saw a lot of press on Napster. Everybody wanted to shut Napster down, and rightfully so, because Napster was in the business of wholesale copyright infringement. At the time of the most recent version of the copyright statutes, which came out in 1976, Congress wasn't really thinking about things like the Internet, or Internet downloading.

Is that why one might get the sense that intellectual property law is changing quickly?

I think as technology increases, intellectual property really has to keep in step, for several reasons. When you invent something new—and the rate of invention, I think, is increasing—many of those things are protectable by patents. For example, you write software code, it could be copyrighted. That's on the invention side. But these new technologies also make it easier to copy and distribute copyrighted materials, and the law has to deal with that. But it's not the first time copyright laws had to do that. For example, there was a big debate when the Betamax cassette recorder came out. I mean, the U.S. Supreme Court had to rule on whether or not a company like Sony could be sued for contributing or inducing others to infringe on copyrights by making a device that facilitated copying.

Still, I think the law does a pretty good job. When you look at the copyright law in particular, you'll find some areas that just make you scratch your head when you read; very complicated issues, royalty schemes, and mandatory royalties. Generally, a person can decide if they want to license someone to use their work. The copyright law carves out some exceptions. Some of those exceptions are a little counterintuitive and the product of complicated technology and lobbying groups that were created to address a particular problem but that make you wonder why they're there sometimes.

How did you get interested in this area of the law?

I was a music guy in high school and college. I come from a music family. I was a band geek all throughout high school and did a lot of different music stuff in college and become a big pro-copyright person.

How did your career evolve from being a recent law school graduate into becoming a litigator?

I always said that just about the time I figured out what it was that I was supposed to be doing, it was time for me to be doing something else. There's a constant evolution. When you get out of law school, you know a lot of law, but you don't know how to be a lawyer. So when I look back on it, or when I talk to young lawyers about their first two or three years in practice, I tell them it is like a residency for a physician. You go out and really learn to be a lawyer. In law school, you study the law and the legal framework, but you don't really know practically how to apply it. So you spend a lot of time really learning how to write briefs, or whatever kinds of legal documents you're writing, to do research, to think critically. The whole analytical framework just gets reversed when you start practicing. In law school, typically, you get a book, and the professor will tell you to read these four cases and let's talk about what they mean [the "Socratic method"]. When you get out in practice, you get a set of facts, and then you have to go out and find what's important about those facts and find cases that deal with those issues to find what the answer is. That's true whether you're in litigation or transactional work. Here's the deal the parties want to do; can they? If so, how? Why can't they? So you really start with the facts and try to find your way through the cases and how those facts should shake out.

In the litigation world, the things that you end up doing differ as you start out and then work your way up. Usually a case will have two to three lawyers, maybe a paralegal, and the senior person, the first chair, who kind of directs where the case is going to go and helps with overall strategy and handles some of the more important depositions. He or she also participates in drafting briefs, but usually more in setting the outline to begin with, then reviewing, revising, and strengthening. The middle person in a three-lawyer case sort of acts as a go-between, does some supervisory work, also a lot of hands-on drafting of documents, maybe appearing in court or conferences. That middle person is also in daily contact with the junior person and the most senior person, maybe once or twice a week. Every case is different, and the stage of the case changes who does what.

I'm still the kind of guy who needs to have a good handle on the entire case. I need to see the documents. I need to see what we're writing. I need to see what we're getting in discovery. I need to get a good sense of where the case is, or you can't strategize effectively.

Did you have a good technical background before you entered into this area of the law?

No, I was a double-major, liberal arts guy. On the copyright side and trademark side, the technical background doesn't really help you. It comes in handy on patents, although I've always been a little bit science-minded and I feel like by the time I get a good working knowledge of it, I'm going to be better suited at getting it across to a nontechnical jury. Maybe a really highly skilled, technical person would have an advantage at the beginning over me, might even have a more thorough understanding of technology even at the time of trial, but if they can't get it across to the jury in a way that rings true to them, I don't think the jury will follow them where they think they're going.

This is a large firm, and it doesn't just specialize in intellectual property law, correct?

That is correct. I mean it depends on who you ask. We think of it as a big firm. We have one hundred and fifty lawyers, but there are firms with thousands of lawyers. Still, anything with one hundred and fifty or more lawyers is considered to be a large firm. This firm does basically everything except criminal law.

And in the firm, how many do intellectual property law?

We have four whose practice is predominantly intellectual property law and an additional eight or so who do some intellectual property law.

How much work is expected from a new hire in the firm?

We ask, we expect, new associates here to bill one thousand nine hundred hours a year, and that is actual time that can be billed to the client. If you take two weeks' vacation, that translates to thirty-eight hours a week billable. It's rare that you can come into work for eight hours and bill eight hours. So there is more time on top of that. There's sorting through your mail, checking your e-mail, whatever is not necessarily billable. So we try to be efficient, we try to make sure we don't waste a lot of time. The billable hours are very important, and the quality of the billable hours is very important. You can have two thousand two hundred billable hours, but if four hundred of those hours can't be used because they took too long or weren't efficient, then they don't count. We also encourage new lawyers to get involved in other things—community service, whatever their passion is—so that they can give back to the community. That's something that's valued. So is mentoring other lawyers and participating in the administration of the firm. So those are all nonbillable things that kind of add on to the time. A fifty-hour week is not uncommon, and sometimes you can have much more. But the nice thing about it is that it doesn't have to be steady. It can ebb and flow a little bit. My advice, typically, to people is to stay on track where you want to be hourwise. My practice was always to stay every day until I met [my] daily goal for billable hours. I think it's dangerous to say that I'll make it up tomorrow, because you might not. It is a lot of work, and it is a lot of stress. The clients' expectations are high. The rates, even for new lawyers, are expensive. And clients expect lawyers to be responsive and accurate and to give them a high-quality product.

That's on an hour model. If you have a contingent-fee law firm, it's a little different. There the model is to have as many cases as you can and spend as little time on each case individually as you can to get a result that is acceptable. The cases I do tend not to lend themselves to that, but some people are very profitable in a model like that.

Who are your clients, and how do they find you?

My clients typically are companies who either own intellectual property or are being accused of infringing on somebody else's intellectual property. Other clients are companies that license technology either from other people or to other people, you know, buy and sell, or are in the business of either creating technology or using technology. So I have manufacturing companies, I have some literary clients, publishers and some individual authors, but most of my clients tend to be companies. I think that's mostly for cost reasons. It's difficult for an individual artist or author or inventor to come up with the financial resources to hire a machine the size of this firm. I think individuals would do that better, more efficiently with a smaller legal shop.

Is your clientele drawn primarily from central Ohio?
In my particular practice, because I do mostly litigation work, I represent companies from here who are in litigation somewhere and out-of-town companies who are facing litigation in Ohio.

Are you responsible for finding clients, or do clients find you?
Both. Sometimes clients will find you in strange ways, but part of what I'm expected to do is to generate business.

How do you do that?
It is a challenge. I do it in two ways. One, I do it by trying to establish a presence as a person who does this kind of work so that when somebody has this kind of need and goes out looking for someone, hopefully they will stumble across me. I do that either by being a member of organizations, or trying to get press or publicity, or writing articles, or just trying to do those kinds of things so that when they Google my name or start poking around, maybe they'll find it. The other way I try to generate clients is by cross-selling other aspects of the firm. It's rare that I'll come up to someone and strike up a conversation and find out that they are being sued for copyright infringement. I mean my timing is never that good, but I might find a company that has some other needs, or companies that have needs that are ongoing. They may not be intellectual property needs. There are certain intellectual property needs that companies don't address, and I make them aware of them. I guess what I do is try to offer the firm's services; even if I'm not doing the actual work initially, hopefully I'll develop a relationship with a client that will be ongoing so that when they have some intellectual property need they'll think of me.

Finding clients is expected of you?
I think so. We definitely want people to be out generating work. I mean it's great when work comes in the door, but you can't always rely on that.

How does the generation of potential clients work? For example, is it "cold calls" from persons seeking legal advice?
I don't think "cold calls" work for this. It's more relationship building. I mean, I will get "cold calls" sometimes, where the person tells me that they got sued and they understand I do this kind of work. Those are great. I also follow cases that are out there, for example, you read about somebody getting sued

and you call them, but that's not terribly effective. Sometimes there are firms that will let out RFPs [requests for proposals] for certain kinds of work, and our firm will respond. This is kind of an invited "cold call"; you don't have a preexisting relationship. There are times when I've called people out of the blue and introduced myself. I tell them that I'd like to get to know them and that I recognize that they probably have counsel, but maybe I can do a better job for you.

Is part of the problem you face in finding clients that companies are unaware that they have intellectual property law problems?

I think that's true a lot. I think there's a big learning curve for clients, even for other lawyers in other large law firms that don't think in terms of those kind of issues. Like they say, if the only tool you have is a hammer, then everything looks like a nail. I think lawyers tend to view the world from the vantage point of what they practice. So I won't be sensitive to a tax issue, but my tax lawyers will be very keen on those. There is some education effort that goes on, both internally in our firm and to the clients and potential clients.

What percentage of your clients have an ongoing relationship with you?

In the litigation world, most of the clients are kind of one-shot. Most companies don't like being in the litigation business. It's expensive, it's time-consuming, and it's stressful. Most companies try not to leave important business decisions up to twelve people [the jury]. So they try to stay out of that world. And the cost of intellectual property litigation is astronomical. Statistics show that in litigated patent infringement cases, legal fees ran around one million dollars for each side. There aren't a lot of companies that want to throw that kind of money around. So they try to stay out of that world, but we do a good job for clients, and I think we can use litigation to build a relationship. Although it is hard because litigation is such an unpleasant process, and even a good result will leave a bad taste in a client's mouth.

Can you describe what transactional work is?

Deals. Helping people register patents and copyrights; also, transactional work can be something as simple as licensing intellectual property. For example, you have a patent, and another company wants to make a product pursuant to that patent. I can arrange a licensing relationship or a purchase of the patent. I also get involved where the deal is not strictly an intellectual property deal, but it has some intellectual property aspects to it. For example, Company A might be buying Company B, and some of Company B's assets are patents and trademarks, so there may be some provisions in the agreement that deal with those things, and I handle them. It may be that Company B is selling some of that technology to somebody else independently of the bigger deal; you've got to figure out how to do this.

Does that work include negotiations with other attorneys?

No, usually the big picture is negotiated among business people, and the lawyers come in and try to hammer out the details.

Do business people have a good sense of what it is they agreed to, or do you have to come in and instruct them that they may have made a mistake and this is how it can be corrected?

It really depends on the deal. Usually, you don't want to tell a business person they can't do what they think they've just done. So the worst you want to say is that you can't do it this way, but we can get the result some other way. And, usually, the business people have a pretty good handle on the deal, but there are always details that wind up in the agreement that business people didn't anticipate, either because they are minute or strictly legal, who knows, but lawyers are conferring on these back and forth while consulting with their clients.

Can you put into percentages what part of your work is transactional versus litigation?

I would say on average it's eighty percent litigation, twenty percent transaction work.

Is that because you've developed a litigation specialty?

I am primarily a litigator. I don't know if I'd call it a specialty. I started in the litigation department, so I've always been a litigator/trial lawyer.

As a litigator, are you involved with negotiation to keep cases out of the courtroom?

It's really dependent on when I get brought into a matter. If it's very early on in the case, which is my preference, where a client will express concern about what somebody is doing or they get a nasty letter from somebody and ask me to take a look at it. Other times, and maybe even more commonly, there's been some back-and-forth between business people, or maybe the other side's counsel, and I usually don't get brought in until everybody's mad. From the beginning, we try and work things out, file different legal documents to try and adjust leverage along the way to get a better bargaining position, to try to get a better resolution.

Can you talk about the different leveraging tools and how you use them?

It's interesting, when you're just negotiating a deal, you have the bargaining power that you have. If you want to go and buy a car, you've got a certain amount of bargaining power, and the other side does, too. There's not a whole lot that you can do to change that. Maybe in the car situation you can use other dealerships for leverage, but the most you'll get knocked off is around $500. In the litigation world, you have some flexibility to adjust your leverage, based on information you learn in the course of the case—maybe documents you've obtained or witnesses you interview or depose. You know, at the very beginning of the case, people are very entrenched in their positions, and there's usually not a lot of wiggle room or they would have worked it out without me. Usually, when the parties go into court, they are polarized to begin with. Along the way, you might take a deposition, and you get testimony out of a witness; and the other side is now nervous about that testimony, and as a result you've got a little bit more bargaining power. You file a motion that is going to be very expensive to respond to, and that maybe gives you some leverage. Or you've got a big discovery process, and in the process you discover some "smoking gun" document that again helps to increase your leverage. There are motions you can file to dismiss certain claims in a complaint. For example, the plaintiff alleges cause of action under eight different theories, and you knock out four of them.

Is the cost of litigation itself a leverage tool?
Sure. It always is, and you always have to think about it.

What is the role of judge in pretrial conferences and settlement?
Judges are designed to be neutral, and all copyright and patent cases are brought into federal courts, and the federal judges are quite good at keeping their distance. If the parties want them to, in certain situations the judges will act as a mediator or will facilitate settlement conferences. Most of the judges I've come across, especially on the federal bench, are very careful not to take in information that might color their view of the case unless it's presented in the way it could be presented at trial. There are certain things you can get in and certain things you can't, ways you go about getting evidence in, and you don't usually get the opportunity in trial to just tell the judge your side of the story. You have to go through a lot of rules and hoops and things. Especially where the judge is going to be the trier of fact [a bench trial], the judge is going to be much more reluctant to engage in trying to bring about a settlement. But there are magistrate judges. Most federal courts have a mediation or settlement facilitation mechanism that is separate from the trial judge. It is usually pretty good, and they will get involved if you want them to. It's voluntary. Judges can intentionally or inadvertently impact a settlement discussion by how they rule, but I guess I'm optimistic that the rulings are based on facts that are presented to the judges and not on a desire on the part of the judge to cause a settlement.

Isn't it the case that judges will make decisions in the pretrial stages of a case that convince one side or the other that they probably should seek a settlement?
Well, you see some of that, but in my experience not a whole lot. You know, certain motions, the court will set for oral arguments and you might get some feedback, but most of the motions in intellectual property are pretty complicated and don't lend themselves to off-the-cuff rulings. Still, there are exceptions to everything. I have had judges come and say I'm leaning to granting this motion, so you ought to settle, but I'm guessing it happens a little bit more in the state courts. State judges are more willing to get involved a little

bit more intimately in a case, take a more active role in bringing about a settlement to a case.

In cases that are strictly litigation work, where you've already described both sides digging in their heels, what percentage of those cases will eventually settle before a trial takes place?

I think the statistics suggest that over ninety-five percent of all civil cases are settled or get dismissed.

And in your practice?

Mine's maybe a little less, say eight out of ten cases go away.

What's special about those twenty percent of your cases that do make it to trial?

Some cases just can't be settled. There are procedural motions that you can file that will make a case go away one way or the other; if there is no genuine issue of material fact, in other words, nothing that a jury has to decide. So if all the evidence construed in the most favorable light to the other side only lets the jury find for you, you win [a summary judgment]. Maybe a better way to say it is, if you look at all the evidence, and there's no way the other side can win, then the court should enter a judgment in your favor and not let the case go to trial. If there's something to talk about that would let a jury go either way, it's not eligible for summary judgment. It needs to be settled or go to trial.

Sometimes the parties are too far apart economically. Sometimes, in terms of what they are willing to settle for, there is either a trademark [or] a patent that needs to have its strength tested. There could be a very important patent, or a line of business, and they're now being challenged by somebody else. Sooner or later, that business might need to take that patent to trial to see if it holds up. Now if it holds up in one case, someone else can still come along and challenge it, and they get their day in court on that issue. It's persuasive to test the strength of a patent in court to see if it will withstand scrutiny. In other cases, not every client wants to license its technology. And trademarks are a big issue, too. If you have a trademark and someone is using a confusingly similar mark, you may want to go to court and see if its mark will hold out. That can be helpful in other cases later on. Sometimes it just a core business piece that's just too important. Other clients—this is rare—just use litigation as their business model. They are in a very competitive industry, and it is important for them to set a standard that they will not be pushed around.

There's a machismo to this, then?

Maybe, but it may just be the way you deal with your competitors. Disney is good example of this. For a long time people said you don't want to mess around with the Mouse, because Disney had a reputation for vigorously defending its rights. So maybe it's not machismo, it's letting people know we will not take our rights lightly. And sometimes there is an extortion value. You get a great big company that's got an important business line, and some much smaller person or entity comes out of the woodwork and says you're infringing on my, whatever it is, but give me five hundred thousand dollars and I'll go away. A lot of companies cannot let this happen. There are too many people who can come out of the woodwork, or they'll show themselves to be too easy of a target. So they need to litigate.

When you litigate, is it usually in front of a jury or a bench trial?
It's probably about half and half. In a patent case, there's usually an earlier hearing in front of the court without the jury to define what the patent covers. The question of what the patent covers or doesn't is a question that the court resolves. The question of whether the accused's invention falls within what the patent covers is reserved to the jury. Those are usually decided separately, and ahead of time the court will construe the boundaries of the patent. In a patent case, in many situations, that's when the case is won or lost. Because there's often not much of a dispute of what the accused's product is or what it does. The question is really whether it falls within or not.

Ultimately, the jury will say if there's patent infringement or not, but the judge will say, I don't think this patent covers shoes with laces and the defendant's shoes clearly have laces, then the case is pretty much done before it can get to the jury.

Can you talk about the process of selecting a jury?
I think that is fairly universal for all litigators. Different courts will handle it differently and will control the number of questions the lawyer can actually ask. It's not usually like it is on television. You get a juror questionnaire ahead of time, and you get information about the jurors. The court will tend to ask a series of questions that are its own questions. Some courts will allow the lawyers each to submit questions that the court will then ask the jury. Sometimes they will let you ask your own individual questions. Sometimes they will let you ask a lot of questions. Once you've gone through all your questions, you have the ability to ask the court to exclude certain jurors because of bias or some kind of cause. Then, after that, typically, each side gets what are called peremptory challenges, the ability to discharge three jurors for no reason whatsoever, as long as it's not a race, gender, or protected-class kind of reason. Sometimes the courts will have you say orally who you want to discharge, or they'll let you submit it in writing so the jurors don't know who's being picked off by whom.

What convinces you to remove a potential juror by using a peremptory challenge?
It depends on the case, but some cases you want people who are really technically minded, in let's say a patent case. You want them on the jury if it's complicated technology or if it's something unusual. Sometimes you don't. If you've got a computer software patent, you really have to think long and hard whether you want a computer programmer. Will he or she understand the technology or think they know more about the case maybe than the

lawyers do? You have to guess how they will respond to the evidence that is presented. I look for people who give me the impression that they just don't want to be there. They're too busy, or they've got other things that they'd rather be doing. Most people on jury duty probably do, but lots of jurors take what they do very seriously. Patent cases can be very long and boring if you're not careful. You need to make them interesting. So you want to look for people who are interested in those things. You look for people who, maybe they're not the software programmer, but they'll be able to relate to that technology.

In areas of the law such as intellectual property, you have people who couldn't escape jury duty determining the outcomes of multimillion dollar patent cases. What is your assessment of the jury system?

I think that by and large juries get it right. By and large, jurors take what they do seriously, and they make decisions based on what they think is right. It may not necessarily be based on all the legal arguments that you present. It's based in many cases on the jurors' sense of fundamental fairness and who they trusted among the lawyers and the witnesses. And a little bit on who they liked, but I think jurors can look at situations even with a less likable party and fall back on their sense of fairness. It's the lawyer's job to make the jury understand what's going on and to help educate them on why what you're asking for is really the more fair choice. There's usually somebody who's happy with the jury's decision and somebody who's not. You know, they say that juries are one hundred percent correct fifty percent of the time.

How long do your trials take, including preparation and actual litigation?

Well, the process from filing a case to having it go to trial can be from eighteen months to two years. Along the way, with your total legal team you can have two to four thousand hours involved with the case. The trial can last anywhere from a week to several weeks. The one statistic I remember off the top of my head was a case I tried in Texas, just myself, I billed one hundred seventy-eight hours in eleven consecutive days [16.2 hours per day]. Trials are pretty intense, at least for me, because the only way I feel can try a case is if I really prepare for it and I am more prepared than anybody else.

Do you enjoy it?

I always say trials are great when they're over. I do like being in trial. I like thinking on your feet. I like the intellectual challenges, the debating points of law back and forth with the court, or responding to objections, and working with witnesses, where you get testimony that supports what you're trying to prove. I think it's a neat process. It is tiring.

Cases are different. I know county prosecutors who will do small criminal matters, and their first time looking at the file is when they are walking up to the podium. Maybe, in a case like that, where your file is twenty-five pages, you can do that. Those cases are fairly straightforward. In the cases I deal with, they tend to have a whole lot more prep work that is necessary to do them well. It would be more fun to have some of the cases where you can just step right in, cases that are straightforward, and you can prove what you need to prove. Then they can be fun.

What's the favorite part of your job?

My favorite part of my job is working with the clients, learning about their business and what's important to them, and then helping them to solve whatever their problem is.

What's the worst part of your job?

There are a few things that are difficult. I tend to internalize my clients' problems a lot, because I'm often the client's last line of defense, and their problems become my problems. I get really invested in that. The other thing that I really don't like is the bickering back and forth with lawyers on the other side. There are some lawyers who feel they cover a lot of ground by doing that, and I think it's just distracting and stressful, and I don't think you need to be necessarily nasty even though we have an adversarial system. Usually it's disputes between reasonable minds and we have an adversarial job to do, but it doesn't need to be uncivil. I think it is important to be very civil with your colleagues within the bar, and when some lawyers lose sight of that, that's always hard for me.

Salene Mazur

The Bankruptcy Attorney

At the time of this interview Salene Mazur was a bankruptcy lawyer in Pittsburgh, Pennsylvania. Bankruptcy is a form of judicial relief
for debtors. Established by Congress under powers found in Article 1,
section 8, of the United States Constitution, bankruptcy courts address
and relieve debtors' financial problems. The law provides for a variety of bankruptcy and debt adjustment processes. These processes
include the liquidation of the assets of individual and corporate debtors to satisfy creditors, the reorganization of corporate finances and
debt payments (Chapter 11 cases), and the rescheduling of individuals' financial obligations to satisfy creditors. Although changes in the
law in 2005 have reduced the volume of bankruptcy filings from more
than 1.4 million in 2006 to 750,000 in 2007, the number of these filings indicates a significant role for lawyers and judges in American
debtor-creditor relationships. (For more details on the law and process
of bankruptcy, the federal courts provide a useful guide, "Bankruptcy
Basics," at http://www.uscourts.gov/bankruptcycourts/bankruptcyba-
sics.html). The interview took place in a conference room at Mazur's
firm that offered a commanding view of Pittsburgh's "Golden Triangle,"
where the confluence of the Allegheny and Monongahela Rivers creates the Ohio River.

Can you describe your practice?

I do Chapter 11 corporate bankruptcy work. I would like to subcategorize
corporate bankruptcy: creditor work, debtor work, and preference work.
I do all three of these. Preference work is a specialty type of law and a
specific type of litigation. It's an isolated provision of the bankruptcy code
that a debtor can sue its creditors. This is my third firm since graduating
from law school. This firm does more debtor work, Chapter 11 debtor
work.

So there is a difference between an individual claiming bankruptcy and a corporate entity claiming bankruptcy?

Yes. Initially, though, the firm founded its practice by doing all personal debtor work, and I had done some as well to get my feet wet. But it's tough work, you have to work very hard, there is a lot of emotion involved, and people don't really have the money to pay you for the time that you need to devote to a case, particularly if it's a complicated case. So I very much prefer the corporate work.

You've done both, and you've shifted to the corporate work?

Yes, I have. When I started I was doing the corporate stuff. I was actually doing general corporate matters, securities work, but then the economy changed. When I graduated from law school, it was 2000, and the economy changed, so all the work dried up, and they weren't doing the deals, because of the dot-com bubble burst. So when all that work dried up, my group in Philadelphia asked me to switch to bankruptcy. You often see that, where you have corporate lawyers pushing to bankruptcy when times are bad and then switching back. I'm in my seventh year now, and there's always been a lot of work in bankruptcy, especially after 9/11.

Can you describe your law firm? How big is it?

This is what I would consider a boutique firm. We do only corporate bankruptcy. Having had experience at both a big firm and a small firm, I very much prefer a small firm, because you don't have all the politics and the competitive nature of a large law firm. We have about fifteen lawyers, and we have in two offices, here in Pittsburgh and in Wilmington, Delaware. There are not many women in the firm, though.

Are you one of the youngest associates?

Yes. It's partner heavy. I think there are six partners and two of counsel, and probably five associates. They just hired two.

Can you discuss the mechanics of moving from associate to partner in a firm?

Whenever you are in a big firm, you quickly learn about the hierarchy within a firm. You're a "first year." You move up to a midlevel associate in your fourth, fifth, or sixth year. It depends on the firm and the size of the city it operates in. It takes about ten years before you're actually a partner. And there are different levels of partnership; again, it depends on the firm, like equity partner versus nonequity partner. But it's definitely that whole you-have-to-pay-your-dues or rites-of-passage thing.

Do you have to move up to the partner level to stay with a firm?

I think so; I mean the whole "women issue" always throws a wrench into the thing because I have to take some time off to have kids. They seem to be amenable to that here, but there again this is a small firm setting. In a larger firm, I don't know, it just depends on the firm, but it always becomes an issue if you have to take off a bunch of time.

How does your firm find their clients?

That actually gets to your earlier question about becoming a partner. As a young lawyer, to become a partner, it is not only your quality of work but also how much revenue you're bringing in. With corporate bankruptcy, it's not like I can go to a networking event and just try to find distressed debtors. It's very, very hard for me to develop my own business book. All of the partners here have been at it for around twenty years, so they're very well established. They have better networking opportunities, lawyer to lawyer. Other lawyers who need to deflect a case know our partners.

You don't have a responsibility to drum up business?

No, I don't. But with this firm it would be great if I did, and they would look upon me more favorably for partner for that. I do get a couple of cases here and there.

Do the partners hand cases over to you that they have secured for the firm?

It depends on the type of representation I'm doing. If it's a debtor case, it's going to involve a big company, and there [are] a lot of moving parts to the representation, a lot of the tasks that need to be done, a lot of writing, but there's a litigation aspect to it, too. Bankruptcy to me is like the hybrid of both litigation and transactional work. I found corporate transactional work kind of boring, particularly as a young lawyer in a big firm where you're just reviewing documents, you're not interacting with the clients, and you're not getting cases on your own.

Here I get all the writing assignments. I am the midlevel at this point, so they will give me the case. I'll write the motions that one needs to file when you're representing a company going through this Chapter 11 process. I like that I'm kind of like this ivory tower academic, doing research and writing. Oftentimes, those motions also have to be argued or presented to the judge, and that's the litigation aspect of it. It can become an adversarial process if someone contests your motion; then you go to court, but it's not an everyday thing.

Can you talk about the kinds of documents you draft on a regular basis?

Discovery creates a lot of work. Things like interrogatories, requests for production of documents, that's all litigation-related work I do. Drafting complaints and responses to them. Motions—in bankruptcy court there are lots of different motions that can be filed, pursuant to specific bankruptcy code provisions, for various types of relief; for example, a motion to authorize the payment of wages to employees. There are all these typical motions that can be filed.

So what is the level of creativity involved in this drafting?

It depends on the case and the nature of the issues. There are lots of boilerplate documents. This is particularly true if you are representing a debtor, where you're fact gathering and filling out forms. If it's a more difficult case—like

I have one where I have to come up with a creative defense for a guy who we are representing, and we think there's a good chance he is going to lose. I really enjoy it because it is writing, not filling in forms, and I love writing, even though it's about law.

Do you engage in litigation?

Yes. Not all the time. In terms of the arguments, because the clients are so big with cases involving a lot of money, the partners argue them. I'll write the motion, I'll do the research, we come together, we brainstorm, and they tell me what the legal theory should be, and I try to flesh it out in the paperwork. I also have to deal with the fallout associated with a bankruptcy, and that involves a lot of interaction with other lawyers and the public. For example, we represented Wedding World, a bridal shop company that went under unexpectedly. They closed their doors, and all these brides were left without dresses, about six hundred brides. The partner told me to just run with the case. I asked him for direction, and I just kept doing whatever he told me to do. So I had to field all the media reporters looking into the case. It was crazy. Of course, I had to look at each of those claims to determine whether they were legitimate and if the company's going to pay them. In a case like that, there's a lot of interaction with people, like the claimants, and I like that; it's not me just sitting all day either doing research and writing or just talking with the people within my firm. It's interacting a lot with other counsel, like claimants' counsel, and the claimants themselves.

What are your interactions with clients like?

It depends on your level in the firm and your boss and how comfortable they are with you dealing with the clients directly. They have me fact finding by talking to the clients. It's fun because it's like your clients become a coworker. I'll call them and ask them to take a look at the paperwork I'm working on. Tell me the facts that I need to approach motions, or please review my recitation of facts and make sure that they are true and accurate. It's keeping them abreast of what's going on. Getting a lot of facts from them about filing their bankruptcy petition and their schedule of statement of financial affairs, their documents. You have to verify the accuracy of these documents under oath.

Do you interact with other counsel?

Are you talking about closing counsel in terms of payments, like, say, these brides? Generally, they don't have counsel themselves. In other cases, like the steel company cases, you have a bank that becomes a creditor, and they'll have counsel. Then you have to file a motion, and then the bank contests your motion, and then you have to resolve the settlement, if you can, with the bank's counsel and come up with documents that you both draft and settle on stipulations. It's a lot of drafting agreements and things like that, so you end up doing that here. Then, in a bankruptcy case, there's a debtors' counsel, and there is also a creditors' committee. It's a committee just to represent the interest of the creditors, and then they have counsel. Then there is a U.S. Trustee's Office, an arm of the Department of Justice [the office is charged with independently monitoring the bankruptcy process to make it more efficient and to prevent fraud]; they are always involved in every case. There is one seated at every hearing, generally, and you have to sometimes correspond with them.

Is there considerable interaction by phone, and are there meetings?

There are meetings that are required by the bankruptcy code; you actually have to have what's called a "341" meeting [Section 341 of the Bankruptcy Code], where the debtor shows up, and every party who has any interest can show and ask the debtor questions under oath.

Your primary function is to protect the debtor in that meeting?

Yes. I find that in terms of the consumer work, that's where the lawyer comes in. You prepare the schedules, and then you go to this 341 meeting, and you basically hold their hand as they testify to the truth and accuracy of their statements.

I never thought I'd be doing corporate work. When I was in law school I was all about civil rights and the public interest, but that aspect comes in personal work, because you are helping people negotiate their financial straits. Even now we'll get a case where extremely wealthy people have businesses on the side and get into very complicated situations. People make deals with shady characters, maybe the Mafia. It's a colorful type of practice. You feel like you're genuinely helping them out because they are ready to commit suicide because creditors are hassling them. For example, in that bridal case, it was a disaster because it was a partnership, a general partnership. So the owners of the company, they ended up becoming destitute after that. They were millionaires, and they had this empire of bridal shops, and instead of creating a limited liability company, they did a partnership, so they were personally and directly liable for all the debts of the companies.

In addition to clients, opposing counsel, and the media, do you interact with bankruptcy judges?

Their staff. You interact with the staff to make sure you're complying with the judge's orders and with all the paperwork that needs to be filed.

Do you interact with anyone else?

There are people who are pushing a lot of paper because there are creditors; for example, in the Wedding World case, there were around five hundred people who had an interest in that case. There are notice requirements if you want something; if a debtor wants something passed, you have to give notice to all the people, all of the parties, who have an interest. That requires hiring an outside service to copy and serve all the documents. It depends on if you're doing this in house or if you're outsourcing it. Either way, though, you have to coordinate all this work. You rely heavily on paralegals in this type of work. It's a lot of different people.

What percentage of your cases are settled before trial?

With the preference litigation, about 90 percent of those cases are settled.

What is preference work?

Let's take a steel company case, for example. They have someone who probably provides them with a specific type of metal, like scrap metal, and then the steel company does something with it. Right now we have a client who owns a scrap metal company. They process it for the steel companies. They'll provide the metal, and the steel company that filed for bankruptcy is supposed to pay them. During the ninety days prior to the bankruptcy filing, my clients are doing regular business back and forth without knowing that the steel company is going to file bankruptcy, but if it looks like the debtor prefers to pay my guy over all the other creditors, those other creditors have a right to sue the creditor who got paid and have the court redistribute that money to all the creditors, not just the alleged preferred creditor. A case that we handled last year was worth eight million dollars of good scrap metal. We had to defend the scrap metal company from a preference suit brought by another creditor. It is very strange and doesn't seem fair because nine times out of ten they're not being preferred; they are working in the ordinary course of business prior to the ninety days of the bankruptcy filing. The logic of the law is that there are some insider creditors who know the bankruptcy is coming, and they pressure the debtor to pay them before they pay other creditors.

That preference work is kind of my niche here, because I've done it for a number of years, and not many other people are doing that.

In preference work you're working for the creditors, correct?

Yes, but I have been on the other side, too, where you file all of the complaints against all of the creditors. Someone makes a demand. They basically look at the debtor's checkbook and just sue everybody who has been paid in the ninety days prior to bankruptcy. The debtor who files for bankruptcy has two years within which to initiate a cause of action to get the creditor to return payments the debtor made to them in those ninety days prior to the filing. The idea is to use that money to pay the other creditors something. So right around the two-year deadline, the debtor will send my client a demand letter for ninety percent of the debt to be paid back. Otherwise, they're going to file a preference complaint against you. They're initiating an adversarial proceeding. Then at that point they file a complaint, we have to file an answer, and we state our defenses in it. I have to set up the invoices to try to argue that my client, the creditor, was paid in an ordinary course of business, that there was no preferential treatment.

Does this involve discovery?

Discovery? No. Most people will try to settle. People just try to get rid of the case.

Is the strategy in terms of the debtor that I'm probably not going to get the whole ninety percent, but I'll get some of it back?

Yes.

And your goal for your client?

I get a comfortable settlement range for them. Most of them are really irritated that they have to pay anything back whatsoever. But sometimes there are circumstances where you don't have a good case, where your guy changed the terms; he made threatening phone calls to the debtor—"you pay me or else"—then you have a crappy case. In that kind of case they're going to have to pay more. Generally, in preference cases, if you settle for twenty percent of the initial suit, then it's an okay deal. Ninety percent of those cases settle.

Can you describe negotiation? How does it take place?

The debtors make their initial settlement demand in the letter, and then they file their complaint. Generally, I'll come up with an analysis of my defenses, and I'll develop a spreadsheet of an analysis of the invoices, and I'll make an offer based on that. Then they come back, and the creditor bears the burden, so I have to do all the work, and the trustee looks at it, gives me some number that he's authorized.

What is it like to be a young, female attorney?

I like what I do now, but it's been a rough road. In Philadelphia, working in these big firms was very tumultuous, a lot of high pressure. Although in hindsight I'm glad that I have experience in that kind of high-pressure setting, because now I feel like I know what I'm doing. Law requires a lot of time, but I still always encourage people to get their law degree. It's a noble profession most of the time.

When I was in law school, I was thrilled to be there. I loved the opportunity, from an intellectual perspective. The downsides are the egos of many of the other students and the extensive time you had to devote to your studies. What drove me as a kid was I really wanted to do politics, and everyone I respected in politics, they all have law degrees. Then there was that kind of pressure you get in high school and beyond, you know, that if you're a smart kid you should be a lawyer or a doctor. A lot of people make a mistake because of this. Who you get in this profession are people who need to validate themselves by achieving at their job and feeling smart in that way and being competitive. There are so many other professions out there where you can still do intellectual work and be paid well for it. If I had to do it again, I don't know. And when I think about doing something else that doesn't pay as well, I have to remind myself that I have to pay off my student loans. That's another issue you could talk about in your book, the heavy, heavy weight of these student loans.

I don't regret it, though, law school; it was a good experience. Fortunately, in this type of discipline, corporate bankruptcy, you will be paid handsomely; there is a lot of money in it to enable you to pay them off.

How long do think a person ends up working to pay off their debt?

Twenty to thirty years. Those are the payment terms. If you're fortunate enough to get those coveted positions, you can pay it quicker. When I came out of law school, there were people making twenty thousand dollars more than I was, but I thought I was doing very well. You have to give up five years of your hobbies, and I tried to maintain a semblance of balance, and I think I did; but seriously, for five years, no hobbies, no activities outside of work.

What's driving away the hobbies?

The work. I don't think it was particularly oppressive, because in a larger firm, when they pay you one hundred thirty thousand dollars a year as a first year and you're twenty-five years old, there is a partner who doesn't have a six-figure debt; they probably had five thousand dollars coming out of law school. They think that you are being very overpaid and that you need to work very, very hard because of it; you need to be at their beck and call. I had a senior partner at a large law firm who told me that I wasn't allowed to plan anything social during the week; it's inappropriate. If you're doing anything social, it's like a drink with your friends at 10:00 P.M. after you've left work. In Philadelphia it's definitely different, and in New York even more so; lawyer's hours are like from 9:00 A.M. to 7:00 P.M. Here it's little bit more laid back, like nine to six. I've heard people say that if you're leaving at six o'clock every day, you should be in here on Saturdays. I probably work fifty hours a week, which doesn't seem that bad because I know there will be peak times where you have to just like work for three days straight. In Philadelphia, I didn't despise it; I just felt like it was what I had to do to garner the salary I was making. That's a sacrifice. People think you're making so much money, but it's a sacrifice, especially if you're single; it's a lot to give up. I enjoyed it, though, and after five years it sort of slows down, you have more control over your schedule. I find that to be true.

It's better in that respect?

Absolutely, especially here in Pittsburgh. I have a life, I have hobbies. That's why I like a smaller firm. And in terms of pay compensation, it's not a lock-step, like in a larger firm where you have a first-year class and a second-year class and they do lockstep with the pay raises. But there will be bonus issues as well, where you'll get a bonus, but only if you've met the billable hours, two thousand hours. It's much more rigid. Here it's more flexible, more informal; for example, you can get a bonus for winning a case.

I want to talk about the women's issue. That's a major issue. I took some women's studies classes as an undergraduate, and I'm so glad I did, because it opens up your eyes about sexism in the workplace. It's so true, particularly in this profession, in my old firm in Philadelphia; it's so odd, because in the academic world, you don't perceive those gender differences. I felt my professors considered me just as capable as my male colleagues. I don't know what happens when you go into the business world, particularly in the legal profession; it changes.

Still, today?

Yes.

With people who are your contemporaries?

Some. I had some associates tell me that I'm acting "like a woman." I've had clients—they're generally older, usually men—who are disrespectful to you because you're a woman. I have had partners who automatically think you're on the "mommy track." And even some office staff act like I'm not a lawyer, because they're used to older men in that role.

Is it a function of age?

It's that, too. It's a weird dynamic because you're young and a woman and you're their boss. I've had secretaries around forty-five or fifty who hated having a woman as a boss. Those are issues that as a young associate you have to deal with, in addition to all these other pressures that you have. I'm sure it's not just in the legal profession.

What's your favorite part of your job?

For me it's, I like the writing, I want to be a writer, and for me to get paid to do that, that's great, that's awesome. I also like the interaction with other counsel, too, it can be fun.

Linda Rice

The Lawyer in Administrative Practice

DURING THE LATE NINETEENTH CENTURY the American judiciary employed a common-law concept—the fellow-servant rule—that made it difficult for workers to sue their employers for injuries suffered as a consequence of the conditions of their jobs or events at work. The early-twentieth-century political reformers known as Progressives sought to provide assistance for workers injured on the job by removing their claims from the jurisdiction of the judicial branch. By 1910 the federal government and most states created systems of workers' compensation. The compensation included payments for medical services, medications, vocational rehabilitation, and, with monthly benefit checks to cover lost wages, subsistence. An executive branch administrative agency, often called a Workers' Compensation Commission, was to impose an insurance fee on employers, retain the fees in a fund, receive claims from injured employees, and distribute compensation from the fund to those with substantiated on-the-job injuries. The Social Security Act of 1935 used variations of this administrative scheme to compensate the unemployed and the disabled. Today other variations on this legal scheme affect the receipt of temporary welfare assistance by poor families (Temporary Assistance for Needy Families, known as TANF) and compensation for the black lung disease suffered by former coal miners. The original intent of these laws was the delegalization of the compensation process and informal agency decision making on compensation claims. However, the administrative agencies operating these programs gradually expanded the rules and regulations about qualifying for compensation, and they permitted the emergence of requirements for due process of law and formal hearings about disputes over the amount of compensation. These changes created a role for lawyers. Today, thousands of lawyers assist the injured and disabled in coping with the rules and regulations of compensation processes. Although many states have

privatized the compensation process by transferring it from a government agency to a private insurance company, this interview describes
the situation in which a state agency considers these claims. Many of
the issues in the claims process, however, have not changed.

Linda Rice is an attorney with a practice before state agencies. At the
time of the interview, she served a workers' compensation clientele from the
offices of Robinson and Rice in Huntington, West Virginia—a medium-sized
city near the point where Kentucky, Ohio, and West Virginia meet. At that
time a small firm of four attorneys and two legal assistants, Richardson and
Rice was located on the ground floor of a two-story commercial-style building on a main street a few blocks from the county and federal courthouses.

Could you please describe your background and education?
Huntington is my hometown. I was born here right after the earth cooled. I have
been here for most of my adult life. I did my undergraduate work at Marshall
[University] in history. I spent a couple of years away as a VISTA volunteer and a
couple of years traveling in the 1960s. [VISTA, or Volunteers in Service to America,
was a federal program to employ volunteers in community improvement projects
in poor neighborhoods. It is now part of the Americorps VISTA program].

What did you do with VISTA?
I was very lucky with VISTA. I got to work in West Virginia, my home state.
Most of the folk they placed in other areas. [I did] community organization in
the central part of the state. I worked with local community action organizations which now have, I believe, become regional community action organizations. They have become a very structured bureaucracy in and of themselves.

How did you become an attorney with an administrative practice?
Actually, I started thinking about it very seriously when I was a VISTA volunteer. That was in the mid-sixties, when I perceived that a lot of social change
was occurring through the judicial system. That was, of course, [the time of]
a very activist U.S. Supreme Court. There have been many, many, many trans-
gressions against citizens in the state of West Virginia by out-of-state interests.
I was thinking I would like to be able to address those things, those practices
I believed needed to be changed.

I went to law school in Morgantown [West Virginia University]. I started
in 1974. [Afterward] I came directly back to Huntington. As I was growing up,
I went to school in almost every part of the county. I have a lot of friends, and
my family is from here. So I figured I had a fairly broad base from which to
grow on, and that, in fact, turned out to be true. I was a solo practitioner—did
a lot of criminal work, domestic work, odds and ends. I practiced for three
years and decided that was just absolutely not what I wanted to do. I stopped.
I came back to the practice of law a couple of years later, after I went back to
school and completed most of the undergraduate requirements for medical
school—and then had better thoughts about that [laughs]. Plus, my former
partner James "Mick" Robinson came to see me at that time and said, "I need

somebody to help me. I have a great idea about how to do a lot for folks in the southern coalfields. I just need help doing it." That was the beginning of Robinson and Rice, and a mass administrative practice—or what grew into a mass administrative practice

Initially, Mick [Robinson], my partner, was from Logan County [a center of coal mining]. His father was a coal miner. Mick was a coal miner. His extended family worked in the mines. His idea was to concentrate in the area of workers' compensation and do a volume practice. So we opened an office in 1984, advertised, used word of mouth, and started building from that. Eventually, what happened was word of mouth led more folks to us. Plus, we would occasionally do some mass advertising. Mostly [now] our business comes from word of mouth. As a matter of fact, we have questionnaires that we ask everybody who comes in as a new client to fill out. One of the questions is, "How did you hear about us?" Last time I looked, well over fifty percent said, "I was referred by my mother, my brother, my sister, my doctor."

How is your practice currently organized?
We were located in Huntington. We opened a satellite office in Logan [in the West Virginia coalfields]. Actually, we have had satellite offices throughout southern West Virginia, because our philosophy has always been that you need to go where the business is to make it convenient for the folks. So we have been in Williamson and Madison. Chapmansville is where we are now. We moved from Logan to Chapmansville. They are satellites—meet 'em and greet 'ems. We do the intakes there, and when clients have problems and need to talk to us about the case, we make appointments [there]. Everybody in the office, all the attorneys, keep office hours in Chapmansville.

We have four attorneys now. At one point we decided we were going to diversify, and we hired attorneys and had a total of nine. And then we decided diversification wasn't really working for lots of reasons. So we started paring down the number of attorneys. We decided to stick with what we knew best, which is administrative law. So that's where we are now. It's manageable.

What sorts of problems do clients bring to you?
Workers' compensation, social security, and we did, but no longer do, federal black lung. It's primarily workers' compensation in West Virginia and Kentucky and social security in West Virginia, Kentucky, and Ohio. In social security the problem is, ninety-nine percent of the time, entitlement to disability benefits. Another one percent is social security overpayment caused either by [deduction at] work or duplication of benefits. With workers' compensation the people who come in the door—and I haven't the stats on this—I would say that well over fifty percent of the people who come through the door have been denied medical treatment by the Workers' Compensation Commission. Of course, once they come in, I talk to them and I say I can help you, one of the issues becomes getting money for them. Which, and this is kind of a backward slap at the people in the Commission, it costs them considerably more to deny treatment in those cases than to pay it.

How would you describe the administrative process?

Administrative law is very, very different from what you see on television and what practitioners of courtroom work do. It's a grinding kind of work. It's routine. The process works very slowly. Litigating issues can run from denial of medical treatment to [eligibility for] permanent partial disability. Some of the cases are extraordinarily complex, and some are very, very simple. In any case you can get one or all of the issues. It gets very complex.

If, generally, someone is considering law school because they are enamored of some show on television or some movie or some romantic notion, you [should] disabuse yourself of that right now. This is ass-grinding work. It's not beauteous and you're out at five o'clock with a lovely person and you go home or whatever. It is ass-grinding work and work at home most nights and on the weekends. If you are an adrenalin junkie it's not the place for you. Personal injury is for you.

About this particular area of the law, I [do] have something very positive to say. It is, for those folks who do not like confrontation, a very good place to be. Workers' compensation law is very collegial. Here we have known each other for years and years. Most of the time, if you need a favor [from the Commission] all you have to do is ask—like briefs going in late. There is never a problem. In what personal injury lawyers call the real world—they don't think we're real lawyers, just scummy disability lawyers right down there or one level above debt-collecting lawyers—people just slice each other up and then have a drink after work. Our bar is very easygoing.

Administrative work, and I would guess this is true of tax work, all administrative work is rule reading and rule abiding. So you better be prepared to read a lot. In the past couple of years they, the Compensation Commission, just love [to] make rules. [The rules] are never five pages. They are fifty-five pages. It's a procedurally driven practice as opposed to substance, so if you don't know the rules, you might as well get out of the ball game. A lot of people are, by the way. It's become kind of burdensome to do a compensation practice. If you have just ten cases, it's not effective to do. People who can't do volume fail. We have five hundred cases at least going. That's easily doable because they don't move quickly and it's routine. It's not like personal injury practice, where every document that comes in your office, say about a guy who had his arm chopped off when a roof collapsed in, it is imperative a lawyer see and digest it. In workers' compensation and to a great degree in social security cases the letters that come into the office are routine and computer-driven. So, only in administrative law can you do this kind of volume. I know lawyers who do two cases a year. Of course, they get settlements of five million dollars or whatever. But I'll do five hundred a year. I couldn't possibly do them if they were all difficult or all of them were nonroutine, but some of them are.

How does the process operate?

What happens? The only thing the injured worker does is file an application for benefits, at least in the past. There is new legislation that is going to change things somewhat. Everything after that ought to happen with some regularity, with the claimant doing very little. For instance, if the person is entitled to the payment of temporary total disability benefits, that is achieved by a treating physician filling a form and sending it to workers' compensation. If they are entitled to the payment or to be evaluated for impairment of [bodily] function, that should happen automatically by the workers' compensation staff. In other words, at some point after temporary total disability time lapses or whatever, they would look at it and say, "You are entitled to an evaluation. We are going to send you to Doctor X to see if your impairment is a result of this injury." So, generally, the only thing [the claimant] has done is file the application.

There are, of course, snags in the system, especially administrative snags in the system. A worker, let's say, gets notice they are not going to be paid temporary total disability because of one reason or another. Generally, it's because they don't have the medical evidence. They'll get [their case] closed, but the doctor has to do extra kinds of things. So they have been denied medical treatment. That's just an example. Other examples could be that they have received an impairment rating, a percentage [that rates the degree of disability], and they don't agree with it. We get folks at that level. But up to that point things happen automatically—should happen automatically. It does in most instances.

At the point of denial of benefits, clients find their way to you?
Yes, they will. I usually tell folks that it is time when you get a notice saying your total disability benefits are being suspended or you get a notice from your doc that you have reached your maximum degree of medical improvement. That's when you need to be talking to a lawyer, because the impairment side of the issue can be simple or it can be very complex depending on the type of injury. The American Medical Association's [AMA] *Guides to the Evaluation of Permanent Impairment*, the fourth edition edition [2001] is the bible as far as workers' compensation is concerned. So all impairments are rated using this book—range of motion and that sort of stuff. But there are add-ons that some doctors won't do. That's how, many times, [clients] find their way here. They have been to a doctor that workers' comp picks. While not wishing to sound especially obstreperous, they don't tend to pick folks who are known for their generosity when it comes to impairment rating. To give you an example of that, carpal tunnel [syndrome] was one early on. There are two portions of the Guides that can be used to determine the impairment when it comes to the hand. Some doctors just wouldn't use one particular portion, which tended to be a little more liberal in terms of percentage [impairment].

Could you describe your clients?
Unemployed, most generally. They may be receiving benefits from social security—I am talking about total disability clients. They may be receiving benefits from social security. They may be receiving a pension from the UMWA [United Mine Workers of America]. Private insurance generally is not in the

vocabulary of the folks with whom I've dealt. So they don't buy any disability insurance from the person who sells them their care insurance.

I would characterize them as generally older, although that dynamic is changing, frankly. The typical client that I would have seen on a permanent total disability case ten years ago would be forty-five or older, usually with a serious back injury, limited educational background, no transferable skills. Regardless of what they did in their employment, those skills wouldn't transfer easily to other kinds of jobs. Maybe illiterate and innumerate. Permanent total disability clients today are people whose bodies are ruined, mangled, because the law has changed. The statutory requirement to apply for permanent total disability is a fifty percent impairment rating—and forty-five is what you get if your leg's cut off. Folks who are going to qualify now and in the future are going to be pretty physically mangled. In these cases their education and transferability becomes less of an issue.

How do clients acquire their disabilities?
Coal mining–that's what I have primarily dealt with. The four industries in West Virginia where you usually find the most severe injuries are coal mining, timbering, glass, and chemicals. The nature of mining has changed, and there's more surface mining now. So the injuries tend to be less. Also, we many times will get folks coming in and saying, "Gees, I haven't filed my [black] lung claim," or "I filed my last black lung claim ten years ago." We get the records and find out, indeed, they had an occupational pneumoconiosis claim in 1995, and they have had continuous exposure to coal dust since then. Then we will send them out to a doctor to make a determination on the basis of occupational pneumoconiosis and whether or not there is an impairment—a pulmonary impairment—as a result of it, and then file a claim.

Do clients come by to talk about their cases?
Yes, and what I am doing about it and why I can't do it faster, which is always a complaint. I have never had anybody come in and say to me, "I'd like to thank you because you did that so quickly." That never happens. In workers' compensation, golly, if it's simple and a continuation of temporary total disability, it can be handled many times with a phone call to the doctor's office and/or a phone call to the claims manager. If it's a hotly litigated permanent total disability issue, it can last for years. And we have had them last for years. It's not a quick process. It's quicker now than it used to be, but it is still not a quick process to resolution on the very complex issues.

How do you assess such cases?
I spend most of my time with clients. The paralegal-legal assistants do most of the paperwork. So the file comes in—I take the client in—and we gather the records from workers' compensation on the particular injury that he or she came in to see me about. We find, for instance, that there are seven other claims [by the client]. So we get copies of everything. Because we do a volume practice—and we can do a volume practice because the work is fairly routine—a great percentage of the letters that we get here every day, and there

are hundreds from workers' compensation, fall into one of four categories. It's only a few of them that are unusual and need to be handled outside of the routine. Because of that, we can use paraprofessionals extensively. Our paralegals—legal assistants—are trained and have been around so long that they can do a lot of the work that at one time was reserved for the attorneys.

Then we sit down and say, "This is what workers' compensation has. This is the complaint the client has. This is how to solve that specific complaint. And here are fourteen other things we can do." When the client comes back in to see me, I say, "Here is the answer to your specific complaint, and I think we can make money happen in other ways. " So then we begin with the next logical step. We answer their one problem, and we have claims that haven't been evaluated. So we insist on evaluations from workers' compensation and, after nine months or a year, we get them. These will be sent and say something like, "Here's three percent, here's two percent, here's zero percent." For each evaluation we have the claimant back in or send a letter saying, "Here's what we think the claim is worth, and we think that it is a fair and right percentage according to the AMA fourth." We will recommend there is no protest and they sit back and wait to reopen if things get worse. If according to the AMA Guides it's not [fair], there are some add-ons, we don't think it was done properly, then we say, "You ought to protest. We will take the [workers' compensation] doctor's testimony or send you out to somebody else." Those are our suggestions. Certainly the clients sometimes come back and say, "My wrist has bothered me and five percent is not enough," or whatever. There are numbers of times when the claimants will say, "Thanks for your advice, but I would like to do it this way. Of course, if it's not unlawful, I'll do what they want me to do." If workers' compensation says, "You get five percent," my client says, "No, I don't think that's enough," I look at the AMA Guides. Sure enough, it may, should have been a little more; then I will lodge a protest.

What do you do if the client decides to protest an assessment by the commission?
Many times in those cases it is just a matter of cross-examining the doctor—taking the doctor's testimony and saying, "Gee, if you use this particular section, what happens? Why didn't [you] use the other section?" and so forth. It can be as complex—as difficult—as sending a claimant to evaluating doctors for opinions with regard to the percentage of impairment. That's thinned out now because the Guides are used exclusively. There are rules on it. The good old days used to be a time of "their doc says you get five, so we send you to two docs who give thirty, and you get thirty [percent disability]."

In this process you have no personal contact with workers' compensation claims staff?
As a general rule, that is true, but a minority of cases do require contact with the claims managers. Usually treatment issues are the ones, or "Was this particular body part included in the claim?" questions. That's a difficult one in some claims. Around 1992 there was a basic paradigm shift in workers' compensation. It has taken until the special session of the legislature this year for that [change] to reach its procedural maturity. Workers' compensation

now is procedurally driven, not substantively driven. The adherence to rules has become more important in the [new] paradigm, rather than whether the [staff] cares about what happens or not. I have never found a lack of empathy in the commission in general. There are certainly [staff] who lack empathy, and certainly people you will hear say ugly, ugly things about folks. But as a general rule I have found them to be amenable to requests.

One of the overriding problems is that they have been so understaffed in the past few years that getting anything done is difficult. There just isn't the time to do it. We have had lots and lots of folks come in because of that, [saying] "I called my claims manager or my case worker, and I can't get anybody to return my calls." It happens a whole lot. Sometimes it's an absolute travesty that [claimants] have to hire lawyers and pay them twenty percent [of the value of the benefit paid to them] to get something simple done. But that happens.

What happens with protested assessments?

The claim goes from the Workers' Compensation Commission to the Office of Judges (OOJ), which is a quasi-judicial body created by the legislature. Then it becomes a litigation issue. It is not like any kind of litigation on any TV show or litigation anywhere else. It's generally a no-hearing process where we submit evidence, the employer has the opportunity to submit evidence, and the Worker's Compensation Commission has the opportunity to present evidence. The judge will sit down, look at it, and make a determination on what should happen. There are appeal routes after that—the Board of Review, which is the quasi-judicial body in the workers' compensation system, and then the Supreme Court.

Across the nation and in this state the management of workers' compensation is being reassigned from government agencies to governmentally regulated private insurance companies. What does this mean for claimants?

It's in a real state of flux right now. In the [2005] special session of the legislature they privatized [workers' compensation]. It is looking more and more like Kentucky. The new legislation, the privatization legislation looks more like Kentucky law—private carriers with some governmental oversight over the distribution of benefits.

[*Point of clarification*: The new law reassigned the administration of workers' compensation claims from a state agency to a private firm that is paid by the state to assess the claims and award compensation. This "privatization" is supposed to control workers' compensation costs.]

But [the changes of the past decade] have hurt injured workers. There is no doubt about it. If you want to compare—and [business leaders] will want to disagree with me on this—the well-being of workers fifteen years ago and today, there is no comparison. Absolutely no comparison. Make no mistake that workers' compensation in this state is about who gets the money and who keeps the money—premiums versus benefits. It has been a political hot potato, and the hot potato has landed in the lap of the worker.

What happens in social security cases?

If [it's] a disability case, those are a one-shot issue. [A partner] does those. I used to do them. Somebody comes in. They have been denied benefits under Title II or Title XIV [of the Social Security Act]   SSI [Supplemental Security Income] or social security disability. There are three stages—initial determination, reconsideration, and a decision by the Office of Judges. We do an intake and gauge—some of it is so subjective—you have to gauge what you think the claimant's chance of success is based on their representations to you. You don't have the record when they come in. If we make a determination that we can help them, they sign all of the required forms. Believe me, it is the federal government, so there are enough of them. They sign all of the required forms, and the documents get ordered. You take a look at the medical records that are available, whether they are from treating sources or from evaluating sources. Then it becomes a waiting game.

Many times when [clients] go in and make the application the company will send them out to have them evaluated by docs that they [the company] have on retainer. They do an examination and a report—the result, not an opinion but a result. Then it's our job to sit down and look over all of those to make a determination about where what we have fits into the regulations, and then make a determination about additionally what we might need in terms of medical verification to prevail before the administrative law judge. During this process and between reconsideration and a decision by the Office of Judges, you can be talking about a time period as long as two years. But that's strictly a disability determination. There are no ancillary issues at all.

What do you regard to be the pluses and minuses of workers' compensation and administrative legal practice?

In the past five years the pluses with me personally have been that I can help this guy, who would not have any idea how to reach some kind of financial security, through my efforts. I get to help people. I know that sounds a bit naive, but it is a good feeling for me. Another plus in practicing this kind of law is you can have almost an immediate impact on your client's lives because some things can be done with just a phone call or just a simple form. In these cases the clients generally think you are a miracle worker, which is really nice to feel.

A minus is its difficulty. Another minus is the frustrations. The people we represent are hurt, broke, and pissed off. The first place that they look to lash out at is at this office. We have abuse heaped here, unjustified. Sometimes it's been six months since workers' compensation did anything. There is nothing we can make them do right now. So I understand the frustration. But sometimes it doesn't take anything to set off some folks that we represent.

As to the process, in the past five years pluses are not coming to mind. They are not just coming to mind. That's terrible, isn't it? I can think back twenty years and find some pluses in pay rates and generally a more liberal attitude to taking care of claimants, but that is in the past. In the past five years it has been one screw after another from the legislature.

Robert V. Eye

Litigating for the Outsider
and the Disadvantaged

Bob Eye practices law for a clientele of social and political outsiders, "have-nots," and criminal defendants at Irigonegaray and Associates, a small firm in Topeka, Kansas. For more than two decades he has defended clients against criminal charges and represented injured parties in civil rights and environmental injury cases. He was interviewed in the conference room of another law firm in Lawrence, Kansas, just days after losing in the defense of a man charged with a murder.

How did you prepare to become an attorney?

I grew up in northwest Kansas out on the high plains in a city called Goodland. I migrated from there to Kansas State University in 1970 and got my bachelor's degree in political science in 1974. I stayed and got my master's degree in political science in 1975. From there I went to a small liberal arts college and taught for a couple of years. From there I went to law school at Washburn University in Topeka twenty-five years ago—1980.

What kinds of legal practice have involved you over the years?

When I first got out of law school, I went to work for the same law firm that I had clerked for while I was in law school. As it has turned out, that is the same firm, although it has gone through a few adaptations, which I am at today. The focus of our firm is litigation. We consider ourselves to be trial counsel that covers a fairly broad range of cases. That was what we did in the past, as well. I would say that year in and year out the bread and butter is really criminal defense in terms of the greatest number of cases that we handle. We do a fair amount of civil rights—plaintiffs' civil rights—and plaintiffs' personal injury. I have also done a fair amount of environmental law, especially nuclear power regulation and fuel cycle regulation. I have also served two years as an assistant attorney general early on in my career as general counsel for the Kansas Department Heath and Environment for a couple of years early in the 1990s.

Who are your clients?

Our clients now are primarily those who have been charged or are anticipating potential charges in state or federal court in criminal cases. We will find ourselves representing criminal defendants who are charged with first-degree murder down to minor drug crimes to white-collar charges. We also still represent a number of people in personal injury claims. On occasion we represent small businesses. I also represent on occasion municipalities, particularly on environmental matters, both as plaintiffs and as defendants—although I have had only one or two environmental defense cases where I have defended someone who has been sued. I have done that on a couple of occasions when I represented local governments—cities or towns.

We do, as I said, a fair amount of criminal defense and personal injury work, and I still keep several environmental case files open over time—some of which are very old projects. There is a highway project here in Lawrence that we have managed to beat back. I started working on it in 1986, so if it were a child it would be in college now, but it's not. It's an open case file that probably has ten or twelve feet of shelf space in my office. It involves protecting a stretch of wetlands that are very rare and very unique to this area.

In addition to our criminal defense clients we are doing an ever-expanding federal civil rights practice. It is sort of a logical extension for our firm, given that you could describe my two colleagues and me—our politics is left progressive. We've always had an interest in civil rights work. It was probably at my insistence that we took some of the civil rights cases and litigated them. They are amongst the most difficult cases I have ever litigated. They are certainly a huge challenge.

Many of these cases arise out of police misconduct or alleged police misconduct, everything from excessive use of force to improper use of criminal databases that invade people's privacy to intimidation of police officer whistle-blowers. Much of it does center on activities of the law enforcement community. Again, it was kind of [a] natural extension of our criminal practice, given that we were frequently in an adversarial position with the law enforcement community. Although I can say we have represented a number of law enforcement officers over the years. I think that they dislike us in terms of the work that we do with criminal clients, but when they are in a jam themselves, frequently they can find our doorstep.

How do clients find their way to your firm?

The majority, I would think, is by word of mouth. The reason I say that is because we are something of an anomaly these days. We don't have a website, we don't do Yellow Pages advertising, so primarily I think it's word of mouth. Also, we do enough high-profile work that, as it turns out, we are in the media a fair amount.

It also allows me the independence to control our caseload, much more so than if we were in a big firm that had corporate clients where you can't really control your caseload very well. The general rule is on our criminal practice is that if a client can meet a proposed fee and expenses, we'll take their case. No matter how egregious the crime, no matter criticism we may get from the public, we'll take the case. We feel that strongly about protecting people's rights in the criminal justice system.

On the civil side we are a great deal more selective. There are certain criteria we have in our firm. If those criteria are not satisfied, we reject the case. For every civil case we accept, we probably reject a half dozen or more. That independence that was always attractive to me, which was one of the reasons I wanted to be a lawyer: I wanted to be able to help people, but I also wanted to be independent enough that I would not be constrained.

Does the firm handle any court-appointed criminal clients?

We have reached a stage in our practice where we are not doing any court-appointed work. All of our criminal clients are retained. We do some criminal representation pro bono [without requiring payment from the client]. As a percentage, I don't know what it is, but at any time we have a number. In fact, our accountant claims an excessive number of pro bono files. Our private criminal practice is concentrated in the Topeka-Kansas City corridor, which includes Lawrence. I have tried a very lengthy criminal case in federal court in San Francisco. We have also gone to other venues around the country.

What happens on your typical day?

I suppose my typical day has me in the office around eight-thirty, and I suspect a good share of my initial activities—assuming I don't have to be in court or a morning meeting—consist of getting caught up on e-mail, correspondence, returning phone calls, initiating contacts that need to be made.

Frequently, we get inquiries for prospective clients. I guess that you would call them cold calls that are seeking enough information to determine if they should go forward and make an appointment for a more in-depth interview. That takes up a fair amount of time. We meet with clients when it is convenient for their schedule and ours. There are probably a couple days a week when I don't have any client appointments at all. That is by design.

I like to keep time open as much as possible just to get the ongoing work that is required in a busy litigation practice done. One of the changes that I have noticed over the years I have been practicing is the tremendous increase in pretrial motion practice. Consequently, that takes up an increasing percentage of my day. I will usually not get out of the office—it's pretty rare I leave the office before six in the evening, and frequently it's well after that. It just depends on what we are up to. If we are in trial, that becomes an all-consuming enterprise. It requires evenings, and I try to keep the workload from getting out of control.

Do you have much contact with other attorneys on the typical day?

Because our firm consists of three lawyers, there is a lot of interaction among the three of us. I don't think every one of our cases is handled by all three of us, but probably in the vast majority all of us have some involvement in it. It does require a good deal of interaction with my two colleagues. We're all about the same age. We all have a similar experience base. Out of necessity, we find either all three or two of us meeting very frequently.

In terms of lawyer-to-lawyer contact, it is frequently dealing with negotiations or trying to push a case toward resolution. The vast majority of cases don't go to trial, which means there is a great deal of interaction with opposing counsel. That includes things as mundane as trying to get a time when everybody can get together for a deposition or mediation to dealing with the more substantial issues in a lawsuit.

What is involved in an environmental regulatory case?
A lot of the regulatory work I did was at the intersection of utility and environmental regulation. Twenty years ago I was counsel for a group of about six hundred small businesses concentrated in the Wichita area that retained me to represent them in a rate case involving the Wolf Creek nuclear plant that was just then coming on line. It was advertised that if that plant went on line it would increase [electric] rates about one hundred percent. Many of our clients said, "we will just leave. We can go to Tulsa, Oklahoma, and do the same kind of work and not work for the utility company just to pay the electric bill." One of the most salient aspects of that litigation was how to attribute costs of externalities, that is, the deaths that could be attributed to the operation of a nuclear power plant and the back end of the fuel cycle—the decommissioning and spent fuel management. These are in many respects accounting questions, but they also deal with complex environmental issues, such as how a fuel cycle works and how it impacts human beings.

Vigilance is not only the price of liberty, but it is the price to keep chronic contaminators, chronic polluters, from engaging in the same practices that have been prohibited. Much of this has been replaced by a regulatory system that deals with permits under either the Clean Water Act or Clean Air Act or with hazardous waste permits so that the litigation process is supplanted by the regulatory process. I think the success of that is uneven. It depends a great deal on the predisposition of certain political leaders as to whether it is aggressive. The less aggressive an administration is in enforcing regulatory standards, the more likely litigation is going to happen. I know of a number of instances when we have taken claims to the state environmental authority or the federal environmental authorities where very clear violations were ignored. That required litigation to try to get a remedy. It's kind of unpredictable how an administration will respond to a particular problem. Much of it is wrapped in parochial politics, contributions, and that network of contacts with constituencies that a particular administration is trying to serve.

I have taken this position for many years.... I believe it is a fundamental violation of the individual's right to become the involuntary repository for environmental contaminants produced by a particular plant. You can see the electronic generating plant from here [points out the window to a smokestack] that is owned by Westar Energy. That plume that we can see from here contains everything from particulates, SO_2, mercury, cadmium. That plume will end up on the food cycle and will end up bioconcentrated and bioaccumulated in human beings without their permission. Courts have said that is permissible because we in our regulatory system have decided to excuse that kind of contamination and involuntary imposition on human beings because it is providing a needed service. I think that is giving the polluters of the world too much leeway. We understate the environmental and the public health impacts and don't fully account for it. One of the things I have, over the years, emphasized is a full cost accounting for that plume—a full cost accounting for the radiation released from nuclear power plants and other facilities, to get an accurate and intellectually honest picture of what an activity actually costs, thereby giving us a much better means by which to choose alternatives. That is probably one of the biggest challenges I have ever had in the environmental field. Then, even if you want to do a full cost accounting, how do you go about doing it? How do you go about monetizing the effect of mercury or cadmium pollution from a particular plant? Economists claim that they can monetize almost anything, and I have hired economists to do just that on occasion.

Did you represent individuals or groups in those cases?

I have done both. Probably the most frequent are ad hoc organizations that form around a particular issue—either trying to stop a highway or a nuclear power plant or a radioactive waste dump or something of that sort. I have represented individual homeowners in claims against neighboring sources of contamination. I have done that a number of times.

What is involved in a civil rights case?

In civil rights cases where we are dealing with, for example, infringement of rights under the First Amendment, where it's not somebody coming into court with an arm that is missing or who have been blinded—but when we are dealing with rights, abstract in a way, but nonetheless real rights are involved. The reason those cases are challenging is that, first of all, the typical case that arises under the First Amendment usually comes in the context of something that is politicized. Taking a politicized claim into the legal system is very tricky business. It's tricky not only because you are dealing with a body politic that has at least to some degree the appearances of legitimacy, but you are also dealing with rights under the First Amendment that, frankly, most jurors don't fully understand or fully appreciate the impact of when they have been abridged. So there is a difficulty in shaping an abstract claim with something a juror can embrace and appreciate. Having myself been subject to a gag order in a case that extended for four years, ten months, and two weeks before it was lifted, and the Supreme Court of Kansas said [it] was wrong to impose it, I have a firsthand sense for what it is like to have one's rights infringed under the First Amendment. It is difficult to put into words other than to say that the constraints are so foreign to what we generally think we are permitted to do that it is like having a burr under the saddle. It's the rock in your shoe. It just never goes away as an irritant. That's on the nonphysical injury side.

When you are dealing with an excessive use of force, then it is the problem to persuade the jury [that] the law enforcement officers that generally come in with an imprimatur of legitimacy and authority that, in fact, they have gone too far. That is made even more difficult by the standards of the federal Civil Rights Act that require a greater burden of proof by the plaintiff to show that there has been an actual infringement of rights by a law enforcement officer. It's no longer is the subject of negligence law, but one has to show it was objectively unreasonable for the law enforcement officers to do what they did and cause an injury.

Federal civil rights cases are very, very difficult. I like doing them. They are a tremendous challenge. I warn clients that this will be unlike anything they will ever engage in either inside or outside the litigation system. My experience, I think our firm's experience, is that government defendants will fight like crazy to avoid having a judgment taken against them. It does undermine their legitimacy to have a big judgment against police officers for excessive use of force. You only have to look at the Rodney King case [a case about the videotaped beating of an African American by Los Angeles police that resulted in the conviction of two officers for civil rights violations, a $3.8 million civil judgment against the city, and urban riots]. It will be generations before the law enforcement agencies involved in that case will rebuild the credibility in the community that they had before.

Is there a difference with criminal cases?

Yes, part of it is the overarching prospect in a serious criminal case context that our client's liberty rights might be seriously curtailed in some circumstances. In contrast with civil cases in which you are dealing primarily with money, damages, in the criminal context there is the concern about the client's liberty rights. Having been in maximum-security prisons on behalf of clients before, that prospect is never very far from one's mind. Because of that we have a particular emphasis on protecting the client's rights and ensuring there is a fair process to get to a resolution.

In criminal cases one has to approach the case from the perspective that the government is going to insist on getting something out of the defendant. It is very rare that the government will back off their case. In the criminal case I try to remind myself that the prosecutor I am dealing with—an assistant U.S. attorney or an assistant district attorney—is answerable to a chain of command. I want to be able to give them something that they can use as talking points when they go to their superior to try to persuade them that the offer we are making is an acceptable one. I try to remind them that, although it is the exception to the rule, criminal cases are lost by the government on occasion. That is anathema to most prosecutors. They like to think they can win one hundred percent of the time, and I have to remind them they don't have a one-hundred-percent track record.

Do you also try to negotiate a settlement in civil cases?

In civil cases it is frequently a matter of finding a magic number of dollars that both sides can recognize as a reasonable compromise. In that regard some of the most effective advocacy we can do with our clients is to show them that the process has pitfalls and uncertainties associated with it that really justify looking at a compromise result. There are some times when you first can't find that compromise, and you find yourself going to trial. But the negotiation process on the civil side is frequently to marshal those expert reports, monetize otherwise very subjective kinds of damage claims, and make that a process that the lawyer on the other side can use as talking points as they go up their chain of command, because usually you are dealing with somebody who is going to be answering to an insurance company. I keep in mind that it is a business decision for them. The subjective dimension of it, the actual life that a client has to live after an injury, is really of very little consequence to them. I keep that in mind that it's a dollars-and-cents calculus for them. That is where it is really incumbent on us as lawyers for the claimants to impress on them that even though for them it is a very subjective kind of injury claim, to the other side it is an objective kind of learned decision. That is a disconnect that we really have to work on bridging.

Has mediation become more common?

Very much. That's a major change I have seen in the last twenty-five years. My own thinking about it has evolved. There are certain cases now that by statute in Kansas require mediation. When you bring a medical malpractice case in Kansas, there is a statutory requirement for mediation. When mediation or alternative dispute resolution became more prevalent, I, frankly, was a skeptic. I was pessimistic about it, and it had the possibility of infringing on peoples' rights to a trial. I was wrong. I was quite wrong. My experience has been that mediation will frequently yield a result that is not only satisfactory to our clients but that is acceptable to adversaries with frequently a considerable saving of time and expenses for the client. They also get to exercise a modicum of control over the outcome that is absent in trials, when you close the evidence and hand it over to a jury or a judge to make the resolution.

How do you begin to prepare for litigation?

If we know a case is going to be filed and require judicial intervention, we begin to take on a role that is more like gearing up for a battle or a game. It becomes, unfortunately, less collegial with our opposing counsel at that point. Then you have to hope you can gain an advantage somehow through the litigation process. I was told many years ago by a law professor something that I always keep in mind. It is a hard thing, and it's still a hard thing for me to accept. It's an even harder thing for clients to accept: "The litigation process really isn't about finding the truth, it's about finding an advantage." Because at the end of the day, what does the client want? They want to win. The truth is sort of secondary as long as they get the result that they really want.

Although that sounds very cynical in a way, in fact, our legal system, given it is an adversary-based system, really is all about trying to find that advantage. So as a case progresses toward trial, we are looking for that piece of evidence, the witness that give us the advantage. Sometimes the advantage arises in the context of how the procedural posture of the call develops—that it is on a fast track or a slow track can sometimes make a high difference as well. We are constantly asking ourselves, how will a jury perceive this case? How will a jury perceive the client? How will they perceive the adversary? It turns almost into a parlor game of sorts at times. Unfortunately, the more years we do this, the more complex the discussions become, and the more nuanced they become. Then it's a matter of trying to predict to a certain extent not only how a jury will perceive it, but then the even trickier part is how a judge may perceive the case and craft evidentiary rulings accordingly. Our experience is that frequently judges will interpret evidence not just in the light of that particular rule of evidence and how it applies to a particular question but how it fits into the broader context of the case, which they should. That really becomes an exercise in trying to predict how a "typical" judge might interpret the circumstances and how particular judges with known idiosyncrasies and known predispositions might interpret it. That is difficult even when you have a fair amount of experience with a particular judge. When you don't have any experience with a judge, then it really becomes an exercise that is much more complicated. You seek input, perhaps, from the other counsel that have dealt with that judge.

As a litigator, do you conduct extensive discovery?

In terms of the written discovery that we do, it focuses on information gathering. We are reluctant in written discovery to ask a lot of open-ended questions because we know who is answering those written discovery requests—it's the lawyers. How do we know that? Because that's how we do it. So if we are seeking things that are beyond the basic background facts, we will usually reserve those kinds of questions for depositions, where we can get someone lying on the record.

Do you consult with experts when preparing a case?

A great deal. That is one of the things I am doing today and most of next week—working with experts in several different cases. It has become, in complex litigation, the standard that experts are an essential part of the preparation and presentation of a case. In a practice like ours—which on any given day we can be handling clients' cases that range from complex medical malpractice to white-collar crime to bank fraud to first-degree murder cases—because the range of topics is so broad, we have a particular reliance on experts to help us understand the basic underlying facts and principles that should come to bear on the case. Ultimately, it is our judgment that has to be exercised about which experts are appropriate and which experts can do the best job for our clients. So we spend an enormous amount of time and resources dealing with experts.

Biologists are an increasingly frequent contact for us in the environmental realm. On occasion I deal with hydrogeologists, particularly on groundwater contamination questions. We deal with people who have an expertise in measuring air contamination. In the environmental realm, the scientific basis for our claims has to be underpinned by experts.

How do you assess the work of juries?

We just came out of a five-week first-degree murder trial that was tried in Lawrence. Our client was convicted. He was a former linguistics professor who was charged with killing his wife. We had the benefit of very skilled jury consultants who had a great deal of experience. They helped us pick one of the best juries we could have possibly gotten. Having said that, we lost the case, but it wasn't because the jury wasn't a good panel.

What goes into [jury selection] is really a blend of intuition and enough social science background that one hopes they can get a profile of a particular juror. One then has to project how that profile juror will respond to the evidence as we think it will come in. I actually heard judges on occasion say that the first twelve people you get off the street are going to be like the next twelve or the twelve after that. To a certain extent, there is truth in that. But we also know that there are defense-oriented jurors and there are plaintiff-oriented jurors and that we have to try to identify and figure out how they will work in our mix. Whenever we can, whenever the client can afford it, we do bring jury consultants on board who have expertise in everything from psychology to social work to sociology to help us identify jurors who will listen to our case carefully and render a decision that we think is consistent with what the evidence is. When we don't have jury consultants on board, then it is just what the lawyers experience and an intuition sense of what jurors are thinking. The process of jury selection, voir dire, is one of the most challenging aspects of trial practice. It is something that is frequently the least prepared for. We have certainly changed that over the years in our practice. We put a good deal more emphasis on that now than we ever have. It is not unusual for us now, particularly in high-profile criminal cases, to seek independent voir dire, where jurors are brought back one by one in the chambers or a room where the only people present are the judge, lawyers, and court reporter to do one-on-one interviews to determine whether or not a juror can serve and do a fair job.

Are there ever problems with the enforcement of the decisions that you win?

Definitely. Fortunately, they are the exception to the rule. If it was the rule, we wouldn't be able to do the kind of practice we do. There are occasions when a judgment is really no more than the paper it is written on. Collecting on it is a more difficult enterprise. There are occasions when we bring other counsel on board whose only function is to try to collect a judgment. That makes it more expensive for the client, but the area of postjudgment remedies is a whole area of law unto itself and requires a different kind of expertise than we generally bring to bear on a case.

Do think the legal process is very political?

Yes, I think it is very politicized. In fact, I am quick to remind people that if they don't think it is politicized, then all they have to do is read the Constitution and recognize the politics of 1789 enshrined slavery. It was a purely political decree. It was to accommodate factions. If they don't think it is politicized, they only have to take a look at Bush v. Gore [2000] and are reminded this is a political process. Many people believe that when a court looks at a case, it is looking on the basis of record, evidence, and the applicable law. Yes, those are obviously the dominant materials, but it is ridiculous to think that a judge or jury, for that matter, is going to check its life experiences at the courthouse door. They are not going to do that. Those are going to be brought to bear. In fact, jurors should bring those things to bear in terms of how they decide a case. Judges do the same thing. That's okay to do that, but we have to recognize, particularly in times when the political trends run counter to the direction we want them to go, that the politicization of the legal process can create outcomes that we have to live with that aren't very favorable. I have represented the Democrats in Kansas in congressional redistricting. Very politicized. It was admittedly very politicized. The legislature carved up the state to accommodate the Republican majority, very much to the detriment of the Democratic minority. The general rule is majority rules, but there is a respect for minority rights that was observed but not particularly manifested.

So is it politicized. It depends on the nature of the case. Obviously, a congressional districting case is very politicized, but a possession of marijuana case in district court is also politicized. Why? Because it is a political decision to criminalize that conduct in the first place. When people come to me and ask, "What is a good major before I go to law school?" I say political science. Because without a firm understanding of the function and structure of the government and the workings of politics in its nuanced versions, I think lawyers are handicapped in terms of advising clients about how to navigate their way. I am biased. My first love was political science.

You would recommend that students study politics before going to law school?

Have the emphasis in the social sciences. In addition to that, having a good sense of how the capitalist business system is structured and functions is important. That is not only in terms of the bigger picture of how corporations are organized but accounting. I had to teach myself accounting. I didn't malpractice anybody. It's a miracle, but I didn't take any accounting classes as an undergrad. I was taking politics of developing nations and Middle Eastern politics and European politics, which is what fascinated me and fascinates me now. The first time I had a utility regulation case, I was faced with accounting problems that were a subject matter and vernacular that I had to learn pretty much from the ground up. So I think that an undergraduate student who wants to go to law school and be a practicing attorney needs to recognize the structure and function of government and politics and also understand the basic economics of capitalism.

What do you enjoy about your legal practice?

In my practice, what drew me to my practice and has kept me there, is the idea that I do not have to compromise my politics. I do not have to compromise my social views. I don't have to seek concessions from the body politic. I am independent. I maintain a very high degree of independence, and I think clients are beneficiaries of that.

The downside of that is when it would be useful to a client to get a politically favorable outcome; sometimes that is difficult to do, because I am sufficiently high profile and sufficiently bigmouthed that on things political, I don't mind stating my opinion, and I've got lots of them. I ran for office ten or eleven years ago. Probably in terms of the moderate right wing of Kansas politics, which accounts for probably ninety percent of everyone, I probably set myself apart permanently, which is okay. So the fact is that we have to compromise on client's claims in order to accommodate a political figure somewhere. Likewise we can't go to these political figures and expect any kind of favorable treatment. Not that we would necessarily seek that, but we know that's not generally in the cards for us. If we get a favorable outcome for a client, it's because we have had to fight tooth and nail for it.

The other thing I would say is I am extremely lucky. Out of law school for twenty-five years, I have never had a job that I disliked. I have gotten to work on the kind of cases that were interesting to me and to get to take up opportunities that gave me the chance hopefully to influence society in a way that was positive. It at least gave me a platform from which to work to further other social goals. For somebody with my predisposition, it is hard to think of a better situation. I have been very fortunate. I have had great support from my colleagues and my family.

Do you think that the law can make for a better world?

I have still a very idealized view of being a practicing attorney, influenced primarily by lawyers like Clarence Darrow, William Kunstler, Leonard Weinglass, Ralph Nader [prominent lawyers who defended workers, victims of discrimination, and consumers], people who have manifested their social and political impulses in their practice. Before I started practicing, the idea of doing that seemed not only natural but easy. In fact, it is very hard. If one considers himself a progressive or left of center politically, in a politics that is pretty hostile to those ideas, it makes them no less valid, but one had to recognize that people are not just going to embrace the idea the First Amendment ought to be interpreted in an expansive way, rather than in a more constrained way. The thing that helped me grow as much as anything in terms of my understanding of the system of the law but how it feels to be a client was when I was sued. I mentioned the gag order earlier. When I represented a group of small-business men in the nuclear power plant rate case, I was seeking a large amount of information that had been given to an internal reporting program at the power plant during the construction. I was stonewalled in getting those documents through conventional means. During the trial, a whistle-blower gave me a very large box of "secret" documents, which I proceeded to use as exhibits in the case. I was sued as a result of that by the nuclear utility. The most difficult thing I did in my practice was represent myself. There is a reason they say a lawyer who represents himself has a fool for a client. I now know that. I would not do it again. But because of circumstances, I had the idea I was the logical person to handle the defense. It gave me an appreciation of what clients go through. How difficult it is to be a client. I now have a standard blood, sweat, and tears speech I give the clients who now come in and insist they want to file a lawsuit. To make them understand there is a cost that goes beyond dollars and cents that they will have to incur that is a very difficult cost, indeed. Sometimes it's even avoidable, but in fact is an aspect that nobody is prepared to deal with coming out of law school because there is no emphasis on putting yourself in the client's place. Now that I have been there, I have a much better appreciation of that.

It's very easy to become jaded to the whole legal process and to look at it as something to be endured rather than cherished and protected. It is my own belief that without a judicial system that is considered to be fair and that renders legitimate decisions on a regular basis, our government would probably not function because of the low ratings the other two branches get.

It gives me a great deal of concern that our judiciary may not be able to function well enough to keep the body politic from sinking into complete disarray. Each lawyer has a responsibility for that. That's a huge responsibility. You might think this is a little misdemeanor marijuana possession. But, in fact, it represents something much more than that. My responsibility is not only to that client but to the process generally, because someday I am not going to be practicing law anymore. I have a responsibility to leave the system in better shape than I found it. It's like the backpackers' ethic. I am going to leave the campsite no worse than I found it and hopefully in a little better shape. While that is easy to say, it's sometimes difficult to do.

I got a call earlier this week. The murder trial I mentioned earlier was the subject of an hour-long program on 48 Hours last Saturday night. I got a call from one of my old high school teachers and assistant football coaches. I graduated from high school thirty-five years ago, and I know I haven't seen him since then. He said, "I saw you on TV." We chatted for a while, and he said, "I wasn't surprised at all that you turned out to be a criminal lawyer. I'm not saying that is good or bad. I'm just saying I'm not surprised." He saw something in me as a kid growing up in northwest Kansas, that I needed to be a part of a process to help people.

Anne E. Becker

The Lawyer in Public Service

BEFORE RECENTLY JOINING THE MIDSIZE law firm of Stewart and Irwin, P.C., in Indianapolis, Indiana, Anne Becker spent more than ten years in public service. This interview concentrates on those experiences when she was Indiana's Utility Consumer Counselor. More than twelve percent of American lawyers work for the federal, state, and local governments, including executive branch agencies and the judicial branch. Although many serve as judges, prosecutors, and public defenders, every federal and state executive department, Congress, and most state legislatures employ legal counsel. Even the smallest of municipalities hire legal counsel on at least a part-time basis. As with Anne Becker, many of these lawyers administer or direct agencies, as well as represent governments in civil suits; offer legal advice; draft and review laws, ordinances, regulations, contracts, and other documents; and hear or advise in executive adjudications of disputes about the regulations adopted by executive agencies. As with Ms. Becker, these lawyers have to become experts in specific sciences and technologies, accounting, the economics of regulated businesses, personnel management, and the politics and policy concerns in their jurisdictions.

Why did you decide to become an attorney?

I'm from Columbus, Indiana, and graduated from Saint Mary's College. I worked in Washington, D.C., for two years prior to law school. Law school had always been in the back of my mind, but I thought it would be helpful to have real-life work experience before I went back to school. Finally, law just seemed intriguing. I had a couple of different jobs in Washington. I was fortunate when I was at Saint Mary's to have a Lyndon Baines Johnson congressional internship with then Congressman Lee H. Hamilton. That internship provided me the opportunity to make some contacts.

When I went back to Washington, I originally worked in a patronage position that opened up at the time I was looking for a job. Hamilton's staff

said, "Take this job so you have some income. It's not a career move." It was
with the Doorkeeper's Office of the U.S. House of Representatives. I had a
wonderful experience working the Speaker's Lobby when Tip O'Neill was
Speaker of the House. It was a restricted area. The press was allowed in that
area, but they were not allowed floor privileges. Cokie Roberts [of National
Public Radio and ABC News] or another reporter would say I need to talk to
so-and-so about a bill or issue. I would go on the floor and convey the message to the appropriate Democratic member. I also told the Speaker how to
pronounce the guest chaplain's name so he or the president pro tem didn't
screw it up on C-SPAN. As I was working this job, I was also volunteering in
Lee Hamilton's office while I was looking for a real job. I ended up working
as a legislative correspondent for a gentleman by the name of Timothy Penny
from Minnesota. He was the first Democrat in a hundred years from his district, and he later had an unsuccessful run for governor as an independent.
I worked for him for about a year.

I started law school in 1985 at the University of Notre Dame. My first
position was at a larger law firm in Indianapolis: Locke Reynolds. I had clerked
at that law firm during the summer between second and third year. They made
me an offer at the end of the conclusion of my summer to come back after law
school. I was at Locke Reynolds for four and a half years as a litigation associate. The litigation practice was mostly insurance defense, handling the defense
of grocery store slip and falls and defense in malpractice—medical and real
estate malpractice.

How did you first come to work for state government?
I left there and went to work for the state. I was recruited by Craig Hartzer,
the number two person at the Indiana Department of Commerce. He had
to...find someone to become general counsel of the department. It was the
waning days of [the governor's] administration when it was difficult to recruit
outside state government, given that the likely candidate of his [Democratic]
party was not considered the front runner to win the gubernatorial election.
At that time the agency was responsible for economic development, community development, some energy recycling programs, administration of grants
and loans for various programs, and community development block grants.
Also, the executive responsibility for the Department of Commerce was with
the lieutenant governor, so I provided legal advice to the Office of the Lieutenant Governor. I was only the second general counsel there. The position was
of recent vintage.

How did you become the state's Utility Consumer Counselor?
When I was at the Department of Commerce I was approached by an individual in the governor's office to consider going over to the Indiana Office
of Utility Consumer Counsel [OUCC]. The governor's staff was looking for
someone to head the agency, and someone had suggested I might be a candidate. This was not a position I was seeking. I first made a beeline to the

lieutenant governor and his staff to say I didn't do this. I was not going to do it without [the Lieutenant Governor's] blessing because I would have left them in a lurch right before election. The feedback I got was go, find out what it is about. We would love to have someone involved in utility issues we know and can trust and call up as a resource. I don't know the whole story, but I was held in high regard by some decision makers in the governor's office. I went and talked. I talked to other people about what it was about and what the responsibilities were and the issues. What I had going for me, in addition to personal relations I had and the goodwill I had with people in state government, was my litigation background at Locke Reynolds. I was asked to head up the OUCC.

What does the OUCC do?

In Indiana, the OUCC has statutory responsibility to represent consumer's interests in all utility matters. The statute is written broadly. The way the statute is written, these could be matters in state, federal court, not just before bodies that regulate utilities at the state or federal level. Practically speaking, most of the activity involved regulatory issues before the Indiana Utility Regulatory Commission [IURC], as well as Federal Energy Regulatory Commission [FERC] and the Federal Communications Commission [FCC]. We also filed lawsuits in state court, which had been unheard of until then.

So the OUCC represents the consumer before other state and federal regulatory agencies?

Yes. In Indiana, all utilities are regulated by the IURC at the state level with the exception of cable. These utilities are monopoly providers, for the most part. [They include] some municipal water and sewer, all electric including REMCs [rural electric membership cooperatives], investor-owned utilities, municipal utilities, local distribution of gas, some municipal gas companies, and, a real biggie, telecommunications—local and within-Indiana calls.

In Indiana the quid pro quo for being a monopoly is agreeing to be regulated. Because there isn't a competitive market for the good or service the utilities provide, when the utility comes forward and files a request to raise its rates, it puts forth evidence supporting its request. The OUCC has the statutory responsibility to review the evidence that the utility provided. Essentially, we then present our own case to the commission [IURC] as to what the rate increase should be, if any. If utilities follow the statute, they can increase rates if justified. The burden is on the utility. Often the OUCC reviews the evidence and might agree on some but not all of the issues; we might disagree; or we might settle.

Are such agencies that represent the public before other public regulatory bodies common in state governments?

The Indiana statute, compared to other jurisdictions, is, in terms of consumer advocacy, pretty broad. The OUCC and its functions are being performed in all states in some form or fashion. In some states it is part of the attorney general's office, and it might be part of a department of insurance, utility regulation, or consumer protection.

What sorts of specific issues does OUCC address?

We represent all consumers, so we approach matters with a broad brush as opposed to specific issues. For example, a particular homeowner or resident or consumer or neighborhood might have a unique issue with a utility. If that issue was minor, we would not raise it. We tried to approach cases in the most cost-effective manner. We took on big issues—big litigated cases.

We also had sections where we would deal with individual consumer complaints, with a hotline and consumer service representatives who could work on [consumers'] behalf. We tracked that data because we became alerted to issues where we could file a request for an investigation or a complaint or actually get the issue resolved. But mostly, the OUCC took in big public policy and dollar issues.

What exactly is the OUCC's role in a rate or utility regulation case?

What is unique about the OUCC and utility regulation in general is that it is so technical and complex. It is not two sides fighting and meeting in the courtroom. The process is very different from civil litigation. It requires a different mind-set. In Indiana and most jurisdictions, a utility does what is called a "prefiling." They file written testimony and cases [about utility] regulatory requests. We—the OUCC—review that evidence and serve discovery based on that evidence. Then we file our own evidence, do our own prefiling with our own witnesses, either disputing the request or raising issues with the commission, such as there are things that the utility hasn't addressed. Or we have these concerns.

What evidence does the OUCC address?

It is a blend of very technical issues on top of rate-making and regulatory issues. Then you have legal issues: rules of evidence, competency of a witness to give testimony, compliance with filing rules, admission to practice. So utility regulation is a blend of engineering, economic issues, accounting issues, and legal issues. Therefore, the OUCC and similar agencies have in-house technical experts, not lawyers, to review the data and information. Then we come up with our own case to rebut the utility.

How does the OUCC define the public interest?

We are charged with representing the public interest, but how you define the public interest varies from administration to administration. I had a good understanding of what the governor's priorities were with respect to where Indiana was and where it should be and what issues were important to him—economic development, for instance. Still, we were our own agency, and we decided what issues we should examine and what things we should fight on behalf of the consumers. The agency received a lot of criticism. For example,

"You didn't do market-based research, how do you know what consumers want and what is best for them?" We got that a lot from telephone companies especially after the enactment of the [federal] Telecommunications Act of 1996. Also, criticism came from some other utilities in gas and electric that were trying to come up with new [stock] offerings and looking for new sources of revenue. After the Act with telephones, the OUCC's response was that we would not tell consumers what provider they should choose. We are not going to direct or steer them. Our responsibility is to make sure the playing field is level. We are to create the framework for a truly competitive market, as well as provide information to the consumer.

Who makes the OUCC's policy decisions about how to pursue cases?

Primarily, it is those in leadership at the OUCC. I created a leadership group with the heads of the different divisions of the agency. We would meet on a weekly basis to talk about the week's events and to look at some upcoming issues. My arrival at the OUCC coincided with upheaval in the industry—electric restructuring and the Telecommunications Act of 1996. There was change and uncertainty in the various industries. Those were challenges the agency had, and they were not unique to Indiana. All consumer advocacy agencies, as well as [utility regulatory] commissions, were struggling with their public policy decisions. Before the advent of people trying to get competition among utilities, it was just rate making. It was a very routine thing. Then there was a big explosion of proposed mergers and acquisitions among utilities. Also, large energy users wanted competition so they could shop for power. These were tough new issues no one had ever addressed before.

What skills did you employ at the OUCC?

No day was ever the same. I'm not sure lawyers in private practice have an appreciation of that. In some ways it was quite enlightening in terms of taking those skill sets you have as an attorney and applying them in such a way that you are not practicing but you are using that knowledge. When I came to the OUCC it was just rate-making kind of issues that arose.

So you helped initiate changes in OUCC operations?

My time coincided with the upheaval of change. For example, when I came on board, the OUCC settled a major rate case with Indianapolis Power and Light. I said, "Hey, that's great, let's issue a press release." The comment was, "We've never issued a press release before. I don't think we're supposed to." We were sort of under the radar. I thought, this is Indianapolis, the state capitol. We had better be selling the settlement. If it is this good, let's go out and talk about it, and give the agency some credit. That is an example of something that hadn't happened before. If you fast-forward, there is now a public information officer who issues press releases on a routine basis to inform consumers that, for example, their gas company has filed a petition for a rate increase and is seeking public input. That is one of the ways we communicated with consumers.

The agency, when I came on board, was structured by discipline as opposed to industry. It made no sense. We would have an accountant who on one day worked on a gas case, a rate case, an electric case, and a telephone case. There was no continuity and no recognition of themes or trends. We reorganized along industry lines: a telecommunications division, an electronic division, a gas division, and a division that is pretty much sewer and water.

We then created the consumers affairs division, and related to that we had the public relations person, as well as the external affairs director who did all the legislative work and helped with the outreach and oversaw the consumer affairs. We also did a number of consumer education publications.

How did you use your legal skills at the OUCC, for example, as a litigator?
In matters that were quite contested and involved a lot of work, I learned not to try the case. I tried to do that, but I decided it was not a great use of my time. I could not try cases on a daily basis and deal with the state budget agency the next day. I took a step back. I would meet with what we called "case teams" assigned to a particular case. I would meet with them and try to steer them. We had people who were so into the trees they couldn't see the forest. If we had a hundred issues on which you could beat up on a utility, I would try to come up with ten. I tried to help steer them in the right direction and prioritize the issues. [However], my day was what I wanted it to be, which is a luxury. I was an attorney, but I didn't have primary case responsibility. That was someone else's responsibility. I would be involved in particular cases, but it wasn't all my responsibility. I delegated that.

Did you draft documents?
I did a lot of editing. I wouldn't be doing drafting, but I reviewed things before they went out—not just legal pleading but expert testimony written by individuals with highly technical backgrounds who are trained to write for a different kind of audience than the audience they needed to write for. I would help shape the testimony in terms of word choice, tenor, and grammar. I also tried to mentor new attorneys and help them with their litigation skills. We had nine attorneys, including me, in an agency of fifty-seven. That gives you some idea of the size of the technical staff. It was one of the largest consumer advocacy agencies in the nation.

Also, there were routine functions to do. There are annual and quarterly fuel audits on the electric and gas sides that accountants do and that I reviewed. I could be reviewing press releases before they went out. That's not a legal document, but in editing it I had a personal sense of what we wanted to emphasize in a particular press release and why we were releasing it—the goal. I helped shape that even though someone else had drafted and worked on it.

Did you have to learn about utility operations?
It was a good thing I wasn't married then, because I would come in the door at seven, seven-thirty in the morning and go home at seven-thirty at night.

I went home with a pounding headache for the first six months. It is so technical and arcane, but it is not rocket science. Once you understand the premise behind utility regulation and the issues that go into it, which can be quite technical, that is the challenge. I had my law degree. I had my litigation background. But here is this niche area of the law. It was a contrast to doing insurance defense. That is why I wasn't happy at Locke Reynolds. You get lost in general litigation. You really do. The friends that I have at that firm have succeeded, I think, because in large part they had a niche area. You got to learn to be a lawyer. You got to acquire the litigation skills.

Then you have to acquire a substantial knowledge and have an appreciation of engineering issues, arcane financial issues, and economic theory. My double major in economics allowed me to get that, especially when we were dealing with the advent of competition and what it took to create a competitive market. I had to learn it. The advantage I had was that we had in-house experts who looked at me as an idiot and a dummy, but they personally helped teach me. Also, there are tremendous resources out there in this business. Michigan State University has a program. It's a two-week program you take a week at a time. It's from morning to night. They bring in speakers from all over the country. It is just for regulators or statutory advocates. Industry people are not allowed in. It is utility school.

Did you have contact with the state's political leaders?

I might go to Indiana General Assembly and meet with individual legislators on a particular piece of legislation. I would share why it was bad for consumers, because there was never anything introduced that was good for consumers. So we were always trying to play defense. I would talk to the press and do interviews. As time went on, I did less of that because we had the infrastructure at the OUCC, and I had a comfort level with its ability to respond to inquiries.

I spoke to various groups. Not so much local groups but larger associations, such as the Indiana Association of Cities and Towns, Indiana Association of Counties, Indiana Municipal Power Agency members, and Indiana Electric Association.

Did you experience any political pressure on the OUCC?

I was working for a Democratic administration. I was a registered Democrat. I was appointed by the governor. I was considered a political appointee and served at the pleasure of the governor, but I was not a person to go to every fund-raiser. In terms of the work, yes, I felt some political pressure. The agency was, fortunately, respected, probably because no one understood all the technical issues and had good people. I would get calls from a legislator about utility questions, but we tried to get ahead of the issues by direct communications to them.

When there was legislation we wanted to take a position on or a more vocal position on, there was concern as to how our activity would affect the governor's legislative package. The question was, "Is the OUCC's position the governor's position?" So there was a lot of discourse between the OUCC and the governor's legislative staff on those issues. Also, the governor's policy staff and legislative staff also didn't necessarily see eye to eye. The staff person who was my conduit to the governor was an advocate for the OUCC.

There were cases before the commission where utilities complained to legislators that misrepresented what had transpired in the case. We had to be sure that we set the record straight. There were cases before the commission where utilities or their representatives would try to backdoor the OUCC. They would try to get people to lean on the OUCC to settle. Those phone calls were made. There was someone in the governor's office who was wonderful and didn't tell me about those phone calls because she didn't want to stress me out. She also didn't do anything about those phone calls. There were other utilities, however, who played by the rules and who never called up the governor's office but called me about problems, even minor problems.

Was your political attention focused on events only in Indiana?

I am a news junkie. It served the agency's benefit that I spent time keeping current on what was going on in other jurisdictions and what was going on at the federal level. If utilities came in and wanted to do something that was unique and different, one of our questions was, Has this been done in other states? It was very helpful to contact my counterparts in other states to gather information. I wasn't figuring out the details. It was more getting enough information to decide if we should move forward on an issue or what we should be focusing on. I delegated the details to the rest of our folks.

Did the OUCC tend to react to what utilities desired rather than seek new policies?

We were more in a reactive mode than in [a] proactive mode. In part, due to the workload we had, we never had the luxury to plan ahead and try to get out in front on a particular public policy issue. If a utility wanted to do something different, it came forth with an initiative. But the OUCC always had a privilege with utilities. They would come in and say, "We are thinking about this. How do you feel?" I met with utilities all the time. I got so sick of meetings because my day got chewed up. [At the OUCC] I have never spent so much time in meetings. Utilities loved meetings where they would give us a heads-up and talk to us. Actually, we might work with them.

Did the OUCC ever negotiate with utilities to settle regulatory matters?

There was constant negotiation. Probably, this is a lot of guess, the overwhelming majority of cases filed with the commission [IURC] are settled. The workload is tremendous because of the number of technical details and amount of information. A lot of material you have to file under seal and sign confidentiality agreements. That part is very different. But one of the reasons we settle so many cases is that the utilities prefer to settle with the OUCC because they never know when the commission would issue its order. Settling with the OUCC and presenting the settlement to the commission provided some certainty as opposed to trying it before the commission and waiting two, four, six, eight months to a year for an order to be issued to implement a change in rates or whatever it wanted to do.

I had a utility tell me one time utilities can deal with good news, they can deal with bad news, but they can't deal with uncertainty. I think my tenure provided predictability with the utilities about what would and what wouldn't and what were the hot button issues that would be contentious. Knowing that they knew what to come in with and what not to come in with.

We got leaned on a lot to settle cases when people confused our statutory role. Our statutory role was to be the consumer advocate, but, if we didn't settle the case, we were the bad guys. People would call up the governor's office or legislators about the big bad OUCC. I would say, if you don't like where we are at, go try it before the commission. Our role isn't to be the body to determine what is in the public's interest. That's the commission. We are the advocate.

What is the role of a state agency such as the OUCC in matters before federal agencies?

The OUCC follows what is happening at the FCC and FERC and gets copies of what is filed. There is an individual at the OUCC, the deputy consumer counsel for federal affairs, who follows the federal stuff. By statute we could appear or intervene in federal matters on behalf of Indiana consumers. An example was the Ameritech-SBC merger [of telephone companies]. Regulation at the federal side is mostly paper handling as opposed to hearings with witnesses. We also filed a request with colleagues in other jurisdictions [states], such as an investigation into billing practice of wireless companies at the state level. There is no [state] regulation of those carriers, but there is at the federal level. We brought such consumer issues to the FCC's attention. We filed comments with FERC on consumer issues, too.

What other tasks did you perform at the OUCC?

I also did human resources. Managing personnel. No one teaches lawyers how to manage personnel. Lawyers in private practice don't have time to chitchat or visit or do nonbillable things. The internal personnel relations are different than at the OUCC. One of the problems with litigating cases at the agency is you have a lawyer perspective, an accounting perspective, and you have the different disciplines. A lawyer might see a case from one vantage point and might want to emphasize certain issues, where nonlawyers might not have an appreciation of those issues but have valid points on some of the technical issues. I had the clash of those different divisions and individuals within the division. I was taken aback at how people who had a tremendous amount of education and who are considered professionals behaved so badly in a professional setting. My small children behave better than these people. There was a time I spent a tremendous amount of time on personnel issues: settling someone down, putting them on unpaid leave, drinking on the job issues. It was not fun. Firing people is not fun, but I was responsible. That was a challenge for me.

We had budgetary issues. The OUCC and the commission are funded by an annual assessment that utilities pay. Even though the agencies go through the budgetary process before the General Assembly, our budgets are pretty much already set. We don't have concerns about the funding drying up. In terms of allocation of dollars for internal resources, computer systems, travel, training, hiring outside consultants, I managed that.

What other aspects of being an attorney affected your role at the OUCC?

Having come from the private sector and a law firm with cachet gave me stature within state government that I would not have had if I had started as a newbie in the attorney general's office. Newbie lawyers in the AG's office are looked down on. It was much easier coming into public service [by having achieved] a level of responsibility and stature from the private sector rather than trying to work your way up.

What do you regard to be the positive results and personal benefits of your service at the OUCC?

I had an opportunity to do truly important work on behalf of consumers. A lot of people lost sight of that. We would deal field hearings throughout the state. You see the elderly on fixed incomes when the gas company is going to raise its rate in response to the changing prices in the market over which it has no control. You see the ultimate impact of market volatility and what competitive markets are having on individual consumers—low-income consumers.

There are utilities that try to pull really sneaky things, although I never thought utilities were evil. Some are much better in playing by the rules than others. If you interact with people, that is a tremendous plus, but there is also tremendous frustration in trying to explain to someone why something is not the utility's fault, or you are not going to fight this particular increase on this particular item because they are entitled to recover it by law. People have a tough time with the fairness issue.

It was interesting to work with people who wanted to make a change in people's lives. It was interesting to be at a meeting and talk about electric restructuring and how we could ensure Indiana benefited from that. It was trying to be prepared for legislation and thinking of ways we could try to shape it.

It was good for me personally because, unlike if I were at a law firm and trying to have a family, I had more control of my schedule as the head of the OUCC. If my children had doctors' appointments, I could take off and take them to the doctor. I didn't have anyone telling me you have to be here or there. I also had the luxury of picking and choosing the things I wanted to work on. I loved the public policy part. I loved the cutting-edge issues and trying to address new stuff.

What do you regard to be the less satisfactory aspects of your service at the OUCC?

Bad things. I was so underpaid. I know how much utility lawyers charge in a private practice. Knowing how much people made in the private sector and how hard you worked and the quality of your work, it was not rewarded.

I also think that undergraduates need to have an appreciation of the tradeoffs of being in public service. There are people in the state government who accept those tradeoffs and are there for life. They are tremendously dedicated. I applaud them. But it's great to be young and poor, but to be old and poor is not so much fun. It is a tremendous experience. I think people in public service get more experience at an earlier stage in their career than at a large law firm carrying a briefcase around for two years waiting to get to do your first deposition. If you are in a niche area of the law in state government—utility or environmental—you are a good lawyer, and you know the law, there will be all sorts of opportunities come your way in the private sector. I also don't think law schools teach you how to practice law. There is only one way to learn, and that is to do it.

Does being an attorney in public service affect your family life?

Yes. You can do some of the things all the time, but you can't do all the things all the time. I have some memories that are good and not so good. I was in negotiations with Ameritech [a telephone company] in a high-, high-rate case with high political pressure. The president of Ameritech was calling the governor personally. It's my first son's birthday. We are in meetings every night. I broke up the meeting after the workday, went home for the birthday, and went to work until 1 A.M. I couldn't always put my family first, but I often figured out a way to do that.

Yet in some ways public service is family-friendly—the benefit package, not the salary. You don't have the billable-hour pressures that you have in a law firm. Now I am in private practice, but I am not full time. That was part of the deal when I came here. But, I will tell you, the woman, irrespective of how participatory the husband is, all the guilt and all the challenges by far the most part fall at the feet of the mom.

III

Criminal Litigation

Crime fascinates Americans. It is the subject of much fiction and television programming. Yet Americans often misunderstand the criminal justice process. For example, police do not spot or detect the commission of most crimes in the United States. If crime is to be discovered, victims or witnesses usually must report it. Studies indicate that people most commonly report robberies, assaults with injury, homicides, and motor vehicle thefts. Least frequently reported are thefts of less than $250. When these studies are coupled with other evidence, it appears that people report crimes out of a sense of duty, to protect others, or to report the taking of valuable property to police and provide evidence to collect insurance. Additionally, the age and income of the victim affect the decision to report a crime to police (U.S. Department of Justice 2008b, Tables 3.33, 3.36). Consequently, numerous considerations by citizens shape the business of American criminal courts. Police address crimes often only after citizens report the crime rather than detect their commission (for overviews of American criminal justice, see Cole and Smith 2008; Neubauer 2007).

POLICE

More than 85 percent of the more than one million American full- and part-time police officers, sheriffs, and other law enforcement personnel are the employees of municipal and county governments. They operate in approximately 17,800 departments consisting of one to more than thirty thousand officers (as in New York City). However, about three-fourths of all local departments have fewer than twenty-five officers. Today most police have received specialized education at a police academy, but, as Michelle Reichenbach notes in her interview, much more is learned when they first patrol the streets. As the interview with Rita Peerenboom demonstrates, the primary duty of most police officers is to patrol the streets by auto looking for traffic offenses and unusual behavior in public places and to respond to radio calls that inform them of citizens' reports of crimes. As the interviews with Peerenboom, and Reichenbach reveal, however, the work of police is much more than making arrests. It is keeping order and serving a wide range of public requests. Only about a quarter of citizen calls are about violent and nonviolent crime or domestic and neighborhood arguments that might result in an arrest. Instead, the public contacts the police about medical assistance, traffic problems, the detention of drunk and dependent persons who pose a risk of disorder, noise and other public nuisances, uncontrolled or noisy animals, burglar alarms, or fires and to report suspicious persons or give information to police (Walker and Katz 2008, 6–14, 236–65).

In performing their tasks, police have considerable discretion. Both patrol officers and detectives receive general assignments from their superiors at the start of a work shift, often through a roll call. Once on the street, department supervisors or communications personnel use radio dispatch to send officers to respond to citizens' calls about crimes or requests for assistance. Peerenboom describes this communications process in a large city. As all of the police officers interviewed for the book note, patrol often requires a routine of driving, observing people, and listening for calls. When not responding to calls, patrol officers cruise a zone or sector of the community or walk a beat. Police tend to look for people or things out of place at specific times of day in a neighborhood; examine public areas frequented by the homeless, drug users, prostitutes, and gangs; study vehicles for evidence of theft; or look for traffic law violators on roads known for speeding. Today, as discussed in Peerenboom's and Reichenbach's interviews, there is an effort to practice *community policing*. The aim of community policing is to have a police officer assigned to work only in specific neighborhoods, to learn the social and criminal patterns of behavior in the neighborhood, to interact with community members to build support for the police and encourage the reporting of crime, and to organize community groups, such as a neighborhood watch to promote order and prevent crime. Often the implementation of community policing involves foot patrols, police consultations with local businesses, churches, and neighborhood associations, and police efforts to have other public agencies address situations that encourage disorder in a community, such as abandoned buildings and illegal dumping (Walker and Katz 2008, 317–35).

As the interview with Michelle Reichenbach reveals, the media depiction of the role of detectives and undercover police officers is more fiction than reality. Many police departments do not have detectives and never do undercover work. Most arrests, approximately 80 percent, are made by patrol officers. What, then, do detectives do? Like Reichenbach, they follow up on crimes in which patrol officers have not made an arrest. Much of their effort is devoted to interviewing people about crimes they regard as serious—almost always crimes involving physical violence. Other cases are documented, but little action is taken to solve them (Walker and Katz 2008, 280–84). Reichenbach also describes how juvenile case investigators play the additional role of attempting to provide effective interventions in an effort to prevent the juvenile from being involved in further disorderly or criminal behavior.

Arrests, as Rita Peerenboom comments, often involve discretionary choices by police. Most police arrests occur when a victim or witness who calls the department can name a suspect. Without a named suspect, the ability of police to *clear* a crime (identify the perpetrator of a crime with or without an arrest) is quite low. According to several studies, forensic science and criminalistics result in less than 3 percent of case clearances or arrests (Walker and Katz 2008, 285–90). Police instead rely heavily on their interviews with victims and witnesses and the use of informants—often petty criminals—to locate and arrest a named suspect.

Legal guidelines serve to limit police discretion. Because police have limited time and cannot enter private premises without an invitation or a *search warrant* issued by a judge and based on *probable cause* or reasonable evidence of the commission of a crime, arrests are not easy. Moreover, with some exceptions, if police lack permission or a warrant to search a private place, the *Fourth Amendment exclusionary rule* prohibits the use of the evidence at trial. Police can arrest when they have witnessed a crime or have information about a fleeing suspect named by witnesses or victims; these are called arrests for *probable cause*. Alternatively, they can issue a *citation*, usually for traffic crimes or offenses against laws regulating business operations, which simply orders the suspect to appear in court at a certain time. Their decisions in these circumstances can be based on the perceived severity of the offenses, the strength of the evidence, the preference of the victim, and the demeanor of the suspect. Otherwise, a police officer or prosecutor needs to assess the evidence, gather information from the public and informants, go to a magistrate or judge, offer probable cause that the suspect committed a crime, and obtain an *arrest warrant*. Dan Hogan (in Part IV) further describes the issuance of warrants. The arrest warrant then can be served by police and the suspect taken into custody. Arrests are mandatory only in a few situations; however, several states require arrests in domestic disputes. Once a suspect is in custody, police must inform him or her of the right to counsel and protection against self-incrimination. Because of the *Fifth Amendment exclusionary rule*, failure to inform suspects of these rights means that the results of the police interrogation cannot be used in court. Failure of police to meet these guidelines can result in the refusal of prosecutors to proceed with a case or judicial dismissal of the arrest.

PRELIMINARY PROCEDURES

After arrest the defendant is normally held until brought, within forty-eight hours, before a magistrate or district judge for an *initial appearance*. Dan Hogan and Rick Savignano describe this process in their interviews in Part IV of this book. Initial appearances also occur for defendants who receive citations and are freed by police. If persons fail to appear, the magistrate or judge has the option to issue a *bench warrant* that police can use to arrest the person. At this appearance all defendants are informed of the charges and are again afforded the opportunity to hire or, because of indigence (poverty), have a lawyer appointed to defend them. For defendants accused of minor crimes, such a shoplifting or petty larceny, drunkenness, marijuana possession, and traffic violations, the judge might proceed to accept a guilty plea and impose either a fine or a brief jail sentence. If a defendant accused of a major crime pleads not guilty, the case is bound over for further action.

The process in criminal cases in these lower courts often focuses on dispute resolution instead of the requirements stated in procedural law. In contrast to an adversarial contest, the judge can inform groups of defendants of their rights and then assign them all a standard penalty—often the situation with traffic offenses. The process is often rapid, and many defendants choose not to have an attorney. The routines of the process neglect the special circumstances of each case in order to dispose of them based on assumptions about the "worth" of the case. Learned norms of behavior toward others and rules of thumb buttress the willingness of judges, prosecutors, and defense counsel to support rapid case disposition and what critics sometimes call "assembly line justice" for lesser crimes. Such rapid processing appears to occur regardless of the caseload of the court (Feeley 1979).

Unless pretrial release is gained by a judge's decision to release the defendant *on his or her own recognizance* (promise to appear in court) or the defendant posts *bail* (property or a sum of money that will be forfeit if the defendant does not show up for trial), the defendant might be detained in jail during this period. As mentioned in the interview with Dan Hogan (Part IV), if a defendant wants to post bail, he or she must normally pay a fee, usually 10 percent of the bail amount, to a *bail bondsman* a private lender. The bondsman then signs papers with the court to pledge that the defendant will appear at court proceedings (Dill 1975).

PROSECUTION

The criminal case then passes into the hands of the prosecutor (sometimes called *district attorney* or *state's attorney* and, at the federal level, *United States Attorney*). Because most crime occurs within the jurisdiction of the states, in all but a few states the prosecutor is a local, usually county, elected officer. In most jurisdictions the press of criminal business means that the prosecutor must hire lawyers as assistant prosecutors. For example, the interview with Traci Cook introduces the reader to a woman who is a lead assistant county prosecutor responsible for managing other assistant prosecutors and handling the prosecution of serious crimes. In large cities or populous counties there can often be hundreds of assistant prosecutors, with many of them specializing in the prosecution of specific crimes. The president appoints U.S. Attorneys, who are regional representatives of the federal Justice Department. As with state prosecutors, the U.S. Attorneys hire assistants such as David Godwin. As with Godwin, once hired, most assistant prosecutors are not subject to firing for overt political reasons. Also, as Godwin notes, the number of prosecutors can result in a bureaucratic structure in which their superiors oversee the discretionary choices of assistants.

In his interview, David Godwin also mentions that U.S. Attorneys can handle both civil and criminal actions in which the federal government is a party. Prosecutors in some states also will deal with some civil cases in which municipal or county governments are a party. Most actions involving state governments and, sometimes, appeals of cases in which the state is a party are the responsibility of a state attorney general's office.

In criminal cases, the prosecutor or assistant prosecutors make a series of decisions about the case. David Godwin indicates that the first decision is to take the case. Normally, this involves either a meeting with police or federal agents or a review of police reports and an assessment of the evidence against a suspect or arrested individual. Often police or federal agents will develop close working relationships, and the prosecutor will advise police so they do not conduct searches or arrests that violate suspect's rights and lead to the dismissal of cases. Sometimes, as he mentions, the prosecutor will recommend more investigation by police or meetings with witnesses. Because police collect most evidence in criminal cases, prosecutors usually do not need to discover and examine evidence held by the defense.

Also, as both Godwin and Traci Cook note, some criminal activities can be violations of both federal and state laws. In these instances, rather than separately prosecuting the defendant under both the federal and state laws (this is not considered *double jeopardy,* or being tried twice for the same crime, because federal law and state law differ), the usual practice is for the Assistant United States Attorney (AUSA) and the county prosecutor to decide who will prosecute. Public defender Luis Guerrero also finds that the federal government leaves lesser crimes of joint jurisdiction to the states for prosecution and defense services.

After review of the evidence and arrest record, prosecutors determine whether there is enough evidence to win the case and whether the police lawfully searched for evidence and lawfully obtained a confession. If not, they can dismiss the case, sometimes called *nolle prosequi,* or nol pros. Alternatively, they might divert some defendants for treatment of mental illness or drug or alcohol dependency. If they decide to proceed with the case, state and local practices require different kinds of *charging procedures.* In states such as California and Pennsylvania, the prosecutor files a document called *information* with the court. The trial judge then, usually at the request of the defendant, holds a *preliminary hearing* to determine whether there is *probable cause* that the defendant committed the crime. If there is probable cause, the case is set for trial. As David Godwin and Traci Cook note, in some states, such as Ohio and West Virginia, and in the federal system the prosecutor must go before a *grand jury*, which in different states can vary in size from six to twenty-three persons. Before a closed session of the grand jury the prosecutor presents evidence about the crime and asks the grand jury to *indict* or charge the defendant with the crime by issuing a document called a *true bill.*

The defendant is notified of these charges and is given the opportunity to plead to them at an arraignment. Meanwhile, the prosecutor and defense counsel have often initiated plea bargaining, or at least some discussions about the case. *Plea bargaining* usually involves the prosecutor granting, in return for a guilty plea, some *mix* of sentence reduction (e.g., from five years' incarceration to three years' incarceration and five years of supervised probation), reduction of charges (e.g., from second-degree murder to voluntary manslaughter), and reduction of counts (e.g., from eight to two counts of burglary). As Luis Guerrero and Traci Cook indicate, in many jurisdictions the bargaining operates according to widely known standards, or a "going rate," for certain crimes, levels of violence during the crime, and defendants with specific criminal histories.

However, variations in plea bargaining occur. Luis Guerrero describes a state jurisdiction in which the prosecutor usually makes plea offers at a regularly scheduled conference attended by the judge. There is limited exchange between the two sides. Most offers at these "let's make a deal days" reflect what is "normal" for the crime. The judge then normally follows the plea bargain at sentence. As discussed by Richard Stearns in Part IV of this book, in federal courts *The Federal Sentencing Guidelines Manuals* (United States Sentencing Commission 2008) set out a uniform sentencing policy for defendants who plead guilty or who are convicted. The guidelines restrict bargaining over a sentence for a specific crime. Consequently, as David Godwin notes, the charge determined by the AUSA precludes extensive bargaining over the sentence. If the AUSA has some indication that the defendant might plead guilty, he sends a written plea agreement to the defense counsel. Bargaining then might occur over narrower issues, such as the place of incarceration. Consequently, even though it is adversarial, the plea bargaining in the federal criminal process is not especially contentious. Finally, Rick Savignano and Richard Stearns, in Part IV, describe the judicial role in plea bargaining in ways that differ from the procedure described by Guerrero, Cook, and Godwin in Part III. Despite the frequency of a plea-bargained outcome, clearly American courts use different procedures to get to that end.

Plea bargaining provides benefits and reduces the costs of managing crime. Through this process a prosecutor, who is a locally elected officer in all but two states and in the federal system, gains a conviction, avoids the costs of trials that tax government budgets, and appeases public demands for the punishment of criminals. As David Godwin mentions, prosecutors also reduce their workload. The defendant can receive less harsh treatment, and his lawyer saves the time and costs of trial preparation, cost often borne by taxpayers. In most jurisdictions plea bargaining results in defendants' decisions to plead guilty in more than 75 to nearly 100 percent of cases.

DEFENDANTS

Defendants usually play a limited role in these pretrial events and in any trial. Studies suggest that they that know the prosecutor is a powerful figure whose decisions can govern their fate. Because most defendants are poor, less educated, unemployed males and lack the family support of the average person, they tend to defer to their defense counsel. They often feel that they are being processed rather than participating in an adversarial process (Casper 1972; U.S. Department of Justice 2008b, Tables 4.7, 4.9, 4.10). Because many, if not most, as Luis Guerrero implies, have strong evidence against them, the aim of their defense counsel is to secure fair treatment and a reasonable sentence.

DEFENSE COUNSEL

The right to counsel requires that defendants can request the services of a lawyer. Defense counsel can be hired by criminal defendants, but income constraints make this a choice available to less than 30 percent of defendants in most jurisdictions. In a smaller number of jurisdictions, the local judge or his or her staff will *assign counsel* for the indigent. Lawyers can register for the assignment, or the judge can randomly or deliberately select them. Although these lawyers are compensated by the government, low pay and sometimes limited expertise can mean less attentive service. A few jurisdictions contract with law firms to provide counsel to indigents.

Much more commonly, the government will create a public agency called a *public defender's office* to represent criminal defendants. Salaried lawyers from the office—assistant public defenders—will defend indigents in the jurisdiction. As Luis Guerrero and Cynthia Short indicate, the press of criminal business in cities or states means that public defender's offices, like prosecutor's offices, are often large, bureaucratically organized government agencies. Also, as they mention, the press of business means that public defenders have many cases in adjudication at any point in time. Because of the assignment of assistant public defenders to specific kinds of crimes and the frequent contacts of public defenders with the prosecutor's office, public defenders often develop specialized knowledge about the disposition of criminal cases. As Luis Guerrero stresses, public defenders become criminal case specialists, and often private counsel call them for advice in criminal cases. The public defender learns to face situations in which, as Guerrero notes, the cases against their clients are strong or "dead bang," as well as clients who are gang members, career criminals, and simply vicious. They also learn "how much a case is worth" and what would be a typical and satisfactory plea bargain for a particular crime.

As with any form of defense counsel, an important activity is discovery. The requirement of open discovery permits them to assess the strength of the prosecution's case and possible evidentiary problems. In criminal cases, discovery usually involves the defense counsel's scrutiny of the police reports on the crime and the arrest, of witnesses' statements to police, and of any reports by forensic experts. Luis Guerrero also notes that counsel will interview witnesses and use investigators as part of their discovery efforts. Formal interrogatories and depositions usually are not needed or are too expensive to conduct. To address evidentiary problems, the defense lawyer can file motions to exclude evidence as the fruit of unlawful searches or interrogations. At hearings on the motions, counsel also hopes to discover errors by police that might free the client. As Guerrero indicates, it is difficult for the defense to win motions, so they tend to use motions selectively. Alternatively, motions on the evidence can affect when and how the prosecutor reacts to defense proposals during plea bargaining. The prosecution usually engages in limited discovery directed at the defendant's case. The Fifth Amendment constitutional protection against self-incrimination ensures that the defendant does not have to answer interrogatories or submit to deposition by the prosecution. Some state and federal courts have imposed additional limitations on prosecutorial discovery.

CRIMINAL TRIAL AND CASE OUTCOMES

As in civil litigation, criminal trials are rare events. Cases go to trial primarily because the defense assesses that the prosecutor's evidence or witnesses are not strong or because, as Luis Guerrero mentions, with a serious crime the potential penalty is so severe that plea bargaining cannot significantly reduce it. As Guerrero indicates, often felony criminal trials last only a few days and feature testimony by only a handful of witnesses. In most of America, the trial judges who superintend civil cases also hear criminal cases. Guerrero thinks that many judges have a pro-prosecution bias in criminal cases. For many criminal defendants, the trial judge often appears as a remote figure who barely speaks at trial. A former criminal defendant once told a scholar, "I feel a judge ain't shit, you know. He's just put up there— he's supposed to be the head of the show, but he ain't nothing" (Casper 1972, 135).

Jury selection and voir dire, the presentation of the case in chief by the prosecution and defense counsel, and judicial management of the admission of the evidence vary little from the format of the civil trial described in the previous section of this book. The major differences in criminal trials occur at the end of the trial. The judge will summarize the evidence and instruct the jury on the applicable law. The judge then charges the jury to either determine guilt *beyond a reasonable doubt* or *acquit* the defendant. This is a stricter standard than the preponderance of the evidence charge used to find a person liable or not liable for a civil wrong. If the jury determines guilt, in all except capital cases the judge (or in six states, in some cases, the jury) must determine a sentence among forms of incarceration, forms of probation, and fines. The choice is dictated in part by standards set by the legislature that either require a mandatory sentence or grant the judge some degree of discretion. As noted in David Godwin and Judge Richard Stearns's discussion (in Part IV) of the *Federal Sentencing Guidelines* and the *Booker* decision, some states and the federal government have further attempted to define sentencing options by requiring the judge to compute the sentence from tables that list sentences for various crimes for defendants. The *Federal Sentencing Guidelines* especially have encouraged federal judges to sentence defendants to very a specific, and often narrow, range of minimum to maximum penalties when convicted of a crime. Penalties are "enhanced" by a defendant's criminal history, aspects of the crime, and certain defendant characteristics. Sentences are set at a lower range when a defendant accepts responsibility for a crime. Except for justifiable reasons, federal judges cannot accept plea-bargained sentences that violate the Guidelines (see U. S. Sentencing Commission 2008, §6B1.2.c.). Other states, such as California, have developed *three-strikes laws* to sentence persons convicted of a third felony crime to an extended period of incarceration. Luis Guerrero describes how public defenders have had to address the disproportionate sentences that can result for defendants who have committed three minor felonies.

Usually, when sentencing, judges will accept freely made plea-bargained sentencing agreements that conform to sentencing guidelines, or they will take into consideration recommendations about the sentence from prosecution and defense counsel. Also, it is typical for judges to request a presentence report from a probation officer so they can evaluate the social and economic status of the defendant, locate him or her on a sentencing table, or assess his or her chances for rehabilitation under different penalties. Much more rarely, the judge can overturn a jury verdict and order a new trial or a dismissal of charges. As with civil cases, the application of the law at trial can be appealed by—in almost all instances—the losing party. In Part IV, Rick Savignano discusses the many elements that go into the determination of a sentence.

A rare kind of case in almost all states, the capital punishment cases that Cynthia Short describes pose special problems. Not only are they time-consuming and expensive to prosecute, but also special rules developed by the Supreme Court of the United States can require a two-phase trial. If a jury finds the defendant guilty at the trial stage, then the jury returns for a penalty phase. The prosecution then must argue aggravating circumstances to convince the jury to sentence the defendant to an execution. The defense counsel can try to offset execution by arguing mitigating circumstances. As Short describes the practice of capital-case defense, a defense team often discovers and presents evidence of mitigating circumstances. Lawyers, investigators, and medical and other experts develop information and arguments for mitigation. The consequence is that extensive discovery must be completed before the penalty phase. The defense might then use their evidence to induce prosecutors to waive the death penalty so that the jury need not conduct the penalty phase.

CONCLUSION

As the interviews in this section illustrate, in criminal cases prosecutors and their assistants and public defenders apply local norms that can supplement, amend, or neglect the law in the books (see Eisenstein and Jacob 1977, 19–39; Kritzer 1990, 68—76). Local norms on the amount of bail, charging, plea bargaining, and sentencing especially can supplement criminal procedures. American criminal justice policy thus emerges as an amalgam of the laws made by legislatures, the street-level decisions of local police, the norms of plea bargaining devised by prosecutors and defense counsel, and the discretion of judges in situations such as bail setting and sentencing. The consequence is that elected officials and civil servants, all political actors, devise criminal justice policy in a context that is often invisible to the general public.

Rita Peerenboom

City Police

Rita Peerenboom is a sergeant with the Milwaukee, Wisconsin, Police Department. The department has about two thousand officers serving the city's six hundred thousand residents. Like many Midwestern industrial cities, Milwaukee's population, which is 50 percent white, 37 percent African American, and 12 percent Latino, is slowly decreasing. Still, Milwaukee has a diversified economy and is home to many prominent American corporations, including Harley-Davidson, Johnson Controls, and Miller Brewing. As with many big city departments, Peerenboom's department is organized bureaucratically. Peerenboom discusses her activities as an officer in two of the three major units of this police bureau—the Patrol Division and her current position in the Administration Division's Communications unit.

How long have you been with the department?
I have been with the department nine years.

In that time, what jobs have you had?
I have been a beat officer, a patrol officer, on both the north side and the south side, and now I'm a sergeant.

What is the difference between being a beat officer and a patrol officer?
I had a line beat, so my beat was one street up and down all night long.

On foot or in a car?
On foot.

As a beat officer, what was your assignment?
My assignment was to patrol one street during my shift, which was second shift, from four to midnight.

Why was that street selected?

Because it's a major street with gang-related incidents. There were several shootings in that area, and the business owners were upset, and I'm sure politics played a big part. We were on that beat.

What was your daily activity or nightly activity on that beat patrol?

Actually, well, parking tickets were a big thing [*laughs*]. Then if you saw a violator in a vehicle at a stop sign, you pulled them over and issued them a ticket. You got to talk to the business owners, who know more about the area. It really wasn't that bad, actually.

Was there high crime activity?

No, not while we were there [*laughs*]. No, since they knew we were there. Most of our things were pedestrian violations or parking tickets or other types of motor vehicle violations.

You didn't encounter a lot of criminals?

Well, we had some of the storeowners reporting shoplifters. Sometimes we [had] people who got pretty loaded, so, you know, you had to lay hands on them, to make sure they got into the squad [car] okay.

What is community policing?

I think it's a good concept if you have enough people to stay in their squad area, to be able to walk and spend some time to meet the people in their area. My husband is a sergeant who spends most of his patrolling as a beat officer and a bicycle police officer. He did that in his squad area. If anything happened, like if the detectives were looking for somebody, he knew where to look. He knew the bad guys and the good guys. He kept a book on them. That to me is community policing because he knew his area very well, plus the people asked about him all the time because he took care of them.

So he developed a rapport with them?

He did. If they had a problem with certain people in the area, he made sure that he was there. That to me is community policing.

Is it tough to accomplish that kind of community policing, given the shortage of officers you mentioned earlier?

Yeah, you never stay in your squad area. You sometimes don't stay in your district.

Because you're needed somewhere else?

Exactly.

Does community policing work?

Absolutely. The presence worked.

What was it like to patrol in a car?

That was on the south side and north side, most of it was on the south side, the southeast of Milwaukee, it was predominantly white. It was working class. Most of the violations were traffic. Traffic was a lot of it. There was domestic violence, too.

Can you talk about that, what it is like to respond to a domestic violence call?

Well, someone hitting someone else, you have a battery. If you live with the person, or have a child with the person, then it's a DV, a domestic violence call. And then whoever is the instigator goes to jail.

Is that the rule, that somebody has to go to jail?

Yes, it's mandatory. If they're both instigators, they both go to jail. I've seen some that were pretty violent. Where the female had to go to the hospital and go on for X-rays and get lots of stitches and things. It's pretty violent out there, you know?

Besides domestic calls, any other calls?

We had our shootings; on the near south side we had gangs, more or less. We'd have our shootings where we'd all respond and we'd have to tape off the area. You may have people who witnessed it. You have to take the license plates of any cars in the area, that kind of stuff. Then the CIB obviously gets involved and takes over—Criminal Investigation Bureau, the detectives.

Did you work second shift on that job, too?

I worked mainly third shift, midnight to eight.

Did you get a briefing at the beginning of the shift?

Yes. You would get your roll call and they'd give you all the major incidents and where they occurred, and what to look out for. That's about it.

And when you went out on patrol, were you an independent actor or was there close supervision by your superiors?

We were independent, most of the time. And the other patrollers who were out there, you knew they would back you up if you had a traffic stop or whatever, because we were mostly one-person squads. It worked, once you got to know everybody, it went okay. You were an independent person; you picked out the car you wanted to go in. For example, if you were a traffic cop, you'd pick out one that had the radar and you picked out your spot where you'd sit.

Sometimes you do park-and-walks. I would do that after the bars closed and things settled down a little. What I would do is park the squad car and I'd walk up and down the blocks, I'd write out tickets, make sure nothing bad was going on, and stuff like that.

The geographic area you worked, what was it called?
It's a district.

How big was the district where you worked?
It was from Lake Michigan to Twentieth Street, about twenty blocks.

How many squad cars worked in that district?
On my shift we'd have eight. Sometimes not, but eight would be ideal. A lot of the times a squad was called out of the district to cover for one area of another squad because we didn't have the personnel.

Was there a division of the district?
You had your squad area, and mine was down by the airport, which consisted of a lot of hotels, things of that nature. Sometimes it got rough, because a lot of people go down there and get drunk and rowdy.

And that's where you kind of did your own thing and decided whether to do traffic, radar, or park-and-walk?
Right, but not until after the bars closed and things settled down.

What time was that usually?
Around 3:30 A.M.

Did you get called out of your squad area?
Many times you would get called out of your area. I was in a calmer area, so most of those things happened in other areas.

In that district, what kind of victims did you encounter?
A wide range of street people who were victims. And there's a big population of gay people on the southeast side. And there would be domestic violence among them, too, and they were more of a violent DV.

Male against male domestic was more violent?
Yeah, and female against female. In that area the DVs were the big thing. And street people, they didn't really cause a lot of trouble, but people would call in because people were in their garbage, or whatever, looking for cans. We had burglaries. On the south side there were a lot of garages burglarized. Not so much of the home invasions, like you see on the north side. Sometimes we would have horrific accidents, because when it would quiet down the roads were empty. I've seen cars go in excess of a hundred miles an hour, running through red lights, with nobody chasing them. There is no way you can catch them. We had horrific accidents because of that.

How did you decide who to stop? How did you decide who to arrest?
You arrest people who are wanted or you arrest people who [*laughs*] just have an attitude, you know. If they are disruptive and they are hampering your investigation, then you give them a disorderly conduct charge. If they are cooperative with things, and a lot of times even if you have something against them, we'll let them go, depending on what it is, if it's not something major.

It comes down to attitude?

It does, it really does, because all you really want to do is solve the problem, you know. Do what you need to do legally and then let everybody do their thing, you know.

How about who to stop?

There's a lot of probable cause. You can just about stop anybody you want to, you know.

And the threshold is now reasonable suspicion, right?

Yeah, it's easier. You know how a lot of people have those big tailpipe things? You can stop them for that. You can stop them for a crack in their windshield. You can stop them for something hanging down from their rearview mirror, you know, that's obstructing their view. You can just about stop anybody for anything, but I never was a vindictive officer. There are many things you can stop somebody for.

You are a busy officer. You don't want to stop everybody, do you?

No, you can't.

What is your strategy, who are you looking for? Is it somebody who looks out of place?

Not out of place, but acting strange. If they're going real slow down alley after alley, that's suspicious. If you see a car parked here and it's running, and there's a driver in there, but they're just sitting there and sitting there. Then you want to see if anybody is walking around and looking for something, things like that. You stop and just ask them what they're doing there. There are other items like expired license plates, or a hole in the trunk where they pulled out the lock, because you don't know if the car is stolen. That's a probable cause to stop.

Can you talk about how you talk to somebody whom you suspect is up to no good, but you have no reasonable suspicion or probable cause? How do you get them to open up, to give you the information you want?

Well, our thing is, when we stop somebody, we have to introduce ourselves, and why we stopped them, and why we're talking to them. Once we do, then they know why we're there. So that gives them a reason to talk or not talk to you. That kind of sets the stage, and if they want to talk to you, they'll talk to you, and if they don't, then, I guess it comes down to your persuasiveness. I've never had a problem because I address them as a person. I never address them as I am a cop, and you have to answer my questions, et cetera. I've never had a problem.

So you tell them they don't have to talk to you, but you'd like them to?

Yeah, but it's not always the truth. You might know that they were involved in something, but you might say, well, that the neighbor said there was a dog walking around and ask them if they've seen it and then you get them talking about what you want to talk about. Even if you have reasonable suspicion, but you don't have backup at the time, you'll do what it takes to keep them there until you get backup.

Did you have drug activity in your area?

Yeah, on and near, the south side more, but there's always drug activity all over the city. There was a lot of drug activity all over. Usually when you went to a shooting, it's because somebody took the drug money, or something of that nature. We find a lot of nickel bags and dime bags and rocks of crack when we pat somebody down. That's common. And they'll tell you how they smoke it, and how they prepare to smoke it. They'll tell you the whole story. Because it's not that bad anymore, you know. You can get a city tag [a ticket] for smoking marijuana, if you don't have so much. It all depends on how much you have. Or if you have a couple of bags and it's, you know, to sell it to someone. Then it's jail time.

Did you spend a lot of time with the assistant prosecuting attorneys? Did you spend time with defense attorneys, judges, social workers, or victims' advocates?

Social workers, not so much, because they don't really get along with police, and police don't get along with them [*laughs*]. The attorneys, the district attorneys, yeah, we do spend a lot of time with them, because our cases have to be reviewed by them. If they have a question, they'll call us in. We always have to go and review cases with them. So yeah, a lot of time with them. Then a lot of times they'll say, "Do you want to take this case to court or do you want to plea bargain?" Which is good for us, because if we spent all this time working on it, we don't want to plea bargain. It's more to our benefit that way.

Do you think that they pay attention to you?

Sometimes.

It varies by what attorney is handling the case?

Right.

Are there times when they have plea bargained something that you didn't think should be plea bargained?

Many times.

More than you prefer?

Right.

Do you go to court a lot?

Actually, yes. For the drug activities or battered DVs, where more often than not, the victim doesn't show up. So it gets dismissed, you know. You wasted your time going to court. But yeah, you have a lot of court time, actually.

How often in a typical month?

In a typical month, if you're an active officer, I would say that you're in court eight or more times.

Is that an overtime activity?

Yes. There were days where, oh, my gosh, there were days we would be there until three o'clock in the afternoon. We would be totally exhausted, and then we'd have to start our shift.

Do you get overtime pay for court appearances?

Oh, yes, there was [*laughs*]. You know, if someone was upset when I arrested them, and they'd say, "I'll see you in court," I would say thanks. It worked to my benefit [*laughs*].

When you do have to go to court, how, if at all, does the prosecutor prepare you to take the stand?

They will go through the case with you. They will tell you what they are going to ask you. They will prepare you for what the defense might ask. You get your report. You review your report, so you know what you said, because some of it could be from three years back. So that helps you when you take the stand, so you know what you're talking about.

Does that happen immediately before the trial?

Well, you get your subpoena to testify, and, if you want, you pull up the case, so you can read it for yourself. The day of the trial, the district attorney will tell you what to expect from the defense. They'll let you know what each side is going for.

Can you talk about your present assignment?

Now I'm a sergeant in the communications division, which is kind of a gravy job and it's kind of not a gravy job, because we have responsibility for the whole city. We overlook the telecommunicator and overlook the dispatch. If the telecommunicator has a call that they don't know how to classify or handle, we help them.

Is the telecommunicator the person who receives the 911 call?

Right, I'm sorry.

Are they officers?

They're civilians. We are there to counsel them and advise them what they should do. We've had calls come in where the telecommunicator has actually heard the shooting, or the stabbing, or heard whatever went down, and we have to be sympathetic to their feelings. Pull them out. You know, get some counseling for them. That's our job. Then the dispatchers, we make sure that the officers are complying with the dispatchers, telling the dispatchers where they are all the time. We also make sure the dispatchers don't get an attitude, because in that role it's kind of easy to take things personally, because the officer might be tired and he might be snapping at you. It's our job to go in there and help the dispatchers understand this. The work is constant. It's really busy.

Is the dispatcher a civilian, too?

Yeah. Then it's our job if there is anything major, like a big explosion and fire. Then it's our job to make sure that everything gets in its place. It's our job to notify the mayor, the chief of police, anybody else who needs to be there. It's our job to get the equipment out and to get that organized.

It gets very hectic at times, and the phone is nonstop up there. We also have an office that has every single district on a monitor, and we monitor them. We prioritize the calls that come in. Priority one is red, priority two is blue, priority three is green, priority four black, and each one has a set time for a response. When it passes that time, the call starts blinking on the screen. That's when we get active and say, "What's going on?" We have been so short of officers that it happens more often than not that we have to take squads out of another district, a whole other district out of their squad area, and put them in another district to help with their backlog, depending on how they're going. It can be kind of stressful. I say it's a great job because you're inside, not outside, you get to park in the garage [*laughs*], and you get to wear short sleeves all year long, because it's climate controlled. That's what's good and what also makes it interesting for me. I get to interact with the people who are higher up in the department and know their views and see maybe a different way the department is going. I also get to know exactly what's going on in the city all the time.

Your communication center, is it countywide, or is it citywide?
Citywide.

Does it take in strictly law enforcement issues, or does it handle any kind of 911 calls?
The fire department is right next to us, but there's a wall separating us from the fire department dispatch. When the telecommunicator gets somebody having trouble breathing, they'll say hold the line, and they'll connect them with the fire department. The fire department will set them up. Now, if it's because somebody punched them or whatever, they'll send them back to the telecommunicator, and we'll get our squads rolling on it. But the first thing is if there is a medical emergency, they immediately go to the fire department.

So for the telecommunicator who receives the call, that's one of their first tasks, to determine whether it's a police or fire?
Yeah, and the same with the fire department.

It's all one number though? 911?
Yeah, well, no. Cell phones are a different animal altogether. When somebody calls 911 on a cell phone, it will go to the sheriff's department, because they pick up all the 911 calls from cell phones in the county. Then, the sheriff determines where it goes, to the fire department or to the police department. And if they send it to the fire department first and the fire department deems that it is a police thing, then they will send it to the police department. And a lot of times, we'll get people grumbling that it took a long time to get service when they called 911. Then you have to ask whether they used a cell phone, and if they did, explain to them the process. Sometimes it takes a little longer than they want.

In Wisconsin, are the sheriff departments law enforcement agencies?
Correct.

Through all of Milwaukee County?
All of Milwaukee County.

What kind of relationship does Milwaukee Police Department have with the suburban police departments?
I'd say we have pretty good rapport with them, because, again, that all comes to us, the communications center. For example, we'll get other departments asking for a Spanish translator, and they're on our border, we don't have a problem helping.

And you deal with each other.
A lot of times they'll come into our city because they're looking for a suspect, but they'll always let us know. We'll always let them know if we're going into their city. It's kind of a mutual thing.

Can you talk about the interaction between you, the patrol or beat officer, and the detectives? How does that work?
Okay. First, the crime scene is pretty much blocked off, and no one is there. The detectives are called, and, well, there is a process. Say there was a shooting. The sergeant gets on the scene. They make sure it's roped off. They clear the house or the area. The sergeant checks the victim and will get information from the officers. Then he'll call the lieutenant. The lieutenant will then take the information and call the Criminal Investigation Bureau. Then the CIB will dispatch their people, either homicide detectives or whoever they have to send to that scene. Then they will begin the investigation.

And they talk to the officers on the scene?
They come to us to find out what happened, and then they'll use the officers to, say, go door-to-door to look for witnesses. They'll also ask us for information about the neighborhood and possible suspects, things like that.

In general, how would you describe the rapport between a beat officer and a detective?
There is not rapport [*laughs*]. In the Milwaukee Police Department, sergeants and detectives are considered the same. They have the same pay. So detectives don't have any supervisory authority over sergeants. When they get on the scene, they think they can take charge. It depends. Personalities always play a big factor in it.

Can you talk about being a two-police-officer couple?
I love it. I like it because he is in the worst district in the City of Milwaukee and I am in communications, so he gives me a better insight, like when I'm looking at things flashing on the screen and I want people out there. He gives me insight as to what is necessary and what is needed at that time and how they

are doing things. Not that I don't already know these things, but he gives me a different perspective that I should take into account. So we kind of feed each other with things that we're doing, and I think it makes us better officers.

So I guess you both understand your jobs?
Yeah.

And you both work the same shift?
We do now, but not always.

How does politics affect your job?
Politics is big. If you know somebody who is up in the department and you do something wrong, but you have their back, it can be corrected. If you are not in favor with that person and you do the same thing wrong, you can get punished.

So it's a matter of internal police politics, then?
Oh, yeah.

Can the average patrol officer avoid that kind of politics?
There's a saying in the department: if you do your job, you're going to be in trouble, but if you don't do your job, you'll be all right [*laughs*]. Because people who are aggressively doing their jobs will obviously get complaints, and they will take the citizen's word over your word. You will be in trouble. People who don't do their jobs will not get complaints. So that's how that works.

The active police officer who you just described, that's the police officer who has to know if his superior supports him or not, and that affects how he'll do his job?
Correct. Absolutely.

So the officer with a supportive sergeant does a better job because of this?
Yeah, and you see it.

What are the pluses and minuses of the job?
The pluses are that living in the city, I know so much that goes on in the city. I know the good spots, the bad spots. The bad side is that you don't have your holidays off all the time. You can't spend it with your family. The hours are sometimes lousy, but the money and the benefits are great, and there is security there, because crime is not going to go away.

I think it's a very rewarding job. If you look at it in the right light, and you don't look at it like you're empowered over somebody else, but that you're just there to solve a problem and work as best as you can to do that, you'll find that it's very rewarding. On this job, you'll meet good people you never would have met if you weren't a police officer. It's just rewarding, you know, to see the little kids smile at you because you're an officer.

So you definitely like your job?
I do.

Michelle Reichenbach

The Detective

MICHELLE REICHENBACH HARDLY LOOKS LIKE a television detective. Although very photogenic, she is neither physically imposing nor tough-spoken. Also, she is far from the sleuth or the crime fighter depicted by the media. However, in several ways she is the "new police"—college educated in psychology and familiar with computers. She is employed as a juvenile crime investigator in an urban/suburban department with approximately 200 officers in a community with 150,000 residents in the Denver, Colorado, area. The community is majority white but with a significant Latino population. Throughout the interview, Officer Reichenbach spoke quietly as she reflected on her career.

Why did you become a police officer?
I was born and raised in Indiana and went to Purdue University, where I majored in psychology and minored in music theory. I moved to Colorado upon graduation and went to the University of Colorado at Denver. I obtained a master's degree in psychology there.

When did you choose policing as a career?
Two years after graduating from Purdue. Throughout college I had planned on being a psychologist. That was my goal. But toward the end of college I took my first criminology course that really intrigued me. I found it fascinating to be inside the criminal mind. It was fascinating to me, and I started thinking about a career in a law enforcement setting.

In college I remember talking to a friend of mine who was a campus police lieutenant. I talked to him about going into the FBI. I don't really remember why at that time the FBI was kind of what I was leaning towards, but it was. He said that if you ever want to have a family, you don't want to be in the FBI. They will bounce you around, and you won't have the stability that you want. I tabled that for a while.

After I moved to Colorado, I really just fell into law enforcement. I had four people throughout the course of my life, starting in high school, who really pretty nonchalantly would tell me, "You should be a cop," or, just out of nowhere, "You would be a good cop." I didn't know why everyone was telling me that, but after a while I realized that they were. And these were people who didn't know each other. They all knew me at different times in my life—some in high school, some in college, some after college. I finally just stopped to wonder why so many people were telling me the same thing. With everyone telling me this, I started thinking that maybe there was something to it and I should look into it, and I did.

What kind of training did you receive to qualify as an officer?

I applied for the city department I work for. I applied to be hired, and, once they hire you, they put you through their own academy. They want to train you according to their own standards. The straight academy portion, which, when I was in the classroom studying, was four months. We learned things like the statutes and the elements of a crime. We learned things about civil law, officer safety. Really, we were in a classroom forty hours a week, learning everything there was to learn about being a police officer. We also had skills training. We would go to the shooting range and learn to shoot. We would go to the driving track and learn emergency driving. We had driving courses where we learned how to drive in an emergency fashion, with quick swerving, high speed, and backing exercises, because a lot of accidents happen when patrol cars are backing. We learned arrest control techniques and the other skills you need as a police officer. Also, during the academy portion, we had PT [physical training] days with a lot of running. That was difficult for me. I'm not really a runner. I worked out since I can remember, but I never ran. That was tough for me.

Then we had an additional three months of field training, which is when you have graduated from the "book part" and you have learned the facts about the job. Then you go out and do the practical parts of the job on the street with another officer right next to you. You're critiqued on everything you do. They want to make sure you can apply your knowledge about being a police officer to actually being one. The field training lasted three months. The total was about seven months.

What was the value of the training?

I had never held a gun. I had no, no prior knowledge of law enforcement at all. For me all of the training was valuable.

What was going onto the streets like?

Very eye-opening. It was so new to me. It was so new to me. First there is the multitasking you have to be accustomed to doing. Patrol officers do a whole lot while they are driving. When you're just driving, you just look where you are driving. But you have to do so much more than that when you are a police officer. Now it's completely natural for me, but at the time when I was brand new, it was very difficult to learn not only how to listen to the radio and know where all my coworkers were and what call they were on, and are they safe and do they need help? To learn to listen for my call sign so I answer the radio when I am called and to learn how to drive safely while still getting myself safely to a location, all that stuff is multitasking. It was tough to learn. You can imagine that it would be very stressful. After I settled in and became comfortable with the job, I was really able to experience everything.

On a personal level, the most striking thing has been this whole underground, secret if you will, way of life that exists right alongside the life that most people normally live. I was raised middle class, and that lifestyle was all I really ever knew. It's easy to think that everyone lives like you do. As a police officer you learn that's not true. You go into people's homes. You see how they live. It just amazed me; it still does, to see the lives that some people live and the conditions they live in. It shocked me at first. Now it just kind of saddens me. It makes me grateful, that's for sure.

Was this lifestyle associated with any groups?

It was more just a poor way of living. A poor way of living and criminal way of living. To go into someone's home and see no furniture, carpets with stains all over them, cigarette burns and dirty dishes stacked everywhere in every room. To know there are people who live like that, and to come into constant, repeated contact with people who are always in trouble with the law. I guess I just never realized, because I had never been a part of it, that there are lots of people who live their entire lives in contact with the police. They are always going to jail and back to jail, always getting in trouble. That's just their lifestyle. I wouldn't say that lifestyle is associated with any ethnic group.

Your first assignment was on patrol?

Yes, one-person cars. Solo. I did patrol for seven and a half years. We worked four days a week for ten-hour shifts. And when I was brand new, I would start, of course, on the night shift. Well, there actually are some people who like the night shift, believe it or not. I would come in at nine o'clock at night and work until seven in the morning. That lasted for maybe a year and a half. Then I went to another. We have three different shifts: one is the night shift, which is 9 P.M. to 7 A.M., a day shift which starts at 6 A.M. until 4 P.M., and the swing shift starts at 3 P.M. and ends at 1 A.M. I have worked all of those.

What was patrol work like?

It is different on the different shifts. What turned out to be my preferred shift was the day shift. If you work day shift, you spend most of your time taking reports on things that happened beforehand and are now over. There are generally not a lot of calls that are in progress. You mostly document what happened and forward your report to a detective for a follow-up investigation. That's also a shift where you spend a lot of your time driving around. You're whole days in your car. The department I work for tries to minimize the amount of time you're in the station. We're really not supposed to be at the station unless we are doing, like, picking up paperwork or booking someone. The majority of the shift is always in my car driving around looking for things that might be suspicious, traffic stops, trying to be proactive. Interspersed with my own activities. Then I would have to keep an ear to the radio because, if dispatch received a call where they needed somebody in my area, then they would dispatch me. I would handle that call and then write my report and then clear [with dispatch].

Swing shift is just busy. You don't have a lot of down time to do self-initiated things. Dispatch has too many calls coming in. You handle one call and have to clear immediately to handle another call. There are more calls in progress as the day ends and the night begins.

The night shift is either very slow or very, very urgent. You can go for a long time with no calls and then get an in-progress call that you have to respond to immediately. Someone somewhere once said that police work is hours of boredom interrupted by moments of sheer terror. That paints a pretty accurate picture.

How do you prepare for a patrol?

We had roll call every morning. It usually lasted maybe half an hour. During roll call that's when we'd get the news, we'd be briefed on the news of the night before our last shift. If it was our first day back after a three-day weekend, we'd be briefed in the activities of the prior three days so we would be up to speed. We would know if there was somebody we were supposed to be looking for and those kinds of things.

Where did you patrol?

When I first started with the department we had beats. The city was divided into—I think—nine beats. We would not always work the same beat. On Monday I could come in and work one area of town, and Tuesday I could work a completely different part of town. That has since changed. We've moved to a sector-based, community-based policy. Now patrol agents work a patrol sector for an entire rotation, which is four months long. So they'll be in the same area of the city every day, for four months at least.

Sectors are larger than beats. The city has only three. The different sectors are different sizes. The areas where the houses are spread farther apart and there are not as many people and businesses—those would be very large sectors.

What did you do while on patrol?

Sometimes you have very, very busy days when you don't have time to keep yourself busy at all because dispatch will keep you busy with all the calls. You clear a call, and they will give you another call immediately, or they will ask for people to clear because nobody will be clear. Then there are some days that are very, very slow. Those are the days or times when you can be pro-active with crime. Instead of just responding to someone calling the police, you actively patrol your area and look for things. Also, I personally would do traffic. I would look for any kind of traffic violation. There are so many out there—traffic violations, red light violations, parking violations. I personally didn't do a lot of speeding violations, but that was just my preference. In traffic you look for anyone who is suspicious—running with a bag in his hand out of a business or things like that.

What sorts of calls did you receive?

Every kind of call imaginable. Really, I think it would surprise you to know how many police matters come up each day. I know that I didn't realize until I became an officer just how many calls the police get every day. It's surprising. People call the police for lots of reasons.

We get calls, of course, for crimes. You have domestics. We had a lot of burglary alarms. Alarms would go off in residences. Most of them turn out to be nothing, but we'll go and have to check those houses. Stolen cars, cars that were broken into, houses that were burglarized, houses that were damaged, and every kind of call that you can think of. Phone harassment, everything. We have assaults. You have fights. You have bar fights. You have school fights. You have husband-wife fights, father-son fights, everybody is fighting! [*laughs*] Sure, we always had fights. Actually, part of what my responsibilities were that I was a crime scene investigator as well. It was a specialty that I took on. So I would be always one of the ones who responded to the fights because I would take pictures of the injuries and any child abuse. We also get calls for things that aren't crimes: neighborhood disputes, out-of-control kids, civil issues.

What sorts of people did you meet during patrol?

Again, you come into contact with everyone imaginable. Of course, we're always in contact with the criminals. One criminal can be very different from the next. Some are hard-core career criminals; crime is their lifestyle, and they're always being contacted by the police. Others may not have much of a criminal record and are contacted because of an isolated event.

Then, you have to talk to the person who reported the problem in the first place before you determine, Do I have a crime? And, if not, then how can I help the citizen resolve the problem? You come in contact with business owners all the time because they are reporting crime to their business. You come in contact with the victims of crime and witnesses all the time.

How does your department's version of a community policing policy affect patrol work and your work as an investigator?

I love it. The way the investigative team is broken down is geographically, by area and high school and feeder schools. I am assigned to a particular high school. All the cases that are generated from that school and its feeder schools, which is a geographical area, are my cases. The sector-based policy is also set up geographically so an officer works the same area [of the community] all the time. What this does for me as an investigator is it gives me a handful of officers who are consistently the patrol officers initially investigating my cases.

I have a good sense of the kind of work that they do and a good sense of their strengths and weaknesses. I know what to expect and how to tailor what I am going to do for a particular case. That's helpful to me as an investigator when compared to every day getting cases written up by lots of different officers.

I also think that sector-based policing helps out the investigation as a whole. With sector-based policing officers get to know a particular area of town very well. They become familiar with the area and some of the people who live there or who are committing crimes there. That means our investigations, from the very start, may have the upper hand [compared to] an investigation done by an officer unfamiliar with the area and the people. The more thorough patrol officers are with their reports, the easier my job is.

Does community policing put you in contact with citizens?

I'm always in contact with citizens. I'm contacting citizens every day. Community-style policing doesn't lessen or increase it that I can tell. Patrol officers do more community contact. We have a team, a neighborhood team, do that. A separate group of investigators sets up community meetings instead of answering calls. I don't do those things. I have in the past spoken, for example, at a Rotary Club breakfast on juvenile issues. Now and then schools will ask me to make presentations or be present at a school event, but it's largely outside the scope of the juvenile investigations division.

Are forensic science techniques used in your job?

We use them all the time. When I was on patrol I was certified as a crime scene investigator. So I've used it more than other people that I work with. I am the one who dusted for fingerprints. I am the one who is lifting fingerprints at scenes that were not major crime scenes. We used fingerprints all the time because the most common crime is trespassing to cars. I love to get a perfect fingerprint, and I did all the time, when kids pried the windows back on a car. You'd get perfect little fingerprints on the inside of the window and a nice thumbprint on the outside of the window. It's perfect. You know exactly what they did. Now as an investigator I don't do that; a patrol officer can do that.

For major scenes, our crime lab responds and does all the forensic processing. DNA evidence is saved for major cases. We are not going to collect DNA if someone spits on a car and wants us to collect it and analyze it. I don't use DNA technology in the job I do because I only work with juveniles.

What do you think you accomplished as a patrol officer?

Seven and a half years day in and day out helping people, its tough to answer what was most significant. I would like to think that, with some of the people I came in contact with, I was a piece in their life that helped change the course of their life. That's probably too grand of an ideal to think actually happened, but maybe one person or two.

Other than that, just day to day I would think I am most proud of having done my job with integrity and having pursued all the leads like I am supposed to do, like a citizen would expect a police officer to do. To do the work honestly, and I think that when citizens see that kind of effort from a police officer and a police department it will create a positive view of police. It helps to have people say, "I had a police officer come to my house and she was really kind and hard-working and she really helped." I think that maybe that's the manner in which I work, and that I was always honest and did everything I did with integrity.

What are your roles as a detective?

I'm on the Juvenile Crime Unit. That means that I get all the crimes committed by juveniles. Of course, juveniles commit all the crimes that adults commit. There are a few exceptions. There is a Crimes Against Children section that handles all the child abuse crimes, and there's a Crimes Against Persons section that handles sexual assaults and homicides. These sections handle those crimes even if the suspect is a juvenile.

How does detective or investigative work differ from patrol?

Well, it differs on a few counts. The first is the work itself. You're investigating crimes in both duties, but the work is a little different. In patrol, you're responding to calls at the start of the incident. You're dealing with the crime as it's occurring or shortly after. You solve as much of it as you can, and make as many arrests as you can right then, but then you write a report and forward it to detectives. When you are on the street, you are on the street by yourself. It's solitary. It's so much more solitary than you can imagine. Sometimes, even when your day is filled with calls, you might handle them all by yourself and never come in contact with your coworkers.

If you're a detective, then you pick up where the patrol officers left off. You investigate the case from that point forward and do everything that needs to be done to complete the case and present it to the courts for prosecution. You basically do the exact same things that patrol officers do, just after they have done all that they could do. Then you do a lot more paperwork. In investigations, you're inside and in front of your computer for a large part of every day. Even if you're working cases by yourself, you have a lot more contact with your coworkers. Even if you sit in your cubicle all day long, which sometimes happens, you're still right across from one another and interacting.

As to your current work as an investigator, what do you do on a normal day? How are you assigned cases? What sorts of crimes or problems do you handle?

My day starts at my computer. My sergeant will have received, by computer, the reports from patrol officers from the night before. He assigns them to a particular detective based on the geographical location of occurrence. Each detective is assigned to work the cases from a specific area of the city. When I first get to work, I look at my newly assigned cases and prioritize them with the ones I'm already working. If there's a case that needs immediate attention, either because of the potential for evidence to be destroyed, or because of a dangerous situation, or because of a juvenile being held in any detention, that takes top priority.

Then, depending on what needs to be done with any given case, I spend the rest of my day working my cases. My ultimate goal is to work a case as much as I can and then to close it, either with an arrest or until new leads surface.

I work different cases in different ways, depending on the needs of each case. Most cases involve interviews—of the suspect, victim, or witnesses. Sometimes I do the interviews over the phone. Sometimes [working the case] means just issuing a summons. Sometimes it means physically arresting someone and booking them, taking fingerprints and photos. Sometimes it just means doing paperwork and forwarding the paperwork to the city or district attorney for the filing of charges. I also collect evidence. Basically, I do everything that hasn't been done that needs to be done in order to close the case and present it, if charges will be filed, to the city or district attorney for prosecution.

Are you in the office or in the field? What do you do in each setting?

For the most part, I'm in the office, which comes in handy on cold, snowy days! Really, to a large extent, I can tailor my days either inside or outside, again depending on the needs of any given case. A large portion of my job involves the computer: looking up reports, writing reports, searching databases for information on suspects. Another large portion of it involves interviews. I prefer to do most of my interviews either over the phone or in person at the police station. I'm inside a lot more than I'm outside. Other detectives choose to tailor things so that they are outside more often. They do the same things when they're outside, except the computer work. They just go about them in a different way.

Could you describe who you come in contact with: the juveniles and their problems, parents, school personnel, victims, and others?

There's no one way to describe all juveniles or all parents or all victims. They're all different. Some juveniles are hardened and certainly seem to be headed for an entire lifetime of crime. They won't cooperate. They're disrespectful. They'll turn around and do the same thing they just got arrested for. Some aren't completely into the lifestyle yet. They cooperate. They're polite. It may take them just once of being in the legal system and they'll learn to stay out of trouble after that.

Parents are the same way. Some are hardened and don't like the police and won't cooperate. They tell their child not to cooperate. Others may not be hardened but may resist believing that their child did anything wrong. They may step in and defend their child, even in the face of all evidence to the contrary. Other cooperate fully and encourage their child to take responsibility. Some even want police help with their child.

School personnel are usually very cooperative. Of course, they have their protocols they have to follow, and sometimes those are at odds with the ones we follow, but almost always we get a high level of cooperation from them. And it works both ways. We try to be there for them as well and help them out when they need us.

Victims can be anyone. They can be victims in the truest sense of the word, people who didn't do anything wrong and were simply targets of crime. Or they can be involved in crimes themselves and turn into victims when what they're involved in goes bad. Some victims are very cooperative and appreciate police. Some aren't. We see the whole spectrum.

What is life like in an investigative unit?

There's a nice mix of teamwork and solo work. I have my own cases to work, and I'm mostly able to work them on my own. I have other detectives in my unit to help me out if I need them, with an interview or arrest or something, or maybe just to bounce ideas off of or get second opinions. There's a lot of information sharing going on, too, about particular juveniles and what interventions might work best with a certain juvenile. I might be familiar with a juvenile, and another detective might be working a case involving that same juvenile. In times like those, I can share what I know about the juvenile to help the other detective, and vice versa. If I were to get a case assigned to me that has a particular juvenile's name on it, and I think, "I've heard this name before; where have I heard this name?" It happens all the time because they're constantly getting in trouble, again and again, and we do repeatedly see them coming back our way. I may get a particular case, and I may wonder what has this kid been involved with, and didn't one of you guys have this kid in on something? What has he been in trouble for? Now I can look that up on a database, and I can see what he has been arrested for. That is different information, very different information from talking to another detective who has interviewed this kid before on three separate crimes and interviewed his family and seen the conditions that he lives in at home. From that you get a very different picture of what is happening in this kid's life. That will help us determine what the best intervention is for this particular kid at this particular time in his life. It helps to have people who have worked longer in the unit than I have who may have seen this kid five years ago. If it's not that, it's just the sheer force of having a backup with you when you go to speak with someone or to find someone to arrest. It's safety.

As an investigator, do you work with patrol officers?

At times I do. I will go back to a patrol officer with a question or a request that they do something if they have done something wrong. Or they didn't do enough. There have been times when something was overlooked, and I am not in a position to correct that because it wasn't my report. So I have to go back to the officer and say, you missed this and can you write me another report that documents this particular thing.

What is an "intervention"?

When I use the term *intervention* I'm referring to the decision I make about what to do with a juvenile offender. In other words, do I write him a summons or file charges in district court? Do I not charge him with anything and, instead, give him a warning talk or talk to his parents? Do I get the school involved, or do I let the school handle the whole incident? Within my area of discretion, I have choices for what to do with a particular juvenile. I use the term *intervention* to describe the decision I make for the juvenile to hopefully get him on the right track.

If I am not going to pursue charges, I have some options to intervene in the kid's life, such as talking to him about his actions. I would do this maybe with a younger kid who hasn't done anything wrong before and is just trying out the criminal stuff. Talking to him, talking with his parents, getting his parents to agree on some different parenting things, some different ways of parenting. Getting him to realize that he really messed up. Asking him to write a letter to whomever he injured. If he stole candy from a teacher's desk, getting him to write a letter to the teacher apologizing. Stuff like that. That's the least drastic intervention that we would do.

Other kinds of interventions happen through the court system, but the court personnel will often be interested in my opinion as the investigator or what I think. We have two courts we put juveniles into. One is our municipal court, which would be the city attorney. On a regular basis they ask us, "What do you think if I offer a plea to this kid? What do you think? Would it be okay with you?" They have different options available to them for interventions. *Intervention* might not be the right term, but I use that term because that is what it is for a juvenile. If you sentence them to community service or you sentence them to a diversion program and allow them to stay clean for a certain period of time in lieu of having a record, that is what it is. It is trying to get them on the right track.

How do you make arrests?

Either on probable cause or arrest warrants. Far and away I arrest on probable cause rather than arrest warrants. Typically with juveniles I am able to elicit their cooperation or that of their parents. More often than not you can call the parent and say, "You have to bring them in. I need to arrest them." That way you can have the cooperation of someone who is a little detached [from events]. Usually I can tell the parents that they need to bring their child in to be arrested and schedule it just like I would any appointment. It's not like I am trying to locate an adult who doesn't go to school during the day and I don't know where he is at every day and who doesn't have a parent who is responsible for him. I can find a student at school; I don't need a warrant or to find a time for him to come down. Sometimes arrest warrants are necessary, though.

Do you ever use search warrants?

Yes. Not too often, but I do. Judges are cooperative in issuing search warrants. I've never had one turned down, although I think I do a thorough job, and I don't ask for them frivolously.

Do you appear at juvenile hearings?

Every time a case goes to court, because I am there. I am subpoenaed for it. However, there have been very, very few times that I have actually gone to court on a case. That tells me that far and away the vast majority of cases are pleaded out prior to going to court in one way or another. There are so many options; there are so many more options for juveniles than for adults. That's because the [juvenile] courts are set up to rehabilitate the juveniles

So you seldom see judges?

Very, very little. The vast majority of my cases just don't make it all the way to court for me to have contact with judges. It's not always that the district attorney is making a plea to lessen something. Often it's the juvenile saying, "Okay, I'm guilty, I did it." And then we go from there. But a court hearing generally does not happen.

What changes would you make in juvenile law enforcement?

The first thing that comes to my mind is that juveniles who have some kind of psychological problem are getting into trouble not because they are criminals but because they have some psychological problems or conditions. Because of my background in psychology, I am in a unique position to see behind some things. From that perspective, I sometimes see kids who are in the system because they are off their medication. That is sad to see, because the system is not what's going to help them. In my opinion the legal system is not going to help them. The medical community, the counseling community is what's going to help them. Sometimes we catch kids we don't want to put through the system. We also get a lot of pressure from victims who say, "I don't care if he is off his medication, he broke into my car," or "He hit my son. I don't care what his personal problems are, he committed a crime." Sometimes we get pressure from the victims, maybe rightfully so because they were victimized, so you have to do something. You just can't let him off. That puts you in a bind because we don't want to do a disservice to the victim. At the same time our job is to protect the victim, it also is to punish or rehabilitate or get help for the perpetrators. Sometimes those things can be at odds. And sometimes I see kids being put in a system that isn't going to help them.

Would more resources alleviate this problem?

Well, there are [resources], but we can't get them the resources. You can't mandate that they use the resources unless the judge mandates it. Sometimes you don't want to put them in the system, but, in order to get them the help they need or the counseling services they need or the medication that they need, you have to get them in the system in order for that to be a requirement. I can't go to them and say that I am not going to press charges against you but you have to get a counselor. I don't have the authority to do that. My position of power is put them in the system and then have a judge say, "Perhaps you shouldn't be in the system. But, since you are, I am going to mandate that you get counseling, or I am going to mandate detention." Unfortunately, a lot of the time they have to get a criminal record to get help.

Traci Cook

The County Prosecutor

TRACI COOK SERVES AS THE Chief Assistant Prosecuting Attorney
for Harrison County, West Virginia. Her office is located in downtown
Clarksburg, West Virginia, a small city about two hundred miles west of
Washington, D.C., that once was a center of a now-vanished glassmak-
ing industry. Clarksburg is the county seat of Harrison County, home
of the FBI Justice Information Services Division (for criminal data and
forensic activities). It has a population of approximately seventy thousand persons. An elected official, the prosecuting attorney is the chief
legal officer of the county. He or she has areas of responsibility in both
criminal and civil cases. In criminal cases, the prosecuting attorney is
the chief criminal law enforcement officer. In civil cases, the prosecuting attorney acts as legal advisor to the County Commission and other
elected officials.

What experiences did you have before becoming a prosecutor?
I went to law school at West Virginia University. I graduated in 1996. From
there, I was employed with a law firm in Wheeling, and I did domestics, social
security, worker's compensation. Then I looked for a job where I would be in
the courtroom, so I worked for the Public Defender's Office for seven years.
When my boss became the prosecuting attorney, he brought me with him to
the Harrison County Prosecuting Attorney's Office.

*Can you describe the structure of the Harrison County Prosecuting Attorney's
Office?*
Well, the prosecuting attorney is an elected official. Then there are assistants
who work in his name. We all work in his name, so any conflicts of interest,
we're done. There are eleven assistants. We all do different things. We have five
felony attorneys, one tax attorney, three juvenile attorneys, abuse and neglect,
and two misdemeanor attorneys.

As chief assistant, what exactly are your responsibilities to the other assistants?

I oversee all the other assistants. I usually will review important cases with them. When I say important cases, [I mean] anything that will be in the news. My boss is an elected official. Any issues that we believe the Supreme Court might entertain or any issues that might directly affect the outcome of the case, I will review those issues with them. I oversee all the plea bargaining in all the trials, and basically the everyday operation of the office, assignment of cases, all of that.

How does the prosecuting attorney oversee your work?

I okay everything through him, obviously. I meet with him, if not daily, then at least three times per week. We review important cases, where they are going, and maybe what we might expect out of a certain case. We talk about job performance of the assistants. He has most of the initial interaction with the police. They will contact him, he contacts me, and then he and I will discuss the case and figure out which way we are going to go and monitor cases.

Roughly how many cases a year does the office handle?

It keeps increasing. At last count, and this isn't necessarily a good representation, I think in felony cases, last year I think we had six hundred fifty to seven hundred felony cases bound over. That's not necessarily a good representation because a lot of cases can go by the wayside. That doesn't include misdemeanors or juveniles or abuse-neglects.

How many cases does the average assistant carry on his or her desk?

It varies, depending on how busy criminals are. Misdemeanor attorneys usually have about three hundred cases, if not more. Felony attorneys, depending on what stage they are in, we are usually monitoring twenty to thirty bound-over cases, in addition to at least ten indictments, in addition to all of the other things that are coming out there, appeals. So I would guess one hundred to one hundred twenty cases at any given moment out there being worked on at different stages.

Can you talk about what happens when law enforcement decides to arrest somebody? How do they get in contact with your office, and where does the case go from there?

It varies depending on the case. If you are looking at a misdemeanor case that isn't that grand, you have law enforcement with the initial contact. They either obtain a warrant, if they weren't there, if they didn't witness it, unless it's a DUI [driving under the influence] or domestic. They'll obtain a warrant, or, if it happened in their presence, they will arrest the person. Once that criminal complaint is filed on the warrant, after they arrest them, they obtain the warrant. It makes no sense, but they do. They file the criminal complaint, then that is sent to us. If it's a felony case, most of the time it happens the same way, unless it is a murder or a rape. So, depending on the severity of the case, we might be involved from the get-go, even on the initial investigation. If there is a murder [for which there is not] even a suspect, when law enforcement arrives they call us. We get involved when the crime scene team arrives. We might advise them if they need warrants for some search. We advise them if there's enough evidence to even arrest somebody. But if it's a murder, sexual assault, home invasion, we'll be contacted before there is any arrest.

Is that in person or by telephone?

Usually by telephone. My boss, if necessary, will arrive on a crime scene. We try to stay outside of the crime scene, because we put ourselves in a position to become a witness. We don't want to do that because it would ultimately conflict us off the case, especially since we practice in his name, his conflict would affect us all. We try to stay away from the crime scene and advise from the sidelines. Even if we are there, we stay away from it.

How would you rate the quality of police work? Is there variation among police departments? Do you have to oversee departments differently?

Absolutely. We have, for example, in our county, all the small-town police. You might be looking at one or two officers. Usually, because they are lower paid, they have less experience. Then you move onto the larger cities—which in our county are Clarksburg and Bridgeport—they are more experienced, obviously, and they have different departments within their police force. They have detectives versus road patrol and lieutenants and on up. The detectives who might arrive on a crime scene, a serious crime, obviously are more trained than a small-town officer. Then you have the sheriff's department that oversees the whole county outside of the cities. They also have a detectives' division, so they have more training than the small towns. Then you have the state police, they are obviously the best trained. There is the most funding for them. Everybody who is in law enforcement is trained at the state police academy.

Do you find that you have to educate police?

Absolutely. I tried on occasion to have trainings, for example, if there is an issue or if we have a new case. We just had a couple of cases that came down from the U.S. Supreme Court that I think directly affect just about every day of police work. I will send out a bulletin to the chiefs and the departments saying, "This case just came down, here is something we can use to our advantage." Yes, we educate them daily. They call us daily.

When a case comes into your office, is there an evaluation of the arrests or allegations of crime?

Based on the volume that comes into our office, we don't do an initial review of the case. The case gets immediately assigned to an attorney, and that attorney is responsible for reviewing the case. For example, Friday I had somebody come in my office who had just received a felony case. They read the criminal complaint and investigation. They gave it to me and asked what I thought. On first blush, I thought this is an illegal search; we will never win that case. So from there we will move to dismiss that case, because anything that was obtained pursuant to an illegal search was illegally obtained, and we will never be able to use any of it. It's really up to the attorney who has the initial contact with the case to review it.

Do the assistant prosecuting attorneys have the authority to dismiss the case on their own, or do they have to review it with you?

If it is a misdemeanor case, they have the authority to dismiss it on their own. But, for the most part, they will come and ask me my opinion, because they don't want to get themselves into a bind with law enforcement. Law enforcement agencies are very territorial about their cases.

Beyond illegal searches, are there fairly frequent reasons for dismissals?

Illegal arrest. Ultimately that leads to an illegal search or obtaining evidence illegally. And illegal arrests, because what the person did is not a crime. Sometimes that happens [*laughs*], it really wasn't a crime.

Are there certain crimes that you wouldn't prosecute?

We have the ability to do pretrial diversions, so if the case is not important to us, we might put it on a pretrial diversion. Then if the person is good, we dismiss it. We give them, like, six months to be good. They're good.

Diversions are those decisions made by the individual assistants?

It depends on the type of case. Misdemeanors, I leave the assistants alone, they know what they are doing. Plus, the volume in the Magistrate Court is unbelievable. We have two attorneys who probably handle in a year approximately seven thousand cases. That's enormous.

What are the reasons for diversions?

Age of the defendant. Sometimes, it's age. They are older and they have no criminal history. The type of crime, it wasn't serious, or the nature of the crime. Some of our laws are very liberal. For example, if you have two people in a bar and one shoves another, that's battery. It carries up to a year in jail; they don't need to go to jail, but they need to have a record. We would do a diversion on that.

Diversion usually results in what kind of outcome?

A dismissal. And, ultimately, they can then expunge their record, so it's not even reflected that they were arrested and then dismissed.

Are people ever diverted to treatment or assigned to the Alcoholics Anonymous program?

As a diversion, not necessarily. Can it be used? Yes, but if we're looking at someone who has an addiction, it's very seldom used. Depending on, again, the person. I had an individual about six months ago who was thirty-five years old, never been in trouble. She was in a car accident and, as a result, was prescribed prescription medication, and it led to an addiction. She stole a prescription slip from her doctor and passed it. That woman doesn't need a felony record—because that is a felony. I mean she had zero criminal history, a very nice woman, a nice family, but she got herself into a bad situation. We put her in drug treatment and pretrial diversion. If she is good in a year, she can expunge her record.

When the assistants get misdemeanors, do they make contact with law enforcement?

Usually it's a high volume in this area. I am not sure how larger cities handle it. We have two attorneys and anywhere from six thousand to seven thousand cases per year. So they're each looking at three thousand to three thousand five hundred cases per year, and that's a lot. In a day, they are in court from 9:00 A.M. until 4:00 P.M. And their cases are usually doubled up, sometimes every fifteen minutes. Usually, they're doubled up and running from magistrate to magistrate. So there's not a whole lot of time for them to sit down and make a phone call. A lot of those cases, depending on their initial review, and unless it's going to a jury trial, a lot of times we meet the victims at the hearing, because those cases move so quickly [and] are such high volume.

Do they meet with the defendant and/or defense counsel before the hearing?

It will be at the hearing. When I was a public defender, we started requesting jury trials in every case. Why? Because people don't have time to try every case, and we knew this. So we use time to our advantage against the State. We moved for a jury trial in every single case. That gives us the pretrial hearing to show up; there is no consequence at that hearing from the State's perspective. You can use it to meet the officer, discuss the case, and meet the victims. We're not looking at a trial at that time. It's kind of like a pretrial meeting if you want. So that gives everybody an opportunity to get together.

As a prosecutor, do you also request jury trials?

Absolutely.

Is it pretty standard that there is this pretrial hearing that is going to serve as a meeting for the parties to become acquainted?

Based on the rules of procedure, as a defense attorney, you have to meet with your clients very quickly, especially on misdemeanors. Often, you're dealing with people who don't have phones. They move all the time, so you might not meet with your client. It was all to their benefit to request it even without the defendant's knowledge, because you only have a certain number of days to do that. If they are in jail, you have ten days. If they're not in jail, you have twenty days to request a jury trial. If not, it's waived. So initially when I got a case I requested a jury trial. Also, it was strategic, because I knew that prosecutors can't try that many cases. Might as well use that to my advantage.

And that results in a plea bargain?

Absolutely

At the pretrial meeting?

Yeah.

Is a magistrate present during that?

Yes. Not for negotiations, but Magistrate Court is very, very informal. I don't know about other places, but here it's very informal. They have a kind of counter, a lunch counter if you will, and we'll stand there and negotiate a plea and the magistrates are standing right there, also. They are not a part of it by any means, and they are not allowed to have any input, but they hear it all.

Given the large volume, there must be some kind of standard rate for a large number of cases.

Absolutely. A lot of cases result in fines, depending on the severity of the case. Some cases we take a lot more seriously, like domestics, depending on the facts and the history. Also DUIs. They're probably the two highest volume cases, and we take those fairly seriously. There are certain sentences that are mandatory, but we're also looking at a county budget and every time we put someone in jail because it's like putting them up at the Hilton for a night. We take that into account, also. It costs us. When I say the Hilton, I mean the Hilton in a small town; it costs us, I think, fifty-three dollars per night to house somebody. There is cost-benefit component to these negotiations.

Are there large numbers of people put on probation?

Yes, unsupervised probation out of Magistrate Court. So, as long as they are not arrested, they'll be fine. So nobody's looking over them to make sure they're not drinking or whatever.

Beyond domestic violence and DUI, are there any other kinds of cases that dominate the misdemeanor docket?

Simple batteries, assaults, those are the majority of cases. Then you have a destruction of property, petit larceny, shoplifting, and simple drug possession thrown in there every so often.

How likely is it that a case will be plea bargained?

I would say more than ninety percent of cases end up in a plea, if not higher. It might even be like ninety-eight percent. It's that predominant.

Who makes the initial offer?

It depends on the case and defense counsel, but a lot of times it's the State, just to resolve the case, and there might be a counteroffer.

A good defense attorney probably knows ahead of time what they're going to get?

Yes, especially in the public defender's office. The public defenders and prosecutors work together all day, every day, and they pretty much know what's going to happen. You know each other's personalities.

So it's a fairly standard courtroom environment?

Absolutely, and there are certain magistrates who you know beforehand will or will not do something. So, as a defendant, there are certain magistrates who you're going to be praying you get, because they're not going to send you to jail. Whereas others have these little schedules, which are unconstitutional, but they have them anyway, schedules that say if you commit this crime you're going to go to jail for X number of days. It's kind of crazy.

There are nonlawyer magistrates in this state?
Yes.

Do you think that is a benefit to certain people or a detriment to certain people?
I think it is a detriment.

Why would you say that?
With all due respect, the magistrates try. They're sent to training, but there are a number of issues that are seen consistently in magistrate court, just by the sheer volume, that are important issues that they don't know how to handle. You know, when I started as a defense attorney, I had to start with: there's this thing, it's called the Constitution; and there's this amendment that's called the Fourth Amendment; and here's what it says, but here's what it really means if you apply the law. When you have to start there, you're in a bad way.

Do you think that quality of magistrates adversely affects defense and prosecution equally, or is it is more likely to affect negatively the defense?
Defense and the defendants.

In felony cases, what happens when the prosecution's office takes over?
With misdemeanors the charging instrument is a criminal complaint filled out by the police officer who swears to it. You are officially charged with a misdemeanor. When you are looking at a felony, there is a criminal complaint that can initiate the felony case, but from there you go to magistrate court and have a preliminary hearing. All that is to determine if there is enough evidence, probable cause, but it really is proving that it's more likely than not that the person named in the complaint committed this crime. That's basically it. Once that's determined, then that case is bound over to circuit court (superior trial court). Once it's bound over to circuit court, the person still isn't officially charged. We then have to go to grand jury, because every person has the right for the return of an indictment, or a formal charge, by the grand jury upon a felony charge. Once that is done, then you are formally charged with a felony case. The type of case determines how quickly we're going to get to the grand jury. If we have a murder case, and it has numerous pieces of physical evidence that need to be tested by our crime lab, we're looking at around six months, depending upon the volume that's at the crime lab, before that ever gets tested. We will pull that case from at least one grand jury, and then indict them in the following grand jury. That could take six months, for example.

Is the grand jury scheduled quarterly?
Yes, they meet every four months. In my county it is January, May, and September, and it varies depending on what county you're in. It's statutorily mandated when different counties meet. Large cities have grand juries going on all the time. They have grand juries literally meeting all the time, in multiples, all

the time. We have one grand jury that comes in at the start of a term of court. They meet for a week and review all the cases. They return indictments at the end of the week, and that's the only time that we have indictments returned.

Is there ever any effort to negotiate a plea with the defendant before a case gets to the grand jury?

Absolutely, and I will tell you that varies from county to county. It depends upon how you want to run your office. When I was at the public defender's office, they basically indicted everybody. So you're looking [at] about one hundred to one hundred twenty indictments per term. With five felony attorneys in our office, you're looking at twenty to twenty-five felonies per attorney. We have new trial court rules that we have to follow. There are certain things that we as the State have to do. With that volume, you might get all those cases done, but they're not going to be done very well. So when my boss took over, he and I decided that we were going to push settling cases. If they're going to be settled anyway, why waste everybody's time and paper, and even the court's time, and do every case halfway rather [than] concentrating on cases that need to be done? As I told you before, you have the right to be charged by indictment. That is a defendant's right. But you can waive that right, as you can waive any right, and agree to be charged by way of what we call an information, which is also a charging document. It looks the same as an indictment, but the prosecutors file that rather than the grand jury returning it. The defendant agrees to be charged by way of information. We can file that felony case against them. We do that regularly, and we settle at least half of our cases before indictment that way. It has led to better results. I know that is a general statement, but our indictments and our cases are now done much better than they were before we were there.

Is there a benefit for the defendant to be charged by information?

There is a benefit. Usually for a defendant, if they commit a felony case, there are usually numerous other charges that are attached to that. Just as a quick little lesson, if a defendant is charged with a misdemeanor and a felony, and they arise out of the same case, same transaction, same event, and we charge them at the same time, the defendant has a right to waive those cases up to the circuit court. With the misdemeanors, they also have the right to object to my moving them with the felony case. What that means is, I would then be stuck trying the same case in two different courts. I don't have my investigators or my police officers file any misdemeanors if there is a felony case attached to it. They merely file the felony. We will take care of the misdemeanors later. We will charge them in circuit court, to keep me out of magistrate court and [to keep from] separating the case. With that, though, when the defendant is bound over on a felony case, it might just be one felony case, but he might have ten misdemeanors attached. The judge will never know that. So the defendant's benefit might be ultimately at sentencing, because the judge doesn't know he committed also all these other crimes when he committed this offense. A lot of times, when we look at property cases, like forgery and uttering [issuing checks without sufficient funds on deposit], there might be thirty-four counts. We charge them with one to get them arrested, get them on bond, get it over to circuit court. When we indict them, we're going to charge them with thirty-four counts of it. They're only bound over on one. The judge won't know about the other ones, or he might only know about three or four. So for the defendant, it's a benefit. We're not hiding it from the judge. He might know in the presentence investigation what the person has done. Ultimately, that defendant doesn't have a record with thirty-four counts on it.

That works into the defense attorney's calculus of whether to allow an information filing to be used?
Absolutely.

Are preliminary hearings frequently used?
It might be waived by the defendant, but they have to be held. There are two ways that we can do a case. Let's say an investigator says this felony charge was committed. I can now have the defendant arrested and just present the case straight to the grand jury, but I don't like to do that. The reason why is that there is a lot to be done between the time the crime is committed and an indictment. Once you get an indictment, you're scheduled for trial. It might be in three weeks. So you want to make sure your case is put together. So my rule is officers' arrest for all felonies. Once they are arrested, they have a right to a preliminary hearing, the defendant does. Basically, it's like a check in our system that says you've been arrested for a felony that's a serious crime. Your bond is probably high. We're going to make sure that there's enough evidence to hold you, because all that the magistrate sees before the preliminary hearing is what's on paper. This is a check in the system. It's due process. Let's see if there is enough evidence.

The preliminary hearing is before a magistrate?
That is correct.

Do you go in and present evidence to show that you have enough to arrest him?
Correct. The rules of procedure and rules of evidence are a little bit lax on the preliminary hearing. It's a lesser standard for us, too. It's merely probable cause; it's not beyond a reasonable doubt. It's just a check in the system to make sure that we're not holding people in jail and/or—because eventually they might make bond—on bond without probable cause.

Do defense attorneys generally participate in the preliminary hearing?
It's a fundamental stage in the process. So before the preliminary hearing they have the right, if they can afford counsel, [they have] to hire counsel, but if [they] can't afford counsel, [they have] counsel appointed. Counsel is present at that hearing. We can go through with the hearing, and a defense attorney might learn things about the case. For example, some of the bigger issues in cases are evidentiary issues, arrest issues, and statements. They might use it as

a discovery tool. Say I'm going to put the officer on the stand. They are going to ask questions to see if they might have an issue as to a legal confession. It's not to be used as a discovery tool, but it is used as a discovery tool.

Is the preliminary hearing scheduled weeks or months before the grand jury indictment?

Yes, it actually runs from arrest. If they are in jail, then they have the right to a preliminary hearing within ten days; if they are out of jail, twenty days.

You mentioned bail. Is there usually a separate hearing to set it?

Bond is done without counsel. It is not a fundamental stage in the process. Once a person is arrested, if they are arrested in the middle of the night, it will be held the next morning. They will be arraigned. People are arraigned every single day. Now we have video conferencing to do arraignment by video. Arraignment is usually done the very next day, and bond is set. Now if preliminary bond is high, the defense attorney might move for the bond to be reduced, but bond is already set by the time we get there.

You request cash, not property bond?

Generally property bond, but bondsmen a lot of times.

So the defendant would have a contract bond with a bondsman?

Correct. They'll post surety, and they pay the bondsman ten percent of what their bond is, sometimes twenty percent. It depends on the bondsman.

How many people are released on their own recognizance?

Very few in our county.

When does the plea bargaining start?

It can start from the get-go. On felony cases it can start at the preliminary hearing, depending on what the case is. There are times when a felony case will be pleaded down to a misdemeanor at the preliminary hearing. For example, it's a grand larceny. Somebody went to J. C. Penney, and they stole a bunch of clothes worth one thousand fifty dollars. One thousand dollars is our cutoff for misdemeanor. We might plea that down at the preliminary hearing to a misdemeanor. If it's third-offense DUI, and we can't find the priors, we might plead that down. The priors might be from New Jersey, some New Jersey municipal court, and we're never going to be able to get someone from the municipal court of New Jersey to come here. So we'll do a lesser DUI for a plea.

So those are the motivations on the State's part?

Absolutely.

Do the defense attorneys feel you out?

Absolutely, they want to always get it down to a misdemeanor.

And they're doing this at the preliminary hearing?

Plea bargaining starts from the moment the defense attorney and the prosecutor meet. From the get-go.

Do you have scheduled meetings to plea bargain? Do you have anything like that?

Not formally. On felony cases I have my attorneys usually start reviewing the cases and sending out plea offers about a month and a half before indictments are going to come about. So about a month and a half before the grand jury meets, I want them to be sending out letters, reviewing their cases, figuring out what it is they're expecting out of this case, and sending out plea offers. I would say about half of our cases are settled that way before indictment. I would say three-quarters of them plead after indictment.

You make the offers?

Yes, most of the time we make the offers.

Did you say you instruct your assistant to make an offer?

No, I have them review their cases and see what they expect out of the case. If they are going to, or they think they can be pled. For example, I have a murder case. We're not going to be pleading that. We're going to go to indictment. I have a sexual assault on a child. We're going to go to indictment. The defense attorney need not even bother me, because I won't be bothered. I won't send out a letter of an offer on that. It depends on the case. Property cases, we try to move them along.

Is there kind of a standard "going rate" for types of crimes?

Yes, but we take that from our judges. We know what to expect if we have gone to trial. I've gone to trial on a case where the judge convicted a woman of seventeen felonies, which would be eight forgeries, eight utterings, and a conspiracy to commit forgery. Everything was run together into a one-to-ten [year] sentence. Because of [experiences like this] I know what the judge is going to do and.the defense attorney knows what the judge is going to do, I'm not going to offer them something that they're not going to get if we were to go to trial. Based on experience, we know what the judges will ultimately do, based on criminal history, based on what the crimes are, how the case is eventually going to end up. So that's what our offer usually is.

So when you're bargaining, usually, your offer is based on the strength of your case and the criminal history of the defendant?

Yes.

Is anything else considered?

The crime, the type of crime. Age of the defendant. I have two cases dealing with burglary, and I've been thinking about this, because the judge is going to be curious about what I'm doing. They are almost mirror images of each other, these two cases. The defendants are about the same age. The events are about the same, but for one issue. You know, defendant A on the one side, who we gave a pretrial diversion to before. He really has no criminal history. He kind of walked through the door, grabbed a purse off his best friend's mom, stole it, off he goes. We gave him a pretrial diversion. He tested positive for drugs. We couldn't get him to come in, but he found his father in the fetal position after having a stroke. That's what kind of led him back down the path. So I have this case over here, defendant B, this guy is a little bit younger, no criminal history until this event, and since then he has committed seven other misdemeanors, unrelated. While he's been on bond he also committed a crime, which was possession of a controlled substance. In addition, this guy pulled a knife on the homeowner when he caught him in the act and was chasing him out [of] the house, even though the defendant has known the victim his entire life. But ultimately the cases are very similar. There are two defendants with no criminal history at the time they committed these felonies. Okay, but they're very similar cases. I'm giving B a felony and giving A a misdemeanor. Now I'm going to have to justify that to the judge. Why, he pulled the knife, and he's committed seven misdemeanors since then. This guy's got nothing. It really depends upon the case, the person, and also the strength of case. If I think a confession is going to be suppressed and that's all I have, I'm going to offer him something.

Do most defendants know they are going to plea-bargain out?
Yes, most of the defense attorneys plan to plea-bargain out. Maybe I should say that.

Do you see much of the defendant during this process, or is it entirely up to counsel?
It is entirely with counsel.

And is the plea bargain conducted in person, by telephone, or other means?
Depends on time. Sometimes by letter.

To what degree do victims participate?
I okay every plea with the victim. Ultimately, it's not their decision. It's the State's case, but I want their input. I'm not going to leave them out in the cold. It was their house that was broken into, not mine. I let them know what I'm going to offer. If it is a high-profile case, or obviously a serious crime, I bring them in. We meet in person. I review, I start at the very beginning. I usually meet them the week that I get the case. I sit them down, tell them what to expect, what I expect out of the case, the ins and outs of how the system works, and I meet with them all the time. I never make a decision without them.

Do law enforcement officers ever try to affect the plea bargain?
Oh, yes, they do. They think everybody should go to prison. It's not going to happen, we can't afford it. It depends on the officer, but there are lots of officers out there who think that they are the last word, and it can get very frustrating at times. I tell them, if you disagree with my plea, you tell the judge. They might disagree with me, we might get into arguments, but ultimately when we get into court, I've never had any officer tell the court that they disagree with me.

Could you describe what cases are more likely to go to trial?
Murders, child sexual assaults, more serious cases. The more time, the more at stake, the less likely we are to use plea bargaining.

When I first started ten years ago as a defense attorney, maybe there were five child sexual assaults a year. Today, we're looking at one per week. It's ridiculous to me. And it's reflected in the change in the sentencing now. Although it's going to be to everybody's detriment, sentencing was just changed. It was fifteen to thirty-five; now it's twenty-five to life. You get more time for sexually assaulting a child than you do for murdering somebody, first-degree murder in this state.

Is the upsurge in child sexual assaults a function of more reporting on the part of victims?
Yes.

Has the murder rate gone up as well?
Yeah, all violent crime is up. Drugs.

Do drugs play a significant role in violent crime?
Absolutely, except marijuana. I would rather have a person smoke marijuana than drink alcohol, because they're less violent. I would say ninety percent of defendants arrested for violent crimes are under the influence of alcohol or some drug other than marijuana. The only crime marijuana users commit is possession of marijuana.

When you decide not to plea bargain, or the bargain is rejected, do you enter into discovery?
It depends on the crime. When a defendant chooses to waive a preliminary hearing that's in exchange for discovery, because I don't have to provide discovery until fourteen days after indictment, the defense attorney will use the hearing to get that discovery from me way ahead of time. If there's a waiver at the preliminary hearing, it's for early discovery, to see the police report.

Do the defense attorneys file motions at this point, and, if so, how many on average?
Yes, they do. The number depends on the case. There are standard motions, like two lines long, that are filed in every case, probably five of these. I have a murder case right now, and I've been in pretrial hearings for the last three days. It depends on the case, it depends on the evidence.

Do you ever do any depositions?
I've done one, in a habeas proceeding. There's no right to a deposition in a criminal case. For as important of an issue as it is, criminal defense attorneys walk into a courtroom much less prepared than a civil attorney, even though there's a lot more at stake.

Does the judge hold a pretrial conference?
No. Under our new trial court rules, we have to have our own discovery conference. I send defense counsel a letter telling them to call me, and whenever it's convenient for them, we'll go over all my discovery. If there's anything else you want, let me know.

In most states, a judge will set trial date whenever a spot is available on his or her calendar. West Virginia does it differently. The trials tend to be held in three or four periods a year, is that correct?

Yes, we have the term of courts. In our county we have three judges, and each has a term of court. This term, for example, is Judge Lewis Marks. We had indictments returned, and then we meet informally in the judge's chambers, defense counsel and prosecutors, we come up with a trial calendar, so everything is scheduled. Then we have the formal arraignment on the indictment. He will tell us motions are due by a specific date—"I want you all to meet and confer and exchange discovery"—so we do it on our own by this date. If you filed a motion for a pretrial hearing, it goes from there.

Does this period of discovery inspire plea-bargain offers from the defense counsel?

It absolutely can. I hate to be redundant, but it's really a function of the kind of case I have. If it's a sexual assault case and the crime lab has a lag time, I might not have the DNA results until a month after indictment. When the DNA results come and they're identified, they're ready to bargain, to take what we offer.

Are the trials you have mostly jury trials?

Yes, there have been only two felony bench trials that have taken place in the ten years I've been there.

Do you do engage in voir dire?

Yes, but I try to limit it. If you read any trial book or go to any conference, they say voir dire is the absolute most important step in trial, and I don't disagree, but I think it's a double-edged sword. If you take up too much of the potential jurors' time, they're tired of you, they're done with you. So I try to be as precise in my questions as possible. There are times when we fail. I try as best I can to come up with questions that will elicit the insight I need, without wasting their time. I could take four hours if I wanted to, but they're going to hate me by the end of it.

Does counsel ask all the questions during voir dire, or does the judge participate?

There are general voir dires that the judge will ask. Then he permits the lawyers to question the potential jurors as a group. We did have a high-profile murder case two years ago where we brought every potential juror in and asked them individual questions. That took four days.

What leads to your request to dismiss jurors for cause?

I love it when they walk up and say the defendant is guilty. We had this guy who, in my opinion, his attorney did a disservice to this guy. There was obviously something wrong with this guy. I hate to put it so bluntly, but I told his defense attorney that she should hire a whore who is a psychiatrist who will find him not criminally responsible because he is insane, and I'll put him in a mental institution for the next five years, because something was wrong with this guy. All you had to do was look at him. It was the safest place for him.

I had heard the stories from the jail, what happened to this guy. He was completely out there. But in that particular case, in voir dire, we had a juror walk up and say, "Of course he's guilty, look at him!" He was dismissed for cause.

I once had a potential juror who was the mother of a client I had defended in a murder case when I was a defense attorney. Not that I didn't do a good job for him, because he's already out. But this was another murder case, and I didn't think she needed to be on that jury. I knew her well from working on her son's case, and I asked her if she honestly can sit in judgment of this person charged with murder, given your son's situation. She said yes. Then the next day she came in, said I was right, she can't be fair. She was dismissed for cause.

Do you use peremptory challenges with any frequency?

We have to. This state is different in a couple ways. First, we have twenty potential jurors, and the State gets two peremptories, and the defense gets six. Try to tell me that's fair. In most states it's an even number. The Prosecuting Attorneys Institute petitions every year to try to change it. Why should the State, the people, have any less rights than the defendant? I know we have to protect the defendant, but not to the detriment of society. We also have unanimous verdicts, too. We do the peremptory challenges all at once. We all ask our questions at the same time, the judge, the prosecutor, and the defense lawyers, then use our two and their six at the same time. It's not like what you see in the movies; we don't use them as we go along.

What is it that gets you to dismiss a potential juror off the jury with a peremptory challenge?

It depends. If I'm doing a sexual assault case, and you have no children, I may not keep you because everybody else has children or grandchildren. If I have a twenty-year-old who stole a car, I'm not going to keep a twenty-year-old guy. I think at times defense attorneys border on unconstitutional behavior and challenge based on race and gender. I think they do it all the time. I don't.

How long do trials usually take?

If you asked the judges, mine run forever [*laughs*]. It depends on the crime. A property crime takes one to two days max. A murder case, possibly two weeks. I used to wonder how they could have these trials that take three months, like in California. Then I talked to a prosecutor out there, and they don't keep the kind of schedule that our judges do. We start at 8:00 A.M., we end at 5:00 P.M., we get a couple ten-minute breaks and a quick lunch, but most of the time we're working, even if the jury is off doing something. It's run like a tight ship. It's all that the judge concentrates on. We never keep the jury waiting, so we get these things in and out. We're efficient.

Roughly, how many witnesses do you normally call?

Average number, for the average case, I would say seven. In a murder case, it might be twenty, because we have to deal with change of custody, where every person who touches a piece of evidence has to testify in court about their handling of it. So that can take up a lot of time and adds witnesses. Whereas in property crime or a malicious wounding case, you might have three witnesses in that case.

What kind of defenses do you see?

[*Laughs*] It's my favorite, the "so'du'it" defense: "Some other dude did it" defense. That happens a lot. A lot, especially in the last five years, of going after the police [interrogations]. We've had confessions that juries have completely disregarded. I wouldn't say they were great confessions. When I read them, I thought, "Let the defendant tell you what happened. Don't tell them what happened and have them agree to what you said." There is a lot of going after the police, a lot.

Overall, how would you rate the effectiveness of juries?

They do their job. I might disagree with them sometimes, but they do their job. I think they take it very seriously. I would love to be a fly on a wall in a jury deliberation.

How would you rate the judges in your county with legal issues, such as the admissibility of evidence and so on? Are they fair?

Yes. I have to say that all three of our judges were criminal defense attorneys; one did DUI, and the other two general criminal defense. I haven't had the opportunity to argue before a lot of other judges, a little bit as a special prosecutor, but they are very fair-minded. I've seen them suppress confessions in a murder case because of the law. I've seen them admit what we call wrongful disposition to children. For example, I had a defendant who confessed to sexually assaulting five different children. I was able to use all those children in each individual case; so if I tried victim A, I could use the other four, too, to make the case against the defendant, and so on. It's evidence that we use to show a lustful disposition towards children. It's admissible. Obviously, the judge and the defense attorney aren't going to agree with a guy who assaults a child, but the judge said on the record, "I don't agree with wrongful disposition, it's a bad law, but based on the law, I have to admit this information." He didn't want me to use it because he thinks it's unfair, but based on this motion and how the law stands, he said he had to allow it. So I think the judges are very fair, middle of the road.

Once the jury comes back with a sentence of guilty, what's your role in sentencing?

It is us versus them. The judge will have a presentence report done on the defendant, so he can learn as much as he possibly can about that particular defendant. In addition, there are times when we learn things from the presentencing report. We make a recommendation to the judge, what we believe is appropriate; the defense makes a recommendation; but ultimately it's the judge's decision.

Is there any bargaining at this ultimate stage in the process?

No. For the most part, plea bargaining is done at that point. We have a verdict.

How are juvenile crimes handled differently from adult crimes?

There are very few crimes in this state that are automatically permitted to be transferred to adult status. I use that very sparingly. In my opinion, a fourteen-year-old is just not the same as a twenty-year-old. They might commit the same crime, but they don't see it the same way. We do treat them very differently, and so does the system. It's not about locking them up. It's about treating them and rehabilitating them. Juvenile proceedings are held *in camera*, not open to the public.

Is there plea bargaining in juvenile cases, too?

Absolutely. When we're at a point where the juvenile is the target of a hearing, that juvenile has a lot of cases pending against him. It's serious. Plea bargaining is used a lot, but it's different. It's not about time, it's about treatment and rehabilitation and what's in the best interest of that child. I think being a defense attorney in a juvenile case is difficult because that's your job, the best interest of the child, and not necessarily just defending them. Defense attorneys have to take a different perspective; judges, too.

We have lockdown facilities, juvenile prisons if you will, but they are the last resort. It is the absolute last resort. We are striving for rehabilitating the child. It's not about putting them in lockdown. It's about meeting monthly, reviewing their cases monthly, with the department and the prosecutors. The judge will review the file every three months to make sure that kid has everything that's available for him. It is the most labor-intensive area in our office.

You have specialists for that in your office?

Yes. Because of judicial reviews, the multidisciplinary team meetings that have to take place regularly, there's no way for felony attorneys to work that into their calendar. Juveniles are just so labor intensive.

What are the positive and negative aspects of your job?

[*Laughs*] Positives? Let's start there. I'm a liberal, which is kind of bad in my profession, but I've come to learn that there are definitely people who need to be separated from society. There is nothing else that can be done with them, and that's a positive for me, when I separate them from society, when I keep another person from becoming a victim. I constantly see victims who have had terrible things happen to their lives, and the only way I can stay positive about it is that there won't be another one.

Negatives. I don't know if there are negatives. Defense attorneys [*laughs*]? I used to be one, seven years. I like my job. I like what I do. I have the chance to help. Even though some people have to be separated from society, I can give somebody a break, too—if they're deserving and might actually use it.

David Godwin

The Federal Prosecutor

DAVID GODWIN IS AN ASSISTANT United States Attorney (AUSA), a federal prosecutor. His office is in the federal building that is just down the
street from the office of Traci Cook. However, as revealed in this interview, federal prosecution is quite different. AUSAs serve under United
States Attorneys, employees of the United States Department of Justice,
who are appointed by the president. There is one United States Attorney's
office for ninety-two federal judicial districts, including at least one district in each state, the District of Columbia, Puerto Rico, and the Virgin
Islands. One U. S. Attorney serves the separate judicial districts of Guam
and the Northern Mariana Islands. Mr. Godwin's primary responsibility is to prosecute federal crimes, largely crimes that involve events that
occur across state lines, such as the importation and distribution of illegal
drugs. Other duties of U.S. Attorney's offices include the prosecution and
defense of civil cases in which the United States is a party and the collection of debts owed the federal government. As in many federal buildings,
security personnel escorted the interviewer to Godwin's office.

Could you please tell me about your path into the legal profession?
I grew up in different communities in West Virginia. The little town of Buck-
hannon has been my home since 1965, when I was in high school. I went to
West Virginia Wesleyan College and graduated in 1972. I spent four years in
the United States Navy as an intelligence officer. In 1976 I started law school
at West Virginia University, and I graduated in 1979.

I am not sure I can really tell you how I got into the law. It was a process of
elimination more than it was a particular goal. I had thought about going to law
school the whole way through college. I took the LSAT [Law School Admission
Test] when I was in college. I really liked the Navy, and I seriously considered
staying. So I got down to the options of staying in the Navy for a career or going
to law school. So I chose law school, and I ended up in a legal career.

How did you first become a prosecutor?

When I was at law student at West Virginia University, I had a summer intern job, two summers, working for the [state] prosecuting attorney in Upshur County. He then hired me when I got out of law school. I became an assistant prosecuting attorney for Upshur County in 1979. He was going to run for judge in 1984 when the judge was retiring down there. I was going to run for prosecuting attorney. Neither job was real lucrative, especially assistant prosecuting attorney. At the last minute, my boss changed his mind. He wanted to stay as prosecutor. I was not the type to run against my boss, so I had a friend who was an AUSA in this district. He had been in law school with me and had been a law clerk with one of the judges here. We talked, and I found out there was an opening on the staff. I called the U.S. Attorney, submitted my resume, and I went through an interview, and he hired me. That was in 1984, June 4, 1984.

So did the U.S. Attorney base your selection to the position on merit and civil service selection, or was it a political choice?

Neither. It's called "excepted service." We are not civil service, at least in the U.S. Attorney's office. Now the attorneys in the main justice divisions in Washington, they are on a GS [civil service] scale. There is job security and regulations regarding the employment. It is not civil service, but it's pretty much a parallel. So I don't serve at the pleasure of the U.S. Attorney. I could be discharged if that were approved by the Deputy Attorney General. It would have to be upon showing of misconduct or incompetence. There are procedures to get rid of an AUSA that are similar to civil service.

You have therefore worked under U.S. Attorneys appointed by presidents of both political parties?

Yes. I've served under the same U.S. Attorney through both of Reagan's terms and George H. W. Bush's term. That was Mr. Kolibash, the man who hired me. That was in President Reagan's first term. Mr. Wilmoth came on when Clinton became president. He didn't stay the entire time. He left in 1999, and I was appointed by the Attorney General and served as U.S. Attorney for the interim period. There is a statute that governs that. It is a way to keep the position filled when there is not a presidential appointee available. Then, Melvin C. Kahle came on board as a presidential appointee in 1999. I left the district on details—special assignments—between 2001 and 2004, when Tom Johnston became the U.S. Attorney in the George W. Bush administration.

How is your office organized?

Clarksburg is a branch office. The headquarters office is in Wheeling, and that will continue. That is where the administrative division and the bulk of the human resources of the district are: the U.S. Attorney, along with the first assistant, the civil chief, and the criminal chief. There are branch offices in Clarksburg, Elkins, and Martinsburg. We have four attorneys in this office for the Northern District (of West Virginia). We have jurisdiction over everything federal in that area. My particular work isn't limited by law or policy to the Clarksburg area. As a practical matter, most of my cases are ones that are investigated in this area—North Central West Virginia. But I also have cases in Martinsburg and Wheeling.

Which federal courts do you appear before?
We have a district judge, the Chief Judge, here in Clarksburg. There is also a U.S. Magistrate Judge here. There is a district judge and a full-time magistrate judge in Wheeling. There is a senior district judge in Elkins, and a full-time judge and part-time magistrate in Martinsburg. The judge there is also a general in the reserves and right now is off in the army.

What sort of cases does your office address? Do they include civil and criminal cases?
The staff does civil business, but I don't. When I first started, I did a variety of work, including civil work, but the staff has grown. Now we have a civil division that operates out of Wheeling that handles all the civil cases that involve the federal government. They handle a wide variety of cases—from the postman kicking your dog to running over you with a mail truck; a VA [Veteran's Administration] doctor is accused of malpractice; social security, tax cases, and bankruptcy, where the U.S. government has an interest at stake. [But] three-fourths of our lawyers work on criminal cases.

How many cases are you currently prosecuting?
Right now I have around twenty in court in some way and another dozen or so under investigation and a couple in appellate courts. Only at one point did I have but one case to work on. I prosecuted the Mountaineer Militia [a white-supremacist organization] when I was First Assistant Criminal Chief, and I had administrative responsibilities. A lot of those were put on hold for a year when I spent the vast amount of my time on that one case. That's not the normal situation. In this district this year about half of the cases are drug offenses, and about a fourth are gun-related. The other fourth are a wide range: fraud, bank robberies.

How do you handle cases that involve the commission of both federal and state crimes?
There are a lot of illegal acts that can be prosecuted by either government or, legally, can be prosecuted by both governments. If you go and talk to state prosecutors, you get a different perspective from different ones, based on their experiences. But it is not a matter of what we decide to "leave" to them. We can't take every case we could take, which could be a substantial part of the state caseload. A lot of things can be tied to interstate commerce. In drug work, we basically have the same statutes.

We make a determination if we are going to work on a particular case for several reasons. If the state is pursuing the same issue, my approach has been that I will call the state prosecutor, and we discuss if they want to continue with it or not. I have never told a state prosecutor, "I don't care what you say, it's our case and it's not your case." I have never ever done that or heard that was done.

One reason I don't do that is that it would be self-defeating. Even though the Constitution allows both governments to prosecute a person for the very same act, double jeopardy doesn't protect against that. The Department of Justice has a policy called the Petite policy [established by the U.S. Supreme Court in Petite v. United States 1960], so that if the state takes a criminal action to disposition, dismissal, plea agreement, conviction, or whatever, we're precluded from proceeding on the same facts unless I get approval from the Department of Justice in Washington and demonstrate that there is some substantial federal interest that the state didn't address. I don't want to find myself in a position where I have a case going and the state takes a plea, and then I have to say I can't go ahead with this case. I don't want to find myself in that situation, so I always try to work out things in advance. I have only had one occasion where I indicted someone not knowing they had already been charged in state court, in New Jersey. I dismissed it. I had only one case where I prosecuted someone for the very same acts for which he had been prosecuted and punished in state court. We had to go through a process to show the federal interest involved was not addressed.

What is the first step in a criminal prosecution?

The most common way a case comes in is a federal agent comes in to see me. He says, "We had this reported. We started on this investigation. Here's what it involves. Is the U.S. Attorney willing to take the case?" They don't want to undertake a case we can't prosecute, because we can't prosecute everything. We have guidelines as to what we can't or won't take. They [the guidelines] are done district by district.

What happens then?

After we have that conversation and we decide to investigate it and see where it goes, I open a file. I work with the investigators to the point where we think there is enough to get an indictment. Sometimes we can use the grand jury to help investigate all the way through, give them documents, have witnesses come in and testify on the record and under oath. Some cases are the kind where the agent does the investigation and then goes before the grand jury. He or she reports to the grand jury.

What law enforcement officers do you work with routinely?

The agent could be any kind of federal law enforcement officers, FBI, DEA [Drug Enforcement Administration] ATF [Alcohol, Tobacco, and Firearms], are the ones we work with a lot. There are also the inspector generals of the different bureaus. We also work a lot with state officers, particularly in the area of drugs. The state officers are the ones who have the kind of contacts in the community that enable them to get into groups of people involved in drugs.

How would you describe your working relationships with law enforcement personnel? Do conflicts arise?

For the most part, the relationship is excellent personally and professionally. The law enforcement officers I come in contact with are competent, well-motivated, and intelligent. They do a good job, and I never have trouble dealing with them personally or professionally. Most of them are willing to consult. When a case is being investigated, I am the consultant, and when it's being prosecuted, they are the consultants. I have never had officers who willfully violated rights. We have to approve things like search and arrest warrants. There have been occasions when there have been turf battles between agencies, but in this area that is ancient history.

Are you in contact with law enforcement officers on a daily basis?

Most days, but not necessarily every day. Sometimes all I do is spend the whole day with them. Either it is in person or on the phone. Sometimes I realize something needs to be done, and I get ahold of them. Sometimes they want to talk about what they are doing and give investigative materials to me.

Who also do you have contacts with in your job?

I also spend time with witnesses. If I am going to try a case, I try to do it about a week before trial. The witness will have already been interviewed by an agent; I will have that. It is also possible the witness may have been before a grand jury, so I have asked them questions on the record there. If there is going to be a trial, I talk to everybody who is going to be a witness at trial. I sit down and go back over what they know. Sometimes I talk to witnesses in the interim to fill out little holes in the case.

All cases that get indicted have to go through the grand jury. The majority of the cases and indictments are based on the investigation of an agent, who reports to the grand jury. A lot of time is spent with witnesses; recently, one whole day. That grand jury—it meets every other month—lasted for two days. The next [session] was almost all agents. Recently one grand jury returned fourteen indictments in a day.

What contact do you have with defense counsel?

I have a lot of contact with defense counsel, but it depends on how a case goes. In one case I am prosecuting right now, it seems I talk to the defense lawyer every day or two. I try to help him sort out issues, as well as see where we stand and whether it's going to be tried or not. Some cases, however, it is a matter of one or two conversations outside of court and two or three hearings in court. I try to maintain good relationships with defense lawyers. They are a diverse group of people, so, like with any group of people, there is a different way you relate to some of them. One you could tell your deepest, darkest secret, others you keep at arm's length, like you were buying a used car from them. [Also,] I am not involved in the bar association. Most of my contact is through work. I don't socialize with a lot of lawyers. Typically, when kids ask me if they ought to go to law school, I say, "Law school is interesting, but you have to remember that you will end up associating with lawyers."

Once a case is filed or an indictment occurs, is there plea bargaining?

The big majority of our cases are settled by plea bargaining. Defense counsel will normally indicate if their client is interested in considering a bargain. Then what I do is send them a written plea agreement. Quite often, it will be signed in the form I sent it. Sometimes, they want to negotiate a few points. Much of it is standard. If you want to plead guilty in this district, this is what you get from me, but there is some diversity among prosecutors.

We decide what they are going to plead guilty to first. Then the penalty flows from the Federal Sentencing Guidelines. They often control what the penalty might be. Even if we charge someone with ten drug counts, they only have to plead guilty to one. Then we talk about the total package. But the weight of drugs from all ten counts will have to be recognized in the plea agreement, or we can't enter it. That's relevant conduct under the Sentencing Guidelines.

Before I left the district on special detail, I was a supervisor, so I played a different role. Then I was detailed to the training center. When I returned, I started over with a clean slate in my work practices. One thing I observed when I was away was that one district [U.S. Attorney's Office] refused to plea-bargain at the last minute. There is a lot of benefit to that. Otherwise, you waste a lot of work preparing for trial. Now I make a point early on in the case to the defense attorney that I will be glad to settle it by agreeing on plea, but that after a certain point I am not interested in discussing it. So, if the client wants to do it, I say, "Let's do it now." I make a point to let them know when we are just going to have a trial.

How are your discovery activities related to plea bargaining?

Discovery is ongoing, but not actual preparation for trial. I was just in court for an arraignment and detention hearing for a person who had been arrested early in the week. Next Tuesday I have to have the discovery materials ready. When you go to an arraignment, the judge or magistrate gives you a week or so to get all the discovery to the defense lawyers. Then you have to follow up on those materials. When you get to a pretrial conference, there are certain deadlines, such as a witness list, notice of use of evidence of other misconduct not charged in the indictment, et cetera.

I try very hard and am usually successful at plea bargaining before I get to that point. That's when I start wasting my time if the guy is going to plead. Before that, I rely on the reports of the police officers about what the witnesses say. If we get down to a pretrial conference at that point, that's when I decide who I am going to call and what I am going to ask each one.

Does the U. S Attorney oversee your charging, plea bargaining, and other decisions?

There is oversight, depending on the case. The U.S. Attorney gives personal oversight when we make motions to get a person a reduced sentence if they assisted the government in an investigation. It's called "substantial assistance." If I want to make a motion like that in a case, I prepare a memorandum for the U.S. Attorney and Criminal Chief explaining the circumstances. I can only file what they approve.

Before I indict someone, I prepare a prosecution memorandum, and it is sent to the Criminal Chief and the U.S. Attorney. They have the opportunity to see what it is about or object to its being brought or ask for changes. They normally ask for changes, but they do not have the authority to order changes.

Dropping more serious charges to allow a plea to lesser charges is supposed to be approved. I always get it approved. I don't know if all AUSAs do. From my experiences in training and supervision and also the year I worked in the Office of Professional Responsibility, I learned it was important to do that. We have an electronic case management system where we track what is going on in our cases. I keep that in good shape, because that is a way supervisors can look at a case and see what is going on. We have a lot of autonomy, but we have local policies as well, Department of Justice policies, and statutes and rules of the court that we have to comply with. I can't go out and indict a ham sandwich.

The U.S. Attorney's Office has a lot of discretion, but it is exercised by assistants and regulated by policy. For example, gun charges. If we have good evidence a person used a gun in a drug case, I am obligated to bring that charge. Under policy, I am required to either require a plea to it or or to have them stand trial on it. An exception can be made to that at the point of charging or at the point of plea agreement. It can't be made on a whim or for convenience. There has to be some reason for it. That reason needs to be approved by the supervisor. Discretion is regulated.

Do the Federal Sentencing Guidelines also control your discretion to charge and plea-bargain?

They affect my work. They are part of the framework for the litigation in each case. They have to be looked at even before we charge. If the Guidelines say the most a defendant can get is six months or probation for an offense, it would be very expensive to bring it to court. Then I might decide that I am not going to do the case because it takes so many resources for the impact it will make.

Plea bargaining is affected by the Guidelines, the charge, the enhancements—Did a person have a gun? Obstruct justice? Is he a leader?—are affected. Of course, the whole sentencing process is affected. I prosecuted before the Guidelines came into effect in 1987. Back then, judges could do pretty much whatever they wanted. There are some things about the Guidelines that help [plea bargaining]. The reductions for accepting responsibility and the government's recommendation [allow] the defendant to see a tangible benefit from pleading. What the Guidelines do is channel and focus discretion. They try to put it on an even playing field for everybody. They give a way for either party to call into question the findings of the judge, too. Prior to 1987 judges weren't subject to that.

As you prepare a case, do you draft various documents as part of your job?

There are some letters. We don't use them as much because of e-mail to defense lawyers. I draft indictments, I draft prosecution memoranda. That's where I document everything about the case and send it up for review [by the U.S. Attorney] before indictment. It becomes a working document for later; it also becomes a witness list. I can go to it and pull out a witness list. I draft discovery disclosures. I draft motions. I draft motion responses, sentencing memoranda, and appellate briefs. Appellate briefs take a lot of your time. Most of the others don't take a great deal of time because there is a format to them. I customize them for a particular case.

I prepare a draft of the document on my computer. I type a draft as fast as I can handwrite it. I don't like dictating. I like being able to go back and edit, and you can't do that with dictating. I generally do a draft of it myself and give it to my legal assistant to put in final form. She takes care of the copies and filing and that sort of thing. We now have electronic filing with the court. So now I file my own documents. The computer reads that it comes from me and not the legal assistant.

How often do you go to trial?

Trials are very uncommon. I haven't had a trial since I returned from training detail in June 2004. I had a trial in 2001. The most trials I had in a single year was about twelve in the 1980s. I have trials scheduled. One, a week away, shouldn't be a trial, but there is a difficult defendant. I have one for October that looks like it probably will occur. They will be held in district court.

Do you have much contact with judges other than in the courtroom?

I very rarely have contact with judges other than in court. I don't think it is good practice for prosecutors to be on a buddy-buddy basis with judges. People who look on that see it as a good ole' boy action or talking about cases out of court.

What do you regard to be the pluses and minuses of serving as an AUSA?

It's a good place for public service. You are where the authority of the government meets the public. You are in a position to use the government's authority under the law to say to people, "We don't do that!" You are in the position to say who is harming the community by their conduct and who put themselves on the outside. You try to weed them out. It is a real good opportunity to fulfill the law and protect the community. Yes, there is personal satisfaction in that. But there are sad things you run into. There are tragic lives. You really feel bad for them. But some defendants fit all the stereotypes and ought to be locked up.

When I had supervisory jobs, I spent way too much time away from home. I would expect that a successful lawyer with similar experience, accomplishments, and ability as mine in the private sector makes significantly more than I do. At the same time, I make an adequate salary. I'm not complaining. Plus, being a government employee, you have other benefits. When you are gone, somebody carries your work.

Are there other reasons why you prefer working for government?

When I was an assistant prosecutor, it was a part-time job, and I was a part-time private attorney for those five years. I did not enjoy the business side. I never enjoyed having a woman who was upset and needed out of a relationship come in and I had to say, "You pay me this and I'll talk to you." I was never comfortable with keeping time and sending out bills. Here we do reports on how we use our time so the Department of Justice has some information on how human resources are spent. But it's not the same thing.

J. Luis Guerrero

The Public Defender

FROM HIS OFFICE IN CHULA Vista, California, Luis Guerrero can look onto a busy street in a Latino neighborhood between downtown San Diego and the Mexican border. His clientele as an attorney in the offices of the Public Defender of San Diego County are indigent criminal defendants. Behind a plate glass window in a foyer painted an institutional green sits a receptionist who easily slips between English and Spanish as she answers telephone calls. Once the interviewer is buzzed into the office, Luis, of medium height but broad-shouldered and athletic, ushers him into a small, sparsely furnished office. Labeled with dates attached on Post-it notes, desk files hold dozens of neatly organized case folders. A sports coat and ties hang on a coat rack.

How did you become a public defender?

I have been working here—as an attorney I officially started in May of 1992—almost thirteen years. I was also a law clerk here, and I worked in other legal capacities for about another year before I became an attorney here.

I was born in Tijuana, just across the border, and grew up in Mexico until I was about eleven years old. Then my family moved here to San Diego. I have pretty much been living here ever since, except for the time I went to law school. I went to San Diego State [University] and graduated from there with a B.A. in economics in 1988. Then I went to law school at Cal Berkeley [University of California at Berkeley, or Boalt Hall] for three years and graduated in 1991. After I finished school, I came here. They offered me a job as a law clerk and whatnot until I became an attorney.

How is the work of this office organized?

Presently we have around one hundred seventy-five attorneys who work for our office. There are about another fifty who work for the alternate public defender's office. Basically, they do the same thing we do, but they take the conflict cases, cases where we have conflicts of interest or whatnot. We have various branch offices: a branch here in South Bay and a central branch where a majority of the attorneys are. Then we have one in North County and East County, and we have a juvenile-dependency branch in the central area that deals with juvenile crime and dependency cases.

I have a supervisor on site, down the hall, and we also have a branch supervisor to supervise all the branch offices. That person is supervised by the public defender. The public defender is hired by the County Board of Supervisors elected by the residents of San Diego. We [attorneys] are civil servants, so if you want to become a public defender, you have to apply and have a law degree. Then you have to go through an interview process, and you then get hired.

How did you learn to be a public defender?

There is no formalized training program required by the state bar or local criminal bar or association of any type. When I was in law school at Berkeley, they really didn't teach you much about being a trial lawyer. They teach you a lot about being an appellate lawyer and learning the different types of laws: torts, contracts, whatnot. They really didn't teach how to be a criminal lawyer, how to be a trial lawyer in particular. When I walked in here, the only experience I had had dealing with trials, what I now do essentially, was the trial practice course I took my third year. It was an optional class. You don't have to take it if you don't want to. I took it because I knew I was going to be doing this. That taught me a little about trial practice, criminal procedure, how you question a witness. It helped me a little bit. Really, when I walked in here, I didn't know what I had to do. I think that's the case with most criminal attorneys. When you start out, you know next to nothing about what you are going to do, what a case is worth, or even how to question a witness on the stand. You don't know how to phrase a question.

What they did with me, and the group of people hired with me, was to put us through a training program. It was an informal thing where we did mock trials. Veteran attorneys from our office would come in and lecture us about how to handle certain things, how to question witnesses, how to cross-examine police officers, or how to deal with all different things about trials. That's really where I began to learn how to do this. The real learning takes place once you start doing it. You make mistakes. You watch other people do it. That's how you learn.

How are cases assigned to you?

All my cases are assigned by my supervisor. The defendants are arraigned in court [after arrest], and then the court appoints us if they find out they [defendants] don't have the money to hire an attorney—which I would say ninety percent do not. Then the court sends the documents here to our office saying that we are appointed. We have to open a case file. The supervisor goes through the documents and sees what the charges are and assigns them to our attorneys based on their experience. Generally speaking, the criminal section is divided into misdemeanors and felonies. The younger lawyers, the first two to three years in criminal practice, will handle only misdemeanors. After a third or fourth year here, you will start seeing some felonies. The way it is now, it could be four or five years until you see some felony cases.

What is your workload?

Right now the computer shows me having close to fifty, but some of the clients have multiple cases. In terms of clients, in the neighborhood of thirty-five to forty. That is typical. This office handles the highest volume of cases of any office in the county. The reason for that is we are a small operation. There is one presiding department [courtroom] of the five or six that handle criminal cases. We have to be more efficient in how we handle things. We have to do more with less. We don't have to be in three separate places at one time, which happens a lot if you're doing criminal cases downtown, where there are fifty departments and a hundred or so lawyers walking around doing different things. It gets chaotic. Down here it is pretty manageable, so because of that we have more cases. There are other reasons, too.

What sorts of crimes are your clients alleged to have committed?

If you are working felonies, like I am now, I'm a level-three attorney. There are five levels. Level-four crimes are murders, serious assaults. We can handle these cases as level threes, but by definition we are to handle the lower level felonies. In any event, the majority of the cases I see involve drugs or are in some fashion drug related. Possession of drugs is a big one, possessions of methamphetamines, in particular. You see a lot of that. You see a lot of possession of stolen vehicles. That is very common, also. Theft from stores by people who have prior convictions: third, fourth, fifth time. People who go into a store and steal a pair of jeans, five DVDs—typically drug addicts who are looking for a way to make a quick buck selling them on the street so they can go and buy drugs. You see a lot of that. Those are the most typical kinds of cases.

Down here, because of where we are, very close to the [Mexico-United States] border, we get a fair amount of border crimes coming to us. The federal government doesn't want to take the money to prosecute them. For example, we get a fair share of people who come across the border transporting marijuana. First-time offenders, for the most part, who get asked in Mexico, "Do you want to drive a car with marijuana? We are going to pay you a thousand dollars." So they do it, and they get arrested with a hundred pounds of marijuana in the car. That would normally be a federal crime, but the feds do not want to spend the money to prosecute those people because there are too many of them. So they send them to us. At one point two or three years back I would say thirty percent to thirty-five percent of our cases—a third of our cases—came that way. It has gone down since 9/11 because of the beefed up security at the border. Still, I believe, twenty percent of our felony cases are from people crossing the border with drugs, primarily marijuana.

What are your clients like, and what is your relationship with them?

I am their attorney. I try to do everything I can do, but you can't practice as a public defender carrying the weight of the world on your shoulders. I have guys who go away for life. There was not a whole lot I could do from the day they walked in the door. For example, I have had a guy who shot his wife in the parking lot of a [grocery store] in full view of twenty people. Shot her—boom, boom, boom—seven times. He didn't kill her. So he was charged with attempted murder—surprise, surprise. What was I to do with that case? I tried my best. I tried to put up an attempted manslaughter argument, saying he did it in the heat of passion. But it is hard to overcome having a guy lying in wait in a car, who gets out of the car, goes out in front of people, and shoots his wife seven times. Do I feel bad because that guy went to prison? I did everything I could for him. That is all I can say, but some people can't handle that. They freak out over the fact a person is going to prison for two or three years. If you are that kind of person, you shouldn't be doing this.

Some people freak out over having to go to a jail cell where there are ten guys. Some of them don't smell so good. Some of them have tattoos running down their arm and on their neck, and they look scary. They [some lawyers] don't want to go in there. If you are afraid of that, then you don't want to do this. I won't say that it doesn't faze me. It does. It's not pleasant to walk into a tank [holding cell]. There have been circumstances when sometimes something riles them up, and they get on you: "How come you can't get me out of here?" "What's a matter with you?" Then one eggs on the other, and pretty soon you've got ten guys getting on you about why you're not helping them out or how come you can't get them out on bail or probation or whatever. You need to know the territory.

How do you prepare cases for trial or bargaining?

We have investigators—in this branch we have twenty attorneys and three investigators. We do, in cases that end up going forward and that do not settle initially, do a fair amount of investigation. Mostly interviewing witnesses—say, in a domestic violence situation, people that know the victim to learn if the wife is a habitual liar, that the wife has a history of violence, or things of that nature.

Are your clients' cases plea-bargained?

After arraignment I first see most clients in jail. After arraignment there is a hearing, with the Deputy District Attorney [prosecutor] and judge, about a week after the arraignment. It is called a readiness conference. It's basically "let's make a deal day." The district attorney makes an offer in pretty much all cases. The exceptions are the real serious cases or the cases that, for political reasons, they don't want to make an offer. However, in ninety percent of the cases we get an offer at the readiness conference.

From experience, you know how much a case is worth. From doing this for years and years you come to understand what features they [deputy district attorneys] look at. The factors they look at are basically the client's history, current crime that is being charged, the facts of the offense—how serious or how strong the evidence is. All those sorts of things weigh into what offer you will get. The D.A. has discretion as to what they want the defendant to plead guilty to and which of the charges they want the defendant to plead guilty to. Typically, the judge has the discretion as to what the sentence will be. Though normally from the district attorney in most cases you will get a guarantee of probation if a person doesn't have a serious history. They [the district attorney] will make an offer, say, "Plead guilty to driving a stolen vehicle with a guarantee of probation." What the sentence will be is actually up to the judge. That's when the judge will weigh in and say, "I think you will get a mid-range sentence, an upper-range sentence, a lower-range sentence," or say, "I'd let him out today with a promise to appear at sentencing, and I'll give him thirty days of community service" or whatever.

What you get from the D.A. is actually an offer. It is a contract you're entering with the D.A. You plead guilty to one charge, and they'll dismiss the remaining charges in exchange for a guarantee of probation or whatever. What we get from the judges is not a contractual promise but rather an indication that is pretty much as a good as a promise. But you can't come in on the day of sentencing and say, "Judge, you told us you were going to do this." If he doesn't do it, you don't have a remedy. The D.A. cannot do that.

How does your experience affect your decisions on bargaining and trial?
The D.A.s get shuffled around. For whatever reason, they continually get transferred to other areas. So they don't stick around as much. I have been here seven years. I know exactly if I am going to try a case, and I know what judges are available, I know who I want to go to, who I don't want to go to, and I know why. I have all the angles covered because of my experience and because I practice in this courthouse. If I would go downtown now, I would be at a bit of a disadvantage because I haven't worked there.

Do you file motions before trial to exclude evidence or for other reasons?
Our motion practice is pretty limited here in state court. We do file—I have one set for this week. When you start out young, and you don't know your way around, you file a lot more motions because you don't know which ones are the winners and which ones aren't. You end up litigating a lot and finding out what you need to be effective. What ends up happening is that as you gain more experience you end up filing fewer motions. As to search-and-seizure motions, I maybe won ten in twelve years. The law is stacked up against us. If you pick your battles, you can win. I got a third-striker who was an alleged Mexican mafia member, a big thing. Nobody liked this guy, who got arrested for possession for sale of drugs in a vehicle. He was on parole. I filed a motion and did research and ended up winning the case. If you know when to strike, you can win.

Do you have much contact with police?
In court, a lot. You get to know the officers from seeing them in court. By and large I think the majority of the officers are pretty honest and do their job. There

are a few who feel they have the burden of saving the world or whatever. They come in and simply embellish. They will try to make things different than they are. In my experience, when they try to do that, it makes things worse for them because it opens the door for me [on cross-examination]. The jurors can see through that. They know when things don't sound right or when things being described don't make any sense because this guy has presented a false picture of what happened. They don't have to do that. They don't have to make a judgment about who the client is or who I am or anything like that. Some do it anyway.

What cases go to trial?

In my experience, the cases that go to trial are the ones where there are real serious charges, like homicide, where the defendant is facing a life term or an excessive amount of years in prison. A person is obviously not going to plea-bargain in that situation. They don't want to sign up for twenty-five years in prison or that kind of thing. Also, situations where the defendant is adamant that he is not guilty, that he did not do any of this, and that he will not plead guilty by any stretch of the imagination to any charge. That doesn't happen a lot, but it does happen. Those are the situations when you find cases going to trial. The stakes are real high, it's a life case, a death-penalty case; there is a lot at stake.

What is the trial like?

I do about ten to twelve trials a year, about one a month. The typical felony trial is probably three to five days long. You have four or five prosecution witnesses and one or two on the defense. A murder trial is two to three weeks, but your average felony trial is not that much different from a misdemeanor trial. When we go to court it is by and large jury trials. There is no sense in having a judge [bench] trial because the sense of most defense attorneys is that most judges are predisposed. They have seen it all. They know every in and out, and so I think they tend to be somewhat jaded. If we have a defense, the judge is less likely to buy it than a jury that is not as experienced in the criminal justice system.

What matters in the selections of jurors?

A number of years ago here in California, after the O. J. Simpson case [the first criminal trial of a former professional football star for two murders that ended in a controversial acquittal by the jury], they [the state Supreme Court] passed a number of rules limiting the voir dire that we could do. The idea being that defense attorneys were bad guys and basically weeding out jurors by asking them all sorts of different questions and just leaving those individuals who were on the social fringe on the jury, doing that kind of thing to hang juries [make them incapable of reaching a decision]. What happened is they limited us; we didn't spend a lot of time on voir dire. Right after I started, you went in, and the judge would have a list of questions—where do you live, where do you work, are you associated or have ties with law enforcement, blah, blah, blah—standardized questions they would ask of everybody [potential jurors]. Unless we had follow-up questions related to those questions asked by the judge, we weren't allowed to do anything. That was it. That's what we got. Over time what they found out was that, because of the lack of information, you started getting outliers on juries. We didn't know anything about these people. A couple of years ago they changed it, so now voir dire is allowed. In the past you could spend as little as two hours picking a jury. Now half a day to a day is how long it normally takes to pick a jury.

How do you assess the quality of the judiciary?

There is definitely a prosecution bias. For example, in this county there has not been a public defender appointed by any governor to be a judge since the early 1980s. It is not because we don't have people who are qualified doing this job. We do. Many of the people who work for this office are often much more qualified than the D.A.s. Often we have more experience, we know more than the D.A.s that sit across from us. Yet it's the D.A.s that get appointed to the bench. It's just a political thing. A lot of them become good judges, don't get me wrong, but you get a lack of diversity of perspective. I always found that to be kind of amusing, because we defense attorneys could be a lot tougher on certain things then the D.A.s, because we have dealt with certain clients and we know where the red herrings are and the kind of punches they [defendants] try to pull. The district attorneys don't understand that side of it because they haven't been in the tank with these guys and talked to them one on one to understand where they are coming from.

Has the adoption of a "three strikes" law in California affected plea bargaining and trials?

Absolutely, initially more so than now. We have been living with "three strikes" for over ten years, so I think the average defendant has kind of grown accustomed to the increase in sentences that came about because of it. So now everybody knows the price of poker is higher. So, for example, whereas before, if you had a guy who comes in with stealing something from a store— petty theft with a prior conviction and he has a strike—instead of the typical sixteen months or two or three years in prison, now he is looking at thirty-two months, four years, or six years in prison. He has only one strike, but it doubles what he used to get. Before, you might have been able to make that case go away for a year in county jail or sixteen months in prison. Now it is going to be thirty-two months at the very least and maybe four years. They [defendants] kind of know that. In some situations it does affect the case, because you get three strikes on three possessions of drugs.

I just had one petty theft where the guy was a third-striker. They [district attorney] wanted to put him away for life because he stole a binder and some other stuff—a set of pans worth eight dollars. He had two prior residential burglary convictions about fifteen years old. He was technically a third-striker looking at twenty-five to life. The D.A. was willing to give him six years—to ignore one of the strikes and give him six years. He [the defendant] did not want to take it. Absolutely not—even the six years. We pushed it forward. I said we were going to trial. Eventually they [district attorney] offered him a year with probation. That case got played out over two or three months because of the three-strike law, whereas before it would not have made it past the initial hearing stage because it wouldn't have [been] that big a deal.

What do you think of private criminal attorneys?

Our office does a better job than most of them. There are a few good ones, but you have to know who they are. We do a better job because we have pooled resources. If I am doing a case and have any question, I can go down the hall and talk to someone who is more experienced and find out what they think of the situation and suggest what I should do. I can go to my supervisor. We have investigators who work for us and do whatever we need within reason. If we need experts, we can hire experts. Everything we need to be a criminal defense lawyer, and do it right, we have it here.

Some of the private practitioners have this, but it is often more difficult [to obtain]. There are a lot of private practitioners I get phone calls from, especially the younger ones I know, who ask me, "I just got this case, I don't know what to do." Somebody is paying them money to handle the case, and they are calling me to find out what the case is worth, what to do, what the various alternatives are! This happens in the courtroom. We are in there with our cases ready to go to war. These guys walk in and ask us, "Are you a public defender?" I say, "Yeah." They ask, "Can you tell me what the D.A. will offer in this case?" or "What do you think about this or that?" They ask us because they don't know.

We are specialists. I work [points] in this courthouse. I know all the judges. I know who they are. I know what they do. I know what they like. I know what they don't like. I know exactly how I am going to play my cards because I know who I am dealing with. A lot of private attorneys don't. It's not that they are incompetent. It's that they don't know.

What changes would you like to see in the criminal process?

The process is overly politicized, especially when it comes to the appointment of judges. Also, in California, with the ballot initiatives, where voters don't know what they are really doing. Three strikes is a prime example. You ask most people, "When you voted for three strikes, did you mean to send the guy who took a pizza to prison for the rest of his life?" they say, "No, that is not what I wanted." But that's what the law does or can do. People don't understand these things. They are politicized, and so people vote out of fear of certain things. That is also happening with the bench. You get a built-in unfairness because of that.

Where in the 1970s some say there were too many rights afforded defendants, the pendulum has swung against them. We have gone too far the other way. We see the Fourth Amendment rights being stripped down so if a [police] officer on the street knows the law, he can pretty much stop anybody and search them. He can say the right taillight was cracked, and that's why I stopped him, or the typical one is, he will pull you over or walk up to you and say, "Can I talk to you?" What are you going to say, "No, don't talk to me?" Or they will go up to a person and say, "What are you doing? What is going on?

Are you carrying anything illegal? Can I search you?" Most people don't think that they can say no to an officer. These kinds of things. The law is in such a state that it allows these kinds of things to go on.

What are the pluses and minuses of practice as a public defender?

If you like the criminal law, if you like being a trial lawyer, it's the perfect job because the business end is weeded out. You don't have to worry about billable hours. You don't have to worry about bringing clients in. You don't have to worry about any of that. You get to practice what you like, and that's all you do.

The bad side of it's that you will inevitably represent some individuals who you don't like as a person. You are going to have some clients who are difficult. They are going to get in your face. They are going to tell you that they don't like you. They are going to tell you that they wish they had the money to hire a private lawyer, when you know in your heart that you are better than any private lawyer they could hire. They don't believe that, and it really doesn't matter what you tell them. That's what they believe. And so you are kind of trying to help them while fighting with them. It's hard, very hard to do. That's when you have to be a true professional and say that, despite the fact this guy is calling me this and calling me that and telling me I am a dump truck and telling me X, Y, and Z, I should put that aside and do what I can do so he can get justice.

Do you plan to stay a public defender?

I am sure I could make more money on my own, but I have talked to people who do what I do as a public defender on the private side. They all say the business side is a drag. Sometimes I do get the urge to venture into other areas of the law. I was an economics major in college, so I do have that side of me, but what I like about this job is that I am very independent. Even though we work for the public defender's office, each one of us makes our own decisions about our cases. Nobody is going to tell you what to do with a case. They can't say, "If they offer you this, you better push your client to take the deal," or "You better go to trial no matter what." We make the decision. The D.A. does not. The deputy D.A.s are told by their higher-ups what to do. If the higher-up says settle the case, they try to settle the case. If the higher-up says you are not going to settle the case, you are going to trial no matter what, that is what they have to do.

We are kind of the last line of defense between the prosecutor, the government, and the people. If we weren't here, the government could run roughshod over people. They could, and they would. Somebody needs to speak up for guilty people. Just because somebody did something wrong, does that mean you have to send them away for twenty years, or should they get a shot at probation? The judges understand that we are a valuable resource for them and that we need to be there to protect these people, that we need to be there to protect the record and let everybody know that these guys are being treated as fairly as possible. That's why, ultimately, most of us are here.

Cynthia Short

The Lawyer for Capital Punishment Defendants

Cʏɴᴅʏ Sʜᴏʀᴛ ʜᴀᴅ ᴊᴜsᴛ ʀᴇᴛᴜʀɴᴇᴅ from a trip to the zoo with her young daughter when she was interviewed at her husband's law firm in Kansas City, Missouri. Working out of space in his firm's personal injury law practice, she serves clients as a mitigation specialist in cases in which the prosecution is seeking the death penalty. Unlike other criminal cases, capital punishment cases have a trial phase. Additionally, as required by the Supreme Court of the United States, if the defendant is convicted, the court then must enter a sentencing phase. During the sentencing phase the judge or jury will have to determine whether the sum of aggravating minus mitigating circumstances requires the death penalty. Cyndy is a mitigation specialist whose job is to try to convince the jury that the mitigating circumstances, such as the mental capacity or life experiences of the defendant, outweigh the aggravating ones so that the defendant can be sentenced to prison rather than death.

Could you please tell me about your path to the legal profession?
I moved around a lot in my youth. I am from a lot of different places. Primarily I was raised in Texas, California, and western Canada. I went to high school in western Canada—Calgary, Alberta. My father was a corporate man, and he took us around the country. He was by education an attorney. So my youth and my teen years I was directed toward the law.

I left Calgary for St. Mary's College, across the street from Notre Dame, where my father had attended both undergraduate and law school. I did not have a vision of what it really meant to go to law school. So as an undergraduate I focused on political science and humanistic studies, without really knowing what law school was really going to mean but knowing all the way through college that I was going to law school. When I picked my law school, my parents were still living in Canada, so I picked a law school in the states that was near the only relative I was close to, my grandparents, which landed me in the state of Missouri. Unknown to me, the state that you pick would likely be the state that you would live in because you might meet your spouse, and you would be making contacts with law firms, with colleagues, that would form the basis for employment. Both of those things happened to me. When I picked the state of Missouri, I unknowingly picked my home. I went to St. Louis University Law School. I continued on through with my Catholic education and was pointed toward service work by emotion, by, really, what was most natural for me. However, law school was a place that really directed you somewhere else. There is a hierarchy that you discover in your first year, that big law firms and corporations are where they want you to go. Frankly, that was also where my family wanted me to go. Not really knowing what I wanted myself, I accepted that in law school.

What was your first position as an attorney?

When I did take my first job, I took a job with a management-side labor-law firm, which was really against what I wanted to do or that which was natural for me. The other thing about me, from high school through college and into law school, was that I was not a natural public speaker. I was not someone who wanted to be out in front of people. Law school was a time when I purposefully started to choose a path that would put me out front and make me speak. I never envisioned a practice where I would be a trial lawyer. So I picked a job initially where I wouldn't be in the courtroom.

When I went into the management-side labor-law firms, I was the second woman who they had ever hired. The first woman they had hired was a very competitive woman who was not happy about having the second woman hired. It was really the first time I ran into sexism. There wasn't anything pleasant about that job. I was doing a lot of writing, a lot of research, and a lot of being in the library that made the law very, very dead in my mind. If I had continued along that path, I think I would have done what a lot of women do, which is honorable. I would have chosen the mommy track and probably not stayed in the law because there was nothing really alive about it for me.

I take it that, looking back, you would have undertaken a different career path at an earlier age?

Had I known that this was the direction I was going to go when I was an undergraduate thinking about law school, I would have looked at law schools that would have provided me a different experience than the one I chose. I would have chosen a law school that put me in the field more often, with a strong clinical program. There aren't many of those. If I had a way to do it again, I would have found methods to be in the presence of Stephen Bryants, a graduate of Yale who has taken a vow of poverty and is in Georgia representing guys who have been convicted and put on death row. I would have found those opportunities if I had really known what I wanted to do.

How did you move into criminal work?

About six or eight months into that practice, I was appointed by the federal court to represent a young woman, Tammy Williams, who had been accused by the federal government of attempting to assassinate Jesse Jackson [an African American civil rights activist]. Jesse Jackson at the time was running for president. I was a first-year lawyer with no courtroom experience who had never been in a jail cell, who had never represented another human being, who had never been in a courtroom, never stood before a judge, really didn't focus on criminal law in law school, and yet was given this enormous responsibility. Fortunately for me, there was a lawyer in St. Louis who I had seen at a seminar. He said that if anybody found them[selves] appointed to a case in federal court and didn't know what they were doing, to call him. I did. His mentoring and his past, the way he ran his practice changed everything for me. Going to meet Tammy Williams, sitting across a mesh window from her in a jail cell, realizing the ridiculous mess of those charges, standing in a courtroom, having everything just feel alive and successfully arguing her case with the aid of that lawyer, I quit the job at the labor law firm without having any job waiting for me. I worked retail until the public defenders had a space for me here in Kansas City. Then I actively pursued public defense work, which is where I really found my passion.

You then became a public defender?

Here in Missouri, I chose a good one for criminal defense work. Missouri has a statewide public-defender system. A lot of its growth happened during my career. I came in at a very good time. It is only one of four states that allow defense lawyers to take depositions. It is a very open discovery state. So we really get to penetrate and probe and interrogate our cases. I have found that to be exciting and great in terms of my ability to represent real people in court and to do it successfully.

I did that a total of fourteen years. I left once, still hearing some of the old ghosts from law school, and went with a plaintiffs' law firm for about fourteen months. Even though it was a great law firm, I didn't have the same empathy for those clients as I did for the poor and for those who were facing the loss of liberty or life.

What sorts of cases did you have as a public defender?

I did mostly felonies. This area just happens to not file very many misdemeanors, so I did the lowest kind of felony, D felonies, all the way up to homicides. Then when I came back from the plaintiffs' law firm, I went into the capital division. All I was doing was capital work. I did that for nearly nine years in the public defender's office, and I continue to do it today. We are in the death belt. Yes, we are. I would say over the course of the last decade I have represented in excess of seventy-five people who faced at the trial level the death penalty.

Once I entered the capital division in 1994, my clients were all over the state of Missouri. That changed my practice. It had been primarily an urban practice, a lot of inner-city youth, a lot of minority representation. Once I went into the capital division, I would find myself in St. Louis, Cape Girardeau, Maryville, anywhere in the state of Missouri. So my practice then was largely in front of elected judges instead of appointed judges. [In Missouri judges are selected by partisan election except in St. Louis and Kansas City, where they are initially appointed by the governor and later become subject to a retention election.] It was with small-town prosecutors. It was really a very diverse practice. For the last decade, I have, in addition to working with different groups of prosecutors and judges and different kinds of clients, I also had to work with different teams of lawyers, which has been a challenge. That is the other way my practice changed when I went into the capital work. When you are doing criminal work most of the time, good criminal lawyers are mavericks. They are "get on the horse and ride on by themselves and take no prisoners" kind of people. Once you get into capital casework, you have to change a little bit and become a team member. It's really interesting with lawyers working in a team. They can be very resistant to that.

You now practice private criminal defense work?

Before I came here, I went with a public interest firm for ten or eleven months that also represented primarily death-penalty people and poor people facing cases in which there is a strong belief that they are innocent. I tried a couple of cases with them and then came over here.

This is a four-attorney firm. It has not historically been one that has worked on criminal cases. We jokingly say I am the pro bono arm of this firm. My work is all criminal. I just tried a case in January for a man who was acquitted of twelve counts of child sex abuse, and we have just filed a civil suit, which I will probably participate in, but that's out of the ordinary for me.

Who are your clients?

Currently my practice is the kind that has to stay small because what I am doing is very complex litigation. Death-penalty cases are comparable to complex white-collar crime. At any given time when I have handled death-penalty cases, my caseload was never higher than eight cases, which is probably three cases too many. Now I am carrying a private-pay case and two cases in which I am what is called mitigation investigator specialist, where I am not the lawyer in the case. I am a consultant investigator for lawyers handling federal cases in Arkansas and Missouri. I have a death case where my client is mentally ill but in the state hospital. He killed his family five years ago. I have been litigating the case for five years. I brought that with me from the public defender's office. The big death-penalty case is a case we believe is an innocence case. It is a reversal from a trial that happened in 1998. I am working on that with a big law firm in town. We literally had to rip it away from the public defender's office. The court appointed me uncompensated, so the big law firm is paying all the expenses. I am not getting paid unless we successfully litigate that. When I was first a public defender [PD], I was what people envision as a PD. I had sixty cases. As I gained experience I moved into a very demanding trial load. I was also manager of an office and carrying a large caseload and training lawyers and frankly was burned out. It was one of the reasons I went into the plaintiffs' law firm. I tried a lot of cases.

How would you describe your clients?

Poor. All of my clients are poor or average-income people. The one, Jim Boyd, whose case I will be trying in the fall, his mother is a teacher, and his father is a manager at Osco Drugs. That's the high end. Everybody else is below the poverty line. I have found over the course of my career that I respond better to that clientele than the rich guy. I have a lot more empathy and fight. What we have seen with death row is that race is a big factor, but the biggest common denominator is poverty. Everyone on death row is poor.

Currently, the mitigation cases have maturity. I seem to get cases where things have gone wrong and we need to fix them. I don't know whether that will continue, because things are always changing. You may have a series of cases where everybody is in it for the first time at the first trial level. You turn another corner, and everybody is at a retrial. You have had a trial years ago, and everything went as bad as it could go, and now by some miracle the court of appeals has given them a second chance. They are at your doorstep saying, "Fix this." I have lots of cases like that. Retrials can be really hard, because there is so much data you have to go through just to get back to the base point, which is part of the issue in a death-penalty case we have going.

How do you spend your time when working on these cases?

A lot of meetings. Particularly once you get into private practice, the first thing you have to do is assemble a team. You have to assemble a team that you feel is competent. That includes lawyers, mitigation investigators, investigators, experts. The experts will depend on who the client is and what the facts are. They could be medical examiners, psychologists, or social geographers when we want the expert to look into the guy's community and show all the ways in which he was not afforded the things that the other kids had. Gang experts. The really interesting thing about being in death-penalty work [is] that you constantly have to be a student. There are so many areas that you have to become familiar with—neurology, neuropsychology. I have clients who are schizoaffective and another guy who is schizophrenic. One case may involve arson, and you have to [have] an expert in arson, and then you have to drop that and let something else come in. It's fascinating in that respect.

What has to be prepared in capital cases?

Death penalty is very unique in that we have two trials and two investigations that we have to run. Typically, as citizens, we want to make decisions based on their behavior surrounding a particular crime. In death-penalty cases, fortunately, we have said we are going to look not only at what the crime was;

we are going to look at the individual who committed that crime. The second phase of the investigation that we are charged with doing is to look at the client from birth until the moment of trial and even prior to birth, because we know that there are biological generational issues that affect his development. We have to understand everything about him or her in order to pass judgment, in order to sentence appropriately. It's a very complex piece if done properly, and a lot of people don't do it that way. If it is done right, jurors by and large won't sentence to death. They see the whole person.

Do you engage in negotiations or make motions during discovery?
Yeah, a lot of it. If you were to draw up a map of the things we do or the lanes we have to run in—investigation, motions, negotiations—there is so much we have to do. Motions is a huge part of it, the legal work, because a lot of the motion work has to be done in order to set up the way in which we want to try the case; also, obviously, to preserve issues that might be important for appeal.

We do an extraordinary amount of discovery. I tried a case a few years ago, a Springfield case tried in Platte County. We started out when they [prosecution] handed us the police reports that started the case. I would say we put those in two large notebooks. When we entered the courtroom to try the case, we had forty banker boxes of material that we had gathered on his life and all the interviews of the witnesses, the depositions of individuals, documents that had been collected. Out of those two notebooks a complex amount of material had erupted.

Do you employ investigators?
Absolutely. When I was a PD we had a mitigation specialist on staff who was a master's-level individual in social work or psychology to help us to identify life issues, such as whether the person might be mentally retarded, whether they had different kinds of mental illnesses, whether they were a sociopath or antisocial. Then we had fact investigators on the team. Sometimes it takes more than one, depending upon how many witnesses we have to deal with. The case we have now, that we are doing a retrial on, we have over three hundred witnesses who are potential interviews or depositions. It takes an army to try such cases. It arose from a large Ozark major-case squad that investigated it, so there were an enormous number of police officers. Then you can just imagine looking at a person's entire life. All the relatives, teachers, medical personnel. A lot of clients have had contact with institutions, mental institutions, Department of Correction. It just starts blossoming out in terms of the numbers of contacts. Witnesses lead you to other witnesses. You have to take a no-stone-unturned approach. Once those stones are turned, you look for more stones. Most of the time, because we can take depositions, one of our sayings is "cases are won and lost in the field." So lawyers have to be in the field. They have to be touching, talking to, working with witnesses and family members and distant family members.

Is there contact with the victims of the crime?

There is a huge movement in the death penalty [community] for something called restorative justice, of which I am enormously optimistic. It encouraged those of us in the community to try to take some of the adversarial stuff out of the process so it is more compassionate to the people who are involved in the process, which is so foreign to law itself. It is such a sterile, horrible place you come into when you come into a courtroom. It is set up for everybody to be angry with each other. Victims are told in these cases that there can be only one outcome, one way to relieve their pain, which is death. There are other ways. With restorative justice, we now hire victims' liaisons to contact the victims—not to get information, but to really find out what they need from us. It's really fascinating what victims often do want.

What have been your experiences with prosecutors in capital cases?

It's a wide spectrum. There are prosecutors out there who are really good, hardworking, ethical individuals who are in for the right reasons. I have found in my practice that the prosecutors in the larger urban offices who have less riding on the line politically are easier to deal with. When you get out to the small towns, where everybody is watching, and they have the first capital case ever in their town, it's harder. They are elected in each of the counties, so it really varies widely, but one of the things you do find is a lot of the prosecutors are unfamiliar with death-penalty law, as are a lot of citizens. I have found many times that we have gone out on cases where the visceral response to the homicide is to come out swinging; before they have a chance to step back and think it through, they have already started talking about the death penalty. They really don't know what they are getting into once they start down that path. Often, they consider the crime and are not looking at the person. So we see a lot of bad decisions made to seek the death penalty. Then it's hard to get out of, once you've made that decision.

In negotiations what you do is you look for ways to get them out of the decision. I have written suggested press releases to help them out or say, this is what it might look like. Time helps us. If we can wait eighteen months, when things have settled down, they can make more reasoned decisions. We have seen better results then in a lot of our cases.

What has been your experience with juries in death-penalty cases?

The whole deal in the death-penalty world is that you don't want to be in front of a jury in a death-penalty case. You are really working to get the death penalty off the table or negotiate it. In this decade, I have no one left on death row, I am proud to say. When I have gone to trial, even running right up to a couple of weeks before trial, I have had almost all of my cases "death waived" by the time I get there. That is by sheer hard work on the mitigation side and being able to get to the prosecutor and say, "here's the life." They have conceded what a life looks like. This isn't Jeffrey Dahmer. This isn't Ted Bundy [serial killers]. It's a poor black kid from the inner city who was abused, who is an alcoholic, whatever the situation was. They don't want to take those to the jury. The ones that have gone to the jury are the death-penalty cases where children are killed, where five people are dead. It would be tough for any prosecutor to back out of those. In those cases in which we have gotten good "life without" verdicts because, one, the state has life without parole, it gives the jurors a good option. Second, we have worked the case very, very hard, worked hard to be credible in front of a jury. We work very hard to find a path to respect and have a relationship with the client that comes through, despite the horror of the crime they committed.

What has been your experience with judges in death-penalty cases?

There is a wide continuum. I often, when I talk or teach in this area, say I would rather have a judge who is a novice in the area of the death penalty than someone who has tried a bunch of death-penalty cases. The judges that have tried cases tend to be stuck in the way they have tried before. Therefore, they are not educable. The ones that haven't tried them before, they are educable. I'd rather be teaching them how to do it than have someone who doesn't do it very well teach them. There are a lot of people out there who do death-penalty work very poorly. I have had really good success with the judges I have been in front of. Every one of the ones I've had, we have had [jury] questionnaires, they have given me the time I needed. My reputation is, because my last name is Short, they call me Cyndy Long. I take a lot of time, and I do long cross-examinations, and I spent a lot of time setting things up and putting things into context. I have been permitted to do that. I spend a lot of time with judges, through motion practice and through the times I am in the courtroom slowly, incrementally mentally preparing them for the trial, like, "It's going to be long"; "We are going to need a questionnaire"; "You're in big territory."

Do you appeal any cases?

I do not handle any appeals. I consider myself a trial specialist. Even within the death-penalty cases I am a specialist in terms of the development of facts, working with clients, developing the stories, doing cross-examinations, doing opening statements, voir dire, all the trial pieces. I am not a law specialist, so I bring someone in who really is a specialist in that piece. Frankly, my belief is that it is such complex litigation, so big, that you couldn't possibly be competent in all the pieces that are there. It's not humanly possible.

With all of the specialization needed in death-penalty law, is there a way for a lawyer to learn it?

There is. Once you are in the area, there are programs called Life in the Balance, which happen every year. The National Association of Legal Defenders puts that on. I teach at that program. I teach at Victor Spence's program in Wyoming. We are developing a death-penalty program. There is a national network of mitigation specialists. I will be teaching at De Paul [University] this summer in a new mitigation program. It's a small community with very passionate, outspoken people who work very hard for very little money at something they are passionate about.

Do you find that politics affects death penalty in other ways that you have not mentioned?

Politics influences this kind of law a lot. It is there all the time, and you are thinking about it all the time. Certainly at the federal level, in order for a case to be certified to become a death penalty, they [U.S. Attorneys] have to go to the Department of Justice, which will be making the decision about whether to seek death. The death penalty is not quite at the level of abortion, but it is at a fever pitch in terms of the way people respond to it. Politicians use it as a lightning rod and come swinging in favor of the death penalty; I think they are afraid to come out and say they are against it, even though we know from studies that people do not vote based on a politician's views on the death penalty. Politics is part of plea negotiations. It affects the prosecutor's concerns about his next election. It is a consideration at every point, particularly in negotiations. When we are in the courtroom, since our case often attracts publicity, we even have to think about how we will phrase things in the courtroom, how we need to deal with and interact with the community in order for us to get what we think will be a just outcome. So I think it's always there.

What are the benefits of having a death-penalty practice?

The pluses are that it is very rewarding if you do it well. It gives you an opportunity for a very diverse practice, in the sense that you're always a student, you are always learning. If you want to be a trial lawyer, it is the ultimate in terms of trial. Civil lawyers, lawyers who do other kinds of work, will often say to me that this is [the] apex of being a lawyer. You are defending a life.

What are negative aspects of having a death-penalty practice?

The flip side of that is it is enormously stressful. It takes a lot of time, a lot of time away from family. My trials have lasted three weeks, four weeks, but often not here. That is hard. I have children and a husband. I have to travel a lot, and that can be hard.

The clients—you have both your rewards with the clients and your frustration with the clients because you are dealing generally with a very damaged or impaired population. It also is very challenging in terms of dealing with [the] horror of homicide over and over. The death-penalty cases are generally pretty horrific events. You have to learn over time to, in the beginning, to come in and in some sense suspend judgment, or you really can't do it.

The Judiciary

The American judge is a representative of the public selected through a political process. These judges hold state or federal office because of a political process of appointment, election, or a combination of executive appointment and retention election called merit selection (McLeod 2009). These various processes all ensure that judges have a degree of legal merit, because politicians do not want to embarrass themselves by supporting incompetents, and a degree of political merit, because their selections depend on the support of popularly elected officials, the leadership of the majority political party, or interest-group efforts. Unlike the judicial selection process in many Western nations, American judges are not part of a career judiciary who enter their profession after university, and not all American judges are attorneys or necessarily have minimal legal education.

As indicated in the interview with Judge Richard Stearns, federal district (trial) judges, as well as Court of Appeals judges and Supreme Court justices, are nominated by the president, and their appointment is confirmed with the "Advice and Consent," or a plurality vote, of the United States Senate. The many studies of this process reveal that presidents overwhelmingly nominate members of their own political parties who have or can readily acquire the support of senators. Some states employ executive appointment or legislative appointment procedures to select judges. In these states, appointment to judicial office often depends on political connections with the governor, governor's staff, or governor's political allies or with members of the state legislature and its judiciary committees. In so-called merit selection states, a judicial nominating commission supplies names of prospective judges to the governor, who then appoints one of them as the judge. After service on the bench, the judge then will face a retention election. Politics can shape the selection of lawyers and laypersons to the nomination committee, and a governor often appoints persons from the commission recommendations who satisfy his or her political interests. The interview with Judge Rick Savignano illustrates how the first stages of this process work in Massachusetts. In the future he will face a retention election, at which time the voters will be asked whether he should continue in office.

Most American states employ some sort of election process in the selection of judges. It can be a partisan election in which Democratic and Republican candidates compete for judicial office, a nonpartisan election in which the ballot does not indicate the party of the candidates, or a merit selection and retention election in which the voters are asked whether to keep in office a judge appointed by the state's governor. As Judge Steven King details the election process, many lawyers do not seek judgeships because of the low pay. Those who do run in states that elect judges, he notes, often lack opponents. If the local bar perceives that the judge is competent, this is especially true. Judicial campaigns are run the same way as for other political offices. Appellate judge Larry Starcher discusses how these campaigns work in a partisan election state. He indicates how a successful judicial candidate needs support from influential lawyers, seeks campaign funds, and develops strategies to attract voters. In recent years, however, the spending of large sums of money for judicial office, interest-group participation, and media advertising have become much more common in state judicial elections. Also, by eliminating some states' regulations of campaign speech, the Supreme Court of the United States has allowed judicial candidates to state their views about controversial legal issues (*Republican Party v. White* 2002).

Once appointed, American judges often attend relatively brief training sessions of a week to a few weeks in length. Many states require such training for non-lawyer judges. The limited training means that many judges learn how to manage conflicts through on-the-job experiences.

JUDGES IN COURTS OF LIMITED JURISDICTION

Both the federal and state court systems feature a set of courts whose judges process the vast bulk of minor criminal and civil disputes that arise in the United States. The names of these courts vary, but they include justices of the peace and municipal, magistrate, and district courts. (The names and jurisdictions of these courts can be found through the National Center for State Courts website, listed in the reference section of this book). In many states the judges of these courts are not lawyers; however, many states require that they attend a training program before exercising the powers of their office (for further discussion of lay judges, see Provine 1986). In the federal judicial system, the federal district judges appoint lawyers as magistrate judges for eight-year terms. These judges can conduct the trials of federal criminal misdemeanors, conduct the preliminary stages of federal felony criminal cases, and even conduct civil trials, with the approval of the litigants.

Despite limited or no authority to consider felony crimes and civil cases with large sums of money, these judges play an important role in the management of quarrels, trouble, and breaches of the peace and the establishment of moral order in their communities (Yngvesson 1993). Perhaps the most common business of these judges is the consideration of the important first appearance in court after arrest of criminal defendants. In most states these judges also will then conduct bench trials

(trials with no jury) that dispose of traffic offenses and police citations or arrests for minor crimes against public order. Also, as noted by Dan Hogan, they might hold bench trials of *small claims,* or civil disputes for small sums of money. Hogan's unique position combines judicial powers common to most limited-jurisdiction lower trial court judges with extensive administrative power over the budget of the limited-jurisdiction (for misdemeanor crimes, small civil claims) state courts operating in Boston.

TRIAL JUDGES

Lawyer judges preside at civil and criminal trials in federal and state courts of general jurisdiction. They have *general jurisdiction,* or authority, over key subjects, including civil claims of more than a few thousand dollars' value and more serious crimes or felonies. (The names and jurisdictions of these courts can be found through the National Center for State Courts website, listed in the reference section of this book). Before trial, judges referee the adversarial contest among the attorneys and interact with them on several issues. As Judges King, Savignano, and Stearns describe them, the judge's activities include *case management,* or ruling on *pleadings,* or requests for the court to consider a dispute, and discovery issues, such as motions about the legal aspects of the complaint, oversight of the collection of evidence collected during the discovery process, and decisions on motions filed by parties to collect and admit or exclude witness testimony and other evidence in their hands or the hands of their opponents.

Judges also receive requests in both civil and criminal cases for *continuances.* These are requests to delay the case because of conflicts in lawyers' schedules, the need for more time for discovery, or lawyers' efforts to jockey for delay as a means to induce the other party to negotiate a settlement. As Judge King suggests, continuances—rather than a shortage of courts and judges or too many lawsuits—is the primary reason for delays in case processing. Also, in response to motions by a party, the judge can issue *subpoenas* and *orders to produce* so the parties have full knowledge of each other's cases, so there are no surprises at trial, and so the parties can focus on key points of conflict.

Throughout these stages of litigation the judge needs information, and so, as Judges King, Savignano, and Stearns describe the job, judges often spend considerable time *studying* motions and settlement proposals filed by the parties—including some they think are not necessary—and *researching* the case and the law. They can also spend time *drafting* orders, warrants, subpoenas, letters to the parties, and other documents. Judges sometimes review and approve or participate in the *negotiated settlement* of a case. Judges Savignano and Stearns describe their role in facilitating negotiated pleas of guilt, or plea bargains, in their courts. However, as with Judge King, many judges do not think that it is their duty or that they have the skills to negotiate case settlements. If they do occur, many times the negotiations occur at pretrial conferences of both sides' lawyers and the judge. However, as Judge King indicates, more and more frequently judges assign cases to the court-ordered mediation services developed by state and federal court systems. Such mediation is especially common in family law cases.

The judge can then *preside* over a trial. As discussed by Judge Saviagno, presiding includes oversight of voir dire, or the questioning of potential jurors by the attorneys; maintaining order and the control of external interference with the *due process,* or fairness constitutionally guaranteed at trial; ruling on motions about the admission of evidence; instructing the jury on the law and charging them to determine which side is favored by the preponderance of the evidence; and then reviewing any jury decision to assess its fairness. Judge Stearns explains that judges can modify jury verdicts in civil cases but that this is a rarely used power.

Judge Savignano discusses another special responsibility of trial judges: the sentencing of criminal defendants after trial. As he notes, state law guides the process, but he still has to take many considerations into account when sentencing a convicted defendant. Judge Stearns describes the quite different sentencing process in federal criminal cases. In 1984 Congress created the United States Sentencing Commission as an independent agency in the judicial branch to establish sentencing policies and practices for the federal courts, including guidelines for the form and severity of punishment of convicted defendants. As noted in the interview with David Godwin, these guidelines shape plea bargaining by U.S. Attorneys, and Judge Stearns discusses how they affect his discretion in the sentencing of convicted defendants.

As Judge King notes, trial judges generally find that counsel do an effective job for their clients. However, sometimes he confronts unprepared counsel or lawyers ill informed about recent developments in the law. Also, as he notes, there is a gradual increase in the number of unrepresented, or *pro se,* parties, whose limited knowledge of the law places special burdens on judges, especially in family law cases. Scholars have yet to assess fully whether the increase in *pro se* representation affects litigants' perception of the procedural fairness of the judge or the distribution of costs and benefits (distributive justice) that result from litigation.

APPELLATE JUDGES

Appellate judges primarily review the application of the law by trial judges. Shortly after trial, a losing party has the option to appeal. Almost all first appeals of state trials, the vast majority of appeals, must be addressed by a state appellate court. (The names and jurisdictions of these courts can be found through the National Center for State Courts website, listed in the reference section of this book). In thirty-nine states an intermediate appellate court (the formal name differs from state to state) hears most first appeals by losing parties. In states without an intermediate appellate court, first appeals go to a state supreme court—again, the formal name differs from state to state. In states with an intermediate appellate court, a second appeal by a losing party goes to the state supreme court. In the federal system, most first appeals go to the United States Courts of Appeals for eleven circuits or regions of the country, the Court of Appeals for the District of Columbia, or the

Court of Appeals for the Federal Circuit, which hears appeals in specialized cases, such as those involving patent laws and cases decided by the Court of International Trade and the Court of Federal Claims. The Supreme Court of the United States can accept second appeals. In rare instances the Supreme Court hears appeals from state supreme courts or other state courts (for details, see Baum 2006; O'Brien 2008, and the United States Courts website listed in the reference section of this book). Also, prisoners can file *habeas corpus petitions* to challenge the lawfulness of their confinement in both federal and state appellate courts.

Most American appellate courts have to hear some appeals, what is called their *mandatory jurisdiction*. However, some appellate courts also can have the *discretionary jurisdiction* to review the claim submitted by counsel for a petitioner and refuse to consider their appeal. Appeals of trial decisions require the lawyer to draft *briefs,* or summaries, of the legal errors that occurred at trial and, on occasion, to make oral arguments before a panel of appellate judges. As Jeffrey Byer indicated in his interview, this is often the function of specialist lawyers. Justice Larry Starcher describes the review of petitions for review in the West Virginia Supreme Court of Appeals, a fairly typical state supreme court. Although appellate procedures vary greatly among state intermediate and supreme courts and federal Courts of Appeal and the Supreme Court of the United States, most appellate courts use either staff attorneys, law clerks who are lawyers who assist each appellate judge, or a panel of judges to screen the cases (Hall 1990). They can recommend that courts dismiss appeals that raise no substantial legal issues and can uphold the decision of the previous court that heard the case. In many state supreme courts and the U.S. Supreme Court, the justices have discretionary jurisdiction and vote whether to consider the appeal. Unlike most appellate courts, as Starcher notes, in West Virginia the lawyers can be invited by the court to argue whether the judges should hear their appeal.

If they deem the appeal to have merit, the judges of the appellate court, either all together (*en banc*) or in a panel usually composed of three judges, will consider the case. They can decide on the written briefs submitted to them, or they can hear oral arguments from the lawyers for the parties. Upon the request of individuals or groups who are not parties in the case, they will allow these third parties to file *amicus curiae,* or friend of the court, briefs to elaborate on the legal issues or potential social, economic, or political significance of the case. As Starcher indicates, most appellate courts readily admit such briefs into the case record.

Rarely lasting more than a half hour per side, oral argument usually features the lawyers highlighting their arguments and the judges asking questions of them. There is no jury. Then the judges confer, vote, and often write an opinion to explain their decision. The assignment of majority "Opinions of the Court" can be done by the chief justice, as in the Supreme Court of the United States; by rotation, as Justice Starcher reveals is the practice in West Virginia; or in other ways (Hall 1990). As Starcher indicates, most appellate judges work closely with their law clerks and interact with the other judges in the preparation of opinions. Judges in the minority can choose to write dissenting opinions, and judges in the majority who disagree with some of the legal conclusions of the other judges in the majority can write a concurring opinion. As Starcher notes, these opinions can have strategic value in shaping the future meaning of the law.

Many appellate courts also have special kinds of cases on their *dockets,* or lists of cases for consideration. For example, in West Virginia the law requires that the Supreme Court of Appeals address workers' compensation appeals. As Justice Starcher notes, these appeals are largely managed by staff attorneys and law clerks and are decided on the basis of the written record; however, they require that judicial time be spent reviewing and evaluating the work of the court's legal staff. This effort indicates that appellate judges do not work alone. Appellate judges, in particular, operate little law offices that are in constant interaction with the little law offices of their judicial colleagues.

Finally, as Starcher remarks, the state and federal supreme courts have administrative duties. They establish the procedural rules that lower court judges must follow, manage judicial branch finances, and interact with the executive and legislative branches on matters affecting the funding, personnel, facilities, and security of the courts. They also can seek to educate the public about the role of courts and work with the bar to improve the operations of the judiciary.

CONCLUSION

The American judge functions as a public representative who is supposed to be a neutral, independent arbiter in the adjudicatory process. As this section and the following interviews suggest, the fact that judges' duties require the use of governmental power to manage family, business, and other social and economic disputes, along with their authority to penalize convicted criminal defendants, defines them as important political figures in their communities and the nation. Their rulings help determine who has and who gets what in American economic and social life. They shape social duties and moral order. The judge thus maintains order but also defines how people are governed in the United States.

Dan Hogan

The Judge of a Limited-Jurisdiction Court

COURT MAGISTRATE FOR CRIMINAL BUSINESS Dan Hogan is a judge of a limited-jurisdiction court, a court that provides bench trials in minor criminal cases and small civil claims and that holds the initial hearing in criminal cases. With a jurisdiction similar to that of the magistrates, district judges, and justices of the peace in other states, for more than two centuries the Boston Municipal Court has heard criminal cases that cannot result in imprisonment, has held initial hearings and set bail in other criminal cases, and has heard domestic abuse, landlord-tenant, small civil claims, and neighborhood-nuisance disputes. The court is a busy, efficient, albeit welcoming urban government center located within walking distance of Boston's historic Quincy Market and landmarks associated with the American Revolution, such as the site of the Boston Massacre and the Old North Church.

Can you describe your duties?

I am the clerk magistrate of the Boston Municipal Court. The clerk magistrate is an appointment of the governor. It has both administrative and judicial functions. The clerk is responsible for most of the administration within a courthouse, the hiring, the firing, the staffing, the allocation of resources, as well as a judicial function. I can issue search warrants; arrest warrants; process criminal complaints; hear small claims, which are civilian or pro se litigants on small claims matters up to two thousand dollars; motor vehicle hearings; motor vehicle appeals; and applications for criminal complaints.

Can you discuss your judicial activities in more detail?

Any time after court hours, the clerk magistrate, following an arrest, can set a bail and admit someone to bail, or could release them, if they read a statement of facts. Within the Commonwealth, if you are arrested, the federal statute says that must be brought within forty-eight hours; the Massachusetts Supreme Judicial Court says within twenty-four. So, if you are arrested on a Friday night, you must have a judicial determination within twenty-four hours. If probable cause is not established, the clerk authorizes the release of the defendant, and that's the end of it. The clerk can also admit to bail, issue search warrants, issue arrest warrants. But on any particular day, when you begin your day, you start by reviewing all the arrests for the city. The police submit an application, which is a piece of paper and an affidavit laying out the facts and circumstances surrounding the arrest. And at that point the clerk either grants or denies the complaint. If the clerk does not find probable cause, the defendant is then ordered released. If the clerk finds probable cause, then we generate the actual complaint itself and prepare and process all the papers in order to proceed to the first criminal session, which is our arraignment session, where the defendant is formally charged. He's told about the offense, the date, the time. Now the arraignment session can be presided over by the clerk magistrate or the judge; it doesn't really make a difference.

Each morning, do you have to review the city's arrests from the night before?
Correct.

Can you estimate how many arrests you review every morning?
Well, it depends. What we do is prioritize all of those arrested over the weekend and held in custody. So we prioritize all the custodies for Monday. So on Monday we could have anywhere from sixty to one hundred people in custody awaiting a determination of bail.

This is for whole city of Boston?
Not necessarily. This is the central division. We are kind of the mother court. There are seven divisions of this court out in the local areas. Most processes that happen out in the other areas will eventually come downtown for a jury trial. We are located with the Superior Court, so, depending on the nature and circumstance of the offense, the outlying divisions could handle it, or it could come in here. We handle a number of different sessions now. Our most recent concern is that Boston has had a significant uptake in gun files. So what we have done is, the DA's [district attorney, the prosecutor] office has asked us to prioritize these cases, so we take all of the gun arrests from throughout the city. All the motions and things. Dispositive motions are done in the lower courts and then brought in here. So we're trying probably three or four jury trials a day, just specifically for guns. So all that takes place. You know, Mondays are custodies, and Tuesdays are all of those people that are released over the weekend and bailed or released on their own recognizance. They have to appear on Tuesday, and that could be another hundred.

You said that the police submit the reason they arrested the individual and that you as a magistrate have to decide whether there is there probable cause. How often do you decide that the police may have made an error or that there isn't probable cause?
I would say probably within a course of a month there are several. For example, there were five people arrested last night on the Boston Common who I

dealt with today. One with the gun, and the police charged the other four on a joint venture theory. As a result of reading them, we just started striking some of the offenses. So they were charged with a possession of a firearm, disorderly [conduct], disturbing the peace, and as a result, once we were finished with four of them, the only offense that we found probable cause for was disturbing the peace. It went from five guys charged with guns, resisting arrest, disorderly person, and disturbing the peace to one person charged with all those offenses and the other four, at the end of it, for disturbing the peace. So the police charged them with everything, and the court then made a decision that was contrary to what the police decided.

Can you also describe how you determine whether they can post bail?
Massachusetts is pretty specific. [In] Massachusetts the rules regarding bail are not necessarily the dangerousness of the defendant. The issue to be decided is whether or not the defendant is likely to appear. So you look at the nature and circumstances of the offenses, the past history in terms of the number of defaults, and so bail can run anywhere from released on their own recognizance to a one hundred thousand dollar cash bond. It's actually one million dollars, but they are required to post ten percent or one hundred thousand dollars cash.

In terms of the criminal practice, do any other things stand out in terms of what you do?
I think one of the most important issues is that the laws are divided in such a way that the Constitution wants to have separate and distinct branches of government. And they don't want all the authority resting on the executive branch. The clerk or the judge within the local courts can issue a search warrant. The chief justice of the Massachusetts Supreme [Judicial] Court cannot. Why? Because the legislature says so. I think that's one of the most important things that we do. At any point of the day or night, allowing the police department to search someone's home, car, person, I think that's an enormous amount of responsibility, and we take that extremely seriously. I think that's one of the greatest things, that there's an independent analysis of the facts before the police department is authorized to go in at any time and rip the place apart, and then whether they find anything or not just walk out and say "oops."

Can you talk a little bit about the mechanics of the search warrant process?
Sure. Massachusetts has very specific rules as to the veracity of the informant. There are all kinds of different issues. The authority of the clerk magistrate is throughout the Commonwealth; it's not defined by certain criminal jurisdictions. So the clerk magistrate can issue a search warrant for anywhere within the Commonwealth with the exception of an invasive procedure. For example, the removal of a bullet from someone's body, or something along those lines. That is only for a judge of either the Boston Municipal Court, the district court, or the superior court. But we do anything from hand-to-hand sales, search warrants of homes, search warrants of cars, as far as tissues and

samples off of cars, bullet casings, bullets removed from homes, all types of issues. Which is great because you get an opportunity to deal with different kinds of cases, you're thinking, and really it's important stuff.

Do officers show up at specific times in your workday for warrants?

No, there are on-call people, The unique part of this city and this criminal jurisdiction is, we don't necessarily have a constituency, like a local court, where it's the peoples' court and it's the people from the community and the neighborhood that utilize that court's resources. Here within the capital city, with the number of banks, financial institutions, law firms located here, every day there is a swelling of a million-plus people who come into and then leave the jurisdiction. And obviously it gets busier around Red Sox time. When the Sox are in town, we get some overanxious fans who want to run on the field. You've got to be able to gauge the different levels of crime. Those are people who may have been out and enjoying themselves a little too much. But we try and treat everybody the same, and that I think is the best part of the job, is you get an opportunity to treat people properly. Here is where the people get their firsthand exposure to what the courts are about. Whether you're on jury duty, whether you're here for a speeding ticket, the majority of the people have no idea what the courts do, and this is their first exposure. So as long as we can treat them reasonably, they leave satisfied. I can give you an example. Historically, when judges heard all the small-claims cases, their appeal rate was probably fifteen percent. Now that the legislature has changed the law and authorized the clerk magistrates to hear all the small claims, the appeals rate is down to about two percent. I think people just want to come in and be heard, and I think we do a pretty good job of that.

In terms of the cases that you hear as a magistrate acting as a judge, you hear civil cases under two thousand dollars, correct?

Under two thousand dollars with the exception of insurance cases. And then there can be no limit.

Is that something unique to Massachusetts law?

I think it is. I haven't seen any other jurisdiction like that. The small claims of two thousand dollars cost the citizen up to forty dollars to file a small claim, where we can give them a hearing, usually in this court within four to six weeks. And you can come in and we'll give you all the time that you want to present your case. Then there is a decision, and obviously there is some appellate remedy.

What is the percentage of people who represent themselves pro se?

Getting larger every day, probably thirty to forty percent.

So a lot of litigants still have lawyers?

The party that tends to have representation is the purchaser of the debt. But most of the debt and collections defendants we see are pro se.

What are your interactions with staff and lawyers?

On a daily basis we begin every morning here with a group of people from the clerk's office and a number of the judges. We talk about a number of different issues over a cup of coffee every single morning. That's when people figure out what their assignments are. The clerk's office deals with every person from all spectrums of society. Because, as I said, this is the first place that they come to when they are not able to resolve their disputes or they need help. They need an order of protection, they come here. The clerk's office staff, more so than the judges', deals with assistant district attorneys, the bar, police officers, outside agencies, the jail, the House of Correction, the Registry of Motor Vehicles. On a daily basis, probably in the area of two hundred calls a day dealing with many different topics. We interact with judges every day. The clerk is also, as a part of their judicial functions, is the actual keeper of the record. As the court is speaking, the clerk's office staff is recording everything that takes place, not only in electronic means but also by hand.

What is the civil-criminal case balance in your workload?

The amount of civil business done in this court exceeds all of the surrounding courts combined. We're pretty user friendly. We've got a pretty knowledgeable staff. Most of our people spend their time on criminal work. There are not as many civil experts as there are criminal experts here. Given the limited resources within the Commonwealth, the resources to each branch have significantly diminished, and we've lost, since the year 2000, probably forty percent of our staff. Something has to suffer, and priority is always given to the criminal defendants in the criminal cases at the expense of the civil cases.

But your court handles both?

We handle both, and a significant amount of it. Because we're divided, and this is the mother court, we are divided into different jurisdictions. The city of Boston clearly has the most number of criminal cases. Once you start going out to Springfield, they have low warrants. Their criminal cases have significantly increased, and their civil remains pretty much constant. They don't do a lot of civil business, but we do probably in the area of seven thousand or eight thousand general civil filings, probably the same number of small claims. And then you've got petitions, civil commitments, and protections. If you group them all together, our civil business has increased. In my opinion, criminal stats are always fluctuating based on the economy. So as the economy begins to go up, criminal cases go down. And we are now experiencing an increase in a number of criminal cases as well. If one has to suffer, we're probably doing around eight thousand five hundred or so general criminal filings, so civil will suffer.

Could you explain your administrative duties and the administration of this court?

The Massachusetts state court system is different from the federal courts, where Congress just allocates X dollars and the judicial branch spends them in a way that they determine to be acceptable. In Massachusetts the executive branch has always tried to give, say, give the judiciary one lump sum and let them spend it. The legislature has disagreed. The governor's budget would give them four or five hundred million dollars, and the legislature says "no." The legislature breaks it down, and they break it down per court, and it's the legislature that decides what court gets what resources. That's always been a source of controversy, because there are those from outside the city that say that "the Boston courts always get all the resources and we don't." I don't know whether that's accurate or not. However, the legislature allocates, and within this particular court, the line item for this particular court, if it's seven million, probably six and a half million goes to the clerk, and a half a million goes to the judge, and there is always all that controversy over who's actually the administrative head of the court. The clerk does all the hiring, does all the firing.

The hiring of whom?

Hiring of anyone within the clerk's office. All of the judges are appointed by the governor, and they have a limited staff. Prior to 1992 the chief justices of the different courts would hire probation officers, probation personnel court officers, anyone but the clerk's staff. The law was changed in 1992, and since that time, the commissioner of probation became responsible for hiring all the probation officers. The clerk is responsible for all the clerks, and the court officers are appointed out of the state administrative office and assigned to the different courts. The legislature has really taken authority away from the chief justice of the local court and divided it between the clerk and the commissioner of probation. All of those people that the chief justice used to appoint and hire, they no longer have that authority. It's difficult because all of those people, who are not responsible to the chief justice, actually have to make the courts run. The probation and the clerk's office are basically what make the courts run. You could pretty much get along in a court on a daily basis with the clerk. The clerk could run everything, the arraignments, with the exception of guilty or not guilty, or presiding over trials, because the probation officers respond to the probation department and the clerk's office does pretty much everything else. That's always been a bit of a controversy between judges and the clerk magistrates, both appointed under the same process by the governor, but not necessarily answerable to one another. It can work very well, or at times it can be a bit unusual.

Can you talk about the difficulties and challenges of administering a big-city court?

I'm the luckiest guy in America to be here, I'm extremely fortunate. As you can see, I have a picture of then Ambassador Cellucci on my window, and out in the front hallway, the vestibule, you will always see Governor Cellucci there, because he's my appointing authority. I've had the luxury of making a number of great appointments, and the people here get the work done. You and I can sit in this room all day long, and the work gets done by the people that

I consider to be the real workers on a daily basis, banging away every single day. I'm extremely fortunate in that regard. I'm fortunate with the resources that the legislature has given me so that we're able to hire capable people, and fewer of them to do the same amount of work. Our technology has helped us an awful lot; we've increased technology. And so I feel pretty fortunate coming in here. The good thing about it is the people that work here. They are very good to me, they're very loyal to me, and I'm loyal to them, and that's what makes it work. In addition, I'm fortunate because this court is so big and so active that my job is never dull.

Given that this court is so busy and you've faced significant budget and staffing cuts, I imagine your job becomes a bit of a juggling act.

It is. There have been a number of issues brought before the court, and people are quick to point out the shortcomings within the process. The process doesn't work all the time, but in the same regard the personnel within the court—it doesn't make a difference whether it's the judge, the clerk, all the way down to the entry-level personnel—they are asked to do so many more things with so many fewer resources. They're asked to be court personnel, public employees, social workers, medical doctors, psychologists. The people who bring in these issues before the court have all kinds of issues, you know, drugs and alcohol. The crime is one thing, but the real issue is what's the underlying problem. I can name a hundred times that people here have given up their jackets and coats, money, transit passes, tokens, have driven people from point A to point B, or to a treatment program. Those are not rare instances and the level of commitment is amazing. I think sometimes our employees get pounded on a daily basis in the media. They don't do this, they don't do that, they're lazy, they're overpaid. That is actually not the case. People here average probably thirty-five, forty, fifty thousand dollars, but they've also been here for twenty-five, thirty, forty years, and it's a very expensive place to live, trying to raise a family, and they do just a great job.

I think that is one of the biggest challenges, that you've got people who come in who are already angry or agitated and the toughest part is trying to deal with them. I think we do a pretty good job of it. These people have mental health issues, and you have to treat them so, and we don't get trained for that kind of stuff. Also, we have to deal with language barriers, so our people have learned different languages, and that's because they're committed and they're dedicated public servants, and I don't believe that they get the recognition. Taking shots at me is one thing. That's what I'm supposed to [be] doing, but taking shots at them, I'll defend them to the hilt because I know what it is that they do on a daily basis. I know what sacrifices they make to be here.

There's a lot of talk about an increase in the number of cases and a litigation explosion. Do you sense that here?

I do. We see a lot of increases in our collections, where you've got firms going out and buying up all kind of debt. One of the biggest issues that we have now is in our small claims; for example, where a defendant fails to appear, and the court gives a judgment and an execution. Some of these constables have been taking that execution, and if the execution is for two or three hundred dollars, they're going out, taking the motor vehicle. It's a fundamental fairness issue that to me is outrageous. You've got someone who owes three hundred, and they've taken a five or eight thousand dollar car, which, quite frankly, the bank owns. Then they hide it, so then that three hundred dollars, by the time they're able to pay, the debt is now six hundred.

And finally, are there any other negatives that come to mind?

To be honest with you, I can't. The only other negative issue is that we have several members of the local media that pound away at us. I have a media person calls me the "al Qaeda of Hackaramma" and [says] that we're all unemployable anywhere else. We have a local guy, Howie Carr. He writes and he just bashes and bashes and bashes, as if anyone employed within the public sector couldn't string a group of words together to form their own sentence. That's just not true. I think that what happens is that we in public service become so afraid to help people out. I think we've lost that mission. Public service is supposed to be about helping people out, and there are things you can do and things you can't do, and there are times, in this particular court, on motor vehicles, on criminal applications, on anything, we almost invariably find in favor of the citizen. The people driving to work at six in the morning, they're going to work, they're raising a family, they're paying huge taxes. This is an expensive place to live. What we try to do here is that we try to treat you reasonably, give you the benefit of the doubt, and sometimes we can't. The problem is the public perception, the media, lawyers, these factors have come together in that perfect storm, and we're all afraid to say, "Let me see if I can help you." Hopefully, I can help you, and if I can't, I can't, and I'll be the first one to tell you that I can't. And I think that public service has lost that a bit of that, and it's a disappointing factor of this job.

Rick Savignano

The State Trial Judge and Crime

RICK SAVIGNANO IS A DISTRICT court judge in Brockton, Massachusetts, home of the late heavyweight boxing legend Rocky Marciano. His court is one of general jurisdiction and hears a wide range of criminal, civil, housing, juvenile, mental health, and other types of cases. However, he largely is assigned to criminal cases. District court criminal jurisdiction extends to all felonies punishable by a sentence up to five years and other, specific felonies with greater potential penalties; all misdemeanors; and all violations of city and town ordinances and bylaws. In felonies not within district court final jurisdiction, the district court conducts probable cause hearings to determine whether a defendant should be bound over to the superior court. The interview took place in Brockton's modern courthouse, located in the refurbished city center outside of Boston. The courthouse reflects Brockton's diverse community, with signs announcing not only the assistance of Spanish and Portuguese translators but also help in the dialect of the Cape Verde Islands, which are located off the western coast of Africa.

Can you explain why you chose to become a judge?

I had been a prosecutor for almost all of my career, at the local level, the state level, and the federal level, and I very much enjoyed that. The reason that I sought to become a judge, quite frankly, was for professional and personal reasons. Personally, I have young kids, three young kids at the time, and the opportunity to serve as a judge gave me a little bit more flexibility with my time. I wouldn't necessarily always be on call for homicides, which is what I was doing at the time. So it gave me a little more regularity in my schedule. More important professionally, it let me stay involved with trial court. I love the trial court. I love criminal trials. I love being involved in them, and it gave me a chance to stay involved in a different role.

How did you become a judge?

In Massachusetts there is a procedure. You're actually appointed by the governor, but to initiate that process you must file an application. You obtain an application from the governor's office. It's fairly extensive. You fill out the application, you send it in, and you wait. When there is a vacancy, they choose to interview certain individuals who filed applications as kind of a prescreening process. You get interviewed for that by a local screening committee appointed by the governor. They then make a favorable or unfavorable recommendation. If you get a favorable recommendation, you meet with the governor. He or she then nominates you. You must be confirmed by what's called the Governor's Council, which are seven elected representatives from throughout the state.

What kinds of cases does your court handle? Specifically, what percentage of your court's work is civil versus criminal?

I would say that throughout the state, particularly in urban courts, such as the court I sit in, ninety-five percent of what we do is criminal and five percent civil. And that civil is a real mixed bag. It's not just what you might think of traditionally, like contracts and torts. We also do an extensive amount of mental health commitments, involuntary mental health commitments, restraining orders, collections cases, and small-claims cases. It's really a diverse range of civil cases.

The criminal cases differ between district courts in the sense of the setting you're in. If you're in a suburban or a rural court, you're certainly going to get more motor vehicle stuff. At a busier urban court, such as Brockton—and we're the third busiest court in the state—we handle close to ten thousand criminal cases a year. We do a substantial amount of cases involving firearms, narcotics, narcotics distribution, shootings, domestic violence, as well as motor vehicle offenses, larceny offenses, breakings and enterings, and so on. The state does a pretty good job of maintaining statistics of what each court does, but we are a court that deals heavily in significant, substantial crimes of violence and narcotics.

As a district court judge, how do cases get into your court? Are you the first court to consider these cases?

Yes, all cases originate and come through the district court. There are certain felonies, however, that we do not have final jurisdiction over, and those are spelled out by statute. Suffice it to say, there is a category of felonies that we do not have final jurisdiction over: those which carry a potential state prison sentence of five years or more and would include things like murder, rape, child rape, armed robbery, and certain other offenses. If those cases [come] through here, which they do on a daily basis, they're arraigned here. They bring themselves to a superior court by way of the grand jury. The prosecutor will seek an indictment through the grand jury to have them brought to a superior court.

The more serious felony cases will come to the district court first for arraignment and then are handed up to the superior court?

For example, we have probably ten or fifteen homicides arraigned in this court each year. They'll be arraigned in this court. We'll set it up for a further hearing in this court, and, in the interim, between the arraignment and the further hearing, the district attorney takes that case, presents it to the grand jury, which issues an indictment, and then that case is transferred to the superior court. And that's what happens with those superior court felony jurisdiction cases; they get indicted and brought over to the superior court.

Do you handle a defendant's initial appearance, or is that handled by a magistrate?

No, it's funny, in Suffolk County, they do use a magistrate to do that and have done so very successfully. The initial appearance here is actually the arraignment. It's a little different than the federal system, which has an initial appearance. In our court, in the district court, arraignments are held in front of judges, so we do handle those. Certain court magistrates are empowered to handle those sessions, but by and large, we do those.

Could you talk a little about an arraignment?

The arraignment is, frankly, my favorite session, because it's the emergency room equivalent of a courthouse. Everything that happens comes through that room, comes through the arraignment, whether it's the people who have been picked up over the weekend for a variety of offenses and held for their arraignment on Monday morning, everything from operating under the influence of liquor to homicide to domestic violence. So you get the whole range of criminal arraignments. You also get, in our arraignment sessions, the restraining orders, where plaintiffs come in and seek restraining orders, which is a fairly substantial amount of our business. Those are heard in there. Petitions for mental health commitments come through the arraignment session. Petitions for substance abuse commitments, which we call Section 35 commitments in Massachusetts. These are for someone who is addicted to alcohol and/or drugs and therefore presents a danger to themselves or others, so we're empowered to have them committed involuntarily for up to thirty days to detox and get some preliminary treatment. All those issues come to us through the arraignment session, so it's really the first line of where we see cases, and it's where we have emotions running high in the audience, and you have people who are fresh off the street from their arrest. It's much more of an immediate kind of feel of justice. I find it to be the most interesting session to be in.

What percentage of your cases are settled before trial?

Criminal or civil? I can speak with more experience to the criminal, because that's where I sit.

Your court is split that way?

I do some civil. I do, I do some civil, but I am primarily a criminal judge, about ninety-five percent. You start with the fact that each year ten thousand criminal cases come into our court, everything from trespass to significant, substantial criminal cases. It would be impossible for us to try ten thousand pure criminal cases. What happens is, in Massachusetts, you come in and you are arraigned. Many of our cases are addressed and resolved on the day of arraignment. A substantial portion of those ten thousand are addressed on that initial day, whether they be minor motor vehicle, larceny by check under two hundred fifty dollars, a twenty-dollar check that bounced, minor trespassing cases, and so on. We make an effort to try to resolve those cases, particularly with people who don't have criminal histories on the first day, on the arraignment day. We'll have them speak with a prosecutor. If they're able to resolve the case, many times it's dismissed on costs, or a small fine. So we try to move a lot of those cases. If any of the cases are unable to be resolved at arraignment—and let's say out of one hundred, twenty-five are resolved, and that's a rough estimate, on arraignment—the seventy-five remaining cases proceed to the next stage, which is called the pretrial conference. The pretrial conference is where the parties get together, they exchange some discovery, they learn a little bit more about the case; and a substantial amount of cases are also resolved at the pretrial stage.

Are you involved in that stage?

I am. Well, we move from different sessions, from arraignment to pretrial to motions to trial, so we do move around. So there is a fair amount of cases that are resolved at the pretrial stage. Not all of them.

Could you talk a little about your role in that pretrial conference as a judge? Do you stand back? Do you get involved?

There are differing styles. The case law talks about judges not being involved in the so-called plea-bargaining process, and I adhere to that fairly strictly. Obviously, at the pretrial, if the case is called, I'll say to the prosecutor and the defense counsel, "Folks, have you had a chance to talk about this case? Do you need a second call? Do you want to see if you can resolve it?" I see that as a perfectly permissible interpretation of the role, facilitating their ability to resolve it. I do not, however, engage in active bargaining, in the sense of, "If you plead to this, I will grant this." I don't do that. I let them. There is a mechanism called the "green sheet" in Massachusetts. It's literally a green piece of paper, and it's a form where the parties put together their proposed deal. The defendant puts down what he or she would accept as a disposition. The prosecutor puts down what he or she is recommending, and then there's a spot for the judge, what he or she would do, and that gets presented to the court. I look at it, I consider the case, I look at the person's record, I make a determination, but I don't engage proactively or significantly in the bargaining process. Other judges, I'm told, are a little bit more proactive. I'm less proactive than others. I let the parties work it out.

So you have a plea-bargain debate outlined on a piece of green paper?

On the sheet, exactly.

Is there a strategy for each party about this, based on the expected punishment, in terms of what they'll suggest?

There is. We have what's called in Massachusetts a defendant cap plea. Let's say the defendant comes in on the green sheet and says, "I'll plea to this charge of operating under the influence and this is what I will agree to do." The prosecutor makes a much higher recommendation, and let's say I agree with the prosecutor. For whatever reason, I adopt the prosecutor's recommendation. The defendant can withdraw the plea and say, "never mind, I'll proceed to trial." That being said, our pretrial sessions are fairly effective. Each judge brings his or her own style into that room on how to resolve cases. Some judges have what's called lobby conferences, where they bring the parties into the office. I don't do that, either. Everything I do is on the record. I just think it's more appropriate. I'm not, like I said, I'm not an active participant in the bargaining process. I'll facilitate it. If they were to say, "Judge, we need a half an hour. We need to go outside and hammer this through." "Go right ahead," I'll tell them, "and try to work it out." I don't engage myself directly in that process. And those cases that are not resolved in pretrial go to the trial session, where there still is an opportunity to resolve it, prior to trial. But in most cases we do go to trial. We try a number of cases, and we have juries comprised of six people in the district court. In fact, I'm in the midst of a jury-of-six trial right now.

Can you discuss the trial activities that occur before the case is presented to the jury, for example, motions and discovery?

Let's say the case is a bit of a complex case, and I'll use the case that I have now on trial as an example of that. The case was not resolved in arraignment. It's a fairly serious matter. It was not resolved in pretrial because, quite frankly, there were triable issues. I think the defense believes it has the chance to prevail, and in this case they very well might. So it's one of those cases that went all the way to trial sessions. There were a number of motions before it actually went to trial. It's somewhat of a paper case. There were a number of discovery motions. Those were heard in the trial session. There were no motions to suppress in this case, but there are in many cases, and that's where they're heard; and again, that's a great session to be in, another one that I like. Because those are issues that I am very comfortable with. I like to write, and I like to research, and so on.

All those discovery- and suppression-type issues get resolved in the trial session. Once everything is complete, the case is set for a trial, and generally we get to trial fairly quickly. I think, statistically, we do a pretty good job from day of offense to day of trial, with some unavoidable exceptions to that.

The day of the trial, we'll have generally nine to twelve trials scheduled that day. Priority goes to those defendants who are in custody awaiting trial. Priority also goes to the oldest cases. We can do about three trials here in a given day. We bring in about forty-five jurors, which is enough. The day of trial I meet with the lawyers on the record in the courtroom. I check if there are any lingering issues, anything we need to know about, for example, do we need an interpreter, are there any motions, is there any evidence counsel wants to exclude in the trial, are there any witness availability issues or exhibit issues. We address all the logistical, mechanical, housekeeping issues at this point, which are mundane, but it's what I used to do, so I really enjoy it. Once you get that all clear, you bring the jury in, you engage in the jury selection empanelment process. We generally pick seven jurors so we have an extra.

What is Massachusetts' voir dire process?
Very limited.

Do you handle it, or do the lawyers have a significant role?
There's some variation. There are certain cases where voir dire in Massachusetts is mandatory. In fact, I had a case a couple of weeks ago where it was mandatory. Cases involving allegations of sexual abuse of minors, cases involving interracial homicide, cases involving interracial rape, cases involving the so-called insanity defense, all require us to have individual voir dire with the jurors, and there is a set standard of amount of questions that we are to ask. In the more generic case, where we are not required to engage in voir dire, it is very limited. There are about eight statutory questions we have to ask. We invite any other questions from the lawyers that they think might be relevant. But it is not asked of an individual juror. It's asked of the jury as a whole, and I know it's a source of some controversy among the trial bar, whether we should have more individual voir dire. In fact, when I used to travel around with the U.S. Department of Justice and meet with lawyers from Texas and all other places, they would regale us with these stories of lengthy individual voir dire. That's a foreign concept to us.

How do you decide on sentences?
Sentencing is an issue I've been involved in as a prosecutor making recommendations to the judge and now as a judge. Sentencing is probably one of the most important functions that we perform. Not only because of its impact on the defendant, which is, of course, the primary concern, but also the impact that it may have on the community and on the victim, and in this state we take into consideration the victim's perspective on what's the appropriate disposition. It's the responsibility that we take the most seriously. There are certainly relevant factors that you look at, like the nature of the circumstances of the offense. What was proven that the person did? You look certainly at the person's criminal history or absence of a criminal history. You listen, of course, to what the victim has to say. We're obligated to do so, and we do. We look at any mitigating circumstances that may be involved. We look at any rehabilitation possibilities that could be accomplished through imposition of probation and other programs. There's a whole constellation of factors that we consider in framing an appropriate disposition. I think most of us as judges, all of us as judges, look at that as probably the most, one of the most significant things we do.

Is the Massachusetts system similar to the federal system in that there is a significant guideline?

No. In fact about eleven years ago, when I was a prosecutor, I was an appointed member of what's called the Massachusetts Sentencing Commission, which was an effort to establish a federal-type system in Massachusetts, and it was comprised at the time of three sitting judges, three practicing defense bar representatives, and three prosecutors. We were all appointed by the governor. It was kind of a lengthy, multiyear project of gathering data and putting together sentencing grids, levels of offenders, and so on. I came in at about the seventh inning of that process. A prior prosecutor had stepped down, and I came in when the process was well under way. The sentencing commission then presented its findings to the governor and to the state legislature. It's never been adopted. It's been kind of a proposal that stayed there. I'm familiar with the federal system, having been a federal prosecutor. I'm not so sure which system is the best. All I know is, and what I recall from being a federal prosecutor, was that there was an awful lot of mathematics involved. There was a lot of adding and subtracting, which seemed a little difficult [laughs].

As a judge now, do you like the fact that you have greater latitude than the federal judges?

I do, and I think most of my colleagues do. I think judges welcome the opportunity to have that kind of flexibility, the ability to go beyond what a guideline might let them do. The secret of guidelines, however—and they are the product of a tremendous amount of work and great effort by the people involved—is that they were guidelines. You could deviate from them. You could have upward departure or downward departure, so long as you made written findings. They weren't cast in granite. You could actually deviate from the sentencing grid. So I think that there was probably some flexibility built in.

But then through court decisions, or whatever, they became set, no?

When I was a federal prosecutor and used to read the decisions that came out of the federal appellate courts, the number of decisions that would be interpreting the numbers in sentencing guidelines would be staggering. I mean, they became literally a lot of hair splitting about what numbers were to apply and what weren't to apply. It was kind of an interesting aspect to being a federal prosecutor.

Could you describe the civil side of your work?

On the civil side, there is a similar system that's been established to kind of process the cases as they go through. The civil cases are filed, and again we have jurisdiction over a full range of civil matters. It goes from contracts to torts and business litigation to dog licensing and gun license renewals. It's a broad spectrum of matters that we handle.

What civil issues get bumped up to the superior court?

The cases that have a certain amount of damages being sought. The threshold is over twenty-five thousand dollars. Now that isn't to say that we can't have recoveries in this court of over twenty-five thousand dollars, but it is to say that if it appears that a case is going to be twenty-five thousand dollars or more, those cases can be transferred up.

So the cases get docketed. Let's talk about more of a traditional civil case: a contract dispute or a personal injury case. Those tend to be driven more by the lawyers than the court. In other words, they file their interrogatories, they have their depositions, they gather their discovery, and a lot of that is lawyer to lawyer without a lot of judicial intervention. In recent years, there's been an effort to impose a little more judicial intervention in that process to kind of push that process along. We have what's called a case management conference, a CMC, a short while into the case where the parties are obligated to come in and report to a judge, or a magistrate, where they stand, whether they've reached any agreements, what's the possibility of resolution, is or is not. It's kind of a pretrial conference of sorts, but it's called a case management conference. After the case management conference, there is, in fact, a pretrial conference in which the parties have to come in and certify that discovery is complete, depositions are done, and they set a trial date. I believe that there is a higher percentage of resolution of civil cases prior to trial than there would be [of] criminal. I think a lot of our matters do get resolved prior to trial, but we do have a fair amount [of] civil activity in this court as well, and we do have certain judges who specialize more in these civil trial matters. I do a lot of the preliminary motions, the case management conferences and the like, but there are judges whose background is more attuned to the civil end, so they do a lot of the trials themselves.

In your court, do you make that split of cases in a formal way, or is it informal?
Informally. In this court, the Brockton court, there are probably five judges who sit here. There's a couple who are informally seen more as civil judges, whereas there are others who specialize in criminal. There are others who do both, and do both very, very well.

How are cases scheduled in your court? Is scheduling handled by a computer?
In our court it's more of a human function of the presiding judge, making the schedule and saying here's our civil docket list. Here we know what our criminal list is going to be. It's always going to be a fairly steady amount. So scheduling comes down to saying that next week the civil cases are going to go to this judge. She's going to hear the civil cases on Monday, Tuesday, Wednesday, and Thursday. The other four judges are going to hear criminal law. It's more of a resource allocation decision made in each individual court. We're not formally designated as criminal or civil or anything such as that.

Could you describe your daily, weekly, monthly interactions with your staff, with lawyers, and with other judges?
Okay, in terms of interactions with judges, we're very fortunate that we work in a big court, and as you may have noticed, in this courthouse it's not just the district court. We have the district court, the probate and family court, the juvenile court, and the housing court. We're all right here. So it's very collegial. There

are thirteen judges who work here, and that's nice. As for my colleagues on the district court bench, my interaction with them is throughout the day. You have to communicate. I'll be in a session where I might have twenty-five things to do, and the other judge's session was able to get through their work, so they can help out. It's a very fluid situation, so communication is really important. As judges we really treasure our colleagues. We're all different. We all come from different backgrounds, we all bring our own experiences to the bench, but we really enjoy that collegiality, and that's one of the great unknowns when you become a judge. You don't know what it's going to be like to work with other judges, and to me that's one of the great joys of it. I really enjoy my colleagues.

Can you use them for advice?

All the time. You know, it's something as simple as saying, "I've written this decision, would you just proofread it for me and tell me if I sound crazy here?" Or, "Have you read the recent case on search and seizure? What do you think of it?" I suppose it's not totally different from what it might be like to be on a faculty, to have colleagues with different experiences and perspectives who you can bounce things off of. It's similar, I would guess, to a college faculty, and to me it's the best part of the job.

The interactions with lawyers are right up there as well. I very much enjoy interacting with the lawyers in the courtroom, outside of the courtroom. Many times a year lawyers on both sides of the bar after a trial will ask to come in informally and ask me to talk about how their trial went. They ask me how they could have done this better, and I make that a quasi-teaching function. I really enjoy working with the lawyers. We have really good lawyers up here.

Do the interactions with lawyers take place strictly within the context of the courtroom?

Right.

Even pretrial conferences?

Right, out in the courtroom, but there's a lot of give and take. There's a lot of discussion out there about everything, and frankly, you'd be surprised in a busy courtroom, like a pretrial or arraignment, and you're out there from nine o'clock to five o'clock with a couple of short breaks, you're interacting with that same group of lawyers all day, a lot of things get said. You know, you learn a lot, and you just get a good sense of the other person. I don't want to say there is a lot of nonlawyer talk that goes on, but I like that kind of give and take that goes on. Having tried cases, I enjoy kind of playing the role of working with the lawyers and seeing how they do. So the interaction with judges and the lawyers is terrific.

Do you sit on the bench sometimes and judge the quality of the lawyers' work before you?

Yes, you do. You keep it to yourself, of course, but there are many times, and you have to understand that every lawyer brings different skill sets, different strengths and weaknesses to each case. As I'm sure every judge looked at me when I was trying a case, probably shaking his or her head and saying, "Why is Savignano doing that?" We do the same, but then it's also a great chance for us to pass on any experience or whatever wisdom we might have about trying cases to practitioners, but I think we miss the adrenaline from trying a case. But I don't miss the sleepless nights, particularly before a murder trial, when you want to make sure your witnesses are coming, what are they going to say, are they going to remember, and all of those intangibles that you can't control. I don't worry about those anymore.

What other work do you do every day?

We don't have legal interns or law clerks in this court for, I don't know if it's traditional reasons or financial reasons. Occasionally, we get a law student who comes and volunteers, but it's not really a major component. I do everything. I do my own typing. And as I said, we spend so much of our time in the courtroom that when we're not there, we're at the library looking up cases, we're typing our decisions, we're doing all of that kind of work, so we're pretty self-sufficient. We do have clerical staff, who really are the backbone of the system, the women and men who get the complaints filed and take care of paperwork and scheduling and all that. In a busy place like this, ten thousand cases a year, we would grind to a halt if we didn't have a great support staff, and we do. Court officers are terrific. You get to know them probably as well as anyone in the courthouse because they're the ones who come in with you and who bring you out, so there's great interaction with them.

Can you describe opinion writing?

Sure. It is one of the aspects of the job that I enjoy as much as any. I really like to write. And we do, particularly in this court, a very healthy dose of motions to suppress. We do a lot of gun cases and a lot of drug cases. With guns and drugs come motions to suppress. So search-and-seizure law is something that we have to be intimately familiar with and conversant in. So in any given year, I probably write fifty to seventy-five decisions on motions to suppress or motions to dismiss or motions to exclude evidence. Whether it's automobile stops, execution of search warrants, pat and frisks on the street. We have a great defense bar that files good and creative motions. We hold hearings. We're responsible in this state, as I mentioned, and virtually every state, for making findings of fact. If there's a motion to suppress on an execution of search warrant or about a motor vehicle stop, I'll hold a hearing, the police officers and whoever else will testify. I'll take notes. I will issue written findings of fact, and then apply the law to those facts and make a ruling. Generally, I write anywhere from five to ten pages on each. I enjoy that. I just really like that. I wouldn't want to do that exclusively. I wouldn't want to be an appellate court judge and simply write all the time, but I like to do it, because it keeps you current in the law.

It adds a creative component to the job?
    It does. I like to write.

Finally, what are the pluses and minuses of the job?
    The pluses are many. The pluses, personally for me, are the practice of law is very demanding, whether you're a defense lawyer, whether you're a prosecutor—which is what I was—whether you work in a big firm, whether you work as a solo practitioner, the demands of being a lawyer are substantial. What I mean by that are the actual hour demands, the responsibility, and everyone goes through it in whatever avenue of the law that they pursue. Whether they're a prosecutor, they're working seven days a week getting ready for a murder trial, whether they're a defense lawyer or a civil lawyer. That's great. It's important that every profession has that. The medical profession has that rigorous internship process and so on. There comes a time, however, where you want to reach a balance, and for me it was I have three kids and I wanted to be able to have some control over my schedule, a little bit more control over my schedule, to be able to coach them, attend whatever they were doing, and be more actively involved. When they were younger I was in the Department of Justice flying all over the place. I was a homicide prosecutor answering pages every night, going out to scenes. It was wonderful work. It was exciting, but it was also demanding. So, from a personal perspective, this job has enabled me to know that I work Monday through Friday. A couple times a year I'm on call to issue restraining orders throughout the night, and so on, but other than that, my hours are pretty regular. I'm able to spend time with my family, which is invaluable. So from a personal prospective, I like that.

    Professionally, however, there are tremendous advantages and rewards, as I've mentioned some of them. I very much enjoy the opportunity to work with all my colleagues. It's been great. The work is challenging. The law is always changing. I like that academic component of it, of having to stay current and be on your toes and know what the changes in the law are. I love the trial work. I like to be in the courtroom, to be actively involved in the quality of justice, ensuring that people get fair trials, that trials are conducted efficiently and appropriately. I like that. I like bringing my experience to bear to make sure that a trial is done well and that the process works fairly for all involved. So those are the advantages.

    The disadvantages: I miss trying cases. I miss the game. It's what I did for a long time. I think if you talk to anyone who was a trial lawyer, before they became a judge, which is a great preparation for becoming a judge, that each of us in some way misses being involved, but not so much that I would want to go back.

    You know, I just want to make sure that I do everything that I can do to make sure that the folks in my courtroom get a fair shake and that's really what it boils down to. That's really what it boils down to.

Steven King

The State Trial Judge
and Civil Cases

FILLED WITH LEGAL PAPERS, PHOTOS of his rafting trips, and assorted memorabilia and awards, Judge King's chambers occupy a portion of the second floor of the La Porte County Courthouse in Michigan City, Indiana. Not far from the shore of Lake Michigan, the downtown business district of the city, a lakeboat casino, and three penitentiaries, his La Porte County Superior Court No. 2 is a trial court of general jurisdiction for the potential adjudication of all criminal, civil, and family disputes arising in the northern portion of the county. However, his court has a docket largely composed of family law cases and other civil actions. Soft-spoken, Judge King reminds the interviewer of the high school teacher that he once was.

Could you please describe how you became a lawyer?
I grew up in LaPorte County near a little town called Wanath, Indiana—an Indian name meaning "knee deep in mud." I graduated from South Central High School, went on to Ball State University to become an architect, and transferred into education. I graduated in 1972 and went into the Peace Corps and served two years in Sierra Leone, West Africa. I came home and taught school in a social studies department for a year. I was accepted at Valparaiso University Law School and graduated in 1978. I went to law school because I have always had a keen interest in government and wanted to be involved in government as a lawyer. Since graduating from law school, I have spent my entire legal career in the Indiana judicial system. I never practiced law. Right out of law school I was a clerk at the Indiana Court of Appeals in Indianapolis for two years. I came back to work on a congressional campaign that did not succeed and went back to Indianapolis to work at the Indiana Supreme Court for two years. Then I came back to LaPorte County, where I served in the capacity of probate commissioner at the LaPorte Circuit Court, which was in essence as a magistrate hearing divorce cases. I did that for eight years.

Could you please describe how you became a judge?

In 1990 I ran for this position on LaPorte Superior Court No. 2 and have been reelected twice—so twenty-three years on the bench altogether. In Indiana we elect our judges in ninety of the ninety-two counties in partisan elections. The election process is akin to any other campaign. We do all the things that other candidates do, such as put up yard signs, appear at public gatherings, and take out radio and TV ads, et cetera. The one caveat or exception to the standard campaign is that we are not, as candidates for judicial office, allowed to take positions on legal issues. For example, I can't come out and say I am for or against the death penalty. They restrict us, and as a result the campaigns lack substance. You may talk about administrative issues in the court you are running for. You can't address legal issues and make claims that "I am going to be hard on criminals" or "I am going to be tough in sentencing." You can't make statements like that.

The first time I ran against an incumbent judge, so it was a contested process. The pattern in LaPorte County has been that if you do an acceptable job, as determined by the local bar association, you are not likely to have an opponent. More often than not incumbent judges who are doing good work are not opposed. I think one of the primary reasons for that is the pay schedule in Indiana for judges falls below what a successful lawyer can make. We are at $110,500. Your successful practitioners with experience can earn more than that. People aren't necessarily going to run for judge for that reason.

What kinds of cases come before your court?

In the county we have five superior courts. They are all courts of general jurisdiction. By local court rule, we divvy up the criminal caseload geographically and by type of case. The court I serve in handles all the criminal cases arising out of the Department of Corrections [DOC] facilities in LaPorte County. We have about seven thousand five hundred offenders housed in this county. Between them and the correctional officers, who might be engaged in trafficking items of contraband into the DOC facilities, [I have] the stabbings and various things that happen in the Indiana State Prison and two other facilities—a medium-security facility and a minimum-security facility. For quite a while the number one criminal defendant in my court was [charged with] battery by bodily waste. He was a prisoner throwing feces and urine at correctional officers. They stopped charging those and are disciplining those individuals internally now. However, I am going to have a murder trial in two weeks involving an offender who allegedly stabbed another offender.

Otherwise, I have a general jurisdiction civil caseload that involves a lot of family law, paternity cases, divorces, child custody and visitation, support, and the whole spectrum of civil law suits: auto accidents, contract disputes, review of local governmental agencies' decisions, zoning issues, real estate cases. Probably the family divorce and paternity cases are approximately fifty to sixty percent of my caseload timewise.

Are there other courts in this county?

What we have in Indiana is state legislation that authorizes the creation of appointed judicial officers to assist elected judges in moving the caseload of the court. Commonly they are used in the juvenile area of law. We call those people magistrates here in Indiana. We have two magistrates in LaPorte County. One of them is the juvenile magistrate, and the other one is assisting with family law matters at the LaPorte Circuit Court and handling the divorce caseload. So they are full judicial officers, and they get paid eighty percent of what judges do. There is a superior court in LaPorte that handles felonies, traffic offenses, and misdemeanor offenses. In this building we have a court that handles that caseload, but we don't have a judge or court officer who is doing solely initial appearances or just limited pretrial stuff. All judges are seeing their caseload through to the end.

What staff do you have to assist you?

I have a court administrator/secretary and I have a bailiff, and I have a court reporter, and I have a law clerk who I hire out of Valparaiso University. It's just twenty miles away. We have about nine thousand six hundred dollars budgeted for the year. The law clerk works full time in the summer and part time during the school year. I did that my third year. It is a terrific experience and a great chance to get an exposure to how courts function and what helps a court decide something a certain way. It is a tremendous opportunity for law students to get a judicial clerkship. That's what I did at the Indiana Court of Appeals and Supreme Court, too. I treasure the experience, because you get to immerse yourself in the theory of the law and work with experienced justices.

What are some of the activities that occupy your time?

One of the things I spent a lot of time doing is signing papers, such as the pleadings that come through the court. That will be the first thing in the morning and at the end of the day and throughout the day. Occasionally attorneys will come in with pleadings that they'd like to have signed on an immediate basis. We try to be accessible to those circumstances. We have lay people who come in who are attempting to file pleadings of one kind or another that may or may not be proper and that may have to be rejected or approved. One of the things that Indiana has done, which complicates a judge's life on a daily basis, is that, in order to address domestic violence, a major problem in this country, we have set up a procedure whereby lay people can file pleadings on forms provided by the court to address situations of domestic violence on an emergency basis.

So we will be reviewing pleadings signed under oath on the forms that have been provided by the court for those people and setting up hearings within thirty days to hear those cases. Every day for about two months forward we have scheduled from eight-thirty to noon and from 1 P.M. to 4 P.M. The time is for hearings of one type or another unless those cases settle, which they do on a common basis. So, in court from eight-thirty to noon, and from one to four, we have hearings of one type or another, a lot of those family, paternity cases, and child-related matters. A large percentage of them involve petitions to modify support, petitions to modify custody, petitions to hold someone in contempt for not paying support or not allowing visitation, petitions to modify visitation, and just the general wrangling that people have over their children, which in bad cases never seems to get resolved. For the most part, in a divorce case things tail away after a couple of years as people get their footing and get over the trauma of divorce.

What else occupies your time?

We have discovery issues between attorneys. In a pretrial context, they are trying to obtain information from the other side that the other side doesn't want to give them. I will have a hearing to determine if that information should be required to be provided. Tomorrow I'm going to have a hearing involving the local police merit commission's decision to terminate a Michigan City police officer for alleged misconduct. The review of decisions by the local zoning board will come before this court.

Do you have many documents to read and review?

Yes, I do. Because my caseload involves people who are already incarcerated, I don't have warrants in my criminal caseload. What I do have is a creature called body attachments that we issue for people who have failed to appear for a hearing involving their alleged contemptuous behavior, most commonly failure to pay child support. In my particular court, we have all of the paternity actions filed in LaPorte County by the local child support bureau enforcement agency, which is set up to assist low-income parents, commonly mothers, to establish paternity and to establish the support obligation. I have maybe two hundred fifty of those cases filed every year. They don't go away, because the children aren't emancipated until they are eighteen. So you compound that times eighteen until they cycle out of the system. We have a lot of support enforcement hearings. People are served with an order to appear, and they fail to appear for the hearing. A warrant or body attachment may be issued for their arrest. So I am issuing those commonly. Once they are arrested, the sheriff lets me know. I bring them into court and as quickly as possible advise them why they are held in jail and commonly release them under an order to appear at another date. Our goal is not incarceration. Our goal is to get people to pay child support and get their attention.

Are parties in family law matters represented by counsel?

Normally they are not. The mother may be represented by an attorney of the child support bureau, the government agency set up to help them. If the bureau seeks the incarceration for contempt after a hearing, they would ask [that] the support obligor [individual who owes child support payments], most commonly the father, be found in contempt of court for being willfully disobedient of the court order to pay child support. They request a remedy that he be placed in jail as a coercive measure. Indiana law provides, because in that circumstance his liberty may be deprived, court-appointed counsel. That's one of the things I have to ask right up front. "Are you seeking incarceration as a remedy for comfort?" If they are, then they are entitled to counsel, which we provide for them.

Do you participate in the negotiation of settlements of cases?

I do not. I have heard of some local judges who do that. I am wary of doing that because I may likely be serving as a fact finder. To participate in the settlement negotiations and know the positions that people have taken might certainly compromise my view of the evidence they present then in court. So we don't do that. We have independent mediators we can refer people to. I did in one auto accident case have an attorney say, "Judge, let's get together and let's have you try to mediate this case." I'm not trained in mediation. Everybody came to this office: the adjuster for the insurance company, the injured party. I found out that I didn't really seem to know much about assisting people in the process. I just got frustrated and told the insurance adjuster she was wasting everybody's time. That is a process I would have to get some training in.

Does court-ordered mediation occur in your jurisdiction?

To a significant extent. It is a process we are using more in civil law, at least in this court. I wish we could use it more in family law, but the fact of the matter is that in divorce court and paternity cases the people commonly can't afford to pay for the services of an attorney trained in mediation or a lay person trained in mediation. We don't have a government agency that can provide that service. Ideally we should, but the limits of government are the limits of government in terms of the costs. That could be very important in family law. So we are using it a lot to settle the routine, garden-variety fender-bender accidents. I probably send sixty percent of my civil litigation that is headed for a jury trial to mediation. I don't require it in every case because the fact of the matter is there are a couple of insurance companies that have taken up the practice of forcing plaintiffs' lawyers to try the cases and prove out the small fender-bender cases as a matter of, I guess, what is cost-effective for their insurance company. There is a lot of grumbling about it. Because mediation in those cases is worthless, they come in with no offer at all. Then what is the point? Everybody's time is wasted. So I don't require mediation in every civil case.

What cases might go to trial?

The cases that go to trial are hard to define. It is common for automobile accident cases that can't be resolved between the insurance company and the injured party to be tried. Most of those will settle, but one of the most common alleged injuries that may not be susceptible to settlement are the soft-tissue injuries that people claim, which are certainly a real thing for a person to suffer but are naturally suspect in the eyes of the insurance companies. We average one jury trial every two months. Bench trials are much more frequent.

When I say bench trials I mean hearings, essentially involving family law or other matters.

Do you have much contact or meet with other judges?

In this particular county we meet usually on an as-needed basis. We don't have monthly meetings. We did that for a while, but that just didn't work out. We are fairly independent. We have some common local rules regarding the criminal caseload and manners of doing business. We are not as cohesive as some other counties around us, with comprehensive sets of local rules. But we have a cooperative approach to transferring cases where a judge might have a conflict of interest and moving the caseload.

How would you assess the quality of the work of the attorneys who appear in your court?

I think by and large attorneys do a good job representing their clients and presenting their cases. There are exceptions in terms of the adequacy of the representation that sometimes raise my concern. Those instances are limited to where I feel that representation may have fallen below the level of what we call adequate representation. To be honest, my criminal caseload is fairly limited, and the offenders who come through my court are all indigent. They all receive a local public defender who is a very experienced criminal defense attorney. Fortunately, I am never seeing the concern about whether the representation was adequate in criminal court. I see it more in family law court, where particular counsel have for one reason or another not prepared well enough for their case or have gotten so accustomed to what they do that they may, as time went on, not have kept up with the law in a given area of family law. I see a lot of very good attorneys, too, who do just excellent work. I also see on occasion, in the civil law area, cases where it appears to be that there are motions and pleadings being filed that could have been avoided, but nonetheless the attorney is billing at a very expensive rate. I guess the phrase for that is called "grinding the case" in terms of billable hours. That is a matter the court has very little ability to control unless it is a totally frivolous situation.

Do you see many self-represented (pro se) parties in your court?

It depends on the economy, but it seems that in the last two or three years we have had a significant increase in the people who are trying to represent themselves. I'll get letters in the mail. I just got one yesterday from a lady down in Arkansas who is a noncustodial parent ordered by me to pay child support. She writes in her letter that her job situation has changed and she would like to see her support decrease. It's not a pleading; it's a letter. I send it back to her and said this doesn't comply with the Indiana Rules of Trial and Procedure, and she should see a lawyer. I have to take a pass on that. I can't give her advice. I have to remain neutral. So it is frustrating because she is probably entitled to some relief, but we'll never know until she makes the effort from Arkansas to get something filed for her that is proper. She can do that herself, or she can contact a local attorney. There is availability of forms to file those sorts of motions on the Indiana Supreme Court's website. Actually, the forms are quite helpful. The Indiana Supreme Court has reached out.

How would you assess the work done by jurors?

I have done about ninety jury trials. I think jury service is a lot like jogging. You tend to dread starting out. When you get to the courthouse and are picked as a juror, you are not happy you got called. Once they get in the process—they probably watch courtrooms at home on television, and they have pre-conceptions that aren't matching up with what they see in court—but once they are selected, I have found that people do a terrific job. They take it very seriously. They have, in ninety-five percent of the cases, reached the decision that I would have reached as a judge.

I used to go back and talk to jurors after the trial to thank them. But sometimes discussions with juries would evolve into discussions of the merits of the case. They would talk about their decision-making process. I went back once and heard something I didn't want to hear, such as that wasn't really the way they should have thought about their vote if they had followed the jury instructions as they should have. Now, when I go back to talk to juries, I just thank them and ask them what we can do to make their service better. I don't go into the merits of the case anymore because I don't want to hear if they have done something that is outside the instructions I gave them. However, all in all, people do just a terrific job as jurors. When they are done, they are very happy that they had the chance to serve. They want to tell their family and children about it. It is kind of a warm and fuzzy thing at the end of a jury trial. They have come together as a group and taken this responsibility and discharged it. They are pleased with themselves.

What is the most difficult aspect of being a judge?

I handle termination of parental rights. That is the death penalty in family law. That is quite simply the hardest thing that I do. I have always felt kind of pleased with my caseload because it does not involve a lot of sentencing of individuals who are not already behind bars. The criminal defendants I have are by and large already in the Department of Corrections. I am not depriving people of their liberty. I have served as special judge and done sentencing. I have found that to be difficult. The other thing that I think is very difficult is child custody decisions in circumstances where there is a lot of rancor between parents. You know that whatever decision you do, whatever legal decision you are making, the parents are not going to take those human steps to address the real problem, their inability to communicate and cooperate. No matter what you do [it] is going to have a cataclysmic and long-standing effect on the relationship of parents with the child and vice versa. Those are very tough.

What problems do you see besetting the courts?

The process is slow by design. I think that courts suffer from being over-worked. We have a lot of stuff coming up at us day after day. I am frustrated a lot of the time by the attorneys who are involved in the case because we can't seem to get a case moving forward and scheduled for a hearing. A lot of the times I will be [at] a preliminary divorce hearing and say I want to set this for a final hearing now. I think it's very important in divorce to get cases set for a final hearing, because that gives a finite context to whatever everybody is doing. If we are having a contested preliminary hearing, I want to get the final hearing set because that gives people a sense that it isn't going to go on and on. There is light at the end of the tunnel, or at least a date on which we will finally resolve the property and get some sort of court order that sets a structure for the postdissolution relationship. We offer dates, and the attorney says, "I'm not available that day, I'm not available that day." Seven or eight dates are offered and we end up five, six, seven months down the road. "We can't get the discovery done, blah, blah, blah." Attorneys are busy people. They want to do their job, so there is all this discovery and exchange of information and depositions to be taken and so on and so forth. They can prolong the process.

What we do in this court is set every other week for jury trials, and the other weeks are set for hearing, especially in family law and paternity. We stack the jury trials four or five deep, and as they settle out, we move cases up. We notify them to be prepared to go. So we are working hard to move them, but there is a lot of stuff coming at us, too. If people are frustrated with it, I don't blame them.

Do you think that other assistance is needed in domestic cases?
Not so much. I don't have any particular feelings that way. I don't sit here saying they should be addressed by another agency, but I think it would be very helpful to have a government agency, a domestic relations counseling bureau.

What do you think of the court-appointed special advocate [CASA] programs?
We have a very good CASA organization in this county. I use them in family law cases when the case involves termination of parental rights, representing the children. A larger pool of cases is child abuse and child neglect, or child in need of service. Those are not in my court. That's where a lot of the CASA work is going on in this county. A great organization, a great concept.

What do you consider to be the pluses and minuses of being a judge?
I find as the years go by working the judiciary, but it also must be true of lawyers, sometimes I grow weary of being involved on a day-to-day basis in the problems of dysfunctional people and the acrimony that attends lawsuits. My biggest frustration is those cases where relationships between the opposing counsel have broken down and become so personal that I have a second layer of problems to deal with on top of the underlying lawsuit. It really makes the work very frustrating. Attorneys in this business can remain zealous advocates without becoming bitter enemies about it. By and large the profession does a great job, but when it goes bad, it is bad. It's just no fun to be involved in that. That can wear you down.

I think if you are looking to go into the law, you need to think about what kind of law you want to be in. There are plenty of lawyers who aren't enjoying their work on a daily basis. Judges have to, by nature. I'm not complaining. I have had a very satisfying career, and I enjoy it, but there are days when I wish I were away from some of the acrimony. Plenty of lawyers working in corporate areas don't deal with the steady diet of problems. If you are going to be in the business, most attorneys are doing just that every day. I think it makes you old.

The attorneys have a job to do, and in a litigious society they have to make sure they aren't going to have somebody looking over their shoulder and saying you didn't do your job. They have to keep their guard up and be the advocate, but I think in a particular area like family law we compound the problems that go with a divorce sometimes by having this adversarial system.

When I first came to this business, I was kind of amazed that in the family arena courts have so much power to make decisions about, for instance, where a child should live. After a year or two of being on the bench, I realized thank goodness somebody has to authority to assist people in this awful situation and can reach agreements about the children. We have set up a system, this adversarial process in family law, which can, without question, aggravate the process. By their very nature, courtroom settings involving custody and visitation involve a lot of negative evidence. It's easier to prove somebody is a rat than to establish that they are truly a good parent, but the more noble side of people isn't so tangible. We have this setting, and I chastise attorneys sometimes about it, "you're making things worse," and they go, "We're doing a good job."

What are the most satisfying aspects of being a judge?

What I like best about my job is I come to work every day and our work product is doing the right thing. Literally, that's what justice is in its simplest terms. Being involved in that process and moving cases through the system—which is our number-one obligation—and providing people with results is a big job. It's a seat-of-the-pants job—day after day, week after week, year after year. I get satisfaction out of that. Statistics can lie, and I don't base my sense of job satisfaction on the raw numbers, but I know what those numbers mean. It's a lot of people's problems went through the system and were resolved. Sometimes like a teacher who has a student come back and say how much they appreciate what they have done as a teacher, I get people who come back years later and say, "I really like what you did or what you said in court at the end of a family law hearing. That made a difference at the time." Because I take ten or fifteen minutes at the end of a contested difficult custody hearing to address the parties and talk to them about the fact that the true answer to the problem is a human one. Lawyers sometimes say you ought to just tape that and play the tape. We've heard it before. They joke that, "Could we be excused when you do that?" but I think it is very important to take that time out and talk to people about solving their problems. Sometimes they do. That's satisfying.

I never see them again. Sometimes the case files get thicker and thicker, and they keep coming back until the children are eighteen. Sometimes they never get together, and that's the great frustration.

My satisfaction, I think, is less tangible in the family law area because it is so human in dimension. There was a lady who was in one of these difficult cases who I ran into in the grocery store. As she entered the aisle at the other end of the grocery store, I saw her. I turned to try and get away from her, because I see her year after year. A lot of the rulings have gone against her over the years. She shouts that day in the grocery store, "Judge King, Judge King." I turned around, and she was as pleasant as she could be. She came down the grocery aisle, and she introduced me to her friend. She said, "I wanted you to meet my friend because she has heard so much about you." I am cringing internally. "You know what, Judge King," she says, "I am going to keep coming back to your court, and I am going to keep coming back to your court and I am going to keep coming back to your court until you get it right." You can't please everyone.

Richard Stearns

The Federal Judge

RICHARD STEARNS IS A FEDERAL district judge in Boston, Massachusetts. The United States district courts are the trial courts of the federal
court system. Within limits set by Congress and the Constitution, the district courts have jurisdiction to hear nearly all categories of federal cases,
including both civil and criminal matters. There are ninety-four federal
judicial districts, including at least one district in each state, the District
of Columbia, Puerto Rico, the Virgin Islands, Guam, and the Northern
Mariana Islands. This interview was conducted in Judge Stearns's chambers in the striking and modern Moakley U.S. Courthouse overlooking
Boston Harbor.

Why did you want to become a judge?

I think I was inspired by example more than anything else. As a young lawyer
I was drawn to trial work, initially as a state prosecutor and then later as a
federal prosecutor. One particular judge, who is unfortunately now deceased,
David Mazoni, was an inspirational figure to me. I liked his mastery of the
courtroom, his knowledge of the law, and just his manner; the way in which
he dealt with lawyers and cases so impressed me that he became more or less a
model for me vocationally, and in imitating him I followed in his footsteps.

How did you become a judge?

To become a federal judge, you have to be nominated by the President of the
United States, and typically the president relies on the advice of the senior
senator or senior representative within the state of his party, assuming that
there are no senate seats held by the party of the presidential office. In making
selections for vacancies on the federal bench, the nomination then goes to a
hearing before the Senate Judiciary Committee and requires about two-thirds
of the Senate for confirmation. In my case, I was selected as a nominee by a
committee that Senator [Edward] Kennedy had developed to screen candidates

for the federal bench, and, as it happened, the president who appointed me, William J. Clinton, was a roommate of mine at Oxford University [*laughing*]. That may dispel any notion that the job came to me strictly on merit.

There is social science evidence that persons who want to get to the federal bench let their interest be known before selections have to be made. Does that strike you as true?

Well, certainly, no one would embarrass themselves by nominating you for a job that you would then decline. Typically, I think the tendency has been recently to make the process more open than it historically was. Rather than whispering in the ear of the appointing authority or someone who had the ear of the president, I think the model Senator Kennedy follows is probably more typical today: actually inviting persons who are interested to apply and having them screened and interviewed by a committee, which then makes recommendations to, in our case, the senior senator.

Can you talk about the kinds of cases your court handles? What percentages are civil versus criminal?

We handle virtually any kind of case. We are a court of limited jurisdiction, that is, we only have the jurisdictional authority that Congress has conferred on us. As it happens, they've conferred a lot. We can be divested of that authority if Congress as an institution chose to do so, and some members of Congress, from time to time, so threaten. The causes of action that are now part of federal law have proliferated, particularly since the beginning of the 1970s. In the earliest days of the Republic, for example, there were essentially twelve or sixteen criminal statutes that actually were prosecutable in the federal courts. Today, we don't know; no one's ever accurately counted the number of actual criminal statutes that have been enacted. We think it's something over three thousand. So, too, on the civil side, what used to be fairly limited jurisdiction, largely confined in the earlier life of the court to admiralty cases and bankruptcy cases, has now expanded to cover almost any kind of case that you would imagine in a state court of general jurisdiction. Anything from employment discrimination to civil rights cases to admiralty cases to appeals from administrative agencies, such as the Social Security Administration, to review of bankruptcy appeals. We also are the trial court for the Federal Circuit, which is the court that oversees the patent system. The patent cases are also on the docket here.

Cases are obviously initiated, either by way of a grand jury indictment or, in the case of a misdemeanor, by an information filed by a federal prosecutor; or, on the civil side, by the filing of a complaint by the way of an attorney. When the case is filed, it's assigned either a criminal or a civil case number. The computer then randomly assigns the case to one of the judges in the court. There is no steering of cases. It's all done by mathematical decisions.

We are not as busy a court in terms of volume as some courts are. We don't have the flood of immigration cases, for example, that you would find in the border districts. Although we like to think, and I think that it's true, that we tend to get a fair number of complex cases, perhaps more so than other courts, because Massachusetts is a center of not only a lot of innovative technology but also because large insurance interests and large commercial interests are present in the state. I think the last time I looked, for example, we were the fourth busiest patent court in the country. Civil cases by far outnumber criminal cases. I think on my docket, currently, perhaps twenty percent of my cases are criminal cases. Eighty percent fall into one civil category or another.

Can you describe in more detail the types of civil cases that your court considers?
Almost anything you can imagine. I would say that, for a lot of complex reasons, the number of actual jury trials that take place in the federal court has been declining, both in criminal and civil sides. The criminal side, one can attribute the decline largely to the imposition of the sentencing guidelines, which were nearly mandatory; now they're discretionary, but they nonetheless tend to still drive most sentencing in the federal courts. So for most defendants, there isn't a great incentive to roll the dice because one loses the concessions that a guilty plea under the guideline system otherwise yields. On the civil side, I think the decline is probably more attributable to the cost of litigation today than it is to anything else. It doesn't mean that we don't have a busy trial calendar. I'm certainly busy enough during the year with trials, but they're not as numerous as they used to be.

What would you say is the percentage of cases that go to trial?
I actually know the number on the criminal side. I think it's around three percent go to trial. On the civil side, I would be surprised if it's two percent, could be a little larger, but I think two percent might be a fair estimate, at least looking at my own civil docket.

What is your role in settling disputes that are settled without a trial? How do you move the cases along, treat motions, documents received, handle conflicts among lawyers, and facilitate settlement, and how do you manage pretrial conferences?
Yes, these are certainly critical stages in litigation. Now, we'll put aside the criminal cases, because by rule we're not permitted to involve ourselves in negotiations of the criminal cases, unlike typically would be the case in state court when I was a state judge. There was no prohibition against my becoming involved in plea negotiations between the government and the defendant. But federal judges are not permitted to involve themselves in those kinds of negotiations.

In civil cases, a case has certain stages of life that it goes through. At the initial stage, there can be a screening of the case through a motion to dismiss, which would most typically be based on jurisdictional grounds. Although, if the plaintiff has failed for some reason to plead the elements of a viable claim, a motion to dismiss may be appropriate, even at the very infancy of that case. More typically, the case will proceed through discovery to a point where the parties either now know enough about the strengths or the weaknesses of their own cases that they settle on their own initiatives, which is true in most cases. Then we proceed to a phase called summary judgment, where again it operates under strict rules, where inferences are all drawn in favor of the non-moving party. But the judge has a fair amount of authority because now the facts have been developed in the case and, if a fact is truly uncontested and it's decisive on one or more of the claims, the judge then has the power through summary judgment to dispose of some or all of the case at that stage.

We are a very case-management-oriented court. Before discovery can begin, there is a preliminary meeting between the judge and the lawyers, where they propose the discovery schedule, and the type of discovery that's going to be pursued, and the time frame over which the case will be litigated. This really was initially conceived as a cost-management device, which is how Congress saw it when it mandated the so-called pretrial conferences, or pre-discovery conferences. They are now more simply a management tool to give the judge a feel for a case. Very often a case at that initial meeting will offer itself, say, for mediation, which we encourage. There is a deduction under federal law that mediation and arbitration are positive things, and parties are urged, as a time- and cost-saving measure, to pursue mediation if it is in their interest. Sometimes that's the case, again, as I said, it develops that the parties will either seek mediation or more typically will come to their own resolution of the case.

Just to clarify, you're not allowed to be a part of plea-bargaining activity in a criminal case.

No, not in terms of attempting to negotiate a result. Obviously, in a criminal context, the rules are stricter. The court is still being asked to rule on motions to dismiss if there's some defect in the indictment in the case, but more typically you're shaping the trial, either through decisions you make on motions to suppress evidence or admissions or confessions on the part of the defendant, evidentiary rulings that would influence the course of the trial. These are all decisions that, as I know as a former prosecutor, will then factor into a defendant's and his lawyer's decision about whether or not it's in his best interest to enter a plea or go to trial.

Although they're so rare, could you talk about your role in the trial itself, first in civil cases, then criminal?

When I say they're rare, I say they're rare in proportion to the number of cases that are actually processed through the court. I don't mean to imply that I rarely preside. I'm in the middle of one now, and as soon as this one ends, we'll start the next one. You can go through sometimes periods of weeks where you don't have trials, but it's also not uncommon to find yourself moving from one trial to another over an extended period of time.

Within the trial, the judge is not expected to be a partisan to one side or another. The judge's role is to enlighten the jury, because in our system juries are the only entity in most cases that have the power to make findings or determinations of fact. To do that intelligently, jurors have to be instructed on something of the law that they're going to be applying or will be applying in the case. So the judge's first job is to help assemble the jury. Screening jurors in federal court is typically done by the lawyers. Then the judge must ensure that the jury is provided with the information that it needs to render an intelligent verdict of a case. Of course, they need legal instructions at the end of the case.

The second task of the judge, and this is encouraged, is to be a guiding presence in the trial. As I say, not to attempt to steer the case towards one conclusion or another—it's important that the judge keeps as neutral a position as he or she can—but to shape the case in the sense of keeping lawyers in focus, helping the lawyers to see what is in their interest in terms of the presentation that they are making to the jury, to spare the jury extraneous or repetitive evidence. Lawyers tend to have a need, if they have evidence, to offer it to a jury even if it has nothing to do particularly with the ultimate outcome of the case. You are making rulings constantly to, again, simply to keep your case on track intelligibly so a jury doesn't decide incorrectly.

Do you ever find yourself in a civil trial modifying jury verdicts?

I've done it, but rarely so. I have enormous confidence in the jury system, and it's in my inclination—and I think this true of almost every judge; in fact, the law encourages it—is to indulge every inference one can in favor of upholding or supporting the jury's verdict in a case. Quite honestly, I think juries do a better job in resolving factual disputes, particularly disputes that involve credibility, than I would as a judge. I've been doing this too long, and I'm afraid that I've become too bureaucratic and too mechanical in the way that I would decide the case, because I've seen it all before. Whereas for jurors it's a fresh experience; they are willing to give a fresh look to the facts of every case. I can't really recall any more than a small handful of instances where I have disagreed with the jury's verdict. The three that come most easily to mind were criminal cases where, in fact, I would have found the defendant guilty, and the jurors, in respect to the presumption of innocence and proof beyond a reasonable doubt, were not as persuaded as I was of a defendant's guilt. Of course, in a criminal case, there's nothing that can be done once a person is acquitted in our system as it can in some other legal systems. On the civil side, again I have very few quarrels with the jury's ultimate determination. Even if I might disagree, if that determination is a credibility-driven one, I don't have any legal basis to overturn the verdict, even if I wanted to. Where I have disagreed from time to time with the jury is over the awards that they give. Sometimes I think it's too much. Sometimes it's too little, and that's something that the judge has a fairly free hand in correcting.

Could you assess the federal sentencing guidelines?

I've actually lived through several generations of sentencing practices. As a federal prosecutor, I began my career before the sentencing guidelines were born. They came into play about two-thirds of the way through my prosecutorial career. Then I became a state judge in a system in Massachusetts where there are really no guidelines. There are recommendations in some cases that developed over the years, but there are no real constraints on the judge in terms of sentencing. Then I came to the federal court. The sentencing guide lines were now in full bloom. I think what happened is that the guidelines sort of lost their way as they began to be interpreted, particularly as courts of appeals began to take a more and more categorical approach to the guideline requirements. What I think was originally intended by its authors to be guidelines—that is, to try to make sensible recommendations to the judge in the hopes of equalizing sentencing among crimes and defendants in some rough fashion—instead became a rigid institution where the ability of the judge, even where the so-called departure was called for, began to shrink as the appeals courts closed the window tighter and tighter over time. I think that's what the Supreme Court was reacting to in the Booker and Fanfan decision (U.S. v. Booker and U.S. v. Fanfan 2005) to try to restore some flexibility to the system in the interest of justice. In my experience, the guidelines generally generate what I think is a reasonable and correct result eighty-five percent of the time. Fifteen percent of the time I think the sentence recommendation is either too low or, more typically, too high, and in the interest of justice I take into consideration the character of the defendant if some different sentence should be imposed. I am pleased with the change that the Supreme Court has instituted in that regard. In fact, I just saw the statistics on how I have sentenced since the Booker decision, and it more or less confirms my intuition. Now that I have discretion over sentencing, if you factor out those sentences where the government, as a reward for cooperation, is recommending a nonguideline sentence, I sentence within the guidelines about eighty-five percent of the time and depart the other fifteen.

Could you describe the nature of your interactions with lawyers?

Well, with lawyers, virtually none. We tend to live a fairly isolated existence in that regard for obvious reasons. You don't want it ever to be thought that lawyers are privately currying favor or whispering in your ear about a case that might be before you. Other than at formal bar functions and interactions directly related to litigation, there's almost none.

They are correct and cordial, generally pretty candid, but, again, they usually occur in the context of case-management issues, or, more typically, I'm sitting on a bench and lawyers are arguing positions, a motion, or the merits of their case before me. Different judges approach that differently. I tend to try to be an active participant, and the oral arguments are presented to the court because I find it a useful way to help inform me on, hopefully, the decision I'm going to make. The hard part about this job is you do have to make decisions. You just can't escape that duty, so whatever help the lawyer can offer is appreciated and elicited, but beyond that there really is very little interaction with the lawyers in their role as lawyers. Obviously, you will come to the bench as a lawyer, and many of your friends are obviously lawyers, but I try, particularly when I am close personally with a lawyer, I try to recuse myself from a case that they might have that would be randomly assigned to me.

Could you describe the role of your staff?

My staff is typical for a federal district judge. I have two law clerks, who basically serve as legal assistants, helping to prepare me for court, analyzing motions as they are filed, making recommendations, letting me know [what] they think the proper disposition of the motion should be. Typically, if we have what is called a dispositive motion, it's one that is going to have a large consequence for the case, the law clerk will draft a memorandum called a bench memorandum, which is a preliminary outline of the facts and major legal points that the parties are making and sometimes will include her recommendation as to what she thinks the outcome should be or, more likely, will suggest questions that ought to be put to the lawyers that don't seem to be clearly answered by the briefings. I follow a different practice than most federal judges; most federal judges hire law clerks annually fresh out of law school and see the law clerk experience as an educational one, with the judge serving as the teacher and the law clerk basically in the role of the student. I didn't like that model. I've hired, rather, career law clerks that have been with me, one that has been with me since the very beginning, the other for almost ten years now. Law clerks are a very important part of your professional life because they are really the only people who you can freely confide in—because, obviously, they're under an oath of strict confidentiality so you can talk with them in ways that you never could with a lawyer or anyone else. In addition to the law clerks, I have what is called a judicial assistant, who is my secretary and does what secretaries do in terms of scheduling my time and doing the finished work product that comes out of the office. We have a courtroom deputy. She's in charge of actually scheduling cases and sitting with me during a course of a trial, swearing witnesses and marking exhibits. For scheduling, we have a docket clerk. Her job is to service the person who has pleadings or files. She sees that they are properly recorded on the docket of the case and then come to our attention, particularly if they are contested motions—which most are—but she keeps the mechanics of the filing system working for us. It's become easier now because most filing in federal courts is now done electronically, so that tends to expedite our ability to actually review motions and stay current with what's being filed at any moment. The last actor on the official staff is the court reporter, whose job it is obviously to keep an accurate record of whatever is said in court during a trial.

Do you have professional interactions with other judges?

Here, in this court, and I think it would probably be true of most courts, yes, in the sense that we are largely a self-governing court. We have a chief judge, who is selected basically by seniority, who presides at a formal monthly meeting where each judge has the same voice and the same vote, but we tend to try to make decisions that affect the court as an institution in a collegial way. Sometimes issues get contested and debated, and there's not unanimous agreement about the course that we should follow, but we do interact in that sense, providing governance for the court. On a more social level, after the law clerks, the next confidant that I have is fellow judges. We tend to try not to discuss one another's cases, just simply to avoid any extraneous influence on the decision-making process. That doesn't mean that we don't talk about general legal principles or issues as they may arise that are going to have an impact on a decision that you might make in a case, and the other judges are a wonderful resource.

Do you feel isolated as a federal judge?

I would, but that I have a second life, which is that I serve as a rule-of-law advisor for an agency called the Defense Threat Reduction Agency, which is very involved in nuclear counterproliferation issues. Currently, terrorism is a major concern. Most of that work is done internationally, so I spend a fair amount of time traveling back and forth between Southern Europe and sometimes Central Asia or Russia doing work for this particular project, and that has created a whole new circle of friendships and interests and soaks up virtually any free time that I have, so I don't feel that I have time to be isolated [*laughs*].

Could you discuss opinion writing?

Everyone has a different expository style, but if you go through, particularly, district court opinions as they're published in federal supplements, you'll find that they almost always follow the same pattern. My concern—and this is why the law clerks are invaluable—is that we get the facts of the case right. If I make an error of law, that can be corrected by the appeals court. It's far less likely that the appeals court will be able to correct a true error of fact that's reflected in the opinions that I write. I believe that the law should be elaborated by the appellate courts. That's their function, not mine, so I try to avoid writing opinions that in effect are mini-Law Review articles. Some of my colleagues disagree. They like writing at length on legal issues. I just don't think that's my job, so I try to write opinions that are very fact intense. The rule with my law clerks is that we don't want anything more than ten to twelve pages. If we can't say it in ten to twelve pages, then we don't really understand the issues of the case. Now there are some cases that are so factually complex that that rule goes by the board, but I think—I mean, it's hard to be a critic of your own writing—but I try to write them in as direct and accessible a fashion as the law permits. I think a trial judge's real responsibility is not to expand or contract or elaborate on the law but to explain clearly to the parties to a case why one is losing and the other is winning. So that's my audience. That's who I'm writing for. In fact, I publish some, not nearly as much as I did earlier in my career. Any opinion that we designate will be printed in the Federal Supplement. After two or three years when I was routinely designating opinions for publication, I realized that I was one of the most widely published and read authors [in] the United States, so I cut back [laughs]. People don't really look to the court opinions very often for binding precedent, so I try to write shorter, more directly, and with the parties in mind, not the legal profession.

Could you describe the pluses and minuses of your job?

I think it's mostly pluses. It's intellectually stimulating; even when you get the occasionally boring task, it's going to be superseded in a minute by something that will have true interest for you. Although I've always said that the quality a judge requires most is not necessarily legal brilliance but the capacity to find whatever is happening in front of him or her at any given time the most interesting thing that you've ever seen or heard. It takes a lot of your focus, a lot of your attention, but I like the intellectual engagement. Being presented problems to solve—not only that, but the solutions that you engender actually have consequences. It means that it's going to be meaningful in someone's life. It's not advisory; it's not theoretical. It's real, and real people have their interests at stake as you approach the decision-making process. I think that's on a positive side; it's one of the real pleasures of the job. The second one I alluded to is the opportunity that has opened for me to branch into other affairs that are not necessarily related to the job but come to me because the job comes with a certain status, which makes me a more attractive participant than [I] otherwise might be.

I think the minus is the one that judges are always pointing to, which is that, compared to others in the profession of equivalent stature, we're not paid very well. Not that we're paid badly, it's just that we're not paid anything like most of us would expect, I think, what we would earn if we were to leave. It's becoming a problem. We have judges who are resigning because they have simply decided that they can't live comfortably and send their children to college on what the salary for a federal judge is today. But saying that, I don't mean to sound as if I'm complaining, because to most Americans it would sound as if we make an enormous amount of money. We obviously live in privileged surroundings. I don't think any law office would ever offer something like the chambers I have here.

Larry V. Starcher

The State Supreme Court Justice

BEFORE HIS RETIREMENT IN 2009, Justice Larry Starcher of the West Virginia Supreme Court of Appeals sat behind a massive desk cluttered with papers and awards in his chambers in the State Capitol in Charleston and handed the interviewers a biographical sketch and resume. Starcher, born "down a dirt road on Henry's Fork" to a mother who was "the only adult present" at his birth, retains his rural West Virginia drawl. Aside from listing his years of service as a lawyer for the poor, trial judge, and Supreme Court justice and his receipt of countless awards from diverse educational and civic groups, the biography contains the line, "successfully avoided the draft." With his poor Appalachian background and vibrant political liberalism, he is something of an anomaly among contemporary American judges. The court of last resort for almost all litigation in the state, his court addresses a diverse range of appeals. As with other state courts of last resort and the federal Courts of Appeals, almost none of its cases reach the Supreme Court of the United States.

Could you please describe your background and education?

I was a poor kid. I'm the first kid in my whole clan, including my older brother and sister, to ever graduate from high school. I come from a family about as country as you can get, I assure you, from up the holler. My parents not only did not encourage education, they discouraged it. They thought you should get a job. As a consequence, Daddy wouldn't have anything to do with it. One evening sitting on the porch he said something like this: "Larry, I wish you'd get this college stuff out of your head. You don't understand. That's not for people like us." At that time I was not encouraged, I was discouraged. I basically ran away to college.

Why did you decide to study law?

I had delivered papers for many years in the small town of Spencer. One of my customers was a man named George Scott. He was a young lawyer who

[had] just been elected prosecuting attorney. We would sometimes chat when I would collect for the paper. He talked me into coming down to watch him in court. So I went down, and I watched a few cases. George Scott would say things like, "You go to Morgantown [home of West Virginia University, WVU]. You get a law degree, and we'll practice together." I'm sure he was just being nice to a kid, but I took it to heart. I decided at that time I would go into law.

How did you prepare for a legal career?

I went to WVU. I majored in political science and minored in English and history and never considered that I had a hard class. For some people they are hard, for me very enjoyable. I loved it. I geared my whole scholastic study at WVU from day one toward going to law school.

The summer of '62 I went to D.C. and worked in the mailroom, the "folding room," for Congress half days and for Congressman Ken Hechler [D-West Virginia, later West Virginia Secretary of State] half days. The summer of '63 I worked in this building [the State Capitol] as a capitol guide. When I worked at the Capitol I had become friends with Joe Burdette, who was the Secretary of State. He was to run for reelection in 1964. I wanted to work in a statewide election, so I carried twenty-one hours my senior year. Then I knew if I dropped out I would come back in summer school, take twelve hours, have enough to graduate, and start to law school immediately. That's what I did. I dropped out of school my senior year and worked Joe Burdette's campaign. I was in every county in the state, and I gave a few little political speeches on his behalf. I learned a lot of things to do and some things not to do [in a campaign]. It was a very educational process.

What were the law school years like?

I went to WVU law school. My first year in law school I worked as a janitor at the University Hospital. The second year I worked at what was called the Office of Research and Development. A job came up. The title was contract auditor, later changed to contract administrator, in what was the business arm of the Office of International Programs. It was a full-time job as a staff person. It paid seven thousand six hundred dollars. A lawyer in a law firm in Charleston at that time started at four thousand eight hundred dollars. So I persuaded the dean to let me go to law school half time for two years. I found myself in my little office with a staff of three and later five. I managed about five and a half million dollars of USAID [United States Agency for International Development] contracts, a series of contracts in East Africa in three countries, four countries, for a short time. I would go into the office about seven-thirty and sometimes study and sometimes get office work ready, then dart across the street to the law school and my classes. Also, I had to go to DC about once a month to meet people at the African Desk at the [U.S.] State Department to get contracts negotiated.

What did you do after law school?

I ended up staying at the university. They kicked me upstairs and gave me a beautiful office. I was assistant to the Vice President for Off-Campus Education for another year. I wrote grants for faculty for fire training, nurse's training. One of the grants I ended up writing for the law school was a proposal for a Legal Services grant [to the federal Legal Service Corporation]. As I wrote it, I said, "I'm burning to get in the courtroom. I have not been in the courtroom in two and a half years." I applied for director of Legal Services. I was there for seven years. Legal Services now is nothing like what it was when I was there. We hell-raised in the 1960s and '70s. We sued people. We brought consumer litigation suits. We fought landlord-tenant suits. We took them to court. It was the heyday of the Legal Services program. We had a six-county program. I was on the national project advisory board. I was pretty active. We did a good bit of community organizing in those days. We organized a group of people we called the Monongalia County Poor People's Association. I had a complaint filed with the U.S. Civil Service Commission against me. Part of the complaint was that I was out "pandering my wares like a huckster in the marketplace."

Today the federal government has put so many restrictions on what Legal Services can do. When I did Legal Services up there, one time I did twenty-some divorces in a day. I mean I lined them up for three months in Taylor County. Those people can't get in now, so what do they do? They just don't get the divorce, or they are doing it pro se, and that makes it very difficult on the court system. Of course, you have two kinds of pro se litigants. You have the poor people who can't afford, who can't pay five thousand dollars for a lawyer. Secondly, you have the guy who says, "Well, I'm smart. I can handle this on my own." He has a right to go out there and hang himself. But [judges] have to accept it as part of the job. We work hard at trying to facilitate [pro se litigation].

How did you end up as a judge?

I was smart enough to know that getting elected to political office is name recognition. It is that simple. They sell more Kellogg's Corn Flakes than Post Toasties for one reason, the advertising. There isn't a difference in the taste. They taste the same. So I got on city council [in Morgantown] and got my name in the paper.

In '72 I ran for sheriff. I did not want to run for sheriff. My intention was to run for prosecuting attorney and then state senator and then the executive. Why did I run for sheriff? A lawyer who was helpful to me also wanted to run for prosecuting attorney. I appreciated that and wouldn't run against him. However, the last day of filing, the county assessor personally paid the filing fee, and I was the sheriff candidate. I won the primary big. I came within three hundred four or three hundred seven votes of beating a former three-time sheriff in the general [election].

I went back to Legal Services. Four years later I ran for judge, in 1976. A bunch of us lawyers were so upset with Judge X, a very lousy judge. He went into office, and he canceled the subscriptions to his law books. Once I followed him into his office. He had no desk, just a table and an easy chair. He was just a caretaker. In the files, not a piece of paper. There just weren't any. He was very harsh, harsh in juvenile matters and criminal sentencing. He was harsh in domestic matters. A group of young lawyers tried to persuade some people to run, contacted some people, and were refused. Finally, they said, "Larry, why don't you run?" They finally persuaded me I could win. Of course, my view on elected officeholders is really quite simple. The real question is who is the best electable candidate. The best person for the job is not necessarily who runs for it. You have to support the person for the job who is electable. It turned out I was electable.

After twenty years as a circuit [trial] judge, why did you decide to run for the state's Supreme Court of Appeals?

Several people tried to talk me into running over the years, some of them judges. I had held all the offices and had been a promoter of education within the Judicial Association. I kept putting it off, not wanting to do it. I said, "I'll never be able to win this race."

What I did when I ran was create some white papers. Little single-page sheets that, when I went to a radio call-in show, I'd set them out. One was [about] an ethical mistake [I had made] in a rape case. I had four of them. When I would be hit with one of those questions, I had a canned answer to give back that was quick, sharp, and catchy. Something like, "I don't deny that I shouldn't have done that and, ethically, I'm wrong. I apologize for that. I shouldn't have done that. But, you know what, I suspect there's some parents around here that don't disagree with the fact that I was concerned about getting a rapist of our college coeds off the street." It actually became a positive. It made me out like a hard-liner, which I really am not, but I turned it around.

So some lawyers talked me into running for the supreme court. They felt we were drifting too far to the right on the court. It was pretty much a business court. What I then did, I said, "This is a statewide campaign. It has to be run differently." We put together a core of primarily, but not all, lawyers, a dozen people. We started doing planning. I made the decision to run after meeting with a couple of Charleston lawyers in early May 1995. We [the committee] met, started talking about setting up a budget, putting a budget together, and figured out how we were going to do that. I had a few things going for me that I thought would mean I would probably win. One, I had been appointed by this court to sit in twenty-three of the fifty-five counties over the past years. I knew many, and maybe most, of the county officials around the state. I had spoken on multiple occasions to the county officials' association. I had the connection at the courthouses that the others didn't have. Also, I had one or more law students as clerks in my office from the day I went to Legal Services in 1969 and as judge. I used work-study students. I paid them sometimes. I forced the county commission to pay them. As a result of that, there was at that time one or more lawyers in every county in this state who had worked in my office while in law school. I had a natural connection there. Now, not all of them were going to be jumping on my bandwagon, but at least I had fingers out there that other people didn't. The third thing I knew was that I would work them into the ground. When they are doing a quality of work that's a two, I'll do ten times two. I will work them into the ground. I'll outwork any of them. I'll cover more space. I'll do a better job. I'll work with people better. I'll touch more bases. I'll get more letters out. I'll do the whole thing better. When I got into it, I said, "I'm not getting into this to lose."

How did you finance the campaign for election to the court?

As judges we cannot, and I did not, raise a nickel. Letters went out for me, and my [campaign] staff helped create those. But they didn't come from me. The financial agent [for the campaign], who was a CPA, sent out lots of letters with his signature. Where did we go to raise money? We had some natural places. One was lawyers, of course. That's not all. I sat down with a [local] phone book, and I personally put a dash by everybody, every name that I knew. My financial people would send a standard letter to them. We went to local law-yers who were on the committee for seed money to get started. We planned. We had a lot of little fundraisers [events]. Some of them raised a good bit of money. One raised very little money but a lot of good will. But I didn't take care of the money.

The first piece of material that went out was designed to raise money for me. I gave ideas, but [my supporters] sent out a letter to every member of the [state] bar signed by a cross-section of twenty-some lawyers—plaintiffs' lawyers, defense lawyers, public service lawyers, very well-respected people— asking to raise money. That went out December 12. Later [the staff] told me they received some money every single working day until about a week before the primary. I find that just phenomenal, [but] I have never looked at the file of contributors, never once. I still have never looked at them.

We spent about four hundred thousand dollars total in both elections, about two hundred fifty thousand of it in the primary. I told the people raising money, "We can't be beat in the fall" [general election]. [At that time] I said, "Don't let people give us that much money. If people want to contribute again, and they tend to want to contribute to a winner, tell them not to give more than half of what they gave in the spring." We turned money away. Toward the end we were saying "no, no, no. We are not going to be able to spend all the money we have."

How did the campaign operate?

We also ended up hiring a lawyer [for the campaign]. He made all the ad buys. When we went into a town, we had a plan we replicated around the state. In the fall I had another individual. One thing I did was I bought an ad in all the little weekly papers every week starting very early in the spring to just create some name recognition. We started with a little TV ad that was made in Mor-gantown for cable TV. It was an introductory ad, a name-recognition thing.

A lot of people talked about it. We ran it really heavy for two weeks or so in November 1995, when no one else was doing anything. The next fall we didn't buy a single big newspaper ad. We just bought in the little rural ones.

I tried to get on the radio talk shows. I tried to see the newspaper editor. I tried to get to the opinion makers, the people who control information flow in the community. So what we would do if we were going into a community? We would say, is there a television station? We've got to get on it. Need to have an interview. Is there a radio station talk show, newscast? Got to get on it. Is there a newspaper editor? Got to get an interview with him. Don't get an interview with him, get it with a reporter. Don't waste your time, no dead time. I'd go to the post office early in the morning. People come to pick up their mail. They are ninety-five percent voters who have boxes. You can meet two hundred people in front of a post office in an hour. Wal-Mart, a lower percentage of voters, but there are people there. Don't waste any time.

Have things changed in the conduct of judicial elections in this state, especially since the four-million-dollar media campaign waged on behalf of the candidates for the court in 2004? Was the 2004 election an anomaly?

I don't think it's an anomaly. I think it is the future. It's the reason I think the future is sad. Now the moneyed interests have learned that they can buy a seat on the court, and they are going to do it. I just hated to see out-of-state interests do what they did. But I don't think the place to make changes is to take away from the people the right to select their judges. Do something about the way you allow money to be used. We only allow a one-thousand-dollar [individual] contribution. If you want to contribute to a judicial candidate—or any candidate—you can't contribute more than one thousand dollars. That's the law, but why not limit the money that people can contribute to [interest groups that aid candidates]? Why not get rid of 527s, first of all [political groups exempted from contribution limitations by federal law]? They say we'll just make judicial elections nonpartisan and that will take the politics out. I say, "No, what are you talking about?" Nonpartisan races, same thing. The business community has now determined to buy the courts. They are going to succeed if we don't figure out some way to put some curtailment on the amount of money that people give. I think we ought to attack the money.

How would you describe life as an appellate justice?

I've had four chapters in my judicial career. The first was when I went into the courts saying we need open courts and better juvenile justice. That was two areas I worked on from 1977 to 1984. From 1984 to 1990 or so I was very heavily involved in alternative sentencing and prison reform. From 1989 to 1997 it was mass litigation. I've done some innovative things, and I've had fun. Then from 1997 I came down here. My rule, and I know it surprises, is that there is more to being a justice than writing opinions. That's what the books show, but the other part of being a justice on the supreme court is the administration of the West Virginia judiciary. We are a 1,196-person public corporation with offices in fifty-five counties with probably one hundred fifty landlords around the state. We have to run that public corporation to serve the public. To be honest, that's the part I like and enjoy much more than doing the casework, although I enjoy the casework.

As to the cases, how does the court address them?

A case is appealed [to this court] from a circuit [trial] court, meaning one of the parties or sometimes both of them do not agree [with the decision], or [it] comes occasionally on what we call a certified question. [That occurs] when one or both parties say, "We don't know what to do in this case. Let's certify this legal question to the supreme court and let them answer it, and we will have some direction on what to do." [Certification] is an area that has grown in recent years. Twenty years ago it was maybe two or three or four a year, but now it's a significant number.

When a case comes here, it comes on what is called a petition. In other words, an aggrieved party at the circuit court level petitions the supreme court, saying basically, "Please take this case and decide it." We take a preliminary review of it. We have a group of clerks that create bench memos on [petitions] being considered. The memos are four or five pages or sometimes eighteen pages thick. The [clerks] are seasoned staff attorneys, not rookies. They are very competent; they know what to look for. They provide us with the bench memorandum.

We read the bench memos before we go into conference. We may want to pull up the briefs [additional written legal arguments made by the lawyer for the petitioner], in addition to the bench memos. I don't very often because I have found the bench memos to be adequate, and I have the opportunity to ask questions of the clerk. Sometimes I agree with the clerks and sometimes I don't. We also [each] have two to four personal clerks and a per curiam clerk. I generally don't talk about the petitions with my [personal] clerks because I don't have time, but they review them for me and send me their notes.

All of the petitions come up at a petition conference [of the justices]. One of the staff clerks will usually present the petitions to us. At the petition conference we can decide one of three things. We vote. We can vote and say we will take that case in, which means it advances to the argument docket. The second thing we can say is we are not going to take that case in. That case is dead. In theory, it can still be appealed to the U.S. Supreme Court, but that doesn't happen very often. The third option is, any justice can say, "Well, I don't know about this. I'd like to hear more about this. I'd like to be able to ask this lawyer some questions." We call that "asking for an oral," which means it is put on the motion docket. The lawyer who is petitioning the court [appellant counsel] then comes [before us] and tells the justices about the case. We will ask some questions. The other lawyer [for appellee] might come down here to watch it or watch it over the Internet [but does not participate in the motion hearing]. Then we will have a conference and decide either no, it does not come in, or we will advance it to the argument docket. Advancing to the argument docket means you have "joined" both sides.

When a case is placed on the argument docket, the clerk of the court sends to the other [appellee] lawyer, information that [the case] is being petitioned. If we take the case, we set up a briefing schedule—ninety days—and about three months down the road it comes up on the argument docket. Both sides then [orally] argue the case. The rule is we are to allow each side thirty minutes, but that varies. Sometimes it is a little more; sometimes it is less, depending on the complexity or simplicity of the case.

What are the voting and opinion assignment rules?

Majority votes. A two-two vote will bring a petition in, because sometimes a justice might be absent or disqualified for some reason. It takes three votes to decide a case. Two-two is not enough to decide a case, so sometimes we have to appoint a temporary justice. Once the case is argued, we go into a decision conference. In our system we already know to whom the case is assigned, which justice is going to write it. They are assigned in absolute rotation. I have been here eight years, and I don't believe anybody has cheated on it. It is as honest as the day is long. It is based on when it is filed. If someone has to be off a case, or whatever, then they flop out of the rotation but back in, in a way that is not dabbled with. There is no reason to.

Does rotation mean you might write a majority opinion but be voting against it?

It has been done in the past, a justice wrote the majority opinion and then dissented. We do not allow that any more. We created a rule that won't allow that. We shouldn't have ever started it, but we did.

How are opinions written?

Once we have the decision conference, the justice who is going to write the case presents the case to the other justices and makes a suggestion. By that time I have made notes on what I think I want to hold. I may change. At decision conference we vote, and most of our cases, sixty-five to seventy percent or more, are five to zero. The contentious ones cause problems. Some are four to one, some are three to two. The dissenters may or may not write a dissenting opinion. I like to write dissenting opinions or concurring opinions because you don't have to cite much law. You just roll out philosophy. Really, you do. It's kind of fun. You just roll it out. You don't have to get too hung up on law to support what you are saying.

I use separate opinions, either a dissent or a concurring opinion, for two things, and I use them strategically. When we are ready to have an oral argument in a case, my [personal] clerks—we talk about the case. We decide first of all which case we have an interest in. Which case do we want to watch? Employment cases we have an interest in. We want to be sure workers are treated fair. If it is insurance company A versus insurance company B, I would probably say who gives a damn and not worry about it. The ones we have an interest in, a human rights case we have an interest in, I will assign one of my clerks to track it as it goes or do special research sometimes. Maybe they will create some questions I should ask at oral argument. After oral argument we go to decision conference, make a decision on the case. My clerks and I will decide if we want to file a concurring opinion or a dissenting opinion. Sometimes in concurring or dissenting opinions we set up a well-reasoned legal decision with law to support it, maybe from other jurisdictions saying this is what other jurisdictions have done, and this is the modern approach to this, et cetera. [It is] setting up what we think might be a positive change in the law down the road. Then somebody might look back and say the concurring opinion or the dissenting opinion in this case is what the law should be. It might be the time to make a change in the law. That's one thing we do.

The second thing we do is, with concurring and dissenting opinions especially, and it really irritates other justices from time to time, we elaborate on what the majority said. The point is, I exaggerate: "what the majority opinion really means is this." It becomes effective. If someone wants a precedent that is a little different, they cite us, so we do that.

After the decision conference the case opinion is written. Generally I give my clerks an oral outline or sometimes a written outline of what I want to start with. Different justices do it different ways. Some justices, Justice X for example, I don't think he has ever written a word. After my clerks write something, I go through the draft. I am a writer, and you can always improve a draft. A really hard case, the clerks and I can go through fifteen drafts. Eventually, a justice gets a finalized opinion he thinks a majority will agree with. You circulate that. All the justices read that. They do read that. Some justices have clerks make notes on them. I read them and make my own notes.

Then we go back into what we call the opinion conference, and we vote on it. If the opinion has three or more votes, then it can be filed [made public]. Or frequently someone says, if you change this, then I'll go along. So there is a lot of negotiation to change language. We filed two cases yesterday, both of them fifty-cent cases. We had an opinion conference last week. The clerk had to cite check them and be sure the cites are all accurate. That's the kind of system we use. Separate opinions can be filed not later than ten days after the end of a term.

West Virginia has a unique rule by which workers' compensation cases can be appealed from an executive agency to the Supreme Court of Appeals without a judicial branch trial. Could you explain that process?

In the workers' compensation system you file a claim [for employment-related injury or disability]. The commissioner of the Workers' Compensation Division makes a decision. If a party is aggrieved, it is appealed to the Office of Judges, the OOJ. The judge hears evidence. If the OOJ affirms a division denial, it can be appealed to the Workers' Compensation Appeal Board, the WACB. If they affirm the OOJ, the worker's case can come to the court [on appeal].

We have a group of younger clerks called workers' compensation writ clerks. They produce a summary of the claimant's appeal, the employer's appeal, and Workers' Compensation Division appeals. I have learned to read through the piles of these quickly. It's unlikely I will see something I haven't seen before. For example [he takes a pile of summaries], the writ clerk here in the summary wants to reverse the WACB order and order the division to grant a partial permanent disability to this person. Here Justice Y marks he would refuse this. Sometimes the clerk will give a summary of the medical evidence and write a note such as "This appeal should be refused." She is supervised by Justice Y. He probably wouldn't do what I do, bring in my two clerks and have them make and then explain [the summary] to me. I think it is a good exercise for them, and I think it is helpful to me.

Here [pointing to the summary] Justice Y has recommended to refuse. Now, he has voted on probably ten of these appeals. Once he has voted on the appeals, he packages them and gives them to each of the other four justices. I'll take them home at night. I don't let them stack up, or you are in trouble. I have a choice—grant, refuse, or oral presentation, which is that I want the clerk to come in and talk to me if I don't understand something. Justice Z gets out of sorts about that, but I say, "If we don't understand it, we ought not to be voting on it." Sometimes the supervising justice will make notes on the documents [on the appeals]. Especially, because of the standards, the Workers' Compensation Board has to be clearly wrong. That is different than probably wrong. I will follow the [clerk's] recommendation more often than not. But all the justices will vote on these. They then go to a clerk for tabulation. Three votes, just like any other case, it's in. Once they get three votes, we divide them to the personal clerks of the justices. They do a more in-depth, thorough [study] and come back with a fairly extensive suggestion. Each of us passes around the ones that come in, the ones we bring in, the recommendation, and we vote up or down.

Now, I doubt we will bring in more than five, six, seven percent of workers' compensation cases. That number [of appeals] has gone down. Just like medical malpractice verdicts have gone down every year. Medical malpractice cases have gone down in numbers every year. The only thing that hasn't gone down is the premiums, because the insurance companies have gone up despite the fact they got everything they wanted in the so-called medical malpractice reform—I call it deform—a couple of years ago.

Does the court allow amicus curiae—friend of the court—briefs?

A goodly number. We have fairly simple rules on that, but some fairly tough rules in terms of timing. I think we all subscribe to the rules. I ask, "What is wrong in allowing a friend of the court brief? It may be helpful, but what is wrong? If you don't like it, ignore it." There have been some instances in which they have been quite helpful, in my opinion. Particularly in tax cases, [such as] an oil-gas tax case when the West Virginia Drillers Association filed a brief, they were very helpful. We have only once, I can think of only once, denied a filing of an amicus brief.

What are the administrative duties of the justices, especially the chief justice?

I believe the chief justice has a bully pulpit and is our CEO [chief executive officer], which is what he really is. He has a CEO role with court facilities. I also, as administrator, created the mental hygiene commission some years ago when I was first chief justice. I have been chief justice twice, 1997 and 2003. As an associate justice, recently I have been made "furniture czar" for the judiciary. Tomorrow morning I'll be working on Calhoun County, lining up furniture for Calhoun County. But also I'll go there personally and help them do some repairs.

What administrative changes in the state's courts has the court made?

Court technology. We have one of the best websites. Three magazines have written us up as one of the three best supreme court websites in America. We are on the Internet. Six courts now do that [webcast proceedings] live. We were the third. I just sneaked that in. I didn't ask for permission. We just installed the cameras, tested them, and got them going. If I had asked permission, they never would have gone along with it. I just did that when I was chief justice.

I created a self-represented-litigant task force about pro se litigants. We have done a variety of things. We make all kinds of forms available on the website, and we have self-help centers, nine of them, through the state. We put them in public libraries. Why public libraries? Librarians are helpers by nature. Clerks are not. They say you need to get a lawyer. The public library is a better place. We work for improvement in court facilities. We had a gender fairness task force that we let die. I reactivated it and expanded it to gender fairness and ethnic issues.

What other changes are you pressing for in judicial administration?

Our mental hygiene law needs to be decriminalized. It [commitment] looks like a criminal case. What happens now? Well, there is a petition filed against a person that says we want to involuntarily, against your will, lock you up not in a prison but a mental institution. Somebody is going to sign a petition. Guess what? Do you know who is going to represent the person who is trying to get you there? The prosecuting attorney will be the person who is saying you need to be locked up, and guess what. We are going to appoint you [the person being petitioned for involuntary commitment] a lawyer just like you were a criminal. Do you know how you are going to be transported to and from the hospital? Not in an ambulance but in a police car. So we have criminalized the whole thing. I want to decriminalize it.

What other changes would you like to see?

The cost of jail is very much in the news. It is breaking the little counties financially and is hurting the big counties, because we are sending people to jail for such little things. I told some county commissioners just the other day, "You need to be talking to your magistrates and your judges. They are the ones who control the spigot. If you want to shut the spigot down, get the courts to slow down on commitments. We can't afford today to pay thirty thousand dollars a year to keep these people in this jail." Somebody has to get to the judicial officials and say, "We don't have to let the prison population keep growing."

What contacts do justices have with the public?

We do a lot of outreach now. We didn't do any before I came here. We now take the court out of this building at least twice a year. We go to the [WVU] law school [each March], where we hear a full argument docket. We were doing that before I came here, but we now in the fall go to another place, too.

In the spring we now go to a high school for the LAWS program: Legal Awareness for West Virginia Students. We get the high schools to identify teachers and seniors in high schools in a county. They take on one of the cases. We set up a court docket that would be of interest to high school kids. We get the briefs and papers in the cases to the students ahead of time and to the teachers. With the help of the lawyers in the case, we coopt the lawyers, we do some planning. We take the court to the community. They [students] come and hear the case argued. We go to lunch with them, and they get to ask questions. After the case is argued, the lawyers also debrief the students, and they follow up, and we write the case opinion pretty fast. So that's one of our programs.

This past year with Brown v. Board of Education (1954) we did some things. I created a little talk called "Brown v. Board of Education: The West Virginia Connection." I have given that speech twenty times. One of my law clerks wrote a play about a schoolteacher, the Carrie Williams case, which is kind of a forerunner to Brown v. Board of Education. We produced the play four times this past year. West Virginia's first African American lawyer, J. R. Clifford, won the case. Judge Marmaduke Dent, one of my favorite judges, was the judge that wrote the opinion. The case was the first time any appellate court in the nation ever said discrimination against "colored people" solely because of their color was—he didn't say unconstitutional, he said against public policy and the law of the land. So it was a significant case. So we do outreach.

What is the relationship between the court and the state bar?

The president of the state bar was just over here the other day touting a couple of things he needed us to do. Lawyers are governed by the court, totally. The bar officers meet with the chief justice as soon as they are elected and three or four times a year on a formal, for-certain basis. From time to time there are certain things they want us to address. The thing they wanted us to address last time was an increase in bar dues.

What is the relationship between the court and the state legislature and governor?

It's a little touchy for political reasons and for separation of powers reasons. It depends on the leadership, too. As chief justice in 1999 I had a very good relationship with the legislative leadership. We worked out a pay raise, worked out other legislation. We can't go over there advocating public policy change. That's not our role. We can go over when asked if it relates to the administration of justice, like adding a new magistrate. We can go over and say, "We don't need a new magistrate—you don't have the caseload." We can become involved in those kinds of things.

What do you regard as your most significant opinion while on the court?

It probably is the arbitration case—the Friedman's Jeweler's case [State ex rel. Dunlap v. Berger 2002]. When you went in to buy a ring, they twisted your arm to finance it. What you didn't know is you're also buying insurance. It only cost like $3.85 or $6.92 for insurance, but you didn't know about it. Then, if you call their hand on it, you found out you didn't have the right to sue. Not only did you not have the right to sue, you had to go [to] arbitration, and the jewelers get to decide who the arbitrator is. Well, there was something wrong about this. We did the case and decided you can't do that. It was appealed to the United States Supreme Court, and they denied cert, which means in essence they upheld our decision [Friedman's Inc. v. W. Va. ex rel. Dunlap 2002]. The case is now being [widely] cited. I think it is the most significant case. We set the bar for companies to get over. They wanted to stick people with this expensive—they talk like arbitration is cheap, but it is not—process that simply defeats the purpose of class actions. Sometimes in class actions the individual amount [of damages] is so trivial that it can't be a case unless it's part of a class. This would be an example. However, if somebody says they are making millions on this, screwing over people, getting people to buy stuff they don't need, then there must be some way for people to redress their grievances.

What do you regard as your most satisfying achievements as a judge?

What I think is probably most satisfying is that I worked hard and somewhat successfully to bring some diversity to the judiciary. It was pretty much a lily-white organization. If you are a believer in and practitioner of affirmative action, then you know it [change] is not easy. It takes work to create diversity. It is a matter of being able to recruit and keep people.

The second thing I have done on the supreme court—and it's based on my experience as a trial judge that is administratively significant and that has resulted in substance to improve the quality of the judiciary—is something the court allowed me to pursue. I'm in charge of the circuit judge law clerk program. Because I used student law clerks—because the law school was there—in my office at Legal Services and as a trial judge, I said I want to propose to the court something I think will do more to improve the quality of the judiciary and justice than anything we could do in the state. That is, we need to get our circuit judges a full-time lawyer-law clerk like in many states. When I came here in 1997, the chief justice and I talked about it, and he said, "Why don't we start it?" We devised a priority system. We went with multiple-judge circuits first. Over a period of five years, by adding ten new ones each year, we ended up with every trial judge now having a law clerk. They [clerks] cannot work more than two years, which is not uncommon. It has just been wonderful. I think every judge in this state would tell you, "That's the most wonderful thing that's ever happened."

V

╼

How to Conduct Interviews and Gather Law Stories

The purpose of an interview with any litigant or legal professional is the collection of a story of a person's experiences with law and courts. To collect the story, the interviewer must ask questions that address the *who, what, when, how,* and *why* of the legal experiences of the interview's subject. Not only do such questions provide factual insights into the activity or inactivity of the interviewee, the persons with whom the interview subject interacts, and the general legal process, but they also convey a sense of what is important to him or her and the role of professional values, norms, and language in his or her behavior. Because people have opinions on thousands of subjects, it is recommended that questions about problems with law and courts and about ideas for improvement of law and courts are focused on the interviewee's *specific experiences*. By doing this, the student gets better informed assessments and avoids the misperceptions of law and courts too often conveyed by uninformed persons, courthouse gossip, and the media.

It is very easy to locate persons for interviews. Although we recommend against interviewing family members because of the potential for less objective assessments, family, friends, and relatives almost assuredly know a litigant, lawyer, judge, or police officer and can help you contact them. You also can contact the public relations officer of a police department or prosecutor's office in a city or just cold-call a law practice. Try to set aside two hours for an interview. Ask if you can call back to clarify any comments. Ask for permission to use tape recorders or written notes. Check with your instructor to see whether college or university policies affect the conduct of interviews submitted as a course requirement.

In this section, we offer four generic examples of interview questions: for litigants; for lawyers, including prosecutors and public defenders; for judges; and for police. In asking questions, the wise student should use these questions as a springboard for more detailed inquiry. He or she should readily ask follow-up questions to obtain further information about each response. For example, if the student asks a public defender, "Do you plea bargain?" and she or he answers "yes," the follow-ups should be "when?" "how?" "how often?" and "why"? Examples from an interviewee's cases are very useful, but try to avoid letting the interviewee lapse into long stories about a single case or an unusual case. Remember that typical workday activity gives you the best perspective of the average real world of law and legal professionals.

These generic models of interview questions will not necessary fit well into interviews with other court personnel, bondsmen, appellate lawyers, nonlawyer judges, forensics personnel, probation and parole officers, or some specialized lawyers or police. However, look at the topics covered in the interviews in this book with some of these people, be creative, and build from some of the ideas in the generic models to learn about *how* the interviewee came into his or her position, *what* his or her daily workday or workweek entails, *who* he or she interacts with or comes into contact with when on the job, and *why* he or she thinks his or her job is important and *what changes* he or she might make to improve the quality of justice delivered by American law and courts. Of course, do not hesitate to ask questions of special pertinence to your project.

When the interview is completed, the interviewer must make some decisions about what in the interview needs to be saved, how to organize the saved material, how to present an evaluation of the material, and how to share it (see Katriel and Farrell 1991). As our interviews illustrate, we have saved interviewee responses verbatim. However, we have eliminated the direct quotation of our questions and provided an introduction to the interviewee to provide a more readable interview. You might want to add descriptive material on the interview subject's appearance, the location of the interview (a messy office? a police car?), and the tone of voice of the subject (polite, angry, sarcastic) to further convey her or his attitudes.

We initially organized the questions in the interview to address specific issues in a specific order related to the topics covered in the introduction. Then we organized the completed interviews into a form that best conveyed the sequence of events in a case. Other interviewers will find that organization is critical to the communication of other meanings about the narratives they collect. However, random presentation is often difficult for readers to interpret. In the introduction to this book, we have presented a minimal evaluation of the interviews. We desired to leave evaluation to the student. However, later in this section, we offer a guide to evaluation of interviews. Finally, interviews ought to be shared. They can be compiled, duplicated, or electronically posted for distribution among students in a class—a sort of class scrapbook. Students can use them as the basis for oral presentations or discussions. Whatever the means of sharing, it is a way for the student to demonstrate his or her information on the representations of the self conveyed in interviews, to compare it with the information collected by others, and to learn more about the diversity that characterizes American law and courts.

SAMPLE QUESTIONS

Litigants: Plaintiffs and Defendants

Note the time and place of the interview.

Note age, gender, race, and apparent socioeconomic status of the subject of the interview.

Could you give me a brief review of *where, when,* and *how* the case [divorce, bankruptcy, auto accident, other civil action, criminal action] in which you have been involved arose?

[*For plaintiff*] When did you decide to sue? What events motivated you to sue?

[*For civil defendant*] When did you receive notice—a summons—of the suit? [*For criminal defendant*] When and how did police first contact you? When did they arrest you? Did they conduct a search? Did they read you any rights or show you any warrants?

Did you have a lawyer? When did you first meet with a lawyer? How did you find the lawyer? Did you have to pay counsel any fees or contingency fee? [*Or*] When was a public defender or appointed counsel afforded to you?

What did the lawyer advise you to do after learning about your case? How often did you meet with your lawyer? Was the lawyer not, somewhat, mostly, or very deferential to your input or directions on the processing of your case?

[*For civil litigants*] How long did the case take to be resolved once you sued or received a complaint? Did you or your lawyer, on your behalf, have to give or arrange a deposition, answer any written questions, or turn over any material to the other side?

[*For criminal litigants*] Was your arrest for a minor crime or something with the possibility of a long sentence? How long were you held before first going to court? If it was for a minor crime, did you plead guilty and receive a fine or other penalty when first brought before a judge or magistrate? If the arrest was for a more serious crime, were you released on your own recognizance or ordered held in jail? Did you arrange bail? If so, how was this done? Did you use a bail bondsman? If so, what did the bondsman do, and what did it cost?

[*For a civil case*] Did the lawyers negotiate a settlement in your case?

[*For a criminal case*] Did your lawyer negotiate a plea bargain? Were you happy with the settlement or plea bargain? Why or why not? Why did you decide to accept or reject the settlement or plea bargain? Do you think the settlement process was fair? [*For civil litigants*] Did you get the money or other result that you wanted? [*For criminal litigants*] Was the sentence satisfactory? Why or why not?

Before trial, did you appear before a judge for any reasons? Please detail them. What occurred? What did your lawyer do? What did the opposition [*or, for a criminal case*] the prosecutor do? What did the judge do, and did the judge make any decision? Please describe these participants' behavior in as much detail as possible.

Did you have a jury trial? If so, how and in what way did the lawyers interview prospective jurors? Did they dismiss any prospective jurors? Why?

Please describe the conduct of your trial. Was it easy to understand the proceedings? Was anything confusing? How helpful was your lawyer in explaining the proceedings and his or her arguments? What did the judge do? Was the jury, if any, attentive?

What was the outcome of the trial? Do you think that the procedures used by the court were fair? Why or why not? [For civil litigants] Did you get the money or other result that you wanted? [For criminal litigants] Was the sentence satisfactory? Why or why not?

Did you appeal? Why or why not? [If the case was appealed, ask what has happened.]

Overall, what do you regard as the most positive and negative aspects of your litigation experience?

Given your experience in this case, what do you think most deserves to be changed in how law and courts operate? How could the change improve the quality of justice provided by law and courts?

Lawyers: Civil and Criminal Practice, Prosecutors, and Public Defenders

Note the time and place of the interview.

Note age, gender, race, and apparent socioeconomic status of the subject of the interview.

When and why did you decide to become a lawyer? Who or what influenced your decision? Did any of the following affect your decision to go to law school: concern for future economic well-being, political ideology, social justice, or religious beliefs? If so, how?

Did you go to law school immediately after undergraduate school? Why or why not? How do you think taking the LSAT [Law School Admission Test], attending law school, and taking the bar examination readied you for legal practice? Do you think any changes need to be made in the training of lawyers? If so, what?

In what sorts of legal practices have you engaged since law school? When did you move into your current position? What occasioned your move into this position?

Now ask specific questions related to the lawyer's current position.

[For lawyers in private civil or criminal practice]

Is the position in a law firm [size?], partnership, independent solo practice, or as house counsel for a corporation? How is the practice organized? What are the advantages and disadvantages of this kind of practice? Do you regard yourself to be a plaintiffs' or a defendants' attorney?

Do you regard yourself as a specialist in any kind of law? If so, what is it? What encouraged you to become a specialist in this legal specialty?

How do you find clients? Do clients find you by word of mouth or because you have met them in social settings? Do you advertise? If so, how, and how effective do your think the advertising is? [*If in a firm or house counsel*] Do senior partners or supervisors assign you cases on which to work?

Roughly how many cases are presently on your desk?

How often do you do pro bono work? If so, in what kinds of cases? Have you ever been *assigned* by the court as counsel in a criminal case? If so, what are the pluses and minuses of such a role?

[*Also, for lawyers in private civil or criminal practice other than house counsel*]

Are most clients cooperative? What do you regard as the most difficult problems in dealing with clients? Why do you think that clients sometimes do not heed your advice?

Do any specific causes or public policies motivate you to take on certain cases? If so, what sorts of cases?

How do you go about collecting fees for cases? Do you use retainers, flat fees, or contingency fees for your service or for different kinds of cases? Do you vary your fees for certain kinds of clients? If so, who?

[*For prosecutors or public defenders*]

When and why did you decide to become a prosecutor [or public defender]? Who or what influenced your decision? How long have you held your position?

[*For an assistant prosecutor, public defender, or assistant public defender*] How were you selected for your position? What do you think matters most in your selection?

[*For prosecutors*] When were you elected to your post? Could you describe how you have campaigned for the post?

How many cases are normally on your desk or are assigned to you?

Who are your supervisors, if any? Do they assign you any specific tasks or give you any guidelines for handling cases? If so, what sorts of supervision do you receive? How closely do you sense that they monitor your work?

What sorts of records of your activity do you have to keep for superiors? Please describe in detail what forms and documents you have to fill out and how long it takes to process them.

[*For a public defender*] How would you describe your clients? When and how often do you normally consult with them in a typical misdemeanor and a typical felony case? What do you discuss?

[*For other lawyers who are government employees*]

Who are your supervisors? Do they assign you any specific tasks or give you any guidelines for handling cases? If so, what sorts of supervision do you receive? How closely do you sense that they monitor your work?

What sorts of records of your activity do you have to keep for superiors? Please describe in detail what forms and documents you have to fill out and how long it takes to process them.

What kinds of specialized tasks do you perform? How did you learn to perform these tasks?

Do you ever negotiate conflicts involving public agencies? If so, when, where, how frequently, and on what issues?

Do you ever appear in court or before public agencies? If so, when, where, how frequently, and on what issues?

[*For all lawyers, prosecutors, and public defenders*]
How many telephone calls do you estimate you answer every day? Who calls you? On what subjects do they call?

How many meetings with clients [if in civil practice], other attorneys, and persons such as court staff and clerks, victims, witnesses, and police [if in criminal practice] do you estimate you have every day? Who do you meet with the most and the least? On what subjects do you meet? How long are most meetings?

Could you estimate how many letters and other documents you draft every day? On what subjects do you draft letters and documents? Could you please give a few recent examples of what you drafted and why you drafted them?

More Specific Questions

[*For lawyers in private civil practice*] Roughly what percentage of your cases are settled without trial? When and why do you negotiate? Who initiates negotiations? Where and how are they conducted? Are there frequent exchanges of offers? Is there something of a going rate, or are there unwritten norms for settling certain kinds of cases? Do you negotiate mostly with other lawyers, insurance companies, or private parties? Are there any specific differences in negotiations that arise from dealing with any of these parties? Could you please give an example of a recent negotiation?

[*For prosecutors*] What aspects of a crime and arrest most affect your decision to charge a suspect with a crime? Why might you dismiss an arrest? How frequently are preliminary hearings and grand jury sessions used in your jurisdiction? How do you prepare for one or both of these events? Do you usually obtain a successful outcome from the review of your charges by one or both of these events?

[*For lawyers in criminal practice, prosecutors, or public defenders*] Do you plea bargain? Roughly what percentage of your cases are settled with plea bargains? When and why do you plea bargain? Who initiates plea bargains? Where and how are they conducted? Are there frequent exchanges of offers? Is there something of a going rate, or are there unwritten norms for settling certain kinds of cases? Are there any specific differences in plea bargaining that arise from dealing with any categories of defendants? Could you please give an example of a recent plea-bargaining process?

[*For lawyers in civil practice or government lawyers*] Do you represent clients or the government before administrative bodies in cases involving disability, workers' compensation, zoning, and other regulatory matters? If so, what do you do in such cases? Do you have to prepare any specific documents? Can you normally negotiate a solution to your client's problem? Do you appear before such bodies or their administrative law judges? If so, how frequently, on what sorts of issues, and what do you do?

[*For all lawyers*] When do you begin to prepare a case for trial? How frequently do you do this? Could you please describe, based on your legal practice, your role in the pleadings? What efforts do you make during the discovery process? What do you try to do during discovery? Do you contact the opposition during discovery? If so, how frequently, and on what issues? Do you regard discovery as a prelude to a settlement?

When do you appear before a judge prior to trial? Why? What sorts of pretrial motions might you file? How frequently do you file them? Why do you file them?

If you have responsibility to litigate cases, what determines whether *you* will ask for a jury trial? If you are involved in a jury trial, when and how do you challenge potential jurors? What do you think of the competency of juries?

What do you think are the most important things a lawyer should do during a trial?

What is your assessment of the range of competencies possessed by the judges before whom you appear?

When do you recommend that a client consider an appeal of an adverse judgment?

Overall, what do you regard as the most positive and negative aspects of your profession?

Based on your personal experience in your current legal practice, what do you think most deserves to be changed in how law and courts operate? How could the change improve the quality of justice provided by law and courts?

Trial Judges
Note the time and place of the interview.
Note age, gender, race, and apparent socioeconomic status of the subject of the interview.

When and why did you decide to become a lawyer? Who or what influenced your decision? Did any of the following affect your decision to go to law school: concern for future economic well-being, political ideology, social justice, or religious beliefs? If so, how?

Did you go to law school immediately after undergraduate school? Why or why not? How do you think taking the LSAT, attending law school, and taking the bar examination readied you for legal practice? Do you think any changes need to be made in the training of lawyers? If so, what?

In what sorts of legal practices have you engaged since law school? When did you move into your current position as a judge? What occasioned your move into this position?

How were you selected for your judicial post? What do you think mattered most in your selection? Were you elected to your post? If so, could you describe how you have campaigned for the post?

What sort of training did you receive for serving as a judge? Did you attend any training programs? If so, how beneficial were they? What did you learn about judging during your first months on the bench?

Are you required to specialize in civil, criminal, family, or juvenile matters? If so, what do you think are the important differences between how a general-jurisdiction judge operates and the activity of a judge in your specialty?

Do you issue warrants? What concerns you most when you consider applications for different types of warrants?

What sorts of pretrial motions related to the pleadings and discovery do you most commonly receive? How do you go about assessing and deciding whether to grant different kinds of motions? Do you think that lawyers file too many motions in civil or criminal cases?

Do you have to issue motions to secure the enforcement of the judgments of your court? If so, when, against whom, and on what issues?

What topics do you normally go over during a pretrial conference? Do you encourage negotiated settlements in civil matters? Do you participate in some way in negotiated settlements in civil matters? If applicable, do you encourage plea bargains in criminal matters? Do you participate in some way in plea bargains in criminal matters?

What do you consider to be your most important responsibilities during jury selection?

What do you consider to be your most important responsibilities during a jury trial? What do you consider to be your most important responsibilities during a bench trial?

How do you go about developing instructions for juries?

Have you ever modified a jury decision? If so, how frequently, and in what way?

If you must sentence a criminal defendant, relatively how important are legislative sentencing guidelines or requirements, a plea-bargained agreement on a sentence, recommendations from prosecution and defense, and a presentence report in your decision? How important is your own sense of fairness?

Overall, what do you regard as the most positive and negative aspects of your position?

Based on your experience in your current office, what do you think most deserves to be changed in how law and courts operate? How could the change improve the quality of justice provided by law and courts?

Police

Note the time and place of the interview.

Note age, gender, race, and apparent socioeconomic status of the subject of the interview.

When and why did you decide to become a police officer? Who or what influenced your decision?

What sorts of tests did you have to take to qualify as a police officer candidate? Did you attend a police academy? [*If yes*] What kinds of training did you receive in police behavior, firearms, the law, and dealing with citizens? After leaving the academy, did you undergo a probationary period of field training? Have you undergone any additional training for specialized police tasks? If so, could you please describe the training? How has training affected your capabilities as a police officer?

Who are your supervisors? Do they assign you any specific tasks or give you any information at the beginning of a shift, at a meeting or roll call? If so, what sorts of information do you receive? How closely do you sense they monitor your work?

What sorts of records of your activity do you have to keep? Please describe in detail what forms and documents you have to fill out and how long it takes to process them.

If you are assigned to patrol, do you patrol a specific sector or beat? What do you look for, and who do you look at as you patrol? Do you concentrate on patrolling specific places or looking for specific kinds of activity by people or vehicles on the streets? If so, where do you go, or what do you look for in public areas? When or what determines when you look for traffic offenses? When are you most and least likely to cite a person for a traffic offense? Does your department require that you meet a quota for traffic offenses?

If you are assigned to patrol, how frequently during a shift do you normally have to respond to radio calls? What are the most common reasons for such calls? Do you frequently have to address calls about events not directly linked to a crime? If so, what are they about—auto accidents, fires, noise, suspicious people and strangers?

[*For police assigned as detectives*] Do you have any special assignments [robbery, vice, juveniles]? What do you do during a shift? How much time do you spend in the office going over other officers' reports of crime and gathering information by phone? When and how often do you go to crime scenes? What do you do there? When, where, how, and on what subjects do you usually interview victims, witnesses, and citizens? How often do investigations result in arrests? How often do you use fingerprints, DNA, and other forensic evidence? Does forensic evidence greatly contribute to many or to few of your efforts to locate suspects? Do you have any contact with insurance companies or their investigators? [*If yes*] When, how frequently, and on what sorts of issues?

Who are the nonsuspect citizens and crime victims with whom you have the most frequent contacts? How do they usually behave toward you? Do citizens and victims ever provide you with useful information about criminal activity? If so, when and why? Do you ever use informants? If so, what kind, how frequently, and for what purposes?

When you stop a suspect or suspect vehicle, what do you do? What do you say? When do you frisk or search a vehicle? When do you arrest? What proportion of your arrests are based on probable cause, on arrest warrants, or are mandatory?

How frequently do you have to obtain search warrants? What is the process, and how do magistrates or judges tend to treat your requests?

How frequently do you appear in court? How in general do the judge or magistrate and defense lawyers treat you?

In what circumstances before and after arrest and how often do you meet with prosecutors or assistant prosecutors? What happens during your meetings with them? Have they ever not prosecuted any of your arrests? [*If yes*] How often, and what reasons, if any, did they give you?

What do you think of the role or lack of a role for police in plea bargaining and the sentences given defendants?

Does your department practice community policing or zero-tolerance policing? [*If yes*] What does this concept mean? How does it affect your everyday activity on the streets?

Does your department have written rules that govern your behavior? Are there specific rules about the use of force and firearms? What is your assessment of the usefulness of such rules? Does your department have a form of internal affairs unit that examines alleged violations of the rules? [*If yes*] What do you think of them?

Have you ever experienced any interference with your work from politicians or local organizations? [*If yes*] Please describe the organization and the nature of the interference.

Overall, what do you regard as the most positive and negative aspects of your profession?

Based on your experience in your current position, what do you think most deserves to be changed in how police, law, and courts operate? How could the change improve the quality of justice provided by police, law, and courts?

EVALUATING THE INTERVIEW

In his interview, Scott Himsel suggested that "reading comprehension, organization of materials, and clear communication," processing information, and effective writing are the skills necessary for becoming a legal professional but that it is also important to ask "life questions" of lawyers. Although it is semistructured, the interview provides such an opportunity. However, after conducting an interview, it is important to reflect on it and communicate what you have learned.

The best way to reflect and communicate what you have learned is to construct what social scientists call a comparative study. Compare what your interview subject has told you—point by point—with descriptive texts on the legal process, criminal procedures, police, or other participants in legal actions. Many of these works are cited in the References, Section VI of this text In constructing this evaluation, consider two questions: Are the responses of my interview subject similar to or different from the generic descriptions of legal jobs and procedures provided by texts? Why do any differences exist?

Then go one step further. Consider the final comments in the interview with Robert Eye and reflect on the broader political implications of the statements and activities of the person whom you interviewed. As suggested in the introduction to this book, the law helps constitute or frame how Americans think and act. Law also is infused with politics and judgments about proper behavior and justice that are established by legislators and judges. Consequently, reflect on how the persons you have interviewed think about the importance and value of the rule of law. What do they see as the costs and benefits of the law? Also, you ought to assess what they expect the law to accomplish. Do they see law and the activities of lawyers and judges—such as negotiation and adjudication—as encouraging social harmony and preventing conflict, as supporting the economic and social status quo, as punishing those persons or businesses they define as disreputable, harmful, or criminal, or as allowing social outsiders and the economically disadvantaged to challenge the politically or economically dominant? What message does the interview subject send about how law makes society and how society makes law?

References

In addition to works cited in this book, in this reference section we offer a selection of some of the best publications and textbooks about the politics of law and courts. A lengthy bibliography on all aspects of law, court operations, lawyers, judges and judicial decision making, constitutional law and rights, and law and courts outside the United States can be found at a website: http://www. polsci.wvu.edu/faculty/brisbin/cover.htm.

Valuable online resources that contain data and information on law and courts include:

The American Bar Association, Division of Public Education, at: http://www.aba-net.org/publiced/

Findlaw at http://www.findlaw.com/

The National Center for State Courts, which contains links to all state courts, at: http://www.ncsconline.org/

The United States Courts at: http://www.uscourts.gov/

The United States Department of Justice, Bureau of Justice Statistics, at http://www.ojp.usdoj.gov/bjs/

WORKS REFERENCED IN THIS BOOK

Bates v. State Bar of Arizona, 433 U.S. 350 (1977).

Baum, Lawrence. 2006. *The Supreme Court.* 9th ed. Washington, D.C.: CQ Press.

——. 2008. *American Courts: Process and Policy.* 6th ed. Boston: Houghton Mifflin.

Bowen, Lauren. 1995. Advertising and the legal profession. *Justice System Journal,* 18:43–54.

Brigham, John. 1996. *The constitution of interests: Beyond the politics of rights.* New York: New York University Press.

Brisbin, Richard A., Jr. 2002. *A strike like no other strike: Law and resistance during the Pittston coal strike of 1989–1990.* Baltimore: Johns Hopkins University Press.

———. 2009. Resistance to the judiciary: The boundaries of judicial power. In *Exploring judicial politics,* ed. Mark C. Miller, 213–230. New York: Oxford University Press.

Brown v. Board of Education 347 U.S. 483 (1954).

Bumiller, Kristin. 1988. *The civil rights society: The social construction of victims.* Baltimore: Johns Hopkins University Press.

Bush v. Gore 531 U.S. 98 (2000).

Carp, Robert A., Ronald Stidham, and Kenneth L. Manning. 2007. *Judicial process in America.* 7ᵗʰ ed. Washington, D.C.: CQ Press.

Casper, Jonathan D. 1972. *American criminal justice: The defendant's perspective.* Englewood Cliffs, N.J.: Prentice-Hall.

Cole, George F., and Christopher E. Smith. 2008 *The American system of criminal justice.* 12th ed. Belmont, Calif.: Wadsworth.

Cook, Beverly Blair. 1969–1970. The politics of piecemeal reform of Kansas courts. *Judicature* 53:274–81.

Dill, Forrest. 1975. Discretion, exchange, and social control: Bail bondsmen in criminal courts. *Law and Society Review* 9:639–74.

Eisenstein, James, Roy B. Flemming, and Peter Nardulli. 1988. *The contours of justice: Communities and their courts.* Boston: Little, Brown.

Eisenstein, James, and Herbert Jacob. 1977. *Felony justice: An organizational analysis of criminal courts.* Boston: Little, Brown.

Engel, David M. and Frank W. Munger. 2003. *Rights of inclusion: Law and identity in the life stories of Americans with disabilities.* Chicago: University of Chicago Press.

Epp, Charles R. 2008. Law as an instrument of social reform. In *The Oxford handbook of law and politics,* ed. Keith E. Whittington, R. Daniel Kelemen, and Gregory A. Caldeira, 595–613. New York: Oxford University Press.

Epstein, Lee, and Joseph F. Kobylka. 1992. *The Supreme Court and legal change: Abortion and the death penalty.* Chapel Hill: University of North Carolina Press.

Ewick, Patricia, and Susan S. Silbey. 1995. Subversive stories and hegemonic tales: Toward a sociology of narrative. *Law and Society Review* 29:197–226.

———. 1998. *The common place of the law: Stories from everyday life.* Chicago: University of Chicago Press.

Feeley, Malcolm M. 1979. *The process is the punishment: Handling cases in a lower criminal court.* New York: Russell Sage Foundation.

———. 1983. *Court reform on trial: Why simple solutions fail.* New York: Basic Books.

Felstiner, William L. F., Richard L. Abel, and Austin Sarat. 1980–81. The emergence and transformation of disputes: Naming, blaming, claiming....*Law and Society Review* 15:631–54.

Friedman, Lawrence M., and Robert V. Percival. 1976. A tale of two courts: Litigation in Alameda and San Benito Counties. *Law and Society Review* 10:267–301.

Friedman's Inc. v. West Virginia ex rel. Dunlap 537 U.S. 1087 (2002).

Galanter, Marc. 1974. Why the "haves" come out ahead: Speculations on the limits of legal change. *Law and Society Review* 9:95–160.

Geertz, Clifford. 1983. Local knowledge: Fact and law in comparative perspective. In *Local knowledge: Further essays in interpretive anthropology,* ed. Clifford Geertz, 167–234. New York: Basic Books.

George, Alexander L., and Andrew Bennett. 2005. *Case studies and theory development in the social sciences.* Cambridge: MIT Press.

Gonzales v. Raich, 545 U.S. 1 (2005).

Greenhouse, Carol J. 1986. *Praying for justice: Faith, order, and community in an American town*. Ithaca, NY: Cornell University Press.

Hall, Melinda Gann. 1990. Opinion assignment and conference practices of state supreme courts. *Judicature* 73:209.

Hastie, Reid, ed. 1993. *Inside the juror: The psychology of juror decision making*. New York: Cambridge University Press.

Kamir, Orit. 2000. Judgement by film: Socio-legal functions of *Rashomon. Yale Journal of Law and the Humanities,* 11:39–88.

Katriel, Tamar, and Thomas Farrell. 1991. Scrapbooks as cultural texts: An American art of memory. *Text and Performance Quarterly*, 11:1–17.

Kilwein, John C. 1998. Still trying: Cause lawyering for the poor and disadvantaged in Pittsburgh, Pennsylvania. In *Cause lawyering: Professional commitments and professional responsibilities*, ed. Austin Sarat and Stuart Scheingold, 181–200. New York: Oxford University Press.

Kritzer, Herbert M. 1990. *The justice broker: Lawyers and ordinary litigation*. New York: Oxford University Press.

———. 1991. *Let's make a deal: Understanding the negotiation process in ordinary litigation*. Madison: University of Wisconsin Press.

———. 2004. *Risks, reputations, and rewards: Contingency fee legal practice in the United States*. Stanford, Calif.: Stanford University Press.

Mather, Lynn. 1995. The fired football coach (or, how trial courts make policy). In *Contemplating courts*, ed. Lee Epstein, 170–202. Washington, D.C: CQ.

Mather, Lynn. 2005. Courts in American popular culture. In *The institutions of American democracy: The judicial branch,* ed. Kermit L. Hall and Kevin T. McGuire, 233–261. New York: Oxford University Press.

Mather, Lynn, Craig A. McEwen, and Richard J. Maiman. 2001. *Divorce lawyers at work: Varieties of professionalism in practice*. New York: Oxford University Press.

McCann, Michael. 2008. Litigation and legal mobilization. In *The Oxford handbook of law and politics,* ed. Keith E. Whittington, R. Daniel Kelemen, and Gregory A. Caldeira, 522–540. New York: Oxford University Press.

McLeod, Aman L. 2009. Differences in state judicial selection. In *Exploring judicial politics,* ed. Mark C. Miller, 10–30. New York: Oxford University Press.

Melone, Albert P., and Allan Karnes. 2008. *The American legal system: Politics, processes, and policies*. 2nd ed. Lanham, MD: Rowman & Littlefield.

Merry, Sally Engle. 1990. *Getting justice and getting even: Legal consciousness among working class Americans*. Chicago: University of Chicago Press.

Miller, Richard E. and Austin Sarat. 1980–1981. Grievances, claims, and disputes: Assessing the adversary culture. *Law and Society Review* 15:525–66.

Nader, Laura, ed. 1980. *No access to law: Alternatives to the American judicial system*. New York: Academic Press.

Neubauer, David W. 2007. *America's courts and the criminal justice system*. 9th ed. Belmont, CA: Wadsworth.

Neubauer, David W., and Stephen S. Meinhold. 2010. *Judicial process: Law, courts, and politics in the United States,* 5th ed. Boston: Wadsworth.

Nonet, Philippe. 1969. *Administrative justice: Advocacy and change in a government agency*. New York: Russell Sage Foundation.

O'Brien, David M. 2008. *Storm center: The Supreme Court in American politics*. 8th ed. New York: Norton.

Petite v. United States 361 U.S. 529 (1960).

Presbyterian Church in the U.S. v. Mary Elizabeth Blue Hull Memorial Presbyterian Church 393 U.S. 440 (1969).

PollingReport.com. 2009. Illegal drugs. Available at: http://www.pollingreport.com/drugs.htm.

Powell v. Alabama, 287 U.S. 45 (1932).

Provine, Doris Marie. 1986. *Judging credentials: Nonlawyer judges and the politics of professionalism.* Chicago: University of Chicago Press.

Republican Party v. White 536 U.S. 765 (2002).

Roe v. Wade, 410 U.S. 113 (1973).

Ross, H. Laurence. 1980. *Settled out of court: The social process of insurance claims adjustment.* Rev. 2nd ed. New York: Aldine.

Sarat, Austin. 1998. Cause lawyering and the reproduction of professional authority: An introduction. In *Cause lawyering: Professional commitments and professional responsibilities,* ed. Austin Sarat and Stuart Scheingold, 3–28. New York: Oxford University Press.

Sarat, Austin, and William L. F. Felstiner. 1995. *Divorce lawyers and their clients: Power and meaning in the legal process.* New York: Oxford University Press.

Sarat, Austin, and Thomas R. Kearns. 1993. Beyond the great divide: Forms of legal scholarship and everyday life. In *Law in Everyday Life,* ed. Austin Sarat and Thomas R. Kearns, 21–61. Ann Arbor: University of Michigan Press.

Sarat, Austin, and Jonathan Simon. 2003. Cultural analysis, cultural studies, and the situation of legal scholarship. In *Cultural analysis, cultural studies, and the law: Moving beyond legal realism,* ed. Austin Sarat and Jonathan Simon, 1–34. Durham, NC: Duke University Press.

Scheingold, Stuart A. 2004. *The politics of rights: Lawyers, public policy, and political change.* Ann Arbor: University of Michigan Press.

Schmidt, Patrick. 2005. *Lawyers and regulation: The politics of the administrative process.* Cambridge, UK: Cambridge University Press.

Serbian Eastern Orthodox Diocese for the U.S. and Canada v. Milivojevich 426 U.S. 696 (1976).

Shklar, Judith N. 1964. *Legalism: Law, morals, and political trials.* Cambridge, Mass.: Harvard University Press.

State ex rel. Dunlap v. Berger 211 W. Va. 549 (2002).

Trubek, David M., Joel B. Grossman, William L. F. Felstiner, Herbert M. Kritzer, and Austin Sarat. 1983. *Civil litigation project: Final report.* Madison: Institute for Legal Studies, University of Wisconsin, Madison.

Tyler, Tom R. 1988. What is procedural justice? Criteria used by citizens to assess the fairness of legal procedures. *Law and Society Review* 22:103–35.

———. 1990. *Why people obey the law.* New Haven, Conn.: Yale University Press.

United States Department of Justice, Bureau of Justice Statistics. 2008a. *Civil bench and jury trials in state courts, 2005.* Available at: http://www.ojp.usdoj.gov/bjs/abstract/cbjtsc05.htm.

———. 2008b. *Sourcebook of criminal justice statistics online.* Available at: http://www.albany.edu/sourcebook/index.html.

United States Sentencing Commission. 2008. *Federal sentencing guidelines manuals.* Available at: http://www.ussc.gov/guidelin.htm.

United States v. Booker, United States v. Fanfan 543 U.S. 220 (2005).

Van Hoy, Jerry. 1997. *Franchise law firms and the transformation of personal legal services.* Westport, Conn.: Quorum Books.

Vidmar, Neil, and Valerie P. Hans. 2007. *American juries: The verdict.* Amherst, NY: Prometheus Books

Wagner-Pacifici, Robin. 1994. *Discourse and destruction: The city of Philadelphia versus MOVE.* Chicago: University of Chicago Press.

Walker, Samuel, and Charles M. Katz. 2008. *Police in America: An introduction.* 6th ed. Boston: McGraw-Hill.

Yngvesson, Barbara. 1993. *Virtuous citizens, disruptive subjects: Order and complaint in a New England court.* New York: Routledge.

CPSIA information can be obtained at www.ICGtesting.com
Printed in the USA
BVOW08s0050310714

361032BV00002B/17/P